September 9–11, 2012
Auckland, New Zealand

I0041867

**Association for
Computing Machinery**

Advancing Computing as a Science & Profession

ICER'12

Proceedings of the Ninth Annual International Conference on
International Computing Education Research

Sponsored by:
ACM SIGCSE

Supported by:
CPIT and AUT University

**Association for
Computing Machinery**

Advancing Computing as a Science & Profession

The Association for Computing Machinery
2 Penn Plaza, Suite 701
New York, New York 10121-0701

Notice to Past Authors of ACM-Published Articles
ACM intends to create a complete electronic archive of all articles and/or other material previously published by ACM. If you have written a work that has been previously published by ACM in any journal or conference proceedings prior to 1978, or any SIG Newsletter at any time, and you do NOT want this work to appear in the ACM Digital Library, please inform permissions@acm.org, stating the title of the work, the author(s), and where and when published.

ISBN: 978-1-4503-1604-0 (Digital)

ISBN: 978-1-4503-1881-5 (Print)

Additional copies may be ordered prepaid from:

ACM Order Department
PO Box 30777
New York, NY 10087-0777, USA

Phone: 1-800-342-6626 (USA and Canada)
+1-212-626-0500 (Global)
Fax: +1-212-944-1318
E-mail: acmhelp@acm.org
Hours of Operation: 8:30 am – 4:30 pm ET

Printed in the USA

Welcome

We have great pleasure in welcoming you to the ninth annual International Computing Education Research Conference, ICER 2012, sponsored by the ACM Special Interest Group in Computer Science Education (SIGCSE). It is especially exciting to be hosting this conference for the first time in Auckland, New Zealand.

This year's conference continues its tradition of being the premier forum for computing education research, from discussions of preliminary ideas to presentation of contributions to the computing education research discipline.

The call for papers attracted a record 54 submissions. All papers were double-blind peer-reviewed by members of the international program committee. After the reviewing, 13 research papers and eight discussion papers were accepted (38%) for inclusion in the conference. There are also ten lightning talks, and we have authors and presenters from seven countries: Australia, Finland, Canada, New Zealand, Sweden, the United Kingdom, and the United States.

The papers span a wide variety of topics, including tools and tool use; conceptions, preconceptions, and misconceptions; attitudes; collaborative learning; research categorization; teacher adaptation to new paradigms; and broad-scale adoption of computing innovations.

The program also includes a keynote address by Jan Meyer of the University of Queensland who will discuss threshold concepts.

We hope that delegates to this conference will not only enjoy the program we have put together but also find the time to explore the beautiful city of Auckland and the wonderful scenery and hospitality of the rest of New Zealand.

Kia Ora Koutou Katoa

Chair Alison Clear
CPIT
Christchurch, NZ

Chair Kate Sanders
Rhode Island College
Providence, RI, USA

Chair Beth Simon
UCSD
San Diego, CA, USA

Table of Contents

Discussion Paper Session 1
Session Chair: Beth Simon *(UCSD)*

Research Paper Session 1
Session Chair: Jacqueline Whalley *(AUT University)*

Research Paper Session 2
Session Chair: Mike Lopez *(CPIT)*

Research Paper Session 3
Session Chair: Amit Sarkar *(CPIT)*

ICER 2012 Organization

General Chairs: Alison Clear *(CPIT, Christchurch, NZ)*
Kate Sanders *(Rhode Island College, Providence, USA)*
Beth Simon *(USD, San Diego, USA)*

Submission Chair: Simon *(University of Newcastle, Australia)*

Lightning Talks Chair: Brian Dorn *(University of Hartford, West Hartford, USA)*

Website: Jan Erik Moström *(Umeå University, Sweden)*

Local Arrangements Chair: Tony Clear *(AUT University, Auckland, NZ)*

Local Arrangements Committee: Mike Lopez *(CPIT, Christchurch, NZ)*
Anne Philpott *(AUT University, Auckland, NZ)*
Amitrajit Sakar *(CPIT, Christchurch, NZ)*
Jaqueline Whalley *(AUT University, Auckland, NZ)*

Registration Chair: Samuel Mann *(Otago Polytechnic, Dunedin, NZ)*

Program Committee Ben-Ari, Mordechai *(Weizmann Institute of Science, Rehovot, Israel)*
Ben-David Kolikant, Yifat *(Hebrew University, Jerusalem, Israel)*
Boustedt, Jonas *(Hogskolan i Gavle, Sweden)*
Caspersen, Michael *(Aarhus University, Denmark)*
Chen, Tzu-Yi *(Pomona College, California, USA)*
Chinn, Donald *(University of Washington, Tacoma, USA)*
Clancy, Michael *(University of California, Berkeley, California, USA)*
Clear, Tony *(Auckland University of Technology, New Zealand)*
Cutts, Quintin *(University of Glascow, UK)*
Eckerdal, Anna *(Uppsala University, Sweden)*
Fincher, Sally *(University of Kent at Canterbury, UK)*
Fitzgerald, Sue *(Metropolitan State University, St. Paul, Minnesota, USA)*
Ginat, David *(Tel Aviv University, Israel)*
Guzdial, Mark *(Georgia Institute of Technology, Atlanta, Georgia, USA)*
Hazzan, Orit *(Technion, Israel Institute of Technology)*
Hundhausen, Chris *(Washington State University, USA)*
Kinnunen, Paivi *(University of Eastern Finland, Joensuu, Finland)*
Lister, Raymond *(University of Technology, Sydney, Australia)*
Malmi, Lauri *(Aalto University, Helsinki, Finland)*
McCartney, Robert *(University of Connecticut, Storrs, USA)*
McCauley, Renee *(College of Charleston, South Carolina, USA)*
Moström, Jan Erik *(Umeå University, Sweden)*
Murphy, Laurie *(Pacific Lutheran University, USA)*
Sajaniemi, Jorma *(University of Eastern Finland, Joensuu, Finland)*
Schulte, Carsten *(Freie Universität Berlin, Germany)*
Tenenberg, Josh *(University of Washington, Tacoma, USA)*
Wiedenbeck, Susan *(Drexel University, USA)*

ICER 2012 Sponsor & Supporters

Sponsor:

Supporters:

Web-scale Data Gathering with BlueJ

Ian Utting, Neil Brown, Michael Kölling, Davin McCall and Philip Stevens

University of Kent

Canterbury, UK

{iau,nccb,mik,D.McCall,plcs}@kent.ac.uk

ABSTRACT

Many investigations of students' initial learning of programming are based on small-scale studies of their interactions with a learning environment. Although this research has led to significant improvements in the understanding of student behaviour (and tool support), it has often been restricted to small numbers of students at single institutions. This paper describes an initiative to instrument the widely-used BlueJ environment to collect data on a much larger scale, and make that data available to Computing Education researchers. The availability of this data has the potential to enable research not previously possible. This paper discusses the type of data that will be gathered, the restrictions placed on identifying students, and mechanisms for associating the data with contextual data gathered outside the scope of the initiative.

Categories and Subject Descriptors

K.3.2 [**Computing Milieux**]: Computer and Information Science Education – *Computer science education.*

General Terms

Measurement, Experimentation.

Keywords

CS1, student behaviour, initial programming, BlueJ, data collection.

1. BLUEJ

BlueJ [6] is a Java IDE specifically designed for beginning programmers. It was originally released free-of-charge in 1999 and is now published under the GPL. The software itself is translated into 17 different languages and is used in introductory programming courses at secondary schools and Universities worldwide. The most common use of BlueJ is in initial programming courses, with students moving on to full-featured professional environments fairly soon thereafter. The BlueJ website lists almost 1000 Universities which have indicated that they are using the software.

Since its first release, BlueJ has been downloaded over 10 million times, with current downloads running at over 2.5 million per

year. This number is influenced by the number of new major releases in any given year, as well as an indeterminate number of downloads where the software is never installed, or is tried once and thrown away, or is downloaded once and installed on many machines.

Since 2009, the standard distribution of BlueJ has contained a function that reports use of the software (including BlueJ version, Java version and operating system) for maintenance and planning purposes. For instance, abandoning support for older versions of Java would have an impact on users of older Apple computers, which makes it important to know what proportion of the BlueJ user base are using them. This data gives a finer-grained picture of the use of BlueJ than raw numbers of downloads (but it still does not allow institutions, or individuals, to be identified).

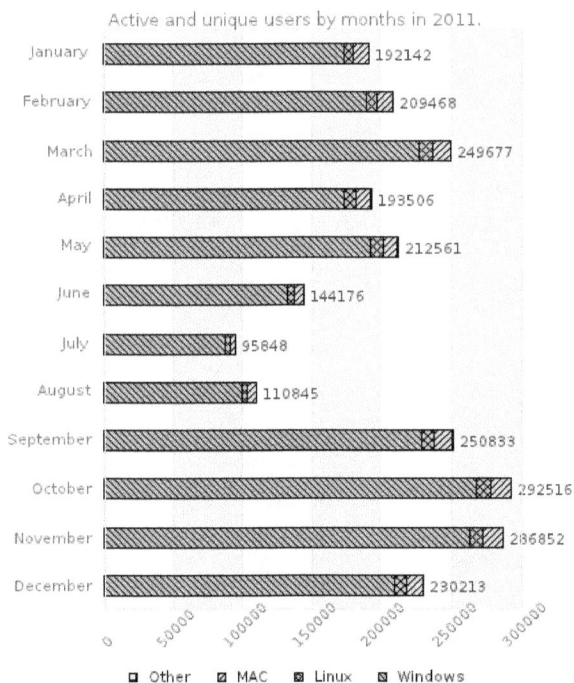

Figure 1: Unique BlueJ users per month in 2011

Data collected by this method is shown in the graph above for 2011 (Figure 1), which reports between 95,000 and 290,000 distinct BlueJ users depending on the month, with distinct peaks reflecting the typical start-date of school and college courses. Data also showed that the average duration of a user's contact with BlueJ (i.e. from first recorded use to last recorded use) was around 90 days, and that BlueJ had been installed in 202 countries around the world, with close to 1,000,000 unique users reported in the US. The 10 countries with the highest numbers of reported active BlueJ users are listed in Table 1.

Rank	Country	Users	% of all users
1	Germany	354123	23.1%
2	United States	327481	21.4%
3	India	136592	8.9%
4	United Kingdom	78005	5.1%
5	Brazil	60978	4.0%
6	Chile	47576	3.1%
7	Spain	38699	2.5%
8	Philippines	36383	2.4%
9	Canada	33417	2.2%
10	Mexico	29717	1.9%

Table 1: Top ten countries for BlueJ use (2011). Includes only users seen more than once.

The number of users is under-reported, as only users whose installation can send an HTTP request to an external website are recorded. This will have a significant impact on reported uses in regions where internet access is not universal (e.g. India, where BlueJ has 200,000 reported installations, but is used in some very large-scale "Standard 10" qualifications), or where local security policies bar internet access (e.g. secondary schools in the UK and USA; and China).

Conversely, the total numbers of users may be inflated by use of BlueJ at sites that routinely re-image PC's between uses, causing users to lose their profile data and BlueJ to consider them as new users on every invocation.

2. BEGINNING STUDENTS' INTERACTIONS WITH IDES

There have been many studies, using many approaches, of students' behaviour in introductory programming classes. Here we will restrict ourselves to discussing those that focused on their interactions with their programming environment, and the resulting program texts.

Thomas et al [7] recorded 4.7 million actions over a six-week period from 141 students using an Ada IDE, but these were very low-level events (e.g. captured from the GUI framework) and data-cleaning proved to be a significant problem, although they did also establish the viability of using such data to answer questions formulated after the data was gathered.

Ahmadzadeh et al [1] collected much coarser-grained data (including source code) from 192 students in the School of CS & IT at the University of Nottingham, mostly focused on compilation errors encountered by students whilst using the JCreator environment.

Edwards et al [3] collected result-focused data from 1101 students over a five-year period. The data gathered was students' work-in-progress as they submitted their evolving programs for testing by,

and feedback from, the Web-CAT tool. They eventually captured 89,879 submissions from two courses using Java and one using C++.

Jadud [5] and Fenwick et al [4] have recently used bespoke extensions to the BlueJ Java IDE to capture student interactions at an intermediate granularity, capturing the input to and output from the Java compiler at every invocation. Jadud captured 42,000 events from 186 students over two years, and Fenwick et al captured 55,000 from 110 students in a single year.

The questions addressed by these studies, in their published output, has been quite diverse, from compilation and editing behaviour to time-on-task and start-time-to-deadline differences. In all cases except Thomas et al, the particular research questions to be addressed were part of the design of the data-gathering apparatus, but in many cases the data proved amenable for use in answering other questions, which became apparent only after the data had been gathered. Some of the studies have gathered very large numbers of event records, and some have involved large numbers of students, but in the published cases, all the students were studying at a single institution, and only in no cases was the tool used to gather the data re-used. We speculate that this was because the tool in question was implemented as an extension to BlueJ, talking to a Web Service fronting a standard database. This allowed not only for simple installation of the back-end, but also (and probably more crucially) simple installation of the front-end in a tool (BlueJ) which the students were already using, and without needing negotiation with those setting up student Labs.

These latter two issues seem to pose a significant barrier-to-entry to those trying to initiate or participate in these sorts of studies. If the instrumented tool is not part of the students' normal working environment, then their use of it will be, at best, artificial and potentially confounded by unfamiliarity with the tool itself. If a tool (or variant of a tool) needs to be specially installed by systems administrators (e.g. for use in a Lab), then that often requires significant lead-time, and it may be difficult to restrict use of the tool to the target population and context.

A further significant barrier to the implementation of these studies across multiple institutions has been the need to undertake paper-based informed consent protocols, requiring significant commitment from staff at all participating institutions, not just the initial investigators'.

3. DATA GATHERING

We propose a data-gathering project that will leverage the widespread use of the BlueJ system to gather more data than the Thomas et al study, from more students than the Edwards et al study, at a similar granularity to the Jadud and Fenwick et al studies. More importantly, we will gather data from students at many institutions around the world, but at a relatively consistent point in their formation as programmers.

3.1 What will be gathered?

One of the important decisions in the design of this work is the selection of the data to be captured by our mechanism. The exact detail of the data will determine the nature of the research questions that may later be investigated using this data. The challenge, therefore, is to capture data that allows as wide a selection of investigations later on, and not restricting its use to a set of previously determined studies.

The aim of capturing data widely (to allow the investigation of as many research questions as possible) has to be offset against issues of privacy and practicality. We have to ensure anonymisation of the data collected, and we have to ensure that the volume of data is manageable, both in the collection phase and the evaluation phase.

This latter aspect is closely related to the question of the abstraction level of the data being collected. On one end of the spectrum, low level events (such as key strokes and mouse events, potentially including every mouse movement) could be logged; at the other extreme, higher level events - such as logical interactions with system components - might be recorded. While low level data offers a more "complete" picture of activity, collection and evaluation is more complex, and often necessitates a transformation into higher-level events anyway, which can be confounded by variability and "noise" in the event traces. Higher level data is easier to interpret, but may exclude investigation of some research questions not previously anticipated.

For the BlueJ data-gathering project, we currently plan to collect the following data, tagged with the UID and timestamped:

- Compilation events – the result of every compilation ordered by the student, including details of any errors reported, and a snapshot of the code submitted to the compiler.

- Code edits, on a line-by-line basis. That is, when a line of code is edited, the modified line will be transmitted once the user moves the cursor to a different line. We will differentiate between single line and multi-line edits, the latter being likely copy-and-paste or reformatting operations, and separately identify edits caused by code-completion actions (i.e. auto-suggested methods names).

- Interactive invocations, including method calls and object creation, on the object bench and in the codepad (i.e. all user code invocation). The object bench is a unique feature of BlueJ which allows students to explore the behaviour of their programs interactively. The codepad is a more traditional direct code entry and execution mechanism which, in BlueJ, can interact with objects recorded in the object bench.

- Unit-testing – recording the execution and results of tests which use BlueJ's integrated JUnit support.

- Project-open and project-close events, giving a handle on time-on-task.

- Debugging – when the debugger is opened/closed, when breakpoints are set, when breakpoints are hit, when 'step'/'continue' are used.

- Use of version control – commit/update commands, through BlueJ's integrated SVN support.

- Location of the user to the "regional" level: the step between the national and the city. For some countries, this will not be available, so only the country will be recorded. Anonymity of institution (if not of individual student) requires this degree of imprecision.

3.2 How much data do we expect to gather?
The data gathering mechanism will use an explicit opt-in approach, with students having to consent to taking part via a pop-up dialogue in BlueJ when they first use it. Students will be able to rescind their consent at any time, and students under the age of 16 will be warned-off (they cannot give their consent under UK law). Therefore, the total amount of data will be determined by the number of overall BlueJ users and the proportion of users who agree to be involved. At current usage levels, derived from the usage monitoring mechanism described above, this will lead to a maximum of around 27,000 users per day, performing on average 3 sessions per day, and generating about 100 events per session over an average period of 90 days. This would mean overall a maximum case of 8 million events per day, or just under 100 events per second, and a total of 3 terabyte of data per year.

3.3 Who will we gather it from?
Students agreeing to contribute data to the repository will not be identified by name or institution. To help to ensure that student names are not accidentally gathered, "class comments" (which is where Javadoc @author tags appear) will be blanked out at source (blanked out rather than deleted to preserve line numbers, etc. for matching to compiler output). We will make no attempt to detect and blank identifying information placed elsewhere in the source.

For every participating user, on every BlueJ installation with which they work, a unique identifier (UID) will be generated and used to tag all the data generated from that place. Using this mechanism, multiple sessions by the same student (in the same place) over time can be linked, allowing longitudinal studies, without identifying the individual. However, an individual student may have more than one UID, either because they work on more than one machine (e.g. in a Lab and at home), or because a particular Lab setup does not preserve students' identity across login sessions. In this case, the user will appear as two users, with histories that are incomplete, but internally consistent.

4. WORKING WITH THE DATA
We intend this project to benefit the Computing Education research community, and as such we will provide access to all the collected data for researchers at bona fide Universities and research institutes. This access will be in the form of SQL-queries on a read-only mirror of the collected data, hosted by us.

We anticipate that researchers working on the data will benefit from collaborating in the production of common SQL-queries and tools and more general approaches to mining the data; and will likely be willing to share the resulting tools with other researchers. To support such collaboration and sharing of resources, we will host a community website for the researchers in the style of the existing Greenroom [2], which supports the sharing and collaborative development of resources through a Wiki-style interaction mechanism.

The data that we collect directly will be anonymised. However, we anticipate that researchers will want to be able to run studies at their local institution where they collect additional data (age, gender, programming experience, etc) about the participants, and then be able to match the data with the participant's user in the database. To support this, users will be able to enter a code (provided by the researchers running the local study) that identifies them in the data. Data retrieved from the database can be restricted by tag, but tags will not be directly retrievable. Thus a researcher can restrict the data retrieved to only that with their tag (i.e. only the users participating in their experiment), but cannot see the tags applied to any other data, effectively denying them the ability to "see" other cohorts within the data.

Beyond this, it is clearly possible for researchers to get students to place identifying material (either at the student or intervention level) into their source code outside the class-comment. But such data will not be indexed in the repository, and so retrieving data on the basis of such material will be highly inefficient (unless pre-filtered on the basis of the indexed tags described above.

Of course, the per-student UIDs are stored locally, and so can be retrieved by a researcher (given the consent of the student) to tie-in with individually collected local data.

Any researcher who wished to identify their own students, or projects, will need to obtain local approval for their experiment (human subjects, or ethical, approval) as required. Approval for collection, use and sharing of the global, anonymised, data has already been obtained by the authors at the institution where the data will be kept.

5. SUMMARY

We propose to instrument the widely-used BlueJ beginners' programming environment to collect anonymised data about students' behaviour. This data will include code-edits, compilation events and other events such as tool invocations. The resulting data-set will be made available to other Computing Education researchers in order to support their research.

We believe that the scale of this data-set will enable not only quantitative differences in research (due to the large number of users likely to be involved in the collection), but also consequent qualitative differences. The large scale means that less-frequently used features (such as the debugger) or rarer error messages (such as private/public access problems) will have enough data that they can actually be studied, where previously this was not possible. The multi-institutional, even multi-national, scope of the data collection will allow comparisons between groups of students which have not been possible in smaller-scale research.

We also believe that this study has the potential to greatly enhance all of Computing Education research, by sharing the large body of data to enable collaborative research by researchers beyond those involved in collecting the data, and by researchers who do not necessarily have the opportunity (or time) to collect their own data at a teaching institution.

6. REFERENCES

[1] Ahmadzadeh, M., Elliman, D., and Higgins, C., An Analysis of Patterns of Debugging among Novice Computer Science Students. In *Proceedings of the 10th annual SIGCSE conference on Innovation and technology in computer science education (ITiCSE '05)* (Caparica, Portugal, 2005), pp. 84-88

[2] Brown, N., Stevens, P., and Kölling, M. 2010. Greenroom: a teacher community for collaborative resource development. In *Proceedings of the fifteenth annual conference on Innovation and technology in computer science education (ITiCSE '10)*. ACM, New York, NY, USA, 305-305.

[3] Stephen H. Edwards, Jason Snyder, Manuel A. Pérez-Quiñones, Anthony Allevato, Dongkwan Kim, and Betsy Tretola. 2009. Comparing effective and ineffective behaviors of student programmers. In *Proceedings of the fifth international workshop on Computing education research workshop (ICER '09)*. ACM, New York, NY, USA, 3-14.

[4] Fenwick, J. B., Norris, C., Barry, F. E., Rountree, J., Spicer, C. J., and Cheek, S. D. Another look at the behaviors of novice programmers. In *Proc. 40th ACM Tech. Symp. Computer Science Education*, ACM, New York, NY, 2009, pp. 296–300.

[5] Jadud, M. A first look at novice compilation behaviour using BlueJ. *Computer Science Education*, 15(1):25–40, March2005.

[6] Kölling, M., Quig, B., Patterson, A., and Rosenberg, J. The BlueJ system and its pedagogy. *Journal of Computer Science Education, Special issue on Learning and Teaching Object Technology*, 13(4), 2003.

[7] Thomas, R., Kennedy, G.E., Draper, S., Mancy, R., Crease, M., Evans, H., and Gray, P. Generic usage monitoring of programming students. In *Proceedings of the 20th Annual Conference of the Australasian Society for Computers in Learning in Tertiary Education (ASCILITE '03)* (Adelaide, Australia, Dec 7-10, 2003).

Evaluating an Early Software Engineering Course with Projects and Tools from Open Source Software

Robert McCartney   Swapna S. Gokhale   Thérèse Smith
Deptartment of Computer Science and Engineering
University of Connecticut, Storrs, CT, USA
[robert|ssg|tms08012]@engr.uconn.edu

ABSTRACT

We developed a software engineering course that emphasizes code maintenance and evolution by having students reverse engineer and modify open-source projects. To evaluate whether this course had the desired effects on student learning, we analyze pre- and post-course survey data using qualitative methods. This analysis, in combination with other data, suggests that the students gained an appreciation and understanding of software maintenance, documentation, and tool use.

Categories and Subject Descriptors

D.2.7 [**Software Engineering**]: Distribution, Maintenance, and Enhancement; K.3.2 [**Computers and Education**]: Computers and Information Science Education

General Terms

Documentation, Design, Experimentation

Keywords

Software Engineering, Maintenance, Reverse Engineering, Program Comprehension

1. INTRODUCTION

There is a predicted shortfall in supplying the need for people trained in software development and maintenance [3]. To meet this growing demand, most institutions now mandate a Software Engineering (SE) course in their undergraduate computing curricula. The objective of this course is to train students in the principles, techniques, and tools useful in both construction ("forward engineering") and maintenance and evolution ("reverse engineering") of software systems. Forward engineering includes design, implementation and testing skills, while reverse engineering includes the skills necessary for extracting the design and structure of existing systems from their code. Most SE courses disproportionately emphasize software construction as opposed to

maintenance and evolution skills. Software engineers in the industry, however, spend a majority of their time in understanding and evolution of legacy software. Hence, we believe that the SE course should focus more on reverse engineering tasks. Additionally, because it is commonplace in industry to use tools to improve the effectiveness and efficiency of SE tasks, the SE course should also train students in such tools.

Maintenance and evolution of legacy software is challenging and cumbersome because it requires understanding poorly written, unstructured code that may have been subject to many fixes and enhancements. Moreover, the documentation can be completely out of date, and very little technical support may be available. It is necessary to emulate these characteristics of legacy software in an academic environment to facilitate teaching SE with a focus on maintenance aspects. We believe that open source software (OSS) projects can exhibit many of these properties, and hence, we taught our SE course using these projects. Reflecting its maintenance-centric focus, next we present the specific objectives of the course and the questions used for the course's evaluation.

1.1 Specific objectives

We want our students to gain skills that are required for maintenance and evolution of software systems. Specifically, we would like them to be able to:

1. Comprehend code sufficiently through reverse engineering to subsequently enhance it.
2. Perform proposed maintenance and evolution tasks.
3. Appreciate that existing architecture imposes constraints on implementing additional requirements.

To comprehend code, a student must be able to discover the underlying structure, such as modules and class hierarchies, as well as being able to discover execution time interactions among the modules. We expect the students to use tools that support these activities, and to be able to express the structure and behavior of both the legacy code and their proposed enhancements using relevant UML diagrams. [10] Given this comprehension, the student should be able to fix and enhance a software system without any undesirable impacts. Performing such tasks should lead to a better understanding of the constraints imposed by the existing architecture.

1.2 Evaluation Questions

We wish to evaluate whether our SE course, taught using OSS projects, accomplished the above objectives. To do so, we examine how student understanding of software maintenance and evolution changes while taking this course. Particularly, we examine whether the students understand:

- The importance of maintenance and evolution in a software project, specifically as a sizeable portion of the overall effort;

- The value and critical consideration of documentation in software maintenance and evolution;

- How reverse engineering can provide sufficient comprehension of existing code to add functionality; and

- How tools can support and improve SE activities.

To evaluate these objectives, we conducted pre- and post-semester surveys, which included both multiple choice and open-response questions, which generated free-text answers. In this paper, we use these free-text answers as our primary data to evaluate these understandings. We also use evidence collected during the conduct and assessment of the course, including the end-of-the-semester project presentations and demonstrations, as a way of triangulating the survey data.

The remainder of the paper is organized as follows. Section 2 describes the course. Section 3 discusses the methodology. Sections 4 and 5 respectively summarize and discuss the results. Section 6 compares prior work. Section 7 concludes with suggestions for future work.

2. COURSE DESCRIPTION

Our SE course is offered early in the curriculum, to sophomores and juniors, after the students have acquired preliminary experience in Java programming and have taken a data structures course. Thus, prior to SE, the students can write, test and debug object-oriented code in Java, use Eclipse, create UML class diagrams, and produce documentation.

The course teaches them how to tackle bigger projects, written by others. The lectures cover SE principles, which the students then apply to their course projects. Through the semester, the students work in pairs on a single project, which they select at the beginning. The overall goal of this project is for the students to propose, plan, and implement an enhancement to their existing system. Teams can either propose and implement their own enhancements, or implement those suggested by the course staff; most choose to implement their own.

Several assignments are connected to this project, to help the students to gain a good enough understanding of the project to be able to implement and test their enhancements. These assignments offer intermediate milestones: in one they create UML class diagrams; in another, after familiarizing themselves with their projects they choose an enhancement; in a third one they describe their enhancement and test plans with use case diagrams, and its implementation using class and sequence diagrams. Midway through the course, students present their progress on the implementation of their enhancements. At the end of the semester, they present their project and demonstrate these enhancements.

3. METHODOLOGY

This section describes the design of the study, how data were collected, and the analysis methods.

3.1 Study Design

We collected data from a single semester's offering of our SE course. The students were asked to complete anonymous online surveys in the first and the last weeks of the semester – referred to as "start" and "end" surveys respectively. As an incentive, they were given points for completing each survey. Both surveys included 15 multiple-choice questions (about student's background, software design and maintenance, and open source software), and these were followed by open-response questions:

16. (start) What are your expectations about what you will learn in this course?

16. (end) What are the main things that you learned in this course?

17. (end) Are the things that you learned different from what you expected? If so, briefly explain the differences.

3.2 Data Collection

Data were collected using the two surveys outside of class time. Students were asked to provide a unique ID with each survey so we could pair up the pre- and post-course surveys for individuals while keeping the data anonymous. The free-text responses were electronically copied and pasted from the survey tool into the Saturate application [12] to support the analysis. Presentations and other participant observations were not anonymous; these data are dealt with here as a unit, rather than on a per student or team basis.

There were 36 students in the class, mostly juniors (start of third year). Thirty-four of the students filled out the start survey, thirty-five filled out the end survey. Three of the students did not answer the "What are your expectations?" question on the start survey; all of students answered both of the open-response questions on the end survey. We observed lab activities and presentations for the whole class.

The data corpus includes all of the survey responses. Supplementary data for triangulation were field notes of participant observation of student activities, including presentations and demonstrations of the enhanced projects.

3.3 Analysis Method

We used thematic analysis [2] as our primary method to analyze the data set consisting of the answers to the three open response questions presented above. Our approach was somewhere between inductive and theoretical: we did not start with a fixed coding framework, but we were influenced by the research questions' focus on software engineering in general and its maintenance aspects in particular. The analysis of the text was at the semantic/explicit level (based on the surface meaning of the text), and we took an essentialist/realist epistemological perspective (meaning is reflected in the language used).

Our analysis procedure was consistent with that presented by Braun and Clarke [2]. Briefly, the analysis proceeded as follows. We read all of the responses to become familiar with the data set, then coded text fragments, originally using in vivo (the students' own words) codes. After that, texts that recurred in the data set were grouped with related texts, related groups were combined, resulting in a set of themes and subthemes that characterize the data. The process of building themes and subthemes was not a linear process: groups were combined and split, codes moved in and out of groups, groups and/or codes that were seen as peripheral to the data were eliminated. The general rules of thumb we used are that we included things that were prevalent in the data, that themes and subthemes were internally similar, that different themese and subthemes were recognizably different, and that the themes were adequate to describe the data set. Ultimately the themes and subthemes could be characterized in terms of what they meant, how they related to each other, and how they explained the data set.

This analysis was performed separately on start and end data. After this, we compared and looked for relationships between the themes and subthemes from the start and end surveys. From these results, we examined the questions in Section 1.2 in light of the end data, as well as the development of the students as a whole through comparison of the start and end results.

A second analysis was done using paired data (i.e., start and end responses from individual students). Using themes and subthemes from the thematic analyses, we compared individual responses to see whether students learned what they expected, and whether the individuals exhibited anything different from what we saw in the aggregate data. This was done via a side-by-side comparison of the coded responses – for each pair we wrote a memo describing the relationship (if any) between the start and end responses.

Finally, we used the participant observations from assignments, presentations, demonstrations, and laboratories to triangulate the above results.

4. RESULTS

In this section, we first present the results from the survey data and then from participant observations. Finally, we relate these results to the questions posed in Section 1.2.

4.1 Survey Data

The survey data were analyzed in two ways, by performing and comparing thematic analyses for the start and end data, then by considering the paired start-end data for each student.

Thematic analyses

Figure 1 presents the results from the analysis of the start data as a thematic map. It has three themes: Technique, Development Context, and Hardware Platform. The theme Technique arose as the most common idea in the start texts. At the beginning, students expected that the course would teach them disciplined approaches to programming. Most of the techniques involved software design and implementation, with some mention of documentation and teamwork. The theme Development Context involved external aspects of the code development process: large scale, or done at work, or done in the real world, or code for someone else. It also involved some documentation and teamwork – these subthemes being part of Technique as well. This theme relates to and provides motivation for the first theme. In the third theme, Hardware Platform, the students hoped to learn how to produce software for multiple platforms (Android or iPhone), but also to see more clearly the interaction between software and its hardware infrastructure. Overall, the start data shows that students expect to learn to design well and code effectively and efficiently – a number mentioned becoming better coders.

Figure 2 shows the thematic map for the end data. It shows three themes: Software Quality, comprised of aspects of a well-engineered product; Engineering Activities and Tools, a collection of means to achieve the end represented by the first theme; and Student Reactions, the students' affective responses to their experience taking the course. Under Software Quality they wrote of the specific qualities they expect in software: reliability, modularity, evolvability and robustness. Similarly, under Engineering Activities and Tools, students discussed specific SE activities such as managing the software lifecycle, understanding requirements, planning, creating artifacts, methodically producing documentation, participating in a team, modifying code, and testing. They also reported organization of work activities and of software modules, use of principles in software production, and techniques of analysis including diagramming and other tools. Student Reactions included surprise that coding is a smaller part of the software production enterprise than they had imagined; negative reactions toward the course or its material, generally that they felt other aspects should have been emphasized; and positive aspects such as learning a lot more or finding the course less stressful than they expected. Overall, the end data show a more detailed understanding of SE, including use of a more sophisticated technical vocabulary. They included modification of existing software and use of tools under Engineering Activities and Tools, evolvability as a desirable Software Quality, and a lot more about documentation under both of those themes (there was also some mention of documentation under Student Responses, reacting negatively to other people's inadequate documentation).

Given these analyses, we looked for relations between the early and late themes. The result, as shown in Figure 3, is that the early Technique theme maps to two late themes, Software Quality, a set of product characteristics, and Engineering Activities and Tools, approaches to achieving that quality. The end results are more specific, with a more technical SE vocabulary. Both of these late themes can be seen as specializations of the earlier Technique theme, with different emphases. General ideas became elaborated during the semester, so that end survey text introduces more specific terms, qualifies the general terms, and increases emphasis on some subthemes, notably documentation. The techniques listed at the start of the semester have become situated contextually as means to the end of producing software, and the qualities of the software have become specific.

Paired start-end responses

We used the student-generated IDs to match up start and end responses for individual students. There were difficulties with the student-generated IDs, however: we had 34 surveys from the start, and 35 from the end, but there were only 15 exact ID matches from survey to survey (and one of these did not answer question 16 in the start data). Based on this limited set, we see a couple of things that did not show up in the aggregate data. First, there was a group of students who could be categorized as "Detailed expectations-negative affective response." These were students who had clear expectations having to do with software development, and were unhappy that the course emphasis did not match what they wanted. While a minority, they accounted for a disproportionate amount of the negative Student Reactions. Second, there was a group of students "Expected coding-

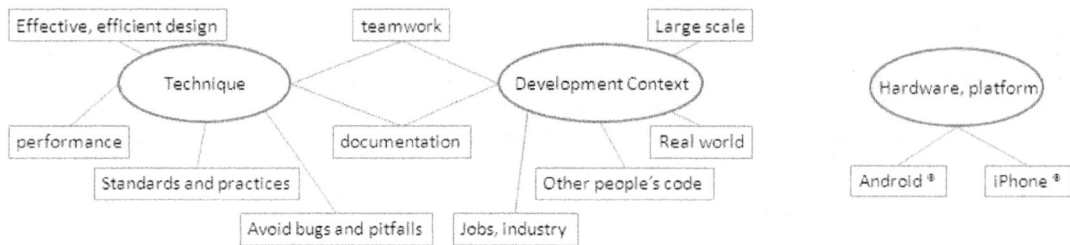

Figure 1: Themes (ellipses) and subthemes (rectangles) in early data

Figure 2: Themes (ellipses) and subthemes (rectangles) in late data

learned maintenance"; students who expected to generate code and learned about modification and evolution. We would have expected this from the aggregate themes. Finally, there was some disconnect between the pre- and post-questions about expected and actual things learned, and the question about whether the student learned what he or she expected. Just under half of the students said they learned what they expected; about half of these were consistent between what they expected to learn and what they learned. For the students who said they did not learn what they expected, the differences they gave were often not apparent in the pre- and post- answers.

Since we had a relatively small set of matched pairs, we looked at the question about differences between expectations and things learned for all students. Of the roughly half who said there was a difference, the most common answer was that they expected more coding or design.

4.2 Participant Observations

We collected data other than surveys, field notes from participant observations, presentations and demonstrations. Specifically we noted that:

- Students were cautious when proposing extensions, out of concern that they would hurt their grade by taking on more than they could do, even though we assured them that they would be graded on what they did.

- All the presentations included UML diagrams, showing students' competence in these.

- Students discovered that they could comprehend and enhance their projects with the help of reverse engineering tools, although the project documentation may not be written in English.

- By the end of the semester, every student team had achieved a functional enhancement of their project, which they demonstrated to the course staff.

4.3 Evaluation Results

These results provide insights into how students' understanding of software maintenance evolved by considering each research question posed in Section 1.2.

Importance of Maintenance and Evolution

The first question determines whether the students realize the importance of software maintenance and evolution.

Subthemes in the end data included modification, evolvability, lifecycle, planning, and documentation; only the last of these occurred in the start data. An example of modification and planning is illustrated in the following:

> Software maintenance and planning are the most important part of the development process.

Participant observation confirmed that students became aware of the significance of maintenance. One team asked advice when it was faced with two choices about how to implement a modification: an easy way would have destructured the code, while the harder way required an implementation of a new structure. The question revealed that they knew that it was critical to avoid destructuring the code.

Value of Documentation

The second question determines whether the students understand the value of documentation in maintaining and enhancing software systems.

Responses about documentation were much more prevalent in the end, such as:

> Documentation and organization of the Software Lifecycle are absolutely critical to successful software development.

> I should document my work and work in a methodical way so that other can understand my work.

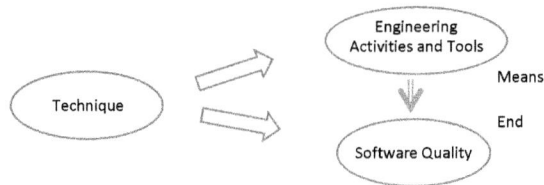

Figure 3: Mapping between related themes in early (left) and late (right) data

We found that the students' thoughts about documentation became more nuanced, and were sometimes explicitly linked to modification and evolvability:

> I really learned the importance of documentation, because if something is not well documented, then it is nearly impossible to add extensions to it.

Reverse engineering and comprehension

The third question asks whether the students understand that reverse engineering can provide sufficient comprehension of the code to add functionality.

Only one student mentioned reverse engineering or re-engineering in the end survey, although many mentioned artifacts that could be obtained from reverse engineering.

> [I]mportance of documentation and the proper ways of analyzing systems. Especially, the tools that we have been exposed to that are so critical to building and reengineering a system

We observed that each team used tools to extract their project designs, and was able to add and demonstrate functionality to their project. This offers some support for the idea that they gained sufficient comprehension from reverse engineering.

Tool Support

The fourth question sought to determine whether the students appreciate the importance of tools in SE tasks.

One student answered the question "What are the main things that you learned in this course?" with

> Use of software engineering tools software testing methods

Another answer to this same question included:

> How to makes Use Case Diagrams, Sequence Diagrams and Class Diagrams.... And the importance in software artifacts, how they are helpful for understanding the code and help with future implementations.

Participant observation revealed that the students wished that they had had the benefit of the tool that extracted sequence diagrams from the code earlier than it was offered.

5. DISCUSSION

In this section, we discuss students' development in terms of themes found in the two surveys, we discuss issues related to the survey design and implementation, and consider some factors that may affect validity.

Student development

The scope and the specificity of the start themes and sub-themes is consistent with the educational level of the students. The Technique theme refers to the quality of the engineered product in general terms: effective design, coding standards and practices, performance, avoiding bugs and pitfalls. These ideas expand into two themes in the end survey, namely, Software Quality and Engineering Activities and Tools. The quality subthemes (reliability, modularity, evolvability and robustness), and the Activities subthemes (planning, lifecycle, requirements, testing) reflect a deeper and more formal understanding of software engineering. The increased specificity and use of more formal vocabulary suggest that the students have matured within the discipline.

Survey Design and Implementation

Although the surveys provided useful data, there were several issues that reduced their effectiveness. First, the short answers to the open-response questions contained limited information. It is reasonable to assume that the themes reflect the things that students saw as most important, but short answers probably do not reflect everything a student learned (or expected to learn). The lack of specific answers about reverse engineering tools may be because nearly everyone saw one or two other things as more important.

Second, the student-generated codes designed to provide us with paired before-after data failed a large part of the time. We do not know whether the generation scheme was too complicated, or if students gave mismatched IDs on purpose; it is possible that the matching-ID pairs are a biased subset of the students. For example, the "Detailed expectations-negative affective response" group may represent a real phenomenon, but the evidence is weakened by these pair-identification issues.

Finally, the content and vocabulary of the multiple-choice questions may have affected the open-response answers. The same multiple-choice questions appeared on both surveys, but the students are presumably different at the end so there may be a differential effect. The first lecture, which was given before the start survey, may also have influenced start responses.

Validity Considerations

One approach to validity includes discussions among the authors. The themes developed in the coding of the start survey were prepared by one of the authors. These themes were checked for transferability to the data collected from the same survey, but from a later class, by another author. The results confirmed the themes, and suggested saturation because no new themes emerged. For transferability, it is important to note that our data were obtained from early-career SE students. Late-career SE students who have more experience and background may respond differently.

Another approach to validation was triangulation using evidence from participant observations, and examination of assignments, presentations and demonstrations. These different types of data provided us with converging viewpoints.

One possible source of bias is that the authors are hoping for success in the use of open source projects in this course. To counter this bias, listening to a course staff member, who was against OSS projects and the chosen tools was useful.

6. RELATED WORK

Several authors have described evaluations of SE courses. Baker et al. [1] taught SE process with an objective of emulating real-world phenomena. Their informal evaluation was based on written feedback in the form of answers to structured questions. Chen and Chong's [4] objective was to teach students how to have effective meetings for software development teams, which they evaluated by measuring the time to completion of the projects, and observing that those projects that followed their meeting approach delivered five weeks early. Hainey et al.'s [5] objective was to teach requirements collection and analysis, which they evaluated using pre- and post-testing questioning. Lee [6] had the objective of empowering teachers to create educational software. Evaluation was by means of an anonymous survey asking respondents about their attitude to the experience. Pfahl et al. [11] evaluated the effectiveness of using simulations to teach software project management. They used pre- and post-tests with an experimental and a control group.

The objectives of our project were to train students broadly in SE activities, with an emphasis on maintenance and evolution. We focused more on software discovery, modification and documentation content, and less on process [1], requirements analysis [5], collaboration and meetings [4] or software creation [5]. Similar to Lee [6], our surveys were anonymous and asked students about their impressions and experiences. Unlike Chen and Chong [4], however, our evaluation was not measurement-oriented. Finally, similar to Pfahl et. al. [11], we plan to compare our course with a control group, the same SE course not using OSS.

A number of authors have used OSS in software engineering courses; Marmorstein [8] provides some examples. Most of these courses had students join existing OSS projects in order to learn about open source software development process, whereas we are simply using open source code for the students to work with independently. With goals similar to ours, Nandigam et al. [9] have used Apache and other open source projects to teach reverse engineering and other software engineering topics.

7. CONCLUSIONS

This paper uses thematic analysis to evaluate whether an SE course taught using OSS projects can impart the importance of software maintenance and evolution to early-career computing students. Our results suggest that this is so: the students came away with an increased appreciation for the significance of maintenance effort and the criticality of documentation. While the results also suggest that students learned the value of reverse engineering and tool use, those results are not as conclusive.

We expect to refine our evaluation techniques as we improve the course. There are potential sources of bias that we can eliminate, particularly in collecting paired start-end surveys, and there are other kinds of data that we can collect from the course. We will also explore formal techniques [7] to collect data through participant observation, and try to better tie these qualitative results to student performance data. Finally, we have collected similar data for a version of this course that emphasizes software development rather than maintenance, which should give us more insights into the effects of the maintenance-centered approach.

8. ACKNOWLEDGEMENTS

We wish to thank the students who participated in the survey. We wish to thank Lisa Kaczmarczyk who helped us design the pre- and post-course surveys. This research is supported by the National Science Foundation under grants DUE-1044061. Any opinions, findings, and conclusions or recommendations expressed in this material are those of the authors and do not necessarily reflect those of the National Science Foundation.

9. REFERENCES

[1] A. Baker, E. O. Navarro, and A. van der Hoek. An experimental card game for teaching software engineering processes. *Journal of Systems and Software*, 75(1-2):3 – 16, 2005.

[2] V. Braun and V. Clarke. Using thematic analysis in psychology. *Qualitative Research in Psychology*, 3(2):77–101, 2006.

[3] S. Canada. Statistics canada. http://www.statcan.gc.ca/start-debut-eng.html, 2012.

[4] C.-Y. Chen and P. P. Chong. Software engineering education: A study on conducting collaborative senior project development. *Journal of Systems and Software*, 84(3):479 – 491, 2011.

[5] T. Hainey, T. M. Connolly, M. Stansfield, and E. A. Boyle. Evaluation of a game to teach requirements collection and analysis in software engineering at tertiary education level. *Computers & Education*, 56(1):21 – 35, 2011.

[6] Y.-J. Lee. Empowering teachers to create educational software: A constructivist approach utilizing etoys, pair programming and cognitive apprenticeship. *Computers & Education*, 56(2):527 – 538, 2011.

[7] T. C. Lethbridge, S. E. Sim, and J. Singer. Studying software engineers: Data collection techniques for software field studies. *Empirical Software Engineering*, 10:311–341, 2005.

[8] R. Marmorstein. Open source contribution as an effective software engineering class project. In *Proceedings of the 16th annual joint conference on Innovation and technology in computer science education*, ITiCSE '11, pages 268–272, New York, NY, USA, 2011. ACM.

[9] J. Nandigam, V. Gudivada, and A. Hamou-Lhadj. Learning software engineering principles using open source software. In *38th Ann. Frontiers in Education Conference*, pages S3H–18–S3H–23, 2008.

[10] Object Management Group. Unified modeling language. http://www.uml.org/, 1997. viewed on April 16, 2012.

[11] D. Pfahl, O. Laitenberger, G. Ruhe, J. Dorsch, and T. Krivobokova. Evaluating the learning effectiveness of using simulations in software project management education: results from a twice replicated experiment. *Information and Software Technology*, 46(2):127 – 147, 2004.

[12] J. Sillito. Saturate application. http://www.saturateapp.com/.

A Case Study of Environmental Factors Influencing Teaching Assistant Job Satisfaction

Elizabeth Patitsas
University of Toronto & University of British Columbia
40 St George St.
Toronto ON M5S 2E4
patitsas@cs.toronto.edu

ABSTRACT

Teaching assistants (TAs) play an integral role in teaching computer science undergraduates in North America. We report lessons in lab TA management, based on a case study which identified environmental factors affecting TAs' job satisfaction. These factors were identified through a series of semi-structured interviews about 23 lab sections taught at the University of British Columbia. We corroborated this with observational sampling of eight different TAs. Identified physical factors affecting job satisfaction include the layout and lighting of the lab rooms. Temporal factors include the intensity and length of the lab sessions. Having a positive social environment (in particular, support from team teaching and staff meetings) was also found to improve job satisfaction.

Categories and Subject Descriptors

K.3.2 [**Computers and Information Science Education**]: Pedagogy, education research

General Terms

Human factors

Keywords

Computer science education, teaching assistants, labs

1. INTRODUCTION AND MOTIVATION

Teaching assistants (TAs) play a vital role in teaching computer science (CS) undergraduates: at many institutions, students spend more time with the TAs than course instructors [7]. In the way we teach CS in large research institutions, we have a culture of high TA use, low student retention, and high failure rates in CS1 [5].

TAs have been found to influence retention [16], and students' performance in labs have been found to be a predictor of success on final exams in CS1 [4]. Within the TA-taught labs, correlations have been found between interaction with TAs and performance on final exams [18]. More interaction and more active observation[1] (as opposed to passive observation) were both found to improve their students' marks, and asocial behaviour of TAs[2] was linked to lower marks. Furthermore, it is known that TAs' favourite part of their job is interacting with their students [7]. In short, the more a TA interacts with their students, the happier they are at work, and the better their students do in class.

Yet, despite enjoying student interactions, TA quality remains an issue [15]. We take the position that the situation is more complex than some TAs just being "bad" – that there are also environmental factors preventing TAs from having quality interactions with their students.

1.1 Research Study

In this work, we seek to answer two research questions (RQs):

RQ1: What environmental factors affect TAs' reported job satisfaction?

RQ2: Knowing that interaction with students is the TAs' favourite part of their work, what environmental factors affect TAs' interactions with students?

Ever since lab-based instruction in CS took off in the 90s [8], the CS community has borrowed environmental approaches to teaching labs from other disciplines. For example, despite the lack of equipment necessitating it, we use workbench-style layouts for lab rooms, taking after physics and chemistry. Like those fields, we have borrowed the three-hour format for labs at our institution – yet our students can save and complete their labs at a later time. We think that we can do better by tailoring the lab environments in CS to the discipline itself, and by identifying and diffusing environmental factors impeding the work of CS TAs.

Although no existing work has examined physical environmental factors affecting teaching assistants' experience on the job, prior work on K-12 teachers has identified physical factors such as lighting, windows, acoustics, the height of the ceiling, the layout of the room, and the number of walls [1, 6]. The social environment has been found to affect TAs; in particular, studies of TAs have found that a lack of social support structures for TAs negatively affects their work [7, 15]. We speculate that, since TAs are less trained than K-12 teachers and generally less experienced, they would be more sensitive to environmental distractions.

---

[1] Active observation is defined to be focused observation on what a student is doing, lasting for more than five seconds.
[2] E.g. checking their email, grading assignments, being outside the room.

2. METHODS

Our study had two portions: one qualitative, and one quantitative. First, we performed semi-structured interviews asking TAs about their experiences teaching labs. In the interviews we made note of what environmental factors the TAs noted as affecting their experience as a TA, and what effect the factor had (positive/negative). Our qualitative approach allowed us to build a theory of what factors mattered to the TAs at our institution; exploratory theory-building is a strength of qualitative approaches. Quantitative approaches, in contrast, are useful for validating and testing theories. The second portion, which was quantitative, allowed us to test the readily quantifiable portions of our theory.

Both portions of the study were part of a larger study of TA experience at our institution; the data used in this paper are a subset of the data collected in the whole study.

2.1 Interviews

We began with semi-structured interviews: we had nine participants, who were interviewed for an hour each. Our unit of analysis is the lab section; each participant was interviewed about *each* lab section they had taught; a total of 23 sections were described by our TAs.

The interviews began with a *grand-tour question*[3], an open ended question which allows the interviewee to set the direction of the interview [19]. We did not directly ask TAs which environmental factors affected their enjoyment of teaching a given section – only what their experience was teaching each different lab section they had ever taught, and how the sections compared to each other[4]. This allowed us to see which factors would emerge without direct probing, or biasing the interview towards the factors that we expected the participants to note. We analyzed the interview data using affinity diagrams [13] to categorize our data and identify patterns in our results.

We recruited interview participants at the course staff meetings of first and second-year courses and at a general event for TAs of the department. TAs with whom the author had worked were deliberately excluded from the study. We interviewed nine TAs, after determining from Guest et al. [11] that at least six participants would be necessary for the study given its exploratory nature and our goal of theory-building. As this was a qualitative, theory-building exercise, we were unconcerned with drawing a random sampling – we wished to generalize from our findings to theory (analytical generalization) as opposed to generalizing from a sample to a population (statistical generalization).

2.2 Observational Sampling

There is a long history of observational methods in the behavioural sciences; *observational sampling* refers to a family of quantitative approaches therein. In observational sampling, the observed behaviours are categorized and tabulated; the time or frequency of particular categories is ana-

lyzed quantitatively. This stands in contrast to qualitative observational styles, where the observer describes the situation at hand, trying to explain or depict the scenario. Like all qualitative methods, that approach is excellent for exploring and generating hypotheses; for validating or testing, however, quantitative approaches are more appropriate.

While the CS education community has used qualitative observational methods in the past, observational sampling remains uncommon (but not unused, e.g. [10]). An observational study was most suited to our larger research study on TA experience – to complement the interviews – and by using this approach we could do quantitative analysis of duration/percentage of behaviours. This approach has been used in the physics education community, such as in Paul et al's work with physics TAs [18].

A common element of all observational sampling methods is the use of an *ethogram*; this is a well-defined catalogue of behaviours. The categories of behaviours are intended to be mutually exclusive and as objective as possible. For example, "active observation" in this study is defined as "the TA is seen staring at a particular student or a student's computer monitor for a duration exceeding five seconds". We cannot know if the TA was actually thinking about the student's work or was just mindlessly gazing in that direction; but this allows for clarity, consisitency and repeatability in our data.

The ethogram we used for observing TAs had five categories: making class announcements, observing students or partner, interacting with students, interacting with partner, and "non-interaction" (Table 1). Each category has several subcategories; the latter category contains subcategories such as working on a computer and being out of the room. This ethogram was adapted from Paul et al's work in observing physics TAs [18]; Paul only looked at student-TA interactions so for this study we added an additional category for logging TA-TA interactions.

A second element in observational sampling is the difference between states and events; in state-based sampling, as we have done in the paper, we are concerned with how long an observed individual remains in a given state. This allows us to investigate duration. In contrast, events are instantaneous. The choice of whether to sample events or states has an effect on the choice of observational method and should be based on the type of research question.

Altmann's 1974 paper [2] on observational sampling is a definitive guide to the different approaches; in the paper she discusses six, appropriate to different research questions and whether one is observing individuals, pairs, or groups. The techniques are applicable to the study of both human and nonhuman animal behaviour, and have a long history of use in both areas.

In our study, we used a technique known in Altmann's paper as *focal animal sampling*; it is also known as focal individual sampling, or when studying a small group, focal group sampling. It refers to sampling all occurrences of specified (inter)actions of an individual or small group [2]. In focal animal sampling, non-social behaviours are straightforward to document; for social behaviours we also need to define receivers and actors. This method is suitable when there is only one or two individuals that we need to observe. In state-based focal sampling, we note the time at which each new state begins; cumulative time in given states can then be computed.

---

[3]Typically, "What has your experience been like as a TA?" Alternate wordings were used.

[4]We would first ask the participants to list all the courses they had TAed, and their duties for each. As we went through the list, we would ask questions like "how did you like teaching your Wednesday section?" or "how was the morning section different from the evening one? Which did you like teaching more?"

Category	(A) Addressing the class	(O) Observing student(s) or partner	(I) Interacting with students	(T) Interacting with partner	(N) Non-interacting
Example subcategories (not full list)	**A:** announcement **L:** lecturing the class on a concept **C:** clarifying text in the lab **W:** writing on the whiteboard	**PF:** passive obs. from the front of class **PW:** passive obs. while walking **A:** active obs. (>5s spent on one student) **T:** obs. partner	**L:** listening to the student **F:** questioning the student **S:** socializing with the student **A:** answering student's question	**G:** discussing strategy **U:** updating their partner **E:** explaining the lab to their partner **S:** socializing	**R:** out of room **G:** grading **C:** using computer **W:** wandering around not observing students

Table 1: Example ethogram codes; the code AW, for example, denotes a TA is writing on the whiteboard.

A trade-off to consider with any observational methods is that between observer fatigue and accumulating a representative distribution of samples. It is standard to take breaks at a consistent periodicity (e.g. sample for twenty minutes, then break for five, repeat) to ensure consistency in sampling. Every five minutes we also switched between which of the two TAs we were focusing on, as logging all behaviours of both TAs at once would have been a strain on the observer. Eight hours of observations were done of four pairs of participating TAs.

3. CONTEXT

The study took place at the University of British Columbia, a large, research-intensive university. The CS Department is home to 55 faculty members, 200 graduate students, and 1300 undergraduate students. In the 2010-11 academic year, the Department filled 153 full-time graduate student TAships and 56 undergraduate TAships.

The study considered only lab TAs. Laboratory sections in undergraduate courses are usually taught by pairs of TAs, borrowing a common practice from labs in the natural sciences and engineering. Sections typically contain 20-30 students, and meet weekly for two or three hours (typically ten times in a twelve week term). The lab rooms are all of similar size and have generally similar acoustics, although the layout varies.

Labs are more common in first and second-year courses. It is common for TAs to meet in weekly staff meetings. Weekly "lab TA meetings" are also held in the two largest first-year courses, in which lab TAs work through the labs in advance.

4. FINDINGS

4.1 The physical environment

4.1.1 Layout of the room

Participants reported having better, and more, student interactions in lab rooms with open layouts than in rooms with traditional "classroom" layouts. We illustrate the difference between these layouts in Figure 1.

Participants who had the experience of teaching in both types of rooms reported preferring the open layouts. As one participant noted, *"the lab layout in [a traditional room] is not as friendly to walking around as [an open room]. When I'd teach [traditional room], I'd walk around a bit, but it is harder. I'd wind up sitting at the front more."*

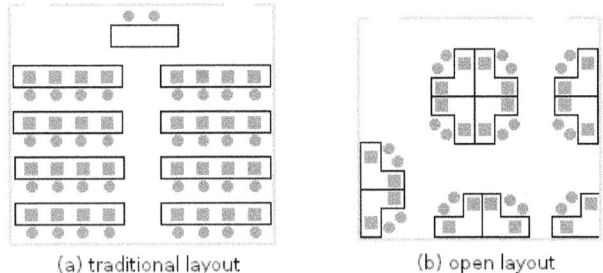

(a) traditional layout (b) open layout

Figure 1: In (a): the traditional "classroom" layout; in (b), an example of an open layout.

We found that TAs who worked in traditional rooms would sit down during lulls in student questions. We noted this in both interviews and observations. While most TAs would periodically take a tour of the room, they tended to make themselves comfortable while waiting for questions – *"[My partner and I] would let the students go crazy with the labs and we would sit at the front. [We'd] try out things on our computers."*

For the TAs in the open rooms, they reported – and were observed – spending those lulls walking around and looking at what the students were doing. As one participant describes it, *"Generally somebody always has their hand up, otherwise it is 'Brownian motion' – walking around slowly, when passing a student I'll a look at them. I'll be looking for students that don't ask questions but need help. If I have extra time I try to be as invasive as possible."*

During these lulls in the open rooms, TAs were more likely to socialize with their students; with the increased opportunity to access students in the room, *"I get to interact with the same group of students, so we develop a friendship sort of thing. It's fun knowing they can turn to me when they need help in lab."*

We observed that TAs in the open rooms spent almost twice as much time interacting with students than the TAs in the traditional rooms, as we saw in our observations (76% of their time vs. 40%). Furthermore, the TAs in the traditional rooms spent much more time doing "non-interacting" activities like texting on their phones (18% of their time vs. 7%). Also, TAs in the traditional rooms did spend much more time talking to their partners than the TAs in the open-rooms (26% vs. 3%). The open-room TAs spent less time overall observing their students (9% vs. 14%) but more of that observation was active as opposed to passively looking at their students from the front of the room.

4.1.2 Lighting

Participants noted better teaching conditions in rooms with more windows, which were better lit. As one participant noted, *"I like [well-lit room], it feels brighter. [The lab I teach in there] feels fun, friendly, not only amongst the TAs but amongst everyone."* The well-lit rooms were described much more positively, with TAs reporting having better moods in those rooms. It should be noted that the layout of the room is not related to the lighting: both types of layouts have a range of lighting.

We noticed that TAs in the rooms without windows were more likely to describe little interaction in their labs when interviewed. We noticed that they described their students as asking fewer questions, and that they would approach their students less often. In our observations of TAs, we found that TAs in the windowless-rooms spent noticeably less time interacting with students, making announcements to the class, and observing their students. Furthermore, the TAs in the windowless rooms also spent more time doing "non-interacting" activities, particularly surfing the web and using their phones.

4.2 The temporal environment

4.2.1 The intensity of the session

Participants preferred teaching labs where there was ample time for their students to complete the lab in the allotted time period, where the intensity was neither too high, nor too low. We use 'intensity' to refer to how often there are gaps, or "lulls" between student questions; a high-intensity lab would have no lulls, while a low intensity lab may involve long stretches of time without any student questions.

TAs in high-intensity labs were less likely to have time to sit down and talk to their students in depth, or have a chance to talk to their partners about their students. These TAs reported lower job satisfaction due to feeling "rushed", not having enough quality time with the students, and feeling bad when their students did not complete the labs on time. Indeed, for these TAs, not having students finish on time was a source of stress. Only the first-year introductory programming course had such high-intensity labs (which were three hours in length); for one participant, the fact that this was the students' first experience with CS added to the stress of the high-intensity labs.

Two courses were reported to have very low-intensity labs, one with three-hour labs and one with two-hour labs. A participant from the latter course reported *"I would have my laptop out and not be disturbed for an hour, hour and a half"* when teaching those labs, which had optional attendance. For the participants in these two courses, the low intensity resulted in boredom for the TAs, and a desire for students to ask them more questions.

The medium-intensity labs were described most positively. These were labs where TAs had regular questions to keep them engaged, but had enough "breathing time" to sit down with students and talk in detail, and restroom breaks.

In our observations, we only observed high-intensity and medium-intensity labs. The difference we saw here was in the frequency at which the TAs switched from student to student: the TAs in medium-intensity labs spent more focused time with their students. The TAs in high-intensity labs did spend more of their time interacting with students, but spent an average of only 7 seconds per student question, while TAs in medium-intensity labs spent an average of 20 seconds per student question.

4.2.2 The length of the session

Participants who taught three-hour lab sessions described their work as more "tiring" than participants who taught two-hour lab sessions. This was true regardless of the intensity of the lab. Three of our nine participants had experienced burnout; they were all on three-hour labs.

Of the nine interview participants, two were no longer teaching labs, both of whom had been on three-hour labs. One tired of the labs due to the stress: *"this term I'm on office hours instead of labs. It's a lot less stressful. [The three hours labs were] very draining... I'm not sure if I want to teach those labs again."* The other TA, from a different class, had much less intensive labs, instead tiring of the three-hour labs since *"there was a lot of time where we were idle... it takes a lot of patience... I needed a break from attending them. The labs were tiring since they were three hours, and most students took half that time."*.

The other interview participants who taught three-hour labs also described them as "tiring" or "draining" – regardless of the described intensity of the activities. One of those participants had spent a term taking a break from labs in favour of marking assignments and office hours, but did resume teaching labs. Another participant on a course with three-hour labs reported that the workload was unsustainable for him, noting difficulty balancing work on his thesis.

The participants who taught two-hour labs, however, did not report finding them "tiring" or "draining", and were all enthused at the prospect of teaching more labs. One participant who had experience teaching both two-hour and three-hour labs noted the two-hour labs as being easier to teach.

In three-hour labs, we saw differences in how TAs behaved between the second hour and the third hour, but no differences between the first and second hours. TAs spent less time giving announcements in the last hour, and more time observing their students. However, how much the TAs interacted with their students did not change over the course of three hours.

4.3 The social environment

All the TAs involved had at some point taught in pairs, which was universally reported as a positive experience for them. Having a partner in the lab contributed to a sense of social support, improving job satisfaction. Friendly relations with one's partner was reported as a motivating factor when teaching, as well as for preparing for the labs, as *"you don't want to let them down or make them do all the work."*

The partner was also there to help out with student questions: *"if there's minor details I don't know I can ask him [my partner]. And if there's something I can't explain, then maybe [he] knows how to do it.... And it's funner when [he]'s around."* The partner would also give the TAs a sense of security – *"I like teamwork. Two's a good number, two is perfect. It's really easy to come to agreement on things. And it's nice to have somebody covering your back."* Indeed, when probed as to whether TAs would prefer to teach solo or in groups, all nine participants reported preferring teaching in pairs, citing the balance of social support with the ease of coordination.

Another source of social support that boosted job satisfaction was staff meetings. TAs felt more valued and had higher job satisfaction when they had staff meetings where the instructor involved the TAs in the discussion, and solicited their feedback. The social support when teaching also contributes to the TAs' growth as teachers; TAs reported finding it highly useful when instructors gave them feedback and encouragement on their job performance, and advice about their work.

The sense of collaboration in the staff meetings that one participant felt was reported as his *"favourite part of being a TA"*. Staff meetings would also provide TAs a chance to talk to their partners – *"[in addition to in lab] we'd also talk in the TA meetings. There's a really friendly atmosphere between the TAs."* Of the nine interview participants, only one participant had a negative experience with staff meetings, where the course instructor was frequently absent, did not listen to TA feedback on the labs, and seemed to have been *"mostly making up the course as he goes along"*. Like the TAs in Bomotti's study [7], this TA reported feeling insufficiently supported and appreciated.

5. CORROBORATING EVIDENCE

Layout. In K-12 education research of classroom layouts, it has been found that open layouts are positively related to teacher satisfaction with the classroom, as was greater ceiling height [1]. Additionally, experience reports in lab-based instruction in physics have favoured open layouts, which are associated with encouraging collaborative learning [12, 3].

Lighting. There is a large body of evidence in the psychology literature that lighting has an effect on mood and cognition [14, 20]. It is hence unsurprising that lighting was found to have an effect on TAs' working environment.

Intensity. Reducing the workload for labs so that students complete them on time has been found in a longitudinal case study to have improved student perceptions of labs and TA job satisfaction [17].

Length. There are a number of possibilities for why length – independent of intensity – would affect TAs' performance. Lower blood sugar levels will result in less energetic teaching. Decision fatigue would also play a role, as teaching is a profession where decision-making is constant [9]. Finally, maintaining an authoritative position amongst the students is a high-effort social activity – something that TAs, as younger teachers, have had less chance to develop stamina for.

Social support. Muzaka's study of TAs [15] – who worked solo – found that those TAs suffered from a lack of social support. Muzaka noted the lack of support structures available to TAs as a negative influence on their work. Furthermore, in Bomotti's study [7], TAs noted feelings of being insufficiently supported or appreciated, and that they felt "overworked, underpaid, and unappreciated." Finally, Bomotti notes that "TAs who plan to pursue college teaching as a career regard high-quality supervision as the single most positive influence on their decision" [7].

6. THREATS TO VALIDITY

With a mixed-methods approach, we can be more certain of our results as they are corroborated by multiple methods.

Each method has its own advantages and disadvantages, but together they can build a clearer picture of what we are trying to study.

As eight out of nine interviewed TAs reported a positive social environment for teaching, we have little to compare socially supported TAs to socially unsupported ones. Also, the choice of student interaction as a proxy for job satisfaction is, by nature, an imperfect measure; hence we only use this to verify the themes which emerged from our interviews. Another weakness in our use of observational sampling is that we did not observe a low-intensity lab, presenting a threat to validity in subsubsection 4.2.1.

We do not claim to have listed every environmental factor affecting every TA, only the ones that were found to matter in our specific context. The time of day of a lab – affecting student and TA metabolism – and the day of week – affecting how "smoothly" the lab proceeds – were each mentioned by only one interviewed TA, and were hence omitted. Room acoustics have been found in other studies [6] to be significant, but was not identified by our participants, likely due to the similar acoustics between rooms.

In subsubsection 4.2.1 we factor whether students completed their work on time into the intensity of the lab; these may be seen as distinct. However, we were unable to examine them individually: the only course where students were unable to complete the labs was one with high-intensity labs.

Similarly, in subsubsection 4.1.1 we were unable to distinguish two factors involved in layout: the physical effect of access to students that the open layout affords and the traditional layout lacks, versus the psychocultural effect of students all facing the front in the traditional layout which is not present in the open layout. While one of the traditional rooms did lack a table at the front for the TAs to sit at, we do not have enough evidence in this study to fully separate these two factors.

As we expected from our study design, we reached saturation in our interviews, with nine participants interviewed. Saturation refers to a state in which no new concepts, or codes, emerge, as more interviews are done. However, bias may be added through the process of interviewing the TAs – as we asked them questions we had generated – and through coding. As the author is a TA herself, it is possible that the analysis was skewed towards reflecting the author's own experiences.

However, by being a peer to the participants, we feel we had their trust; we feel TAs were as a result more open and honest during interviews, and behaved normally when under observation. We speculate that had a faculty member run the study, we would not have heard anecdotes about being uninterrupted for "an hour, an hour and a half", nor would we have observed some TAs spend nearly a tenth of the time playing with their phones.

7. SUGGESTIONS FOR INSTRUCTORS

We have identified five environmental factors affecting TAs' job satisfaction in our case study: the layout of the lab room, the lighting of the room, the intensity of student questions, how much time is allotted to a given lab session, and the social support given to the TA.

Based on the model that we have constructed from our findings, we make four suggestions to course instructors on how to manage their labs:

1. Avoid scheduling three-hour lab sections, and ensure that the students can comfortably complete the labs in the allotted time. Three-hour labs tire out your TAs.

2. When writing labs, consider the intensity for the TAs. Further, TAs are demotivated when students do not complete labs on time.

3. Provide a positive social environment for your TAs. Actively solicit their feedback during staff meetings, and collaborate with them in making changes to curriculum and course policies. Furthermore, our participants reported working in pairs to be a source of social support for them.

4. Schedule your labs in rooms with the best physical environment you can – with a layout that supports TAs having easy access to their students, and good lighting. As TAs reported feeling pressure to give students in introductory courses (CS0 and CS1) a positive impression of the field, we suggest prioritizing those courses when assigning lab rooms.

Additionally, we suggest to those on space committees, or facing renovation, to design lab rooms with open layouts, ample windows, and proper lighting.

Improving the job satisfaction of TAs promotes a healthier teaching environment, and in turn, a healthier learning environment for the students. It also promotes retention of TAs to the courses they are assigned to – resulting in a more experienced teaching staff in subsequent terms.

8. ACKNOWLEDGMENTS

We thank our study participants for their involvement. Patrice Belleville and Meghan Allen supervised the study, and we were assisted by Steve Wolfman, Kimberly Voll, Michelle Craig, Steve Easterbrook, Jonathan Lung, Velian Pandeliev, Andrew Petersen, Jon Pipitone, François Pitt, Fabio Silva and Daniel Zingaro.

9. REFERENCES

[1] S. Ahrentzen and G. W. Evans. Distraction, privacy, and classroom design. *Environment and Behavior*, 16(4):437–454, 1984.

[2] J. Altmann. Observational study of behavior: Sampling methods. *Behaviour*, 49(3/4):pp. 227–267, 1974.

[3] R. Beichner, L. Bernold, E. Burniston, P. Dail, R. Felder, J. Gastineau, M. Gjertsen, and J. Risley. Case study of the physics component of an integrated curriculum. *American Journal of Physics*, 67(S1):S16–S24, 1999.

[4] J. Bennedsen and M. E. Caspersen. An investigation of potential success factors for an introductory model-driven programming course. In *Proceedings of the first international workshop on Computing education research*, ICER '05, pages 155–163, New York, NY, USA, 2005. ACM.

[5] J. Bennedsen and M. E. Caspersen. Failure rates in introductory programming. *SIGCSE Bull.*, 39:32–36, June 2007.

[6] F. S. Berg, J. C. Blair, and P. V. Benson. Classroom acoustics: The problem, impact, and solution. *Lang Speech Hear Serv Sch*, 27(1):16–20, 1996.

[7] S. S. Bomotti. Teaching assistant attitudes toward college teaching. *Review of Higher Education*, 17(4):371–393, 1994.

[8] D. E. Comer, D. Gries, M. C. Mulder, A. Tucker, A. J. Turner, and P. R. Young. Computing as a discipline. *Commun. ACM*, 32:9–23, January 1989.

[9] S. Danziger, J. Levav, and L. Avnaim-Pesso. Extraneous factors in judicial decisions. *Proceedings of the National Academy of Sciences*, 108(17):6889–6892, 2011.

[10] S. Garner, P. Haden, and A. Robins. My program is correct but it doesn't run: a preliminary investigation of novice programmers' problems. In *Proceedings of the 7th Australasian conference on Computing education - Volume 42*, ACE '05, pages 173–180, Darlinghurst, Australia, Australia, 2005. Australian Computer Society, Inc.

[11] G. Guest, A. Bunce, and L. Johnson. How Many Interviews Are Enough? *Field Methods*, 18(1):59–82, Feb. 2006.

[12] M. C. Holmes. An integrated environment approach to physics teaching in higher education. *Physics Education*, 27(3):138, 1992.

[13] K. Holtzblatt, J. B. Wendell, and S. Wood. *Rapid Contextual Design*. Elsevier, 2005.

[14] Igor and Knez. Effects of indoor lighting on mood and cognition. *Journal of Environmental Psychology*, 15(1):39 – 51, 1995.

[15] V. Muzaka. The niche of graduate teaching assistants (GTAs): perceptions and reflections. *Teaching in Higher Education*, 14(1):1–12, 2009.

[16] C. O'Neal, M. Wright, C. Cook, T. Perorazio, and J. Purkiss. The impact of teaching assistants on student retention in the sciences: Lessons for TA training. *Journal of College Science Teaching*, 36(5):24–29, 2007.

[17] E. Patitsas and S. Wolfman. Effective closed labs in early CS courses: Lessons from eight terms of action research. SIGCSE '12, 2012.

[18] C. Paul, E. West, D. Webb, B. Weiss, and W. Potter. Important types of instructor-student interactions in reformed classrooms, 2010. American Association of Physics Teachers Summer Meeting.

[19] D. Siegle. Qualitative research, 2002.

[20] J. A. Veitch and S. L. McColl. A critical examination of perceptual and cognitive effects attributed to full-spectrum fluorescent lighting. *Ergonomics*, 44(3):255–279, 2001.

Education and Research: Evidence of a Dual Life

Joe Miró Julià
Dept. Mat. i Informàtica
U. de les Illes Balears
07122 Palma de Mallorca,
Spain
joe.miro@uib.es

David López
Dept. of Computer
Architecture
UPC- Barcelona TECH
Barcelona, Spain
david@ac.upc.edu

Ricardo Alberich
Dept. Mat. i Informàtica
U. de les Illes Balears
07122 Palma de Mallorca,
Spain
r.alberich@uib.es

ABSTRACT

To study the differences of the CS Education and Research communities we have studied the collaboration networks of 6 CS Education conferences and 7 CS Research conferences. Results show that both communities behave differently when collaborating to create technical papers. It could be said that the CS Education community has introversion traits: there is a higher tendency to only collaborate with nearby colleagues.

Categories and Subject Descriptors

K.3 [**Computers and education**]: Computer and Information Science Education

General Terms

Human factors

Keywords

Collaboration, Education and Research communities, Social network theory

1. INTRODUCTION

Few would dispute that collaboration is essential in the advancement of scientific knowledge. It is through conversations and discussions with others that new ideas appear or disappear, and the best ones are refined and strengthened. This collaboration might be through face to face contact or by reading and studying the works of others. In any case it usually begins from published material and ends with more publications others will read, discuss, and write about. Not all collaborations revolve around publications, but the most fundamental ones do: Studying and building on other peoples' work or writing with a colleague creates a profound and permanent imprint in the community. Ideas diffuse and improve through this work of authors and readers. It can be said that it is the collaboration that creates a community

and that the publications that gather its knowledge is the community's best description.

And so, it is natural that one would study publications to understand the characteristics, the behavior even, of its authors. This is studied by the field of informetrics. As can be seen in Judit Bar-Ilan's [1] excellent and comprehensive introduction to informetrics' methodologies there are many ways to study publications.

One is to classify the papers by their type. This has been done for the CS Education (CSE) community by D. Valentine [10]. He classified the SIGCSE papers in six categories that he colorfully called Marco Polo ("I went there and I saw this"), Tools, Experimental, Nifty, Philosophy and John Henry.

A second way is to study which are the most referenced papers and conferences. This was done by R. Lister in a series of papers. In one of them [4] he studies all the citations in ICER's first 3 editions. He presents how many references were to books, journals and conferences, and which were the most cited ones in each category.

A third way is to study who writes with whom. This face to face interaction is probably the most fundamental way of collaborating. They are studied through *collaboration networks:* very large graphs where the vertexes represent authors and the edges symbolize the coauthorship of a paper. Mark Newman, in a seminal paper [6], studied many scientific collaboration networks from medicine, high-energy physics and CS. Erten and others [3] studied over 50 000 papers from the ACM Digital Library.

To our knowledge the CS Education collaboration network has barely been studied. We have only found a study of Spain's local CS Education conference [5]. We believe that a comprehensive study of the major conferences is particularly interesting: it is "our" community and it is important that we know *who* we are and *how* we are. The natural thing is to compare the results with the other CS community: the (for lack of a better name) CS Research (CSR) community. Note that we do not want to imply that CSE work is not research. Inasmuch as they improve knowledge, it *is* research, although we must acknowledge that the formal methods used in many papers still lack behind other research areas [9].

The CSE and CSR communities are formed by the same body: CS university professors. The differences between the two communities, this dual behavior, can be particularly enlightening and useful to understand the differences in the nature of both communities and if those differences are useful or detrimental to the fields.

In this paper we study and compare the CSE and CSR communities. We do so by focusing on the collaboration networks of 6 'standard' CSE and 6 'standard' CSR conferences. We also study ICER which is a research conference, and thus CSR, but focused on CS Education. This distinguishes it from other CSR conferences as its matter of study is more in the social sciences realm than in the engineering one. Among them we analyzed the coauthorship of some 26 000 authors through more than 15 000 papers. The results show a significant difference in the collaboration patterns between the two, with the most significant results arising from the study of the evolution of the networks through time. Our results show differences between researchers and educators: the CSE community has a greater tendency than the CSR one to stick with nearby colleagues. Also, we have found that newcomers have a harder time integrating into the CSE community. In one word: we are introverts.

2. METHOD

To study the CSE and CSR communities we will use social network theory [8], and in particular collaboration networks. In these networks[1] each node represents an individual and two individuals are linked if they have collaborated in a well defined way. The aim of the network is to capture a specific type of collaboration, in our case, working directly together in the creation of a paper. Therefore the network is formed by the *authors* of the technical papers in a conference and two authors are linked if they have *coauthored* a paper. This specific type of collaboration networks has been studied before. Most interesting for us are the study by Newman [6] of the Networked Computer Science Technical Reports Library (NCSTRL) and the one by Erten and others [3] of the ACM Digital Library. We have used their studies to validate ours.

To create the networks used to study the CSE and CSR communities we had to choose a set of publications. We decided to concentrate on conferences, mainly because we already had experience on some of them. We did not include journals, the other main type of publication, because we believe the dynamics of both types are different, and therefore eliminating this variable would simplify interpreting the results. We also limited the study to technical papers. Panels and other special events were not added for two reasons: the information available from the different proceedings was not consistent; and, more importantly, we had difficulties in comparing data from conferences, if each had its unique events. We consider the collaboration existing among panelists or the presenters in, say, SIGCSE's *Nifty Assignments* to be very different to the one present in a joint paper making it hard to compare the results. We also decided not to include ITiCSE's Working Group Reports. This was a tougher decision. We finally decided not to add them because the reports are *not* included in the conference proceedings and, again, it represents a unique type of collaboration, making the comparison between conferences difficult or even meaningless.

These networks capture the interactions of authors over time. In just one conference the interaction is too small to be of interest: it is only over several editions and a large set of papers that the structures of the networks emerge. We set

the criterion of having information of at least 10 editions of each conference. This is not a problem for CSR conferences, but surprisingly more so for CSE ones.

To select the CSE conferences we searched the databases of ACM, IEEE, and the American Society for Engineering Education (ASEE). We also did a general Internet search. Even though we only needed the table of contents or conference program and not the whole proceedings, we found only 7 conferences with at least 10 years worth of data. We found, and discarded, several others with data for only sporadic editions. We also discarded the ASEE Annual Conference, in this case because it was very large with over 400 papers per edition. We already had one conference of similar size (Frontiers in Education) and it had posed serious technical difficulties, to be commented on later. The six selected conferences are:

- ACE: Australasian Computing Education Conference,
- FIE: Frontiers in Education,
- ITiCSE: Innovation and Technology in CS Education,
- Jenui: Jornadas de Enseñanza Universitaria de la Informática (Spain's CS Education Conference),
- SEE: Conference on Software Engineering Education and Training, and
- SIGCSE: Technical Symposium on Computer Science Education.

Details of each conference can be found in Table 1.

Most of these conferences started around 1996. To establish a common time frame we selected the editions taking place between January 1996 and September 2011.

To select the CSR conferences we searched for conferences with most similarities: starting dates, number of editions, and sizes —measured in number of authors and papers— to the CSE ones we had. We also wanted them to cover as many CS fields as possible to reduce any field-bias there might be. Of course, the matches were not always perfect, and in particular, we did not find any CSR conference as large as FIE. The selected conferences are:

- ASE: International Conference on Automated Software Engineering.
- ASPLOS: Architectural Support for Programming Languages and Operating Systems.
- ICSE: International Conference on Software Engineering.
- ISCA: International Symposium on Computer Architecture.
- SIGMETRICS: International Conference on Measurement and Modelling in Computer Systems.
- SPAA: Symposium on Parallelism in Algorithms and Architecture.

Details of each conference can be found in Table 2.

We used the same time frame as before: January 1996 to September 2011. The only exception was ASPLOS. We chose it because this conference was held every other year until 2008. In this sense it is similar to ACE, that also was not an annual conference until 2003.

To these conferences we added ICER. It is different from the rest in that it is younger, 7 editions, but it is a special case with its research orientation over CSE matter. As we will see, it has aspects of both types of conferences.

Once the conferences were selected, and the information downloaded, we created a BibTEX format file for each and we had to face an ugly reality: many authors appear under different versions of their names in different papers. This

---

[1]We will be using the social sciences terminology instead of the usual graph terminology: network instead of graph, node instead of vertex, link instead of edge.

	ACE	FIE	ITiCSE	Jenui	SEE	SIGCSE	ICER
Number of editions	12	15	16	15	16	16	7
Number of authors	560	8218	2322	1712	913	2272	178
Number of papers	383	5668	1603	1132	602	1454	111

Table 1: Characteristics of the six CS Education conferences and ICER

	ASE	ASPLOS	ICSE	ISCA	SIGMETRICS	SPAA	NCSTRL	ACM DL
Number of editions	14	15	16	16	16	16		
Number of authors	1710	1114	2961	1231	1453	1230	11 994	81 279
Number of papers	880	426	1617	560	687	661	13 169	51 503

Table 2: Characteristics of the six CS Research conferences, the Networked Computer Science Technical Reports Library (NCSTRL) [6] and the ACM Digital Library [3]

is a complex problem. We had to assign a unique code to each author. This is a time consuming and painstaking process, that grows much faster than linearly, and was the main reason we did not include the ASEE Annual Conference in our study. It is also the reason we did not even attempt to create a single network encompassing all the conferences.

The assignment has to be done manually, specially due to having authors of many different nationalities, and therefore different national naming customs. For instance the N. in Lillian N. Cassel is a middle name and she also might, and does, appear as Lillian Cassel. But the G. in Daniel G. Morales is the first of the two family names existing in Spanish speaking countries, and he might, and does, appear as Daniel González. Furthermore, if there were a Daniel Morales it would certainly be a different author. You must also deal with different ways of spelling non-ASCII characters (Rossling vs. Roßling), nicknames, short-fors, misspellings, name changes due to marriages and other factors.

After assigning the codes it was possible to automate part of the process of creating the network and calculating its main parameters. We did so using some home-made programs and the statistical application R [7]. An important part of our contribution is the compilation of this data and can be found by anyone interested at `http://bioinfo.uib.es/~recerca/Colab/`.

3. RESULTS

We analyzed the 13 networks of the 13 conferences and compared the CSR to the CSE ones and ICER. A summary of the results is shown in Table 3. We studied them through the values used in *classical* collaboration network and we developed new measures to help us understand them better. We found a clear difference between CSR and CSE.

Given that we have few instances of each type of conference, most of the statistical analysis is done through descriptive statistics, although we also did hypothesis testing. Most of differences gave a statistical significance from moderate to high, although we are aware that with so few data points, even with small p-values, the statistical evidence is weak. It is with this caveat that we provide the computed t statistic and p-values.

3.1 Giant components

In a collaboration network the individuals are connected in clusters that model the internal structure of the network. One of the most characteristic traits is that a large percentage of the individuals are connected into a single very large cluster called the *giant component*. The existence of this giant component together with the fact that the paths within it are usually short create the concept of a small world. In Milgram's famous "six degrees of separation" experiment it took only 5 or 6 acquaintance links to ship a parcel from a random person in mid-western US to a person in Boston. In the CS communities it takes just a few joint papers to get new concepts and ideas worked on and diffused through a large portion of the community. Without a giant component authors are connected through direct contacts with only a small portion of their colleagues. The giant component contains the essence of the community and we could even say that without a giant component there is no community.

All studied scientific communities present a giant component. In his paper, Newman studied collaboration networks from different fields, from medicine, to high-energy physics to CS, and found that almost all of them had a largest component comprising over 80% of the authors. The smallest one was that of CS, at 57%. Erten, in his study of the ACM DL found the component to comprise 49% of the nodes.

These values are in agreement to what we have found on the CSR networks. Although there is one abnormally small case (ASE, 17%), four of them are quite close to the numbers of the NCSTRL and ACM DL, ranging between 43% and 52%, while the other one is quite larger (ISCA, 83%). On the other hand, the CSE conferences had a much smaller giant component. The largest (Jenui, 46%) is smaller than the median of the CSR networks. The rest range between 24% and 38% with ITiCSE trailing at a very small 14%. Therefore, the giant component in CSE networks is smaller ($t = -1.8$, $p = 0.05$; $t = -1.8$, $p = 0.01$ if we remove ASE), a bit over half the size of the CSR ones.

So now the question is why is there this essential difference between the two types of communities? The two most famous models used in social network theory are the Erdös-Rényi random graph model [2] and Watts and Strogatz small world model [11] and neither provide insight or ways to compute the size of the giant component. So we had to create our own analysis.

We started by focusing on the network characteristics that are normally computed. The values of interest would be the Average Authors per Paper, the Average Papers per Author and the Average number of Collaborations per Author. It would seem natural that the more papers an author writes, the more coauthors a paper has, and the more collaborations an author has, the larger the component. Unfortunately this

	CS Education	ICER	CS Research	NCSTRL	ACM DL
Size of Giant Component	14% – 46%	49%	(18%) 43% – 83%	57%	49%
Avg. Papers per Author	1.51 – 2.05	1.80	1.39 – 1.75	2.55	1.8
Avg. Authors per Paper	2.29 – 2.61 (3.10)	3.00	2.74 – 3.85	2.22	2.32
Avg. Collaborations per Author	1.59 – 3.11	3.31	1.70 – 2.51 (3.60)	3.59	3.36
Percentage of Newcomers	45%–67% (79%)	48%	51% – 68%		
Percentage of M papers	4.0% – 6.5% (8.5%)	8.4%	5.6% – 10.3%		
Percentage of E Papers	22% – 39%	35%	35% – 57%		
Percentage of I Papers	18% – 24%	23%	5% – 16%		
Percentage of N Papers	30% – 54%	34%	(18%) 35% – 40% (50%)		

Table 3: Data of the networks. We show ranges, with the numbers in parenthesis representing outliers. The data of NCSTRL is from Newman [6] and the one of the ACM DL is from Erten et al. [3]

approach does not yield an answer although it does provide some interesting insight.

On the one hand it does seem that the authors in the CSE community have a clear tendency to write with less people ($t = -3.2$, $p = 0.006$). The average number of authors per paper ranges from 2.29 to 2.61, with Jenui being an outlier at 3.10, while in the CSR conferences the range is from 2.74 to 3.85. On the other hand there seems to be a disposition to write more papers ($t = 1.6$, $p = 0.08$) in these conferences. This of course could be because the authors have less conferences to choose from. But whatever the reason, in the CSE conferences there are from 1.51 to 2.05 papers per author while in the CSR it goes from 1.39 to 1.75. These two effects seem to cancel each other out, as the number of collaborations per author is very similar in the two fields.

Summarizing, although the average number of collaborations is similar in both communities, in CSE we tend to write more often but with less people. An introvert pattern starts to emerge.

3.2 The MEIN Classification

To further study the network we focused on the changes that occur when new papers and authors are added to it. The addition of new papers and its authorship make the clusters appear and evolve. We have created parameters to study this effect.

We differentiated between *newcomers,* authors who write to the conference for the first time, and the veteran *oldtimers.* First of all we took a look at how many newcomers arrive each edition. Evidently, on the first edition of a conference everybody is a newcomer. The ratio of newcomers reduces after the first year and quickly stabilizes. It does not vary much among conferences or among types of conference and it is surprisingly high: the average for the last 3 editions is 62% of newcomers for CSE and 60% for CSR.

We then studied how this influx of newcomers and the papers written by oldtimers change the network's clusters. To do so we had to create a classification of the papers depending on how they modify the clusters. We considered that:

- *Newcomers* enter the network by either creating a new cluster or joining an existing one;

- *Oldtimers* either work with people from their own cluster, thus not changing its membership, or with people from other clusters, thus merging them.

If we consider just one edition, we basically have as many clusters as papers. Only as editions accumulate larger clusters form. If we consider the situation after edition $E-1$ we have a given cluster set that will be changed by the papers in edition E. To model this we have created a classification of the papers, called the MEIN classification, as follows:

- If oldtimers that belonged to different clusters in edition $E-1$ collaborate in a joint paper in edition E, perhaps with newcomers, their clusters will *merge*. The paper that caused the merge is called a type M paper.
- If one or more oldtimers from a single cluster collaborate with one or more newcomers, then their cluster will *extend* with the new authors. Such a paper is said to be of type E.
- If all the authors of a paper are oldtimers belonging to the same cluster, the collaboration is *internal:* there will be new links within the cluster, but its membership will not change. This is a type I paper.
- Finally, if all the authors of a paper are newcomers, they create a *new* cluster. Such a paper is called a type N paper.

Papers from the first edition have no type.

Note that M trumps E: a paper written by oldtimers from different clusters plus newcomers is considered a type M paper. Also note that we are not considering the changes that happen when combining two or more papers. For instance, two type E papers with the same newcomer might merge two existing clusters. We do this because, in a sense, we are trying to capture the *collaboration behavior* of the authors. When individuals choose to write a paper with others they are choosing, probably unknowingly, how the clusters will change. But they have no control on the changes that occur by the actions of their coauthors.

We classified each paper and computed the percentages per type. The proportions of M, E, I and N papers for the complete paper set for each CSE and CSR conferences is shown in Figure 1. Its analysis offers us a much clearer picture of how the giant component evolves and explains the difference between CSR and CSE conferences: CSR is more M and E, while CSE is more I and N.

Despite there being approximately the same percentage of newcomers on both types of conferences, in the CSE conferences there seems to be a slightly higher tendency for them to come 'alone' through N type papers: the median is 45% in CSE vs. 40% in CSR ($t = 1.5$, $p = 0.09$). In CSR, on the other hand they come more often through a collaboration with oldtimers, as the difference in E type papers show ($t = -3.9$, $p = 0.002$): it ranges between 22% and 39% for CSE with clearly higher values (35% to 57%) in CSR.

The difference between the behavior of oldtimers is more

pronounced. In CSE conferences we very much prefer to write with people we are already connected to as the clearly larger percentage of I papers show. In CSE the range is high and narrow: 18% to 24%; in CSR it is lower and wider: 5% to 16% ($t = 5.8, p < 0.001$). For both type of conferences the percentage of M papers is small (median of 6% for CSE, 8% for CSR, $t = -2.3, p = 0.02$). But the small-world network model explains that these few merging links are essential to create a large interconnected component. This small 2% difference is a big difference.

The introversion is confirmed.

3.3 The ICER story

So, what about ICER? Although it is a CSR conference, it is focused towards CSE, and threfore it is worth studying if the ICER community behaves more like the CSE or CSR ones. We already know that ICER papers do not follow CSE conference patterns. Simon and others [9] found that, while 88% of the ICER papers can be clearly classified as research papers, this is not so in the majority of CSE conferences: for instance in ACE only 35% of the papers could be considered research papers.

Interestingly, its network parameters do not show values that are in between those of CSR and CSE. Rather, part of its parameters are within the CSE range and the other part within the CSR one. Its cluster size, at 49%, is larger than any CSE conference and completely in the CSR range, almost identical to ICSE, ASPLOS or SIGMETRICS. The same can be said for the Average Authors per Paper, larger than any CSE except Jenui, and with values similar to those of ICSE, SPAA and SIGMETRICS. On the other hand, its Average Papers per Author is larger than any CSR conference and very similar to FIE and ACE. It is harder to say how it aligns when looking at the Average number of Collaborations per Author. It is larger than any CSE conference and any CSR one except ISCA (a clear outlier), but its value is similar to the one obtained by Erten for the ACM DL and Newman for NCSTRL.

If we look at the MEIN classification, it aligns very closely to CSR in the M and N categories. But, on the other hand, it has more Internal type papers than any CSR or CSE conference. In the Extension type papers we find the only parameter in which ICER is an inbetweener: it has almost as many as the CSE with most (Jenui) and almost as few as the CSR with least (ASE).

ICER is unique, but is not halfway: it has the blue eyes of one, the auburn hair of the other.

4. DISCUSSION

We have established that there is a difference in the collaboration networks of CSE and CSR conferences, with the CSE community being more introvert than the CSR. Is this a 'good thing' or a 'bad thing'? Neither: we are what we are. But there are two aspects related to this introversion that we believe deserve further attention: the integration of the newcomers and the small size of the giant component.

We have seen that in the CSR community newcomers have a higher tendency to enter into an existing cluster through an E paper, while in the CSE they arrive on their own through an N paper. This naturally reminds us of that long standing mentorship program researchers have: the advisors and their doctorate students. To our knowledge young professors with inclination toward education issues just "fall into it" (often against all odds) rather than being "received into it." We are not advocating there be a doctorate program in CS Education, nor that entering the field must come through a mentor, but we believe that more care must be taken to encourage young professors with education interests and help incorporate them into the CSE community through some kind of organized mentoring. It would help transfer skills from the veteran to the novice, speed up their progress, preserve the knowledge of the community, and result in an improvement of the community as a whole.

With respect to the small size of the giant component, our results show that we write as much, but with less people, and those tend to be nearby colleagues belonging to our same cluster. More study is needed to understand which are the borderlines we constrict ourselves to, but it does seem that we much prefer to work with people with the same environment as ours. Note that many papers begin by defining the character of the university, e.g. as a liberal arts college, and thus it would seem that the community believes that teaching depends on the charter of the institution. And this is consistent with ITiCSE having a largest component —we do not dare call it "giant"— of only 14%. From this perspective, this would be due to the "European" character of this conference. Despite the recent creation of the European Area of Higher Education, Europe can still be considered a "fragmented" university system, with large structural differences from country to country. For some reason the differences in environment prevent in some measure the creation of a common teaching workframe. It seems that deep down we believe that although a for loop or virtual memory is the same in Paris than in London, teaching the concept in French is different than doing so in English. Should this be the case, we are letting inexistent differences interfere with our teaching views and methods.

We do believe that we care about newcomers and that a small giant component does not imply a lesser community. On the contrary, it is a common observation among those who attend CSE conferences that the atmosphere is much friendlier and that there is a clear will of the attendees to help each other rather than compete with each other. But this friendlier, more helpful attitude, this latent collaboration, does not translate into joint projects that become joint papers. It might be due to funding, although SIGCSE, which can be considered an American conference where funding is available, shows no difference to the rest. So what is needed?

The first step is to present the facts, and thus this paper. And just this might make a big difference. There is plenty of anecdotal evidence that the knowledge of the collaboration structure influences the choice of partners: all mathematicians know their Erdös number (their distance through coauthorship to Paul Erdös) and, only half-jokingly, seek to lower it when starting a partnership (http://xkcd.com/599/). Another case is that of Jenui. It was studied in 2004 [5]. Interestingly, the study shows that Jenui and ITiCSE were strikingly similar at the time. This study was presented to the Jenui community in 2004. In 2011 Jenui and ITiCSE are at opposite ends of the spectrum. Jenui has more M and E papers than any other CSE conference, has the largest number of collaborations per author, and its giant component stands at almost 50% while ITiCSE's giant component remains tiny. Maybe all we need is to know how things are.

Merge paper type percentage

Internal paper type percentage

Extension paper type percentage

New paper type percentage

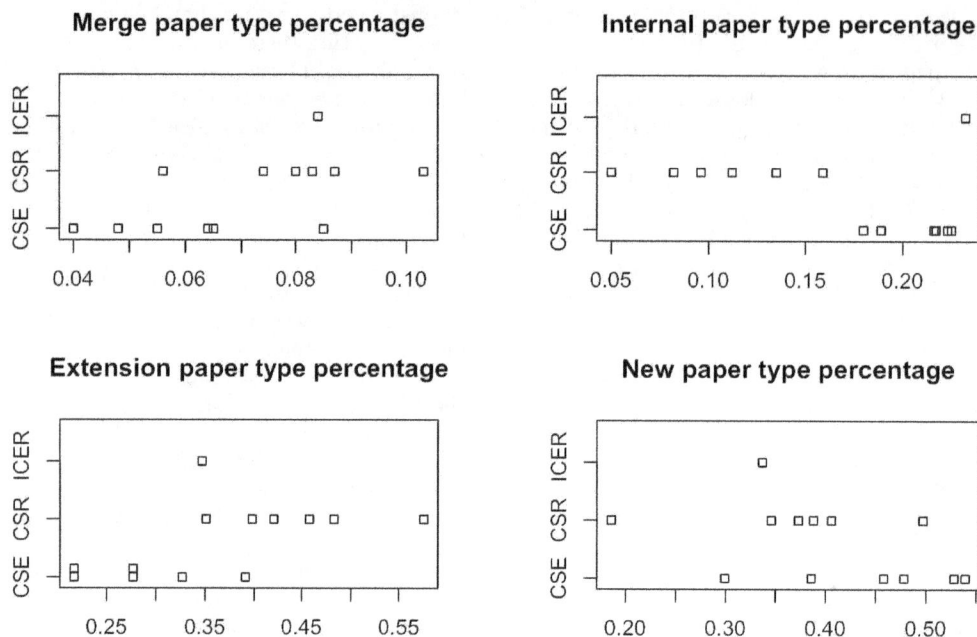

Figure 1: Percentage of Merge, External, Internal, and New papers in the 13 conferences.

5. CONCLUSIONS

We have shown that the CS Education and CS Research communities have substantial differences: CSE authors have a higher tendency to write more papers with less authors and they show a higher preference to write with people of their same cluster. Also newcomers have to find their way into the community rather than being ushered into it. For all this we consider the CSE community to be more introverted than the CSR one.

It does seem that CSE authors have a hard time working out of their local environment. And it would seem there is nothing wrong in "working locally". But real advances in education theory are those that work globally. We must look beyond our classrooms if we want to find robust teaching methods and prove their validity.

This is just a first look at the CSE collaboration networks. We must look deeper into them, and probably create new analysis tools, if we want to understand the influence university structures, national boundaries, funding, and other aspects have on the behavior of the CS Education community.

6. ACKNOWLEDGEMENTS

The research reported in this paper has been partially supported by the Spanish government and the UE FEDER program through projects MTM2009-07165 and TIN2010-21695-C02-02.

7. REFERENCES

[1] J. Bar-Ilan. Informetrics at the beginning of the 21st century – A review. *Journal of Informetrics*, 2(1):1 – 52, 2008.

[2] P. Erdös and A. Rényi. On random graphs. I. *Publicationes Mathematicae*, 6:290–297, 1959.

[3] C. Erten, P. J. Harding, S. G. Kobourov, K. Wampler, and G. Yee. Exploring the computing literature using temporal graph visualization. In *Conf. on Visualization and Data Analysis (VDA)*, pages 45–56, 2003.

[4] R. Lister. CS research: We are what we cite – so where are we? *SIGCSE Bull.*, 40(4):16–18, Nov. 2008.

[5] J. Miró and R. Alberich. La colaboración en el Jenui, a quién nos parecemos y a quién no. In *Actas de las X Jornadas de Enseñanza Universitaria de Informática, Jenui 2004*, pages 179 – 186, Alicante, Julio 2004.

[6] M. Newman. Who is the best connected scientist? A study of scientific coauthorship networks. In E. Ben-Naim, H. Frauenfelder, and Z. Toroczkai, editors, *Complex Networks*, volume 650 of *Lecture Notes in Physics*, pages 337–370. Springer Berlin / Heidelberg, 2004.

[7] R Development Core Team. *R: A Language and Environment for Statistical Computing*. R Foundation for StatisticalComputing, Vienna, Austria, 2005.

[8] J. P. Scott. *Social Network Analysis: A Handbook*. SAGE Publications, 2000.

[9] Simon, A. Carbone, M. de Raadt, R. Lister, M. Hamilton, and J. Sheard. Classifying computing education papers: process and results. In *ICER '08* , pages 161–172, New York, NY, USA, 2008. ACM.

[10] D. W. Valentine. CS educational research: a meta-analysis of SIGCSE technical symposium proceedings. In *SIGCSE'04*, pages 255–259, 2004.

[11] D. J. Watts and S. H. Strogatz. Collective dynamics of 'small-world' networks. *Nature*, 393:440–442, June 1998.

Threshold Concepts and Threshold Skills in Computing

Kate Sanders
Mathematics and Computer
Science Department
Rhode Island College
Providence, RI USA
ksanders@ric.edu

Jonas Boustedt
Faculty of Engineering and
Sustainable Development
University of Gävle
Gävle, Sweden
jbt@hig.se

Anna Eckerdal
Department of Information
Technology
Uppsala University
Uppsala, Sweden
annae@it.uu.se

Robert McCartney
Department of Computer Science and
Engineering
University of Connecticut
Storrs, CT USA
robert@engr.uconn.edu

Jan Erik Moström
Department of Computing Science
Umeå University
901 87 Umeå, Sweden
jem@cs.umu.se

Lynda Thomas
Department of Computer Science
Aberystwyth University
Aberystwyth, Wales
ltt@aber.ac.uk

Carol Zander
Computing & Software Systems
University of Washington Bothell
Bothell, WA USA
zander@u.washington.edu

ABSTRACT

Threshold concepts can be used to both organize disciplinary knowledge and explain why students have difficulties at certain points in the curriculum. Threshold concepts transform a student's view of the discipline; before being learned, they can block a student's progress.

In this paper, we propose that in computing, skills, in addition to concepts, can sometimes be thresholds. Some students report finding skills more difficult than concepts. We discuss some computing skills that may be thresholds and compare threshold skills and threshold concepts.

Categories and Subject Descriptors

K.3.2 [**Computers and Education**]: Computers and Information Science Education—*Computer Science Education*

General Terms

Measurement, Experimentation

Keywords

threshold concepts, threshold skills

1. INTRODUCTION

While learning computing, students acquire both theoretical concepts and practical skills. Some of these theoretical concepts may act as "threshold concepts": ideas within a discipline whose learning fundamentally changes the learner's viewpoint of that discipline. The idea of threshold concepts has been useful as a way to both organize disciplinary knowledge and explain why students have difficulties at certain points in a curriculum. [7]

Most investigations of threshold concepts in computing to date ([15] for example) have identified potential concepts that are effectively aspects of learning to program. In our own investigations [35], we identified pointers as a potential threshold concept in computing: we observed that students exhibited the characteristics of being in a liminal state as they acquired this concept [18], a state in which they struggled to apply their knowledge by writing code. Programming involves conceptual knowledge, but it is also a skill that improves with experience – something you do, not just a concept you know.

When we interviewed students about threshold concepts, they often emphasized problems with learning how to apply the concepts through programming rather than the concept itself. One interpretation of this: *The acquisition of particular skills, and not the concepts related to these skills, can act as thresholds.* This interpretation, plus descriptions of aspects of programming in the literature, led us to re-examine threshold concepts interview data with a focus on skill acquisition, to see whether Threshold Skills exist, and (if so) to see how they compare to Threshold Concepts.

The structure of the paper is as follows. In Section 2 we review three things: skills, knowledge, and threshold concepts. In Section 3 and Section 4 we more formally state the research questions that this paper addresses and discuss our methodology. Our findings are discussed in Section 5:

what the analysis says about threshold skills in computing. Section 6 presents some quantitative results about retention in a course where the students gain experience applying concepts that they previously learned. Section 7 looks at the relationship between threshold skills and threshold concepts and possible implications of these results. Finally, in Section 8 we provide conclusions drawn from this work and suggest further work that might follow.

2. BACKGROUND AND RELATED WORK

Our examination of threshold skills comes from our belief that writing computer programs is a skill, not simply a collection of concepts: an effective programmer knows the concepts and also knows *how* to write programs. This section discusses skills, knowledge – the relationship between theoretical and practical knowledge as well as the distinctions between declarative and procedural knowledge – and threshold concepts.

2.1 What is a skill?

Terms such as "skill" have been widely used in the discussion of what students should be learning, but without a clear consensus on their definition. [9] For purposes of this paper, we start from the *Oxford English Dictionary* definition:

> Capability of accomplishing something with precision and certainty; practical knowledge in combination with ability; cleverness, expertness. Also, an ability to perform a function, acquired or learnt with practice. [27]

In particular, the second part of this, the *ability to perform a function, acquired or learnt with practice*, is consistent with our experiences with things like programming.

Examples of skills are easy to find. Ryle [30] suggests making omelettes, conducting battles, designing dresses, persuading juries, and running experiments. While some conceptual knowledge is needed for all of these in varying degrees, intuitively, they primarily involve non-conceptual knowledge – knowledge that cannot easily be written down in the form of propositions and communicated – and all are best learned by practice.

Using the above definition, we can identify many skills in our interview data. Some are involved in programming such as using pointers, recursion, and data structures; others are non-programming skills such as object-oriented design and writing reduction proofs.

There exists a considerable body of research on students' learning programming skills like reading and writing code [21, 17], debugging [14], and software design [11]. These studies all report that students have severe problems in developing their skills.

2.2 Epistemology - what is knowledge?

When discussing skills, we cannot avoid discussing epistemological aspects: what is knowledge? The concept of knowledge has been discussed using different and partly overlapping terminology in different contexts. We give a summary of aspects of these discussions, including our own use.

2.2.1 Theoretical and practical knowledge

Research in professional education has considered the different kinds of knowledge using the terms *theory* and *practice*, with the understanding that a professional needs to master both area-specific practices and their related theories. However, the view on the relationship between theoretical knowledge and practical skills in educational contexts varies. In Western culture there is agreement that theory and practice are opposite parts of a dualistic opposition; knowledge is regarded as either theoretical or practical [16, 24]. In discussing the quality of student learning, Entwistle [13, p. 3] writes: "In the student learning literature, there has been an emphasis on conceptual understanding to represent high quality learning, but this had to be broadened to cover additional skills and ways of thinking, both academic and professional." There is a longstanding debate on the relationship between theory and practice in higher education. Dewey argued in the beginning of the 20th century, that theory should be the foundation of professional education [32], but at the same time he sought "intelligent practice" [8, p. 125]. He rejected theory without deep understanding as well as practice learned as procedures removed from their meaning. Shulman comments on Dewey's research saying: "he argued that only theoretical learning *situated in practice* would be rich and meaningful" [32, p. 524, italics in original].

The complex relation between students' learning of concepts and their learning of practical procedures in the lab is seen in science education, see e.g., [31, 1]. In computer science education it is generally accepted that students need to learn both theory and practice to become skillful professionals. It is further widely acknowledged that not only the theory but also the practice can cause great problems in students' learning. For example, du Boulay [4] discussed domains that programming students must learn to master, including the syntax and semantics of a programming language and different programming skills.

2.2.2 Declarative and procedural knowledge

In mathematics education research the terminology "conceptual" (or declarative) versus "procedural" knowledge is frequently used. McCormick [20, p. 149] explains that conceptual and procedural knowledge relate to "a familiar debate in education, namely that of the contrast of content and process ... In mathematics education the argument has been about 'skills versus understanding'." Procedural knowledge is often discussed as less advanced and preceding conceptual knowledge.

In the language-instruction domain, there exists a comparable dichotomy between declarative and procedural knowledge:

> Language teachers and language learners are often frustrated by the disconnect between knowing the rules of grammar and being able to apply those rules automatically ... [M]any native speakers can use their language clearly and correctly without being able to state the rules of its grammar. Likewise ... students may be able to state a grammar rule, but consistently fail to apply the rule when speaking or writing. [25]:

2.2.3 Knowing what and knowing how

We are making a distinction between knowing *how* and knowing *what* similar to that in the philosophical literature. Knowing what includes the kind of conceptual understanding that has been discussed as threshold concepts. We focus on knowing how, as described by Ryle:

(a) When a person knows how to do things of a certain sort (e.g., make good jokes, conduct battles or behave at funerals), his knowledge is actualised or exercised in what he does. ...His intelligence is exhibited by deeds, not by internal or external dicta.

(b) When a person knows how to do things of a certain sort (e.g., cook omelettes, design dresses or persuade juries), his performance is in some way governed by principles, rules, canons, standards or criteria. ...But his observance of rules, principles, etc., must, if it is there at all, be realised in his performance of his tasks. [30, p. 8]

Ryle's description of the difference between knowing how and knowing what is a philosopher's; a similar idea is discussed by Norman in the context of engineering design:

Knowledge *of* – what psychologists call declarative knowledge – includes the knowledge of facts and rules. ...Declarative knowledge is easy to write down and to teach.

Knowledge *how* – what psychologists call procedural knowledge – is the knowledge that enables a person to perform music, to stop a car smoothly with a flat tire on an icy road, to return a serve in tennis, ...Procedural knowledge is difficult or impossible to write down and difficult to teach. It is best taught by demonstration and best learned through practice. [26, pp. 57-58]

Both Norman and Ryle provide support for the notion that concepts and skills are different. Moreover, Ryle provides some examples of skills that are non-physical – designing dresses, persuding juries, and playing chess. [30]

2.3 Threshold Concepts

The theory of Threshold Concepts was developed by Meyer and Land [22, 23] as a way to understand the learning of concepts that change the way a learner views a discipline. A subset of the core concepts in a discipline, threshold concepts are described as having the following characteristics:

- *transformative*: they significantly change the way a student looks at things in the discipline.

- *integrative*: they tie together concepts in ways that were previously unknown to the student.

- potentially *troublesome* (as in [28]) for students: they are conceptually difficult, alien, and/or counter-intuitive.

- probably *irreversible*: they are difficult for the student to unlearn.

- often *boundary markers*: they indicate the limits of a conceptual area or the discipline itself. [22]

Generally speaking, Threshold Concepts are "conceptual gateways" (or barriers): things the student needs to understand to go further in his or her discipline. Examples given in [22] include *limits* and *complex numbers* in mathematics, and *opportunity cost* in economics.

In previous work, we identified three computing concepts that fit the description of Threshold Concepts: abstraction (including the ability to move flexibly from one level of abstraction to another), object-orientation, and pointers. [10, 5] These papers did not discuss skills, although many of the student interviews we empirically build on involve an element of skill as well as conceptual knowledge.

Another characteristic of Threshold Concepts is that the learner can find him- or herself in a "liminal state" while learning [23], characterized by an incomplete change in perspective, or an oscillation between the old and new perspectives. In [12] we found that computing students' experiences are consistent with those in [23]: the students may take significant time being transformed, they may react emotionally, and they sometimes use mimicry as a coping mechanism. Moreover, the analysis identified different kinds of partial understandings that students possess within the liminal space:

1. An abstract/theoretical understanding of a concept;

2. A concrete understanding – the ability to write a computer program illustrating the concept – without having the abstract understanding;

3. The ability to go from an understanding of the abstract concept to software design or concrete implementation;

4. An understanding of the rationale for learning and using the concept; and

5. An understanding of how to apply the concept to new problems.

If we consider software design and implementation to be a skill, then the second of these is an example of having the skill without the conceptual understanding, and the third and fifth illustrate connections between skills and conceptual understanding.

Previous research has indicated that learning certain skills might exhibit characteristics akin to learning threshold concepts. From computer science, Sien and Chong [33] propose object-oriented modeling to be a threshold concept. From mathematics education, Worsley, Bulmer and O'Brien [34] propose that the technique of substitution and solving ordinary differential equations are candidates for threshold concepts. These problems seem close to our view of skills as thresholds. However, none of the articles pursue the question how these skills relate to threshold concepts.

3. RESEARCH QUESTIONS

This paper addresses the following research questions:

- Are there skills whose acquisition acts as a threshold for computing students?

- If yes, how do these "threshold skills" compare to threshold concepts? Specifically, what characteristics do they share (and fail to share) with threshold concepts?

4. METHODOLOGY

For this project, we re-analyzed a set of semi-structured interviews concerning threshold concepts, looking for references to skills. In addition, we examined quantitative data regarding student performance in a course where a significant part of the learning involved new skills, while the related concepts were already familiar to the students.

4.1 The interviews

The interview data consist of sixteen semi-structured interviews on the topic of threshold concepts. Participants included graduating students at six institutions in Sweden, the United Kingdom, and the United States. For analysis, the student interviews were transcribed verbatim; where necessary, they were translated into English by the interviewer.

Fourteen of these interviews used a script that began by addressing the troublesome criterion, asking students for concepts they found difficult at first (places where they were initially "stuck"). From these, we selected one concept to pursue in depth and addressed the transformative, integrative, and irreversible criteria in that context. We do not examine the boundary marker criterion in detail, since our interviews were only about core concepts and did not focus on the disciplinary boundary of computer science. These interviews formed the basis for a previous study of threshold concepts [10, 5, 19, 18], and the full interview script is found in [5].

To further explore the concept of transformation, we conducted two additional interviews with a variant of the original script in which we explored the transformative criterion first. The questions in the script were modified as needed to fit the new order. In these additional interviews, the participants spent more time discussing transformation and less time talking about how troublesome a concept was, how it felt to be stuck, etc. With regard to skills, however, there was no notable difference.

4.2 Analysis of the interviews

This is an exploratory study. Until now, thresholds have been discussed in terms of concepts. We report here on a preliminary investigation of how, in computing, skills might be, or be part of, these thresholds. As a result, we chose to do a primarily qualitative analysis.

We began by reading and re-reading the interview data, looking for quotes related to skills. Once we were satisfied that skills played a significant role in most of the interviews, we conducted a deductive thematic analysis. [6] Each of the characteristics of threshold concepts – transformative, integrative, troublesome, and irreversible – was examined by at least two researchers. The researchers assigned to a particular characteristic re-read all the interviews and coded extracts related to that characteristic, considering them in relation to skills. During the analysis, the need to practice emerged as an aspect of skills, so two researchers examined that as well.

4.3 The quantitative data

In Section 6, we discuss quantitative data that provide some further support for the hypothesis that skills can be thresholds. These data quantify student performance in a course required for all computing students at the institution where one of the authors teaches. They were gathered from 2005-2011.

5. QUALITATIVE FINDINGS

In this section, we present the ways in which the threshold concept characteristics are manifested in the context of skills as well as the relationship between skills and practice.

5.1 Transformative

Mastery of a threshold concept transforms a student's perception of his or her discipline. Mastering a threshold skill transforms what students can *do* – and their vision of what they can do. They can solve problems they couldn't solve before or solve them in a better way.

In discussing transformations, the students often emphasize their newly acquired skills. For example, Student 15 reports that after taking data structures, he could do more, and he *knew* he could do more.

> [I began to] really think about it [programming] on a deeper level of how I could do things ... faster ... seeing how I can make all those data structures that are in use, and then if I wanted I could make my own or combine them. I did that over the summer for an internship. And I couldn't have done that before. I wouldn't have ever thought of that.

True mastery of a skill means it becomes almost automatic. Before Student 2 mastered the skill of writing C++ code with pointers, for example, he'd "randomly try something different until it works, which sometimes I thought I had the answer and sometimes I didn't." He wasn't "really sure *how to use it*" [emphasis added]. Afterwards, "then it's almost like it's a tool and you don't even think about using it. You say I need to do this. Okay, done."

Sometimes there is a complex relationship between a threshold skill and a concept. For example, Student 6 had heard in lecture that object-oriented programs are made up of a collection of cooperating objects and had practiced writing object-oriented code for some time, when he finally got it. "It was just the relation between the two. This class was just going to do this job and that's it. And this class just needed that information. So it accessed the other class." This change in understanding was accompanied by a significant change in his perception of what he could do: "[I]t was, like, sitting down, I could add my own class. I could come up with stuff and just go nuts with it on my own." In this case, the threshold seemed to include both a concept and a skill, tightly connected together.

Student 1 went a step further and reflected on the process of transformation. He noted that he had learned several design patterns, and each time, the process was the same. He struggled for a while, then understood why the pattern was useful and how it worked, and eventually became comfortable using it. Find the quote in Section 8.

5.2 Integrative

Learning a threshold concept is integrative, in that it exposes connections between concepts in the discipline that were previously unknown to the learner. There seems to be an analogous notion with threshold skills, but related to their application to tasks or problems: once a threshold skill is attained by applying it to some task, the learner sees other places where the skill could be applied. These other places can be tasks that the user could already perform, but using different techniques. Student 1, for example, was able to find recursive solutions for a lot of tasks that he had done before using iteration, and in procedural as well as functional languages. Student 2 discusses how the application of a skill to different problems can lead to this sort of integration:

[T]he only way to make that is really just through doing it multiple times or seeing examples where it's done. And saying oh, I can use it this way. Oh, I never would have thought of that. ... And then when it's off that base knowledge you can start making different connections.

Gaining a skill in one context may lead to improved understanding in others. Student 4 had problems dereferencing pointers in C++, but figured out how to do it when doing problems in assembly:

I can't explain why assembly made it more clear than C++. The only thing I can think of is that in assembly you rely on those references heavily, because you don't have a ... whole lot of registers ... you can't declare too many variables.

5.3 Troublesome

Threshold concepts can be difficult for students as they are associated with troublesome knowledge (as in [28]): knowledge that is inert, ritual, conceptually difficult, or foreign. Although the researchers were trying to elicit troublesome concepts in these interviews, the students frequently discussed skills. They reported having difficulties not when they listened to a lecture or read the text, but when they had to *do* something. Students report this problem in a variety of different contexts. Student 14 talked about the difficulty of learning to program:

I remember from the first year how when I was going into the lectures I could see the way that you were doing things and I could mentally work it out for myself, but when it came around to doing it ... it was if sometimes I was hitting a brick wall.

Similarly, Student 2 reported that he understood how recursion "theoretically worked" but still, "writing an application" took time, and Student 4 talks about the difficulty of writing code using pointers:

So, before pointers I thought programming wasn't that hard. And then I got into pointers and the doing part; I was just lost.

The students may have understood the concepts and been unable to apply them, or perhaps they didn't fully understand them until they could apply them. In either event, however, they definitely perceived applying the concept to be the troublesome aspect of learning.

5.4 Semi-irreversible

One of the features used to describe a threshold concept that it is probably irreversible; once learned it is difficult to "unlearn" or even to "think back" to how a concept was viewed before understanding. Irreversibility seems somewhat weaker with skills – skills can degrade over time through lack of use, but they do not completely go away. The student stays transformed, and knows where the skill applies, but it may be necessary to review or practice to regain or maintain skills.

Student 7, for example, discussing pointer manipulation and the need to review:

I haven't written a C++ program in a while so if I was going to go back and code that again I'd have to dig out my old code and kind of review and look at it. I'm not sure that I can create it from scratch on the fly.

Student 4 agrees and describes how if she is "doing it every day then if you ask this question, [I] can explain it a lot better."

We saw some examples of skills that seemed to be irreversible once attained. Student 10 remembered having difficulties when learning object-oriented programming, but is unable to explain why from his current perspective:

It just made so much sense to me right now that it's hard to think back at how I didn't understand it.

5.5 Associated with practice

As suggested by the definition in Section 2, skills are closely related to practice: part of the definition of a skill is that it is attained or learnt through practice, where practice is "repeated exercise in or performance of an activity or skill so as to acquire or maintain proficiency in it."[27] In our data, students describe using practice in both ways: to initially acquire a skill, and to maintain proficiency.

While learning a skill, students talk about the need for repetition or drill, to try many examples. For example, Student 3 gives advice and discusses his experience learning to use pointers:

... draw lots of pictures. For example, write a lot of programs that have lots and lots of pointers. Write lots of linked lists and manipulate them as much as you possibly can. Dereference them and find out, do a lot of cout statements and find out exactly where you are in memory. ...
I made sure that the address was exactly what it was supposed to be pointing to because then I would get the address, I would go into the debugger and get the address of the object...
Yeah, I saw it update and all that stuff. Yeah. I saw when it got to a null value and I changed my code. It went out of bounds. I made all the mistakes.

Student 10 thinks that practicing your skills is the essential thing that creates engineers:

I think really the engineers need to learn that to be successful in engineering; to be successful in life you need to somehow sometimes just buckle down and just really work at it for hours – slave away at it.

The use of practice to maintain skills is closely related to whether threshold skills are irreversible.

6. QUANTITATIVE SUPPORT

Here we provide support for the notion of threshold skills seen in formal education, where teachers observe that it is the nuts and bolts of programming that stymies the students. Section 5 discusses skills as thresholds with evidence obtained from student interviews. Here we see direct support of programming skills as a threshold. We report on a third-year C++ course where students are expected to previously have learned fundamental programming concepts. We present empirical evidence that the students have not yet acquired the associated programming skills.

At one author's university, students start out in typical CS1 and CS2 courses at the home university or at a regional college or university. The majority learn Java; fewer than 5% have seen C/C++. To be admitted to the program, students must have had success in CS1 and CS2: receive a grade of B- or better (greater than 2.7 on 4.0 scale).

The first required course in the third year, is somewhat a repeat of CS2 conceptually, but in C++. Concepts taught in CS2, elementary abstract data structures such as linked list, stacks, and queues are used as foundations; algorithm complexity is formalized and recursion is revisited. A focus of the course is on pointers, memory management, and object-oriented design and programming in C++. There are discrete math topics not necessarily covered in their CS2 course: induction; introduction to propositional and predicate logic; recurrence equations. While topics other than programming are covered, the focus is on programming with the mantra by faculty that a student must be a competent programmer to be able to succeed to the next course.

Students in this course report that they do not find the programming concepts new. Yet, it has been repeatedly observed that they struggle with using pointers and memory management. The statistics (available numbers from different terms offered 2005 through 2011), seen in Table 1, support the observed difficulty with the skill.

Course Offering	Drops	Inadequate Grade	Number of Students	Not Successful
1	5	2	30	23.3%
2	5	1	22	27.3%
3	4	3	34	20.6%
4	2	9	26	42.3%
5	5	14	51	37.3%
6	3	6	39	23.1%
7	11	8	73	26.0%
8	6	2	36	22.2%
Totals	41	45	311	27.7%

Table 1: Students not successful using C++

Only students who dropped the course after performing poorly on the midterm exam are counted in Table 1. These students would likely not have succeeded with a satisfactory grade. Students completing the course with unsatisfactory grades to continue to the next course (less than 2.0 on a 4.0 scale) typically are inadequate at programming.

This course highlights the threshold skills of using pointers and managing memory. The students were successful in CS1 and CS2, but many, nearly 30%, still have difficulties crossing this skill threshold. Students are confused by pointers, references, pointers to pointers, and references of pointers. While the concept that memory holds an address is straightforward, students struggle with implementation, with the application of the concept.

7. DISCUSSION

While we do not have a definitive answer, our data suggest that the answer to our first research question, "Are there skills whose acquisition acts as a threshold for computing students?" is yes. Different aspects of threshold skills are mentioned in relation to various skills and, as shown in Section 5, the skill of *using pointers* shows up in relation to each of the threshold skill criteria.

Transformative: When learning pointers, a student went from making "random" changes to code in order to make it work, to being able to use pointers routinely, to solve problems he couldn't solve before.

Integrative: Understanding pointers in assembly language helped a student to understand how to use them in C++.

Troublesome: a students describes how when he started using pointers, he went from thinking "programming wasn't that hard" to being "completely lost."

Semi-irreversible: Students say they could use pointers even though it had been some time since they had done so – but it would require review.

Associated with practice: A student's advice on learning pointers includes many practice activities: drawing lots of pictures, dereferencing many pointers, verifying addresses in the debugger, and so forth.

From these data, it appears that using pointers is an example of a skill that exhibits both threshold concept and skill attributes. Students emphasize that the skill of using pointers, not the concept, is the threshold.

In answer to our second question, threshold skills are both like and unlike threshold concepts.

Threshold concepts are transformative, integrative, and irreversible. A good example is user-centered design: the notion that software is designed for other people to use. Introductory students don't generally think in this way (and judging by the software on the market, not all computing professionals do either). The idea, once grasped, transforms the way students view their profession; it affects many aspects of software design, development, and testing; and because it is such a fundamental shift in perspective, it is unlikely to be reversed.

Threshold skills can be transformative, integrative, and (semi-)irreversible – but in different ways from a threshold concept. A skill is **transformative** if it changes what students can do – and their vision of what they can do. It is **integrative** if it can be used in different contexts. Sometimes it broadens the list of problems students can solve; sometimes it gives them a new and perhaps better way to solve problems they could already handle. It is **semi-irreversible** if it can be regained with practice, without having to start again from scratch. It is rarely learned in a single aha moment; generally it must be acquired with practice.

Threshold skills and concepts can both be **troublesome** in much the same ways. Some skills, such as recursion, may be perceived as *foreign*; without the perspective of how functions are invoked, a function calling itself may seem like nonsense. A skill can be *inert* if a student has the ability to use it in a narrow context but not in others: for example a student who uses stacks effectively in a data structures course but fails to use them when they apply to problems in a later course. A skill cannot be *conceptually difficult*, but it can be complex and demanding to learn and maintain.

It may be that skills are more likely to be thresholds in computing than many other disciplines. When students learn the concepts related to their native language in elementary school, such as nouns, sentences, and paragraphs, they already have a skill – speaking the language – to which they can tie these concepts. In many university-level subjects, the students build upon skills developed in primary and secondary education. When our students learn computing, they are generally learning skills and concepts at the same time. This may be especially challenging since knowledge of skills is partly tacit. Polanyi writes: "*There are things that we know but cannot tell. This is strikingly true for our knowledge of skills.*" [29, p. 601, italics in original]

An implication of this is that we may need to identify the skills that are hard for students to attain, and to allocate more time in our instruction for practice. Students may listen to the lectures, read the book, believe that they understand – and maybe really understand – and still be unable to apply a concept. Students having difficulty with C++ even though they have demonstrated competence with Java supports this notion. As a discipline, perhaps we need to develop drills comparable to the scales played by musicians or athletes' practice.

Another implication is that acquiring skills is particularly important for retention. Whether or not students understand the related concept, what they focus on is the skill. There is external feedback: the program doesn't compile, the recursion causes a stack overflow, or the program simply doesn't do what it's supposed to do. As a result, lack of a skill not only blocks their progress, but frustrates and discourages them in an immediate way that failure to understand a concept might not.

Finally, we have observed that the problems related to gaining skills does not only apply to beginning students: more advanced students report similar problems e.g., with pointers or design patterns. Skills, therefore should also be considered in more advanced courses. One may ask whether the traditional assignment and assessment forms in Computer Science (problem solving and projects) cover the individual student's needs for gaining the appropriate skills.

8. CONCLUSIONS AND FUTURE WORK

In this paper we looked at skills as thresholds, suggesting that their learning exhibits analogous characteristics to those seen with threshold concepts. Here is a quote from Student 1 that displays several of the characteristics of threshold skills discussed earlier, with our annotations in square brackets and italics:

> There's like a big gap between the theoretical good software design, and the how do you implement it well *[The difference between concept and skill]*. And I found design patterns are a nice way for me to bridge that gap *[Integrates theory and practice]*. But it takes, you know, a month or so of just working with one to really understand when it's appropriate, how to use it to its full advantage *[Need for practice to attain skill]*. And then if I don't use it regularly, I forget how to structure it *[Need for practice to maintain skill]*.

This student appreciates that skills are important in computing as well as concepts.

Our research into threshold concepts has shown that what students describe as problematic about learning a concept is not always understanding the concept in its abstract sense. They often think they understand the general meaning – the principle. Instead, the perceived difficulty is to handle the details of specific applications. It may be interesting to consider this in relation to the Biggs [2] and Bloom [3] taxonomies. To recognize and re-tell something is less advanced than using it. To draw useful conclusions from the experiences of using something is more sophisticated than just using it.

What does it mean to know a concept? To become truly familiar with a concept in programming, it is not enough to know the conceptual idea, its principles and rules: one must also be able to use the concept unhindered in its applications – to make things with the concept. Only then the concept is understood in its deeper meaning. Hence, we found it interesting to look the combination of concepts and the requisite skill.

We still do not know if threshold skills always relate to one or more threshold concepts. In our previous research we suggested pointers as a threshold concept candidate. Following from the present findings we now further suggest that pointers also exhibit the characteristics of what we describe as a threshold skill. We believe there is a need for further research in this area. We hope that the threshold concept theory will provide a useful framework to study how these skills are learned and maintained, and how they complement conceptual computing knowledge in our students.

9. REFERENCES

[1] C. von Aufschnaiter and S. von Aufschnaiter. University students' activities, thinking and learning during laboratory work. *European Journal of Physics*, 28(3):51–60, 2007.

[2] J. B. Biggs and K. F. Collis. *Evaluating the quality of learning : the SOLO taxonomy (structure of the observed learning outcome)*. Academic Press, New York, 1982.

[3] B. S. Bloom, editor. *Taxonomy of Educational Objectives: the Classification of Educational Goals. Handbook 1: Cognitive Domain*. Longman, New York, 1956.

[4] B. du Boulay. Some difficulties of learning to program. In E. Soloway and J. Spohrer, editors, *Studying the Novice programmer*, pages 283–299. Lawrence Erlbaum Associates Inc., 1988.

[5] J. Boustedt, A. Eckerdal, R. McCartney, J. E. Moström, M. Ratcliffe, K. Sanders, and C. Zander. Threshold concepts in computer science: do they exist and are they useful? *SIGCSE Bull.*, 39(1):504–508, 2007.

[6] V. Braun and V. Clarke. Using thematic analysis in psychology. *Qualitative Research in Psychology*, 3:77–101, 2006.

[7] P. Davies. Threshold concepts: how can we recognise them? 2003. Paper presented at EARLI conference, Padova. http://www.staffs.ac.uk/schools/business/iepr/docs/etcworkingpaper(1).doc (accessed 25 August 2006).

[8] J. Dewey. Science as subject-matter and as method. *Science*, 31(787):121–127, 1910.

[9] C. Dörge. Competencies and skills: Filling old skins with new wine. In N. Reynolds and M. Tursanyi-Szabo, editors, *Proceedings of the key competencies in the knowledge society: IFIP TC 3 International Conference, KCKS 2010*, pages 78–89, 2010.

[10] A. Eckerdal, R. McCartney, J. E. Moström, M. Ratcliffe, K. Sanders, and C. Zander. Putting threshold concepts into context in computer science education. In *ITICSE '06*, pages 103–107, Bologna, Italy, 2006.

[11] A. Eckerdal, R. McCartney, J. E. Moström, M. Ratcliffe, and C. Zander. Categorizing student software designs: Methods, results, and implications. *Computer Science Education*, 16(3):197–209, September 2006.

[12] A. Eckerdal, R. McCartney, J. E. Moström, K. Sanders, L. Thomas, and C. Zander. From *Limen* to *Lumen:* computing students in liminal spaces. In *ICER '07: Proceedings of the third international workshop on Computing education research*, pages 123–132, New York, NY, USA, 2007. ACM.

[13] N. Entwistle. Concepts and conceptual frameworks underpinning the ETL project. Occasional Report 3 of the Enhancing Teaching-Learning Environments in Undergraduate Courses Project, School of Education, University of Edinburgh, March 2003, 2003.

[14] S. Fitzgerald, G. Lewandowski, R. McCauley, L. Murphy, B. Simon, L. Thomas, and C. Zander. Debugging: finding, fixing and flailing, a multi-institutional study of novice debuggers. *Computer Science Education*, 18(2):93–116, 2008.

[15] M. T. Flanagan and J. Smith. From playing to understanding: the transformative potential of discourse versus syntax in learning to program. In R. Land, J. H. F. Meyer, and J. Smith, editors, *Threshold Concepts Within the Disciplines*, chapter 7, pages 91–104. Sense Publishers, Rotterdam, 2008.

[16] J. P. A. M. Kessels and F. A. J. Korthagen. The relationship between theory and practice: Back to the classics. *Educational Researcher*, 25(3):17–22, 1996.

[17] R. Lister, T. Clear, Simon, D. Bouvier, P. Carter, A. Eckerdal, J. Jackova', M. Lopez, R. McCartney, P. Robbins, O. Seppälä, and E. Thompson. Naturally occurring data as research instrument: analyzing examination responses to study the novice programmer. *SIGCSE Bulletin*, 41(4), 2009.

[18] R. McCartney, J. Boustedt, A. Eckerdal, J. E. Moström, K. Sanders, L. Thomas, and C. Zander. Liminal spaces and learning computing. *European Journal of Engineering Education*, 34(4):383–391, 2009.

[19] R. McCartney, A. Eckerdal, J. E. Moström, K. Sanders, and C. Zander. Successful students' strategies for getting unstuck. *SIGCSE Bull.*, 39(3):156–160, September 2007.

[20] R. McCormick. Conceptual and procedural knowledge. *International Journal of Technology and Design Education*, 7(1-2):141–159, 1997.

[21] M. McCracken, V. Almstrum, D. Diaz, M. Guzdial, D. Hagan, Y.-D. Kolikant, C. Laxer, L. Thomas, I. Utting, and T. Wilusz. A multi-national, multi-institutional study of assessment of programming skills of first-year cs students. *SIGCSE Bulletin*, 33(4):125–180, 2001.

[22] J. Meyer and R. Land. Threshold concepts and troublesome knowledge: Linkages to ways of thinking and practising within the disciplines. ETL Project Occasional Report 4, Universities of Edinburgh, Coventry, and Durham, 2003. http://www.ed.ac.uk/etl/docs/ETLreport4.pdf.

[23] J. H. Meyer and R. Land. Threshold concepts and troublesome knowledge (2): Epistemological considerations and a conceptual framework for teaching and learning. *Higher Education*, 49:373–388, 2005.

[24] B. Molander. *Kunskap i handling [Knowledge in Action; in Swedish]*. DAIDALOS, 1996.

[25] National Capital Language Resource Center (NCLRC). The essentials of language teaching: Strategies for learning grammar. `http://www.nclrc.org/essentials/grammar/stratgram.htm`. Accessed March 13, 2012.

[26] D. A. Norman. *The Design of Everyday Things*. Doubleday, New York, 1990.

[27] *Oxford English Dictionary Online*. Oxford University Press, March 2012. http://0-www.oed.com.helin.uri.edu/viewdictionaryentry/ Entry/ 180865 (accessed April 07, 2012).

[28] D. Perkins. The many faces of constructivism. *Educational Leadership*, 57(3):6–11, 1999.

[29] M. Polanyi. Tacit knowing: Its bearing on some problems of philosophy. *Reviews of Modern Physics*, 34(4):601–616, 1962.

[30] G. Ryle. Knowing how and knowing that: The presidential address. *Proceedings of the Aristotelian Society, New Series*, 46:1–16, 1945.

[31] M. Séré. Towards renewed research questions from the outcomes of the european project *Labwork in Science Education*. *Science Education*, 86(5):624–644, 2002.

[32] L. S. Shulman. Theory, practice, and the education of professionals. *The Elementary School Journal*, 98(5):511–526, May 1998.

[33] V. Sien and D. W. K. Chong. Threshold concepts in object-oriented modelling. In *7th Educators' Symposium@MODELS 2011 - Software Modeling in Education - Pre-Proceedings*, pages 55–64, Carl von Ossietzky universität Oldenburg, 2011.

[34] S. Worsley, M. Bulmer, and M. O'Brien. Threshold concepts and troublesome knowledge in a second-level mathematics course. In *Symposium Proceedings: Visualisation and ConceptDevelopment, UniServe Science*, pages 139–144, The University of Sydney, 2008. UniServe Science.

[35] C. Zander, J. Boustedt, A. Eckerdal, R. McCartney, J. E. Moström, M. Ratcliffe, and K. Sanders. Threshold concepts in computer science: a multi-national investigation. In R. Land, J. H. F. Meyer, and J. Smith, editors, *Threshold Concepts Within the Disciplines*, chapter 8, pages 105–118. Sense Publishers, Rotterdam, 2008.

On the Reliability of Classifying Programming Tasks Using a Neo-Piagetian Theory of Cognitive Development

Richard Gluga
University of Sydney
Sydney NSW Australia
richard@gluga.com

Judy Kay
University of Sydney
Sydney NSW Australia
judy.kay@sydney.edu.au

Raymond Lister
Univ. of Technology, Sydney
Sydney NSW Australia
raymond.lister@uts.edu.au

Donna Teague
Queensland U. of Technology
Brisbane QLD Australia
d.teague@qut.edu.au

ABSTRACT

Recent research has proposed Neo-Piagetian theory as a useful way of describing the cognitive development of novice programmers. Neo-Piagetian theory may also be a useful way to classify materials used in learning and assessment. If Neo-Piagetian coding of learning resources is to be useful then it is important that practitioners can learn it and apply it reliably. We describe the design of an interactive web-based tutorial for Neo-Piagetian categorization of assessment tasks. We also report an evaluation of the tutorial's effectiveness, in which twenty computer science educators participated. The average classification accuracy of the participants on each of the three Neo-Piagetian stages were 85%, 71% and 78%. Participants also rated their agreement with the expert classifications, and indicated high agreement (91%, 83% and 91% across the three Neo-Piagetian stages). Self-rated confidence in applying Neo-Piagetian theory to classifying programming questions before and after the tutorial were 29% and 75% respectively. Our key contribution is the demonstration of the feasibility of the Neo-Piagetian approach to classifying assessment materials, by demonstrating that it is learnable and can be applied reliably by a group of educators. Our tutorial is freely available as a community resource.

Categories and Subject Descriptors

K.3 [**Computers & Education: Computer and Information Science Education**]: Computer Science Education

General Terms

Human Factors, Design, Measurement

Keywords

Programming, Neo-Piagetian, learning standards, assessment

1. INTRODUCTION

Kramer [8] asserted that the key difference between top-performing and under-performing software engineering students is "The ability to perform abstract thinking and to exhibit abstraction skills". He also posed the question "Is it possible to teach abstract thinking and abstraction skills?" If the answer to Kramer's question eventually proves to be "yes", and abstraction is eventually taught explicitly and taught well, then it will be because Computing Education Research found ways (as Kramer expressed it) to "measure students abstraction abilities" using tests that "examine different forms of abstraction, different levels of abstraction and different purposes for those abstractions".

Neo-Piagetian theory provides a way to describe the abstraction abilities of novice programmers [9, 4]. However, if Neo-Piagetian theory is to be useful, then it needs to be learnable by computing educators who are not necessarily computing education researchers. Having learned Neo-Piagetian theory, those same computing educators need to be able to apply it reliably. To that end, we have developed an online tutorial system for Neo-Piagetian theory.

In this paper, we describe our tutorial, and report an evaluation of how well the tutorial enabled twenty computer science educators to classify programming assessment tasks. Before doing so, however, in the next section we review Neo-Piagetian theory within a programming context.

2. NEO-PIAGETIAN THEORY

The Neo-Piagetian theory of cognitive development [11] is a derivative of Classical Piagetian theory [13]. Classical Piagetian theory focuses on the intellectual development of children as they mature. That is, Classical Piagetian theory focuses on a child's development of general abstract reasoning skills as they grow older. Neo-Piagetian theory instead states that people, regardless of their age, progress through increasingly abstract forms of reasoning as they gain expertise in a specific problem domain. In Neo-Piagetian theory, a person irrespective of age, can display abstract reasoning abilities in one domain, but not necessarily in an unrelated domain. This is the key difference between Classical Piagetian and Neo-Piagetian theory.

Neo-Piagetian theory defines four stages of cognitive development. Those stages are, from least mature to most mature, *Sensorimotor, Pre-Operational, Concrete Operational* and *Formal Operational* [9]. These four stages are described respectively in each of the next four subsections.

The subsection describing the sensorimotor stage is brief, because that stage is relatively well defined and is not taught by the online tutorial. The subsections describing the higher three stages contain: (1) a description of the Neo-Piagetian stage; (2) an example programming exam question representative of that stage; and (3) an explanation as to why the example question requires a minimum abstraction ability at that Neo-Piagetian stage. The descriptions of these stages are adapted from Lister [9] and are taken near-verbatim from the tutorial system. (The use of bold font in those subsections reflects the use of bold font in the online tutorial.) The example questions and explanations were produced collaboratively by the authors of this paper.

2.1 The Sensorimotor Stage

The sensorimotor stage is the first and least abstract of the Piagetian stages. In the context of programming, Lister defines the sensorimotor stage as being exhibited by "students who trace code with less than 50% accuracy" [9].

2.2 The Pre-Operational Stage

Typically, pre-operational students can trace code. That is, they can manually execute a piece of code and determine the values in the variables when the execution is finished. However, they **tend not to abstract from the code to see a meaningful computation performed by that code**.

For the novice who is thinking pre-operationally, **the lines in a piece of code are only weakly related**. The thinking of the pre-operational student tends to focus on only one abstract property at any given moment in time, and when more than one abstract thought occurs over time those abstractions are not coordinated, and may be contradictory.

A pre-operational student uses **inductive reasoning** to derive the function of a piece of code by **examining input/output behavior**. That is, the pre-operational student chooses a set of initial values, **manually executes the code**, and then inspects the final values.

Example Exam Question: What is the output of the following code?

```
int a = 3;
int b = 7;
int c = 0;
int[] data = {1, 6, 5, 2, 3};

for (int i = 0; i < data.length; i++) {
    if ( data[i] > a &&  data[i] < b) {
        c++;
    }
}

System.out.println(c);
```

Explanation: This is a tracing exercise where the correct answer can be obtained by a pre-operational student by manually executing the code one line at a time. A higher understanding of the code as a whole is not essential (i.e. realizing that the code returns the number of elements in the data array between the values of a and b). If the array 'data' was much larger, a pre-operational student would not be able to manually execute the code to derive the answer.

2.3 The Concrete Operational Stage

Concrete thinking involves **routine reasoning about programming abstractions**. However, a defining characteristic of concrete reasoning is that **the abstract thinking is restricted to familiar, real situations, not hypothetical situations** (hence the name 'concrete').

A concrete operational student can write small programs from well defined specifications but struggles to write large programs from partial specifications. When faced with the latter type of task, the concrete operational student **tends to reduce the level of abstraction by dealing with specific examples instead of with a whole set defined in general terms**. That is, rather than solving the problem for the general case, they write code to solve a simple subset.

Concrete operational students are capable of **deductive reasoning**. That is, given a piece of code, **a concrete operational student may derive its function just by reading the code**. While they may also try manual execution of the code to help confirm this interpretation, they would not simply report the code's function in terms of input and matching output sets.

Example Exam Question: The following piece of code shifts all elements in the data array one place to the right. The last element in the array is rotated to the front of the array. Modify the function to do the opposite, that is, shift every element one place to the left, and rotate the first element to the last position.

```
public int[] shiftRight(int[] data) {

    if ( data.length < 2) return data;
    int temp = data[length-1];

    for (int i = data.length-1; i>0; i--) {
        data[i] = data[i-1];
    }

    data[0] = temp;
    return data;
}
```

Explanation: To answer this question correctly, a student must understand all the abstract relationships in the given code. A student operating at the concrete level will see most if not all of the changes required: copy the value from the appropriate array location to the temporary variable, reverse the loop direction, change the assignment in the body of the loop and put the temporarily saved value into the appropriate array location. A pre-operational student may make some of those required changes, the most likely being the change to the assignment in the body of the loop, but the pre-operational student is unlikely to make all the required changes, as he does not understand all the abstract relationships between the lines of code.

2.4 The Formal Operational Stage

A person thinking formally can **reason logically, consistently and systematically**. Formal operational reasoning also requires a **reflective capacity** - the ability to think about one's own thinking.

Formal operational thinking can involve **reasoning about hypothetical situations**, or at least **reasoning about situations that have never been directly experienced** by the thinker. It also involves an awareness of what is known for certain, and what is known with some probability of being true, which in turn allows someone who is thinking formally to **perform hypothetico deductive reasoning**, that is, make a tentative inference from incomplete data, then actively, systematically seek further data to confirm or deny the tentative inference.

Writing programs is frequently referred to as an exercise in problem solving. Problem solving can be defined as a five step process: (1) abstract the problem from its description, (2) generate subproblems, (3) transform subproblems into subsolutions, (4) recompose, and (5) evaluate and iterate. Such problem solving is formal operational.

Example Exam Question: Write a program that will read in an arithmetic expression from the console and print out the result. For example, given the input **3*8/4+(6-(4/2+1))**, your program should output the answer **9** on a new line. The program should gracefully handle all exceptions.

Explanation: To answer this correctly, a student is required to use problem solving skills as described above. This involves logical, consistent, systematic reasoning about programming abstractions in an unfamiliar context to piece together a working solution. A student at the formal operational level would abstract functionality into objects and methods and piece together a solution that is correct and adheres to best-practice design patterns.

3. THE TUTORIAL STRUCTURE

A participant using the tutorial works their way through several phases, as shown in Figure 1. The tutorial is a component of a larger research system called ProGoSs (Program Goal Progression) [6], which aims to provide a mechanism for modeling student learning progression over an entire degree, in terms of the topics and learning objectives in curricula such as the ACM/IEEE CS curriculum guidelines [1, 2]. An essential component of such modeling is a way of describing cognitive development, in terms of a suitable theory or framework. ProGoSs can support any suitable theory or framework, not just Neo-Piagetian theory. In an earlier paper, we described a tutorial for Bloom's Taxonomy, which can also be used within ProGoSs [7]. All tutorials supported within ProGoSs share the same broad phase structure. In the following subsections, we describe each of the tutorial phases, explaining the design rationale for each.

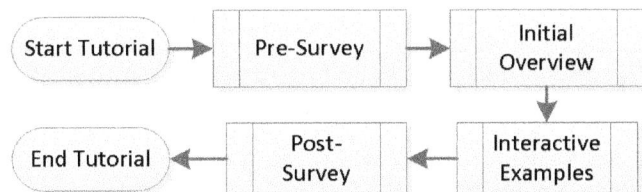

Figure 1: Tutorial Stages Flowchart

3.1 Pre-Survey Phase

The tutorial commences with the pre-survey phase. In this phase, participants are asked to provide their level of experience in computer science education (i.e. tutors/teaching-assistants vs. lecturers/professor) and to self-rate their ex-

isting confidence at correctly classifying programming exam questions using Neo-Piagetian theory, based on any prior knowledge. We refer to this confidence judgment as the *Initial Confidence* (IC) score. It is expressed as a percentage (100% indicating complete confidence). We collect this data for two broad reasons. The first reason is that we use this data to evaluate participant perceptions of the effectiveness of the tutorial. The other reason is that it calls upon the user to perform a metacognitive judgement of the feeling of knowing (FOK) and such activation of metacognitive processes can improve learning [10].

3.2 Initial Overview Phase

In the Initial Overview, as shown in Figure 2, participants read descriptions of each of the three Neo-Piagetian stages. Each description is accompanied by an example exam question representative of that stage and an explanation as to why that stage of Neo-Piagetian reasoning is required to answer the question. These descriptions and examples were described near-verbatim earlier in this paper, in Sections 2.2, 2.3 and 2.4. The design aim of the Initial Overview was to provide a description and example for each Neo-Piagetian stage that would fit on a typical browser screen and could be read in three to five minutes, thus providing an overview of all three Neo-Piagetian stages in 10 to 15 minutes. The Initial Overview is not intended to be a comprehensive introduction to the three Neo-Piagetian stages.

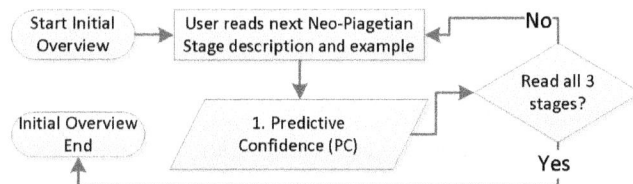

Figure 2: Tutorial Initial Overview Flowchart

After reading each description and example, a participant self-rates their confidence at being able to recognize other exam questions as also requiring that same stage of Neo-Piagetian reasoning. We call this the *Prediction Confidence* (PC) score. These scores are expressed as a percentage, one for each Neo-Piagetian category. A participant must rate their Prediction Confidence on all three Neo-Piagetian stages before they may proceed to the next phase of the tutorial, the interactive examples.

3.3 Interactive Examples Phase

After completing the Initial Overview, participants then step through fifteen interactive examples. In each interactive example, the participant is presented with a programming exam question, and is asked to identify the minimum Neo-Piagetian stage required to produce a correct answer. Space does not allow for all fifteen examples to be presented in this paper. Readers are invited to create an account and log in to the tutorial (http://progoss.com) to read all fifteen interactive examples.

A screen shot of the interface is shown in Figure 3 where a participant has classified Example 4 as pre-operational. The participant has self-rated their confidence in that classification as 90% (On-Task Confidence, or simply OTC) and has provided via a text box an explanation for that classification.

The tutorial asks for the participant's confidence and explanation in accordance with the recommendation of Chi et al. [3] that "Eliciting self-explanations improves understanding". (The explanations by participants also sometimes uncover aspects of interactive examples needing improvement).

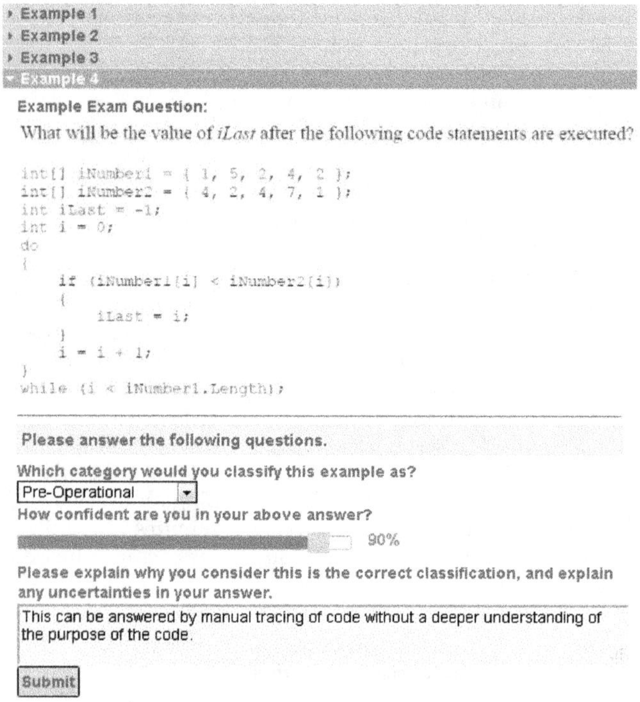

Figure 3: Participant classifies Example 4 as pre-operational and self-rates confidence

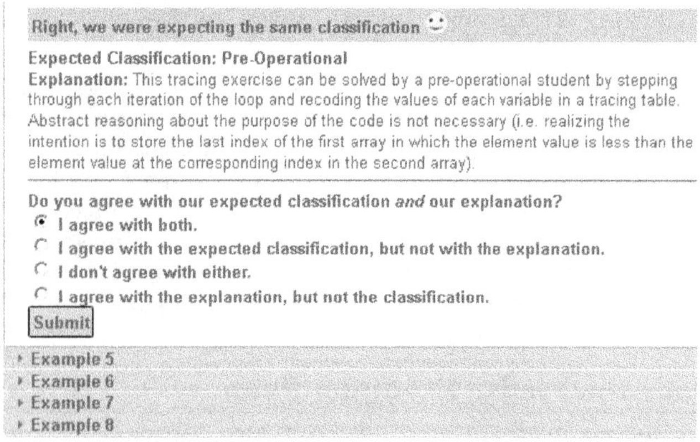

Figure 4: Participant reviews nominated classification for Example 4

After a participant has recorded their classification for an exam question, and also their confidence and explanation (as shown in Figure 3), the participant clicks on the "Submit" button. The interface then presents the system-nominated classification for that example, along with a justification, as illustrated in Figure 4.

The system-nominated classifications for each of the fifteen examples were developed collaboratively by three of the authors of this paper, all of whom are computer science

education researchers with an active interest in cognitive development and learning progression in programming. That does not necessarily guarantee that each nominated classification is the only correct interpretation of Neo-Piagetian theory, but rather the nominated classifications serve to provoke further reflection and discussion among participants (as discussed in the next two paragraphs). However, for the purposes of carrying out the evaluation in this paper, we will regard these nominated classifications as 'correct' classifications. Therefore, the percentage of times a participant's classification matches the nominated classification is referred to as the participant's On-Task Accuracy (OTA).

After being shown the nominated classification for a particular example, and an explanation for that nominated classification, the participant is then presented with a closed-option response to register their agreement or disagreement with the classification and explanation (as shown in Figure 4). The percentage of times a participant agrees with a nominated classification is referred to as the participant's Agreement Score (AGR). When a participant disagrees, a text box is provided so that the participant can explain why.

After registering their agreement or disagreement with an example, the participant moves to the next interactive example. This process continues until all fifteen examples are completed. The flowchart in Figure 5 captures the process of working through all 15 interactive examples.

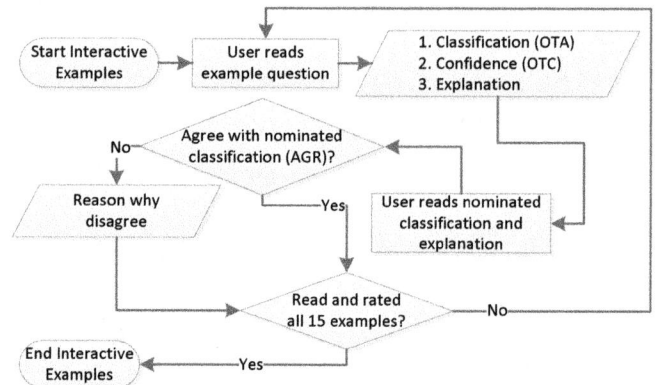

Figure 5: Tutorial Interactive Examples Flowchart

3.4 Post-Survey Phase

After completing all fifteen examples, participants complete the short Post-Survey. Participants are asked to self-rate their Final Confidence (FC) at being able to classify programming questions according to Neo-Piagetian theory. Participants are also asked to comment on whether they found the tutorial useful and efficient, and whether they would consider using Neo-Piagetian theory when devising future assessment tasks.

4. EVALUATION RESULTS

We conducted an evaluation on two aspects of our work: (1) to assess the effectiveness of our tutorial at teaching computer science educators how to classify assessment tasks according to Neo-Piagetian theory; and (2) to elicit feedback on the perceived value of classifying exam questions according to Neo-Piagetian stages.

4.1 Participants

Twenty participants completed the interactive tutorial. Eleven of these were Computer Science professors or lecturers who have taught or are currently teaching first year computer science subjects. The other nine participants were postgraduate students or computer science researchers who have tutored or are tutoring computer science subjects (also referred to as teaching assistants in some parts of the world). Some of the participants completed the tutorial in their own time and at their own pace in private, while others completed it in a workshop (but still coded each question individually and independently).

4.2 Pre-Survey Phase

The average Initial Confidence for all twenty participants was 29%. Out of these twenty participants, only five had encountered Neo-Piagetian theory before in some limited capacity (probably via Lister's paper [9]). Those five participants self-rated their initial confidence as between 50% and 74%. The remaining fifteen participants self-rated their initial confidence as between 1% (lowest allowed value) and 40% (s.d. 23). The eleven Lecturer/Professors had a higher average initial confidence than the nine tutors (39% vs. 17%).

4.3 Initial Overview Phase

Figure 6 summarizes the quantitative results from the initial overview and the completion of the fifteen interactive examples. The vertical axis is an average percentage score, from 0 to 100. The horizontal axis is grouped into the three Neo-Piagetian stages. Within each Neo-Piagetian category, the chart shows four values. These values are, from left-to-right and as described in the previous sections, the participant Prediction Confidence, On-Task Confidence, On-Task Accuracy and Agreement.

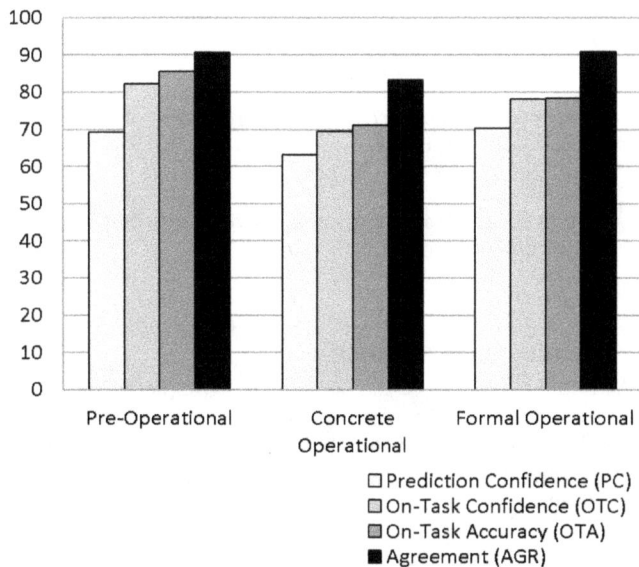

Figure 6: Aggregate participant results per Neo-Piagetian stage

The average Prediction Confidence (PC) scores for all twenty participants were 69%, 63% and 70% for the three Neo-Piagetian stages. The Lecturer/Professors exhibited higher average prediction confidences than the tutors (76%, 73% and 79% vs. 62%, 52% and 59%).

These PC averages indicate that the material presented in the Initial Overview phase was not sufficient for participants to become confident that they had a solid understanding of the framework (especially the tutors). This was further reflected in the post-survey. One participant commented "doubling the number of examples will help with the initial comprehension of the classifications". Another noted "what might be better is a more comprehensive list of [initial] examples to start off with". These comments suggest a misunderstanding of the goal of the Initial Overview. The goal of the Initial Overview is not to provide a comprehensive introduction to Neo-Piagetian classification. Instead, the goal is merely to give a quick overview of Neo-Piagetian theory, to prepare the participants for the 15 interactive examples.

4.4 Interactive Examples Phase

For the 15 interactive examples, the average On-Task Confidence, across all twenty participants, were 82%, 69% and 78% for each of the three Neo-Piagetian stages. These averages are higher than the respective Prediction Confidence averages, suggesting that the Initial Overview had prepared the participants better than they had thought. The Lecturer/Professors had a slightly higher average overall on-task confidence than the tutors (82% vs. 74%). However, that difference in average confidence was largely due to a single tutor exhibiting an average confidence of only 37%. The next lowest average confidence of any participant was 67%. The concrete operational category had the lowest average confidence rating, suggesting it may be the most problematic of the three (as middle categories often are).

On-Task Accuracy averages were 85%, 71% and 78% for the three Neo-Piagetian stages. These are close to the respective On-Task Confidence ratings, suggesting participants were fairly accurate in their self-reflection. Despite their higher initial confidence, the On-Task Accuracy average of the Lecturer/Professors was almost identical to the average accuracy of the tutors (78% vs. 77%),which suggests that the major determinant of accuracy was the tutorial, not prior exposure to Neo-Piagetian theory.

The Agreement Scores (i.e. agreement with the nominated classification) were 91%, 83% and 91% for each Neo-Piagetian stage. This high agreement indicates that participants generally accepted the nominated Neo-Piagetian classifications, even when they had made a different classification choice. The most debated examples were those targeting the concrete operational stage.

4.4.1 Individual Participant Results

Figure 7 shows the result averages for each participant. The columns from left to right are: Participant ID (PID); Experience (EXP) where L/P is Lecturer/Professor and T is tutor or teaching assistant; Initial Confidence (IC); Prediction Confidence for the three Neo-Piagetian levels (PC1 for pre-operational, PC2 for concrete operational, and PC3 for formal reasoning); On-Task Accuracy (OTA); On-Task Confidence (OTC); Agreement (AGR) as an average across the fifteen questions; and the Final Confidence (FC). The results are divided into two sub-sections, showing the averages for the eleven Lecturer/Professors, and the nine tutors/teaching-assistants. The average and standard deviations are shown at the bottom of the table for all twenty participants.

PID	EXP	IC%	PC1%	PC2%	PC3%	OTA%	OTC%	AGR%	FC%
29	T	1	10	10	10	53	72	73	70
30	T	1	60	56	85	87	82	100	74
31	T	40	77	47	51	87	78	100	72
32	T	30	80	70	78	73	82	100	81
33	T	10	22	31	30	60	37	100	29
36	T	20	100	80	80	80	85	87	70
60	T	25	65	40	48	80	67	93	73
63	T	1	50	40	60	93	71	100	90
92	T	26	90	90	90	80	90	93	90
T AVG		17	62	52	59	77	74	94	72
50	L/P	21	66	80	93	87	90	93	90
51	L/P	12	50	46	45	80	72	93	60
56	L/P	30	90	89	91	87	92	80	91
47	L/P	74	79	76	91	93	77	100	81
55	L/P	70	82	80	94	67	68	60	58
78	L/P	60	89	78	75	53	77	53	80
11	L/P	30	100	76	94	93	91	93	90
77	L/P	30	80	100	100	73	95	80	80
87	L/P	50	100	80	89	67	90	93	70
44	L/P	1	20	20	27	80	77	100	85
43	L/P	50	75	75	75	73	74	93	75
L/P AVG		39	76	73	79	78	82	85	78
TOTAL-AVG		29	69	63	70	77	78	90	75
TOTAL-SD		23	27	25	26	12	13	14	15

Figure 7: Participant Result Summary

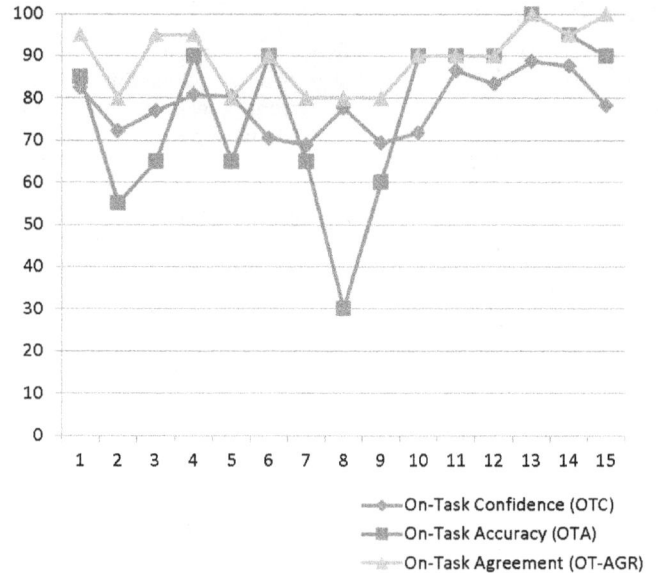

Figure 8: Aggregate participant results for each of the fifteen interactive examples

4.4.2 Learning Progression

The 15 interactive examples are not a summative assessment exercise. Instead, it is intended that participants will further develop their understanding by classifying, and reflecting upon, these 15 examples. The chart in Figure 8 indicates that participants do learn and improve as they progress through the 15 examples. That chart shows the average On-Task Confidence, On-Task Accuracy and Agreement scores (as percentages from 0 to 100 along the y-axis) for each of the fifteen interactive examples (numbered 1 to 15 on the x-axis). For the first half of the interactive examples, the accuracy of the participants varies considerably from question to question. From example 10 onward, On-Task Accuracy is consistently at 90% or higher. (Note, however, that none of examples 10 to 15 were from the concrete operational category.)

4.5 Post-Survey Phase

The average Final Confidence was 75% with a standard deviation of 15. Nineteen of the twenty participants self-rated their understanding as between 50% and 90%. One participant self-rated at only 29%. Ignoring that participant lifts the average Final Confidence to 83%. Whether it be 75% or 83%, the Final Confidence average is a large improvement on the 29% average Initial Confidence.

In the closing feedback comments, all participants were generally positive about the tutorial, although some suggested more examples are needed. The post-survey also presented participants with a set of six yes/no check-box statements:

- 12 agreed (7 of 11 lecturer/professors, 5 of 9 tutors) that "The tutorial helped me change the way I think about programming assessment"

- 14 agreed (7 lecturer/professors, 7 tutors) that "I now have a better appreciation of the different competence levels required to solve tasks"

- 12 agreed (7 lecturer/professors, 5 tutors) that "I may consider using Neo-Piagetian theory for classifying some of my own exams or assessments in the future"

- 4 agreed (3 lecturer/professors, 1 tutors) that "There is too much ambiguity to use Neo-Piagetian theory for classifying programming tasks"

- 17 agreed (11 lecturer/professors, 6 tutors) that "I found this exercise useful"

4.6 Completion Times

As noted earlier, 15 of the participants completed the tutorial in one sitting and under our supervision, so we were able to capture the time it took them to complete the tutorial. The average was 67 minutes. The slowest participant took 96 minutes.

5. DISCUSSION

Figure 8 shows that Example 8 had an unusually low On-Task Accuracy of only 30%. There are two broad reasons why this example could be especially problematic: either (1) it is a poor example, and needs improvement, or (2) perhaps the mapping of Neo-Piagetian stages to programming remains a work in progress. Example 8 is as follows:

Interactive Example 8 Explain in plain English, using a single sentence, the purpose of the following function.

```
function whatDoIDoFunction(x, array) {
    var y = 0;
    var i = 0;

    for(i = 0; i < array.length; i++) {
        if(array[i] == x) {
            y++;
        }
    }
    return y;
}
```

Thirteen participants initially classified Example 8 as concrete operational, offering explanations such as the following: "requires holistic understanding of a simple, specific piece of code"; "the student needs to be able to reason about the high level operation of this code"; "the student needs to understand the relationships between the lines of code and how the code works as a whole". However, the system-nominated classification for Example 8 is pre-operational, for which the system-explanation is as follows:

While this is not a tracing exercise, a student might solve this by substituting some specific values for x and the array and tracing one or two iterations of the loop, which should reveal the purpose of the code (i.e. inductive reasoning). A concrete operational student will answer this without the manual tracing (i.e. deductive reasoning), although this would be hard to distinguish from the answer. This code is a particularly simple iterative process on an array. Based upon cues such as the use of "for", a pre-operational student might surmise that the code scans across the array, without completely understanding exactly how it scans across the array. After making such an assumption, a student can then answer the question by focusing solely upon the "if" within the loop, and its associated increment to variable "y". The student need not be worried about how successive iterations of the loop will affect each other. Such a student might be considered to be late pre-operational.

As Figure 8 shows, 80% of the participants agreed with this system-explanation. One of the participants who disagreed argued as follows:

"I believe this is another borderline question (that is, bordering between pre-operational and concrete operational). In the explanation of what these two categories are, there is the idea of using specific input or concrete examples to make inductive leaps. It is unclear at what level of simplicity/complexity we start to cross into the concrete operational category."

This participant makes a valid point, especially given that the tutorial's own explanation for Example 8 (shown above) ends with "such a student might be considered to be late pre-operational", which is a further indication that this example may be a border-line classification. In the remainder of this discussion, we take this opportunity to extend upon the system-explanation for Example 8, to further clarify what aspects of the code in an "explain in plain English" question render a question pre-operational or concrete operational. In

so doing, we restrict the discussion to code that performs an iterative process on an array.

The case made in the above system-explanation for Example 8 consists of two arguments: (1) the pre-operational student may answer the question by tracing, and (2) the student may answer the question by paying most attention to a small portion of the code. We discuss these arguments in turn.

Provided a pre-operational student is resourceful enough to choose suitable data for the parameters in Example 8, that student may successfully answer the question inductively – that is, by tracing the code. Such a student must pay attention to the "if" condition, and ensure that there is data that will sometimes make that condition true and sometimes make it false. The ability to construct suitable data is non-trivial, and is possibly a step on the road to thinking concretely, but for cases like the simple piece of code in Example 8 we argue that choosing suitable data is within the capability of some pre-operational students.

The second argument, that the student may answer the question by paying most attention to a small portion of the code, is perhaps less clear when we imagine a pre-operational student answering Example 8 correctly, but more clear when a pre-operational student answers a similar question incorrectly. Murphy *et al.* [12] provide such a case. They described an experiment where students were required to read and explain a piece of code of similar complexity to Example 8:

```
double num = 0;

for(int i=0; i < numbers.length; i++ ) {
    if ( numbers[i] > 0 )
        num += numbers[i];
}
```

When students were asked to explain what that code did, Murphy *et al.* found that many students gave an answer like "It sums all the numbers in the array". An error like that is to be expected from a student who pays little attention to most of the code, but instead focuses on a single line of code, the assignment statement within the loop. An incorrect answer like that is clearly pre-operational. However, we argue that there is only a small difference of degree, and not a difference of kind, between a student who focuses on one line within a loop, and a student who focuses on two lines within that same loop. For both the code used by Murphy *et al.* and the code used in Interactive Example 8, if a pre-operational student does focus on the two lines within the loop, there is a good chance the student will correctly guess what the code does. An "explain in plain English" question that is evidence for concrete operational reasoning is a question where the student must give serious consideration to most of the lines of code, and understand how those lines interact.

By either tracing code, or by focusing on one or two lines, a pre-operational student has a very good chance of correctly answering an "explain in plain English" question when the code is such that: (1) the loop scans across the entire array, (2) each iteration of the loop either changes or uses a single, unique element of the array, (3) the same operation is performed in each iteration of the loop, and (4) no iteration of the loop has any affect on any subsequent iteration. An example of code that meets these four criteria is a loop that increments all the elements of an integer array. For such a loop, the pre-operational novice can ignore most of the code and focus upon the incrementation. A pre-operational novice reads the incrementation declaratively, as if the loop is not a sequential process. A loop control variable such as "i" is read mathematically, as "let i be any element of the array".

Both the code in Example 8 and the code used by Murphy *et al.* breaks the third criterion, because of the the "if" expression. While those two pieces of code are therefore not trivial, we believe (as argued above) that both pieces of code are explainable by pre-operational novices. However, as examples of code increase in sophistication, and the number of broken criteria rises, pre-operational novices will be less likely to understand the code.

Note that we are not arguing that a given pre-operational novice will always perform consistently when explaining different pieces of code, such as the two pieces of code in this discussion. Recall that earlier in this paper, in the description of the pre-operational stage, we wrote that "The thinking of the pre-operational student tends to focus on only one abstract property at any given moment in time, and when more than one abstract thought occurs over time those abstractions are not coordinated, and may be contradictory." Sometimes a pre-operational novice will focus upon the most salient features of a piece of code, and sometimes that pre-operational novice will not. Many experienced educators will have encountered a (pre-operational) student who appears to understand one piece of code, but not another, when the educator believes both pieces of code embody almost identical programming concepts.

6. CONCLUSIONS

The results from our evaluation indicate that our tutorial is effective at introducing Neo-Piagetian theory, within a programming context, in about an hour of study. The tutorial is freely available at `http://progoss.com`.

Participants however commented that more interactive examples would be desirable. A revised version of the tutorial may thus have a large database of different examples which are used at random. Users would complete any number of these examples until they felt confident. Perhaps a system operating like PeerWise [5] could be used to build a large repository of exam questions. Participants would submit their own exam questions and have these classified to a Neo-Piagetian stage by other users. Such a large repository of questions, classified according to Neo-Piagetian theory, would be a useful community resource.

7. ACKNOWLEDGMENTS

We thank the Smart Services CRC for partially sponsoring this project and our colleagues who gave their time to test the tutorial. Support for this project was also provided by the Office of Learning and Teaching, an initiative of the Australian Government Department of Industry, Innovation, Science, Research and Tertiary Education. The views expressed in this publication do not necessarily reflect the views of the Office of Learning and Teaching or the Australian Government.

8. REFERENCES

[1] ACM/IEEE. Computer science curriculum 2008. http://www.acm.org/education/curricula-recommendations, 2008.

[2] ACM/IEEE. Computer science curriculum 2013. http://www.sigart.org/CS2013-EAAI2011panel-RequestForFeedback.pdf, 2011.

[3] M. T. H. Chi, N. Leeuw, M.-H. Chiu, and C. Lavancher. Eliciting self-explanations improves understanding. *Cognitive Science*, 18(3):439–477, 1994.

[4] M. Corney, D. Teague, A. Ahadi, and R. Lister. Some empirical results for neo-piagetian reasoning in novice programmers and the relationship to code explanation questions. In M. de Raadt and A. Carbone, editors, *Australasian Computing Education Conference (ACE2012)*, volume 123 of *CRPIT*, pages 77–86, Melbourne, Australia, 2012. http://crpit.com/confpapers/CRPITV123Corney.pdf.

[5] P. Denny, A. Luxton-Reilly, and J. Hamer. The peerwise system of student contributed assessment questions. In Simon and M. Hamilton, editors, *Tenth Australasian Computing Education Conference (ACE 2008)*, volume 78 of *CRPIT*, pages 69–74, Wollongong, NSW, Australia, 2008. http://crpit.com/confpapers/CRPITV78Denny.pdf.

[6] R. Gluga, J. Kay, T. Lever, and R. Lister. An architecture for systematic tracking of skill and competence level progression in computer science. In D. B. Varthini, editor, *2nd Annual International Conference in Computer Science Education: Innovation and Technology*, number 2, pages 65–69. Global Science and Technology Forum, 2011.

[7] R. Gluga, J. Kay, R. Lister, S. Kleitman, and T. Lever. Coming to terms with bloom: an online tutorial for teachers of programming fundamentals. In M. de Raadt and A. Carbone, editors, *Australasian Computing Education Conference (ACE2012)*, volume 123 of *CRPIT*, pages 147–156, Melbourne, Australia, 2012. ACS.

[8] J. Kramer. Is abstraction the key to computing? *Commun. ACM*, 50:36–42, April 2007.

[9] R. Lister. Concrete and other neo-piagetian forms of reasoning in the novice programmer. In J. Hamer and M. de Raadt, editors, *Australasian Computing Education Conference (ACE 2011)*, volume 114 of *CRPIT*, pages 9–18, Perth, Australia, 2011. http://crpit.com/confpapers/CRPITV114Lister.pdf.

[10] D. Moos and R. Azevedo. Self-efficacy and prior domain knowledge: to what extent does monitoring mediate their relationship with hypermedia learning? *Metacognition and Learning*, 4(3):197–216, 2009.

[11] S. Morra, C. Gobbo, Z. Marini, and R. Sheese. *Cognitive Development: Neo-piagetian Perspectives*. Psychology Press, 2007.

[12] L. Murphy, S. Fitzgerald, R. Lister, and R. McCauley. Ability to 'explain in plain english' linked to proficiency in computer-based programming. In *Proceedings of the eighth international workshop on Computing education research*, ICER '12, Auckland, New Zealand, 2012.

[13] J. Piaget and B. Inhelder. *The Psychology of the Child*. Routledge & Kegan Paul, 1969.

Social Sensitivity Correlations with the Effectiveness of Team Process Performance: An Empirical Study

Lisa Bender, Gursimran Walia,
Krishna Kambhampaty, Kendall E. Nygard
North Dakota State University
Computer Science Dept. 2740
Fargo, ND 58108
+1 701-231-8562

{lisa.l.bender, gursimran.walia,
k.kambhampaty, kendall.nygard} @ ndsu.edu

Travis E. Nygard
Ripon College
300 Steward Street
Ripon, WI 54971
+1 920-748-8783

NygardT@ripon.edu

ABSTRACT

Teamwork is essential in industry and a university is an excellent place to assess which skills are important and for students to practice those skills. A positive teamwork experience can also improve student learning outcomes. Prior research has established that teams with high levels of social sensitivity tend to perform well when completing a variety of specific, short-team, collaborative tasks. Social sensitivity is the personal ability to perceive and understand the feelings and viewpoints of others, and it is reliably measurable. Our hypothesis is that, social sensitivity can be a key component in positively mediating teamwork task activities and member satisfaction. Our goal is to bring attention to the fact that social sensitivity is an asset to teamwork. We report the results from an empirical study that investigates whether social sensitivity is correlated with the effectiveness of processes involved in teamwork and team member satisfaction in an educational setting. The results support our hypothesis that the social sensitivity is highly correlated with team effectiveness. It suggests, therefore, that educators in computer-related disciplines, as well as computer professionals in the workforce, should take the concept of social sensitivity seriously as an aid or obstacle to team performance and the teamwork experience.

Categories and Subject Descriptors

K.3.2 [**Computer and Information Science Education**]: Computer Science Education.

General Terms

Experimentation, Human Factors, Measurement, Performance

Keywords

Computer Science, Collaboration, Social Sensitivity, Teams, Empirical Study

1. INTRODUCTION

Teamwork is increasingly important in today's world. Although, individual work is also highly valued, software development projects are increasingly complex and tend to involve many sophisticated tasks and require the collective work of individuals to accomplish. Thus it is important to prepare students as future practitioners and provide them with positive teamwork experiences. Complex projects require people to interact with each other, as well as with computing technologies. Project development processes are often difficult due not only to the complexity of the technologies, but also to the complexity of social interactions between the project team members. Previous research asserts that the ability to use soft skills to navigate interpersonal relationships and negotiate social interactions is critical to team success [1, 2]. With current academic standards and curricula, many students graduate with the technical, hard skills that they need, but they often lack necessary soft skills that are critical to team success [3]. Soft skills are not only important to teamwork in industry, but also in a classroom environment. Research results show that interpersonal and small-group skills are essential to positive cooperative learning and improved learning outcomes [4, 5]. Begel and Simon studied recent college graduates who were hired by Microsoft and found that while the new hires generally did well, there were numerous problems with communicating and collaborating with others [6]. Rademacher studied students at a large university and found that a lack of soft skills often prevented students from getting hired or caused problems once they began working in industry [7].

One factor that can greatly influence collaborative team performance is team composition. Much research has been done on team composition, but no single attribute stands out as key to superior performance [22-26]. Intriguing questions were raised by a recent study, that established that group intelligence depends less on how smart individual group members are and more on team dynamics, including how well team members communicate and collaborate [8]. These researchers found that social sensitivity, which is the personal ability to perceive the mind and mood of others, made the largest contribution to a group's overall intelligence and was a primary predictor of team effectiveness in accomplishing short-term tasks.

Motivated by these findings, a major goal of this research is to investigate if the connection between social sensitivity and team performance extends to students in computing fields who carry out longer-term tasks within major projects in addition to the short-term tasks. Another goal of this research is to determine if social sensitivity impacts team process activities (i.e. brainstorming, dependability, etc.) involved in team projects. We wanted to see if SS had an effect on any of these process activities to better understand how SS affected team performance. One last goal is to investigate whether social sensitivity impacts the satisfaction of the team members. By looking at these three measures, we hope to gain a more complete picture of the impact of social sensitivity on the overall effectiveness of a team.

To accomplish these goals, we conducted an empirical study that investigated the effect of social sensitivity on the performance of project teams consisting of computer science and management information system students who worked on semester-long projects. These student projects were completed in multiple stages, each building upon previous work. The results indicate that social sensitivity of subjects is positively correlated with their performance on the group projects. This suggests that social sensitivity is a key factor in the success of complex projects, such as those carried out by software development teams. Our results also show that social sensitivity is positively correlated with many of the process activities performed in team work and with team member satisfaction.

2. BACKGROUND AND RELATED WORK

Teamwork is essential throughout organizations in all areas of society, including industry and education. Increasingly, the complexity of today's problems cannot be solved by an individual and require the resources of a team. Wuchty et al. has report that over the last 50 years, more than 99 percent of the work in scientific subfields, from biochemistry to computer science, have experienced increased levels of teamwork and that the best research now emerges from groups [10].

The prominence of team collaboration has created the need to study what makes teams effective. In academia, the more effective a team is, the greater chance there is for learning and success. The educational benefits of teamwork are well documented in the educational literature [11]. Working in teams leads to an improvement of learning outcomes [5] and is positively associated with students' self-assessed quality of learning [12]. Collaborative learning, which involves teamwork, directly engages the learner with the subject matter. This allows for better absorption of the material [13], increases socialization and exposure to different student ideas which can improve student retention [14], and can lead to an intense level of information processing that encourages cognitive growth [13]. Contrary to the many benefits of positive teamwork, student learning is hindered from participating on dysfunctional teams and they often develop negative opinions of the value of teamwork [15].

Researchers find that measures of team effectiveness are concerned with two aspects: task performance effectiveness and measures of team member affectiveness (e.g. satisfaction, participation, and willingness to continue to work together) [16, 17]. A major team-related factor that can affect project performance and the effectiveness of a team is the interaction of individual personalities. Other factors affecting the project performance include team communication, information sharing, cooperation, and coordination [18, 19]. One of the main factors contributing to poor performance is project team composition [2]. This suggests that careful consideration in the formation of teams is important.

Teamwork is different from project management in that it focuses on team formation as well as team member attitudes and behaviors; not just on the successful accomplishment of the project [20]. There are many factors to consider when forming teams, and their impact on team composition has been widely studied. Educators use many criteria to form teams such as gender, race, prior class or work experience, personality, problem solving style, and/or grade point average and have developed multiple guidelines for assigning people to teams [21]. Within the field of Software Engineering, some of the factors include the effects of personality composition [22, 23], team member abilities [24], team roles [25], diversity [26], shared mental models [2], and team member satisfaction [2]. Chan et al. [1] suggests that soft skills are the primary factor that should be considered for achieving good project performance. They argue that higher levels of soft skills within the team facilitate the application development skills and domain knowledge skills necessary to achieve good project performance. In the spirit of this study, our work has produced new knowledge by considering a soft skill that Chan et al did not interrogate (social sensitivity) and investigating how it affects the team performance.

Social Sensitivity (SS) is the ability to correctly understand the feelings and viewpoints of people [27]. Salovey and Mayer [28] view social sensitivity as an element of emotional intelligence and identify some of the characteristics of socially intelligent people which include the ability to admit mistakes, to accept others for who they are, to enhance other's moods, to be social problem solvers, to be flexible thinkers, and to have an interest in the world at large. They also recognize that the appraisal and expression of emotion often takes place on a nonverbal level. The ability to perceive nonverbal expression ensures smoother interpersonal cooperation. By perceiving, empathizing, and then responding appropriately, people experience greater satisfaction, more positive emotions, and lower stress. Such positive emotions aid in creative thinking and enable flexibility in arriving at alternatives to problems. Sternberg et al., identified additional behaviors reflecting SS: thinks before speaking and doing; displays curiosity; does not make snap judgments; makes fair judgments; assesses well the relevance of information to the problem at hand; and is frank and honest with self and others [29]. Kosmitzki et al., noted important characteristics include being good at dealing with people; has extensive knowledge of rules and norms in human relations; is good at taking the perspective of other people; adapts well in social situations; is warm and caring; and is open to new experiences, ideas, and values [30]. These characteristics suggest that high levels of SS could be a benefit for teams.

Every person has a certain level of SS, but there is evidence that people who choose technical careers have less of it on average than the general population [31]. More specifically, Baron-Cohen et al. [31] provide evidence that engineers, mathematicians, physicists, and computer scientists are typically less socially sensitive than their peers in the humanities, arts, and social sciences. This suggests that people in these technical disciplines have more difficulty decoding what others are thinking and feeling. Although this research did not address teams specifically, it suggests to us that teams of technical people may be challenged in the area of social sensitivity. Computer professionals and engineers are stereotypically viewed as introverted independent specialists who find it exceptionally difficult to work in teams. The observation made by Baron-Cohen et al. [31] may explain why computer professionals and engineers find team skills difficult. This finding especially aroused our interest in studying SS and its effects on team performance.

A major inspiration for our study comes from the work of Woolley et al. [8] whose study established a correlation between

SS and effective teamwork. They describe a collective intelligence that predicts group performance and is grounded in how well groups interact and work together. In other words, team performance was not driven by the intelligence of the individuals on the team, but rather by collaborative groups who conversed easily and contributed equally. In particular, groups whose members had higher levels of SS were more collectively intelligent. They found that neither the average intelligence of the group members nor the intelligence of the smartest member played much of a role in the team performance. Woolley stated that the groups where the conversation was more evenly distributed were more collectively intelligent and had better performance on the tasks. The tasks (e.g. brainstorming, puzzle solving, negotiating, decision making, and typing) in their study were short-term contrived tasks requiring hours, rather than months, to complete. Thus, those team members had little opportunity to develop longer-term working patterns and problems. Our study extends this research by interrogating the effects of SS on teams that worked together for longer durations—the better part of an academic semester—and produced a complex series of deliverables during that time. In many ways our study closely approximates a real working environment.

In order to proceed with our study, we needed an accurate test to determine an individual's level of social sensitivity. There are several methods for testing social sensitivity. The one we chose to use is referred to as the "Reading the Mind in the Eyes" test which was created and validated by Baron-Cohen et al. [31]. This test gauges the accuracy of individuals in judging someone's emotional state by looking at their eyes. An individual is presented with a series of 36 photographs of the eye-area of actors. For each photograph, the individuals are asked to choose which of four adjectives best-describes how the person in the photograph is feeling. This test was originally developed to measure an 'advanced theory of mind' in adults, which is the ability to identify mental states in oneself or another person and it has been found to have test-retest reliability [32]. Alternative techniques for measuring social sensitivity, such as the George Washington Social Intelligence Test [54] and the Vineland Social Maturity Scale [33] were rejected due to reported inaccuracies or the inclusion of factors irrelevant to our research [33].

As mentioned in Section 1, the researchers of this study also investigated if SS impacts specific team process activities, and if so, which activities are impacted more than the others. There are many team process performance activities to consider and their impact on team effectiveness has been widely studied [34]. The activities we believe were most pertinent to our project goals consisted of brainstorming, dependability, focusing on tasks, sharing responsibility, performance, research and information sharing, questioning, discussing, listening, and teamwork, and are briefly described as follows.

a) *Brainstorming* [35] is a technique used by groups or individuals to help identify opportunities and challenges, solve problems, and generate ideas.

b) *Being Dependable* is defined as being trustworthy [36]. A dependable person shows reliability, responsibility, and believability [37].

c) *Focusing on Tasks* refers to how well a team member stays focused on the task at hand and gets work done. It refers to a team member who is self-directed and does not need other team members to remind in order to get things done.

d) *Sharing Responsibility* refers to how good a team member is at doing their fair share of the work. All team members must work together to maximize team performance and a team member's productivity can be negatively affected if they are over-burdened with tasks.

e) *Performance* quality refers to the accuracy or precision of output [38]. Low quality performance by one individual can have serious consequences on the team's product (e.g. causing the need for extensive rework) and team effectiveness (e.g. team member frustration).

f) *Research and Information Sharing* refers to how well a team member gathers research, shares useful ideas and defends or rethinks ideas.

g) Communication [39] is essential to effective teamwork and involves **Questioning, Discussing**, and **Listening.** Questioning is important to clarify meanings and to understand the rest of the team members. Discussing ideas is important to the interchange of information. Team members also need to listen to each other in order to hear and consider their team members ideas and develop mutual knowledge.

h) *Teamwork* is composed of communication, collaboration, cooperation, and compromise. Good teamwork requires that team members cooperate with each other, consider others feelings and needs, and offer to help each other out. Collaboration refers to working together and sharing responsibility. Compromise is important so that team members avoid unnecessary arguing over details that may cause the team to lose focus on the main objectives.

These activities are common team processes used to achieve project objectives. In addition to analyzing overall team performance and satisfaction, we also analyzed the level of impact SS has on these team processes in order to better understand the impact that social sensitivity has on team performance.

3. STUDY DESIGN
This study was designed to analyze the relationship between the SS of student teams and the quality of work in computer science team projects. We investigate whether the student teams with higher average SS were positively correlated with their actual performance on the project as measured by grades. This study also analyzed the relationship between SS of individual students and some of the common process activities in teamwork as measured by averaged scores given to an individual by their teammates.

A randomized experimental design was used in the study in which participants were tested to determine their SS scores and were then randomly assigned to teams of three participants each. Each team worked to complete a major semester-long project on an ethical issue related to current computer technology in society. The project consisted of four deliverables: three written deliverables and one team presentation. Grades were collected for each deliverable. The team members completed self and peer evaluations after each of the written deliverables and completed a post-survey at the end of the project. The details of the study are provided in the following subsections.

3.1 Study Goals and Hypotheses
The following hypotheses were formulated:

Hypothesis 1: Student teams with higher average social sensitivity scores perform significantly better on the project.

Hypothesis 2: Students with higher social sensitivity scores are perceived, by their peers, to perform better on each team process activity (e.g., brainstorming, dependability, etc.).

Hypothesis 3: Student teams with higher social sensitivity scores have significantly higher levels of team member satisfaction.

3.2 Independent and Dependent Variables

The experiment manipulated the following independent variable:

a) *Social Sensitivity Score*: Each student participant completed the "Reading the Mind in the Eyes" test [31] in order to determine their individual social sensitivity score.

The following dependent variables were measured:

a) *Team Performance*: This measure includes the total points earned by each team—the sum of scores on four project deliverables submitted throughout the semester.

b) *Teamwork Activities*: These activities include: *Brainstorming, Dependability, Discussing, Focusing on Tasks, Listening, Performance, Questioning, Research and Information Sharing, Sharing Responsibility*, and *Teamwork*. The measures include the average of the peer evaluation scores that an individual received from their team members for each of the ten activities..

c) *Team member satisfaction:* This measure includes each individual's level of satisfaction with their team on the project at the end of project.

3.3 Participating Subjects

Out of the 98 graduate and undergraduate computer science and management of information systems students enrolled in the Social Implications of Computing course, 76 students chose to participate in the study. The goals of this course are to raise awareness of real world ethical issues involving computing and to help the students understand different methods used to understand, analyze and respond to many of the ethical dilemmas involving computer technologies. The participating subjects (17 out of 18 females and 59 out of 80 males) worked together in teams on a project involving a multi-vocal response to an ethical issue related to the world of computer science and technology.

3.4 Artifacts

The major course project consisted of four deliverables: a project proposal, an interim report, a final report, and a final project presentation based on computer-related ethical topics. Each team chose a different ethical issue (such as privacy related to biometrics or social networking) and met throughout the semester on their selected topic in order to produce these deliverables. The main idea was to have each member of the group focus on the viewpoints of one of the issue's stakeholders and then, as a group, discuss the views that these diverse stakeholders may have on the ethical question. The team was also tasked with tracing the consequences of alternative actions to their logical conclusions and then evaluating the impact these actions would have on the stakeholders. This was done to help the team members gain an understanding of perspectives other than their own and to produce artifacts that contained ideas that would not have been articulated by working independently.

3.5 Experimental Procedure

The study steps are described as follows:

a) *Step 1 – Test Subjects for Social Sensitivity:* At the beginning of the semester, the "Reading the Mind in the Eyes" test [31] was administered to measure each subject's SS. To ensure that the subjects had a clear understanding of the adjectives used in the test, a glossary was provided that contained a definition and sample sentence for each of the emotional state choices. The glossary basis was provided by the work of Baron-Cohen et al. [31]. The students were encouraged to read through the glossary prior to the test and to refer to it as needed during the test. The survey was administered online, the responses were analyzed for completeness and individual SS scores were assigned.

b) *Step 2 – Forming Student Teams:* Thirty-four teams were formed by randomly assigning three students to each team. At the end of the semester 32 teams still had three students each and one team had two students, due to one student dropping the course.

c) *Step 3 – Actualizing Team Projects:* The students worked in teams on specific semester-long projects where each team produced a project proposal (PP), an interim report (IR), a final report (FR), and a final presentation (FP). Most groups chose a topic from a list of ideas provided by the instructor, although students could pursue any topic that was approved by the instructor. After the project was approved, the teams performed the necessary research to write a project proposal. The proposal required them to articulate ethical questions that they planned to investigate, justify the questions' importance, identify major stakeholders and ethical values, specify their research methods, and plan the project. Half way through the semester, each team submitted an interim progress report that described the project goal, objectives, and scope, research methods, evidence to support ethical viewpoints, and potential stakeholder actions. Near the semester's end, each team gave an oral presentation on their project and submitted a final written report which strengthened viewpoints from the interim report, applied ethical tests to the potential stakeholder actions, and evaluated the feasibility of these actions.

d) *Step 4 – Evaluating Team Projects*: Each deliverable was scored using detailed rubrics to structure the grading. All grading was done by the same researcher (who was not the instructor) and all team members received the same score for each assignment. The team performance (i.e., *the total team score*) was measured by summing each team's score from all four deliverables.

e) *Step 5 – Peer-Self Evaluations*: After each of the written deliverables, the student participants completed an evaluation for themselves and for each of their team members. These evaluations were performed by each student outside of the classroom. This allowed for more privacy, decreasing the chances that fellow students would see how others filled out the evaluation and allowing the students to be more honest in the assessment of their teammates. It also allowed the students more time to fill out the evaluation and be more thoughtful and complete in their assessments. Each participant rated the quality of each team member's participation (including self participation) on 10 candidate activities of an effective team as described in Section 2. Participants rated each of the 10 activities on a 5-point Likert scale (4 –Excellent, 3 – Good, 2 – Average, 1 – Poor, and 0 – Fail) and provided comments to justify the ratings.

f) ***Step 6 – Post-Study Survey:*** At the end of the semester, a 19 question survey was administered to the students to collect data regarding the self-perceived effectiveness of each team including their level of satisfaction, whether members felt valued, whether effective feedback occurred among team members among other questions.

3.6 Data Collection and Evaluation Criterion

Because this study investigates the impact of SS on team performance, only teams that had at least two team members consenting to participate in the study were included in our analysis; and only the consenting team member's SS scores, team performance scores, and peer evaluations were collected. After this elimination process, 28 out of 34 teams remained in the study.

Individual student SS test scores for each of the 76 participating subjects are shown in Figure 1. Most subjects scored in the range of 19 to 25, with the SS scores ranging from a minimum of 9 to a maximum of 32 out of a maximum score of 36 correct.

Although both self and peer evaluations were collected for each consenting participant, only the peer evaluations were used so that we could understand how a team member is perceived by their peers. Our reason for only using peer evaluations is that individuals are less accurate at judging themselves as opposed to judging their peers [40]. Because evaluations were collected after each written deliverable (PP, IR, FR), each participant had three ratings for each teamwork activity from each team. Using the peer assessment data (not self-assessment data), average scores (on a scale of 0 to 4) received by each participant for each of the ten activities (e.g. brainstorming, dependability, etc.) were calculated. We then analyzed the correlation between the individual SS scores and the scores the individual received on each activity.

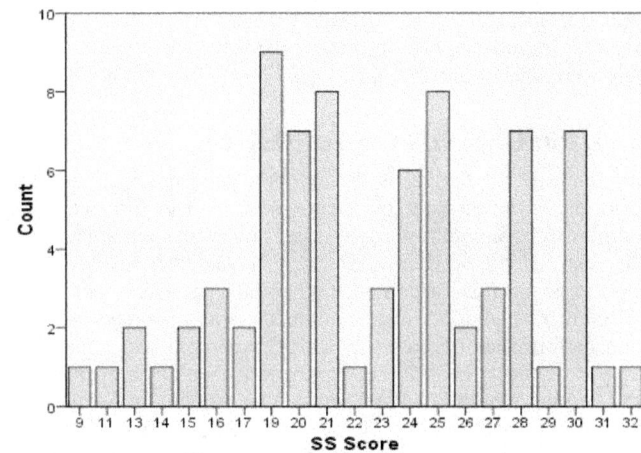

Figure 1. Individual Social Sensitivity Scores

4. DATA ANALYSIS AND RESULTS

This section provides analysis of the quantitative data that includes student's SS scores, their team's project performance, and their individual peer-rating on each of the ten team activities. This section is organized around the three hypotheses presented in Section 3.1. An alpha value of 0.05 was used for all statistical analysis and r^2 value of 0.30 was used for correlations. The preliminary results on hypothesis 1 have been reported earlier [9]. This paper details the results for the entire three hypotheses and combines the results across all hypotheses to draw conclusions.

4.1 Analysis of the Effect of Social Sensitivity (SS) on Team's Project Performance

This section analyzes the connection between the student's SS and their performance on the team project. Individual SS scores were combined into one average team SS score. The performance of each team (i.e., *total team score*), was calculated by totaling the scores of the four deliverables. This analysis was performed for each of the 28 teams.

To test hypothesis 1, we ran a linear regression test to see whether the average SS scores of a team were positively correlated to the team's performance. The results show that the team SS score had a significant positive correlation with the total team score (p =0.001; Pearson's R = 0.383; r^2 = 0.16). We also analyzed the relationship between individual SS scores (shown in Figure 1) and team performance and found a significant positive correlation (p =0.009; Pearson's R = 0.297; r^2 = 0.09). Furthermore, we analyzed whether the team SS scores were correlated with the team performance on each of the four deliverables. The results showed that the team SS scores had a strong and significant positive correlation with their performance on the project proposal (p=0.004), interim report (p=0.003), and final report (p=0.05). The result, however, did not show a significant correlation between teams' average SS and performance on the final presentation (p=0.382). Therefore, based on these results, we show that teams with higher average SS performed significantly better on their project.

4.2 Analysis of the Effect of Social Sensitivity (SS) on Performance Activities

Results of the significant correlation between SS and team performance encouraged us to look deeper into possible connections between SS and the activities that are often performed by teams. This section analyzes the connection between the student's SS score and their performance on each of the ten team performance activities.

In order to identify the aspects of the team process that were positively affected by SS, we analyzed the teammate's perceptions of their other team members. As stated previously, after each written deliverable, the participants evaluated the individual performance of each team member on 10 common process activities that could have affected team work. The peer ratings were averaged across all deliverables for each category (shown in Figure 2). This procedure was performed for each of the 76 individuals participating in the study.

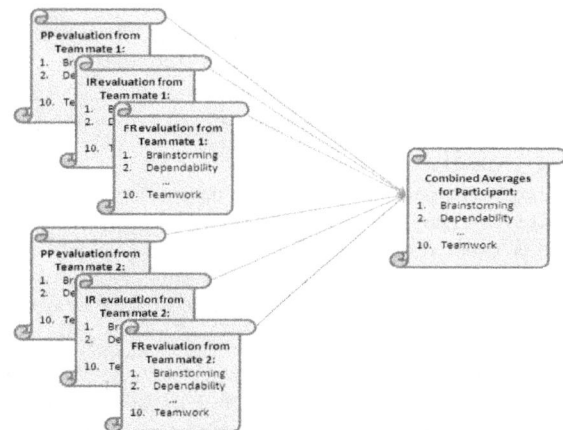

Figure 2. Aggregation of Category Rank Data

To test hypothesis 2, we ran bivariate correlation analysis tests to see whether the individual SS scores were positively correlated with each of the averaged rankings of the individual performance of each activity.

Overall, the results show a significant positive correlation with eight of the ten performance activities. The correlations between individual SS and each of the other team performance activities are shown in Figure 3 and our major observations are summarized as follows:

a) Of all ten process activities, *performance* had the most significant correlation indicating that people with higher individual SS were perceived as producing high quality work.

b) The other individual process activities that showed a significant positive correlation with SS included *brainstorming, dependability, discussing, focusing on tasks, sharing responsibility*, and *teamwork*. These results are reflected on in Section 6.

c) The results did not show a significant correlation between individual SS and either questioning (p =0.390; Pearson's R = 0.588; r^2 = 0.35) or listening (p=0.346) (p =0.346; Pearson's R = 0.674; r^2 = 0.45). This means that team members were perceived as being equally good or bad at questioning and listening, regardless of an individual's level of SS.

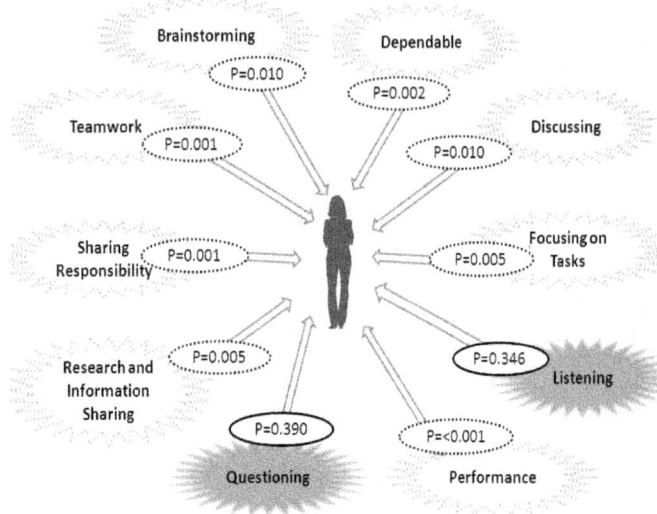

Figure 3. Correlation between Individual Social Sensitivity and Team Performance Activities

4.3 Effect of SS on Team Member Satisfaction and Viability

Although task performance effectiveness is obviously important to overall team effectiveness, researchers also recognize the importance of team member satisfaction to team effectiveness. We wanted to determine what type of correlation, if any, there was between a team's average SS and team member satisfaction with their other team members.

The students were asked to rank how satisfied they were with their team members (Step 6) on a 5-point Likert scale. To test hypothesis 3, we ran a linear regression test to see whether the average SS scores of a team were positively correlated to the how

satisfied team members were with the other members of the team. The results showed that the team SS scores had a strong and significant positive correlation with the satisfaction with individual team members within the teams (p =0.028; Pearson's R = 0.679; r^2 = 0.46). In other words, the higher the level of the average team SS, the more team members were satisfied with their other team members. There was not a significant correlation between individual SS and team member satisfaction. This implies that having a higher SS score does not mean that you are more satisfied with your team members; however, the fact that teams with higher average SS are more satisfied means that these teams are more likely to participate and continue to work together in the future.

5. THREAT TO VALIDITY

Although the results of this study are encouraging, there are certain threats to its validity. One threat is language proficiency. Approximately fifty percent of the students in the course are international students. Even though each of these students had passed an English proficiency exam, some may have struggled with the language. To improve construct validity in the "Reading the Mind in the Eyes" test, a glossary was provided that contained a definition and sample sentence for each of the word selection choices used in the test. Students were encouraged to read through the glossary before they took the test and refer to it as necessary during the test. However, because the students were not supervised while taking the test, we do not know how extensively the glossary was used. Feedback from students suggests that some groups struggled with language barriers during the semester as well, which could be a confounding factor and hinder success.

Another threat relates to the peer evaluations and perceived pressure for conformity. Although the peer evaluations were performed outside of the classroom to reduce the pressure the students may feel by possibly having their evaluations viewed by other students, some students could have still felt the need to give favorable ratings to their team members, whether these ratings were warranted or not.

6. DISCUSSION OF RESULTS

Our fundamental finding is that SS is a good predictor of team performance in carrying out major student team projects with complex tasks and multiple deliverables over long periods of time. This extends previous research that showed that SS had high impact on teams accomplishing well defined, short-term, relatively simple tasks. Task complexity is an important factor in team performance because the difficulty of tasks can impact the success of the team [42]. Complex tasks within large projects have many opportunities for errors and they can be hard to identify. Stressful environments can easily be created by these types of projects and can hinder team performance (e.g. impair decision making, decrease speed and accuracy of task performance) by adversely affecting team coordination and ability to engage in team activities. These difficulties can ultimately discourage a team. The effects of project duration on team performance comes into play as team members become more intertwined and interdependent, the impact of one member's lapse can disrupt the entire team's performance.

Another interesting finding in our study is that the study supports Baron-Cohen's assertion that engineers, mathematicians, physicists, and computer scientists are, generally, less socially sensitive. All participants in our survey are majoring in scientific or technical disciplines and their mean SS score of 22.59 was lower than the original general population sample mean SS score of 26.2 of Baron-Cohen et al [31]. This suggests that these students find it more difficult to perceive and understand the feelings and viewpoints of others. An awareness of this can help educators better recognize possible reasons behind team difficulties and help students focus on techniques for managing that social deficit.

Not only do our findings speak to the importance of SS on the effectiveness of team performance, we also found that SS is generally a good predictor of the effectiveness of team process performance activities (e.g. brainstorming, dependability, focusing on tasks, sharing responsibility, performance, research and information sharing, questioning, discussing, listening, and teamwork).

Social sensitivity was positively correlated with the brainstorming activity. As described above, it is well established [26] that a socially sensitive person's tendency to be a flexible thinker and their general ability to perceive, empathize, and appropriately respond to team members may aid in brainstorming. We speculate that by creating a positive climate in which team members experience greater satisfaction, more positive emotions, and lower stress most likely aid in creative thinking and enable flexibility in arriving at alternatives to problems.

Socially sensitive individuals were also seen as more dependable. If a team member is not dependable, they place a burden on the other team members to make up for the missing production of the undependable team member which can adversely affect the team's effectiveness and team member satisfaction [41, 42]. We also speculate that a socially sensitive individuals ability to admit mistakes, accept others for who they are, to think before speaking, to make measured and fair judgments, to be frank and honest with others, being warm, caring and good at dealing with others [26, 65. 66] aid in being considered trustworthy and dependable.

Peers also viewed socially sensitive individuals as very self-directed and responsible in sharing the work load. Avery et al. [43] state that taking responsibility for one's own work on a team is one of the most important factors in ensuring a productive team experience.

Socially sensitive individuals were also seen as producing high quality work, were very good at sharing ideas and information as well as discussing issues and interacting respectfully with others, and excelled at consistently collaborating, cooperating and compromising as necessary to meet goals. This could be because socially sensitive people can recognize and take actions that demonstrate consideration for the feelings and needs of others. This sensitivity promotes cooperation. Cooperation can enhance communication and information sharing. Also, this ability to recognize emotions and use this as feedback may also allow them to recognize problems before they evolve into larger problems and also use this emotional information to improve team processes.

Researchers have found that high performing teams are interactive groups that share information to build high levels of trust and responsibility. This is important to overall knowledge integration and team satisfaction [44]. Social sensitivity can play a positive role in increasing information sharing and building trust within teams.

Not only did we find that SS is a good predictor of the effectiveness of team performance (task) effectiveness (one of the two elements of overall team effectiveness), but we also found that SS is a good predictor of team member satisfaction (part of the other element of overall team effectiveness. These findings provide compelling insights into the significance that SS plays in overall team effectiveness and thus shows that SS is an asset for a team.

7. CONCLUSION AND FUTURE WORK

Our results establish that both task performance effectiveness and affective measures of a team are positively correlated with the SS of members. This is valuable knowledge for managers and educators. Although we recognize that teams need members with the correct skill set and knowledge, by using SS as an additional input, more effective teams can be composed.

Using quantitative data related to work in teams, our work demonstrates correlations between SS and performance on team processes. These correlations tempt us to assert that high SS causes high performance. We expect that our future work with qualitative analysis will support this connection. We know that some groups faced interpersonal challenges and we plan to investigate whether such challenges were better-overcome in teams with socially-sensitive individuals.

Assuming that SS is a contributing factor rather than simply correlated with team success, then this type of research raises many exciting questions of interest to people across academia. How much SS is needed for success? Can just one socially sensitive team member make a difference? Can SS be learned? Authors such as Anthony Mersino have published techniques for improving emotional intelligence [45]. If these techniques can be effectively applied to improve SS, then team performance can also be improved. In any case, it is our hope that a greater understanding of SS will result in better learning experiences in the college classroom and better productivity of software engineering teams.

8. REFERENCES

[1] Chan, C.L., Jiang, J.J., and Klein, G. 2008. Team Task Skills as a Facilitator for Application and Development Skills. *IEEE Transactions On Engineering Management*. 55, 3 (Aug. 2008), 434-441.

[2] Ikonen, M. and Kurhila, J. 2009. Discovering High-Impact Success Factors in Capstone Software Projects. In *SIGITE'09* (Fairfax, Virginia, USA, October 2009), 235-244.

[3] Smarkusky, D., Dempsey, R., Ludka, J., and de Quillettes, F. 2005. In SIGCSE '05 (St. Louis, Missouri USA, Feb. 2005).

[4] Bacon, D.R., Stewart, K.A., and Silver, W.S. 1999. Lessons from the Best and Worst Student Team Experiences: How a Teacher Can Make the Difference. *Journal of Management Education*. 23, 467-488.

[5] Hsiung, C.M. 2010. An experimental investigation into the efficiency of cooperative learning with consideration of multiple grouping criteria. *European Journal of Engineering Education*, 35(6), pp. 670-692.

[6] Begel, A. and Simon, B. 2008. Struggles of new college graduates in their first software development job. In *Proceedings of the 39th SIGCSE technical symposium on Computer science education* (Portland, OR, USA, 2008). ACM.

[7] Rademacher, A. "Evaluating The Gap Between the Skills and Abilities of Graduating Computer Science Students and the Expectation of Industry." M.S. thesis, North Dakota State University, 2012.

[8] Woolley, A.W., Chabris, C.F., Pentland, A., Hashmi, N., and Malone,T.W. 2010. Evidence for a Collective Intelligence

Factor in the Performance of Human Groups. *Science 2010.* ePub ahead of print doi10.1126/science.1193147

[9] Bender, L., Walia, G., Kambhampaty, K., Nygard, K.E., and Nygard, T.E. 2010. Social Sensitivity and Classroom Team Projects: An Empirical Investigation, *Proceedings of the 43rd ACM Technical Symposium on Computer Science Education - SIGCSE 2012: Teaching, Learning, and Collaborating.* February 29 – March 3, 2012 Raleigh, North Carolina, USA.

[10] Wuchty, S., Jones, B.F., and Uzzi, B. 2007. The Increasing Dominance of Teams in Production of Knowledge. *Science,* vol 316, (May 18, 2007)

[11] Wells, C. 2002. Teaching teamwork in information systems. In E. Cohen (Ed.), Challenges of IT education in the 21st century, pp. 1-24. Hershey, PA: Idea Publishing Group.

[12] Oakley, B.A, Hanna, D.M., Kuzmyn, Z., and Felder, R.M. 2007. Best Practices Involving Teamwork in the Classroom: Results From a Survey of 6435 Engineering Student Respondents. *IEEE Transactions On Education,* vol. 50, no. 3, (August 2007)

[13] Springer, L., Stanne, M.E., and Donovan, S.S. 1999. Effects of small-group learning on undergraduates in science, mathematics, engineering, and technology. *Review of Educational Research,* 69(1), ppg. 21-51.

[14] Felder, R.M., Felder, G.N., and Dietz, E.J. 1998. A logitudinal study of engineering student performance and retention v. comparisons with traditionally-taught students. *Journal of Engineering Education,* 87(4), pp. 469-480.

[15] Swan, B.R., Magleby, C.S., and Todd, R. 1994. A Preliminary Analysis of Factors Affecting Engineering Design Team Performance, Proceedings of the ASEE 1994 Annual Meeting, Edmonton, Alberta, Canada, June, 1994.

[16] Cohen, S.G. and Bailey, D.E. 1997. What Makes Teams Work: Group Effectiveness Research from the Shop Floor to the Executive Suite. *Journal of Management.* 23, 3, 239-290.

[17] Hackman, J.R. 1983. A Normative Model of Work Team Effectiveness, Technical Report #2, Research Program on Group Effectiveness, Yale School of Organization and Management, November, 1983

[18] Bradley, J.H. and Hebert, F.J. 1997. The effect of personality type on team performance. *Journal of Management Development.* 16, 5, 337-353.

[19] Faraj, S. and Sproull, L. 2000. Coordinating expertise in software development teams. *Management Science.* 46, 12 (De. 2000), 1554-1568.

[20] Smith, K.A., and Imbrie, P.K. 2004. Teamwork and project management (3rd Ed.) New York, NY: McGraw-Hill. BEST Series.

[21] Haller, C.R., Gallagher, V.J., Weldon, T.L., and Felder, R.M. 2000. Dynamics of peer education in cooperative learning workgroups. *Journal of Engineering Education,* 89(3). Pp. 285-293.

[22] Gorla, N. and Wah Lam, Y. 2004. Who Should Work With Whom? 2004. *Communications of the ACM.* 47, 6 (Jun. 2004), 79-82.

[23] Shen, S., Prior, S.D., White, A.S., and Karamanoglu, M. 2007. Using Personality Type Differences to Form Engineering Design Teams. *Engineering Education.* 2, 2, 54-66.

[24] Felder, R. and Brent, R.. 2001. Effective strategies for cooperative learning. *Journal of Cooperation & Collaboration in College Teaching.* 10, 69-75.

[25] Beranek, G., Zuser, W., and Grechenig, T. 2005. Functional Group Roles in Software Engineering Teams. In *HSSE '05* (St. Louis Missouri USA, May 2005), 1-5.

[26] Pieterse, V., Kourie, D., and Sonnekus, I. 2006. Software Engineering Team Diversity and Performance. In *Proceedings of annual SAICSIT 204* (Somerset West South Africa 2006), 180-186.

[27] Greenspan, S. 1981. Defining childhood social competence. *Advances in Special Education.* 3, 1-39.

[28] Salovey, P. and Mayer, J.D. 1990. Emotional Intelligence. *Imagination, Cognition, and Personality.* 9, 3, 185-211.

[29] Sternberg, R.J. *Handbook of intelligence, 2nd ed.* 2000. (359-379). Cambridge, U.K.: Cambridge University Press.

[30] Kosmitzki, C. and John, O.P 1993 The implicit use of explicit conceptions of social intelligence. *Personality & Individual Differences,* vol. 15, pp. 11-23

[31] Baron-Cohen, S., Wheelwright, S., Hill, J., Raste, Y., and Plumb, I. 2001. The 'Reading the Mind in the Eyes' Test Revised Version: A Study with Normal Adults, and Adults with Asperger Syndrome or High-functioning Autism. *Child Journal of Psychology and Psychiatry,* 42, 2, 241-251.

[32] Hallerback, M.U., Lugnegard, T., Hjarthag, F., and Gillberg. C. 2009. *Cognitive neuropsychiatry,* 14 (Mar. 2009), 127-143.

[33] Pedrini, D.T. and Pedrini, B.C. Vineland Social Maturity Scale Profile. Retrieved August 18, 2011 from http://www.eric.ed.gov/PDFS/ED079342.pdf.

[34] Mesmer-Magnus, J.R., and DeChurch, L.A. 2009. Information Sharing and Team Performance: A Meta-Analysis. *Journal of Applied Psychology,* vol. 94, 2, pp. 535-546.

[35] Osborn, A.F. 1957. *Applied Imagination: Principles and Procedures of Creative Problem-solving, 2nd ed.* 1957. New York: Scribner.

[36] American Heritage Dictionary, Retrieved December 27, 2011 from http://ahdictionary.com/

[37] Maxwell, J.C. 2002. The 17 Essential Qualities of a Team Player: Becoming the Kind of Person Every Team Wants. Nashville, TN: Thomas Nelson Inc.

[38] Jenkins, G.D., Mitra, A., Gupta, N., and Shaw, J.D. 1998. Are financial incentives related to performance? A meta-analytic review of empirical research. *Journal of Applied Psychology,* 83, pp. 777-787.

[39] Katzenbach, J. 1997. The myth of top management teams. *Harvard Business Review,* 75(6), pp. 82-92.

[40] John, O.P. and Robins, R.W. 1994. Accuracy and Bias in Self-Perception: Individual Differences in Self-Enhancement and the Role of Narcissism. *Journal of Personality and Social Psychology,* vol 66, no. 1, pp. 206-219.

[41] Costa, A.C., Roe, R.A., and Taillieu, T. 2001. Trust within teams: The relation with performance effectiveness. *European Journal Of Work And Organization*

[42] Conlon, D.E., Meyer, C.J., and Nowakowski, J.M. 2005. How does organizational justice affect performance, withdrawal, and couterproductive behavior? In J. Greenberg & J. Colquitt (Eds.), *Handbook of organizational justice* (pp. 301-327). Mahwah, NJ: Erlbaum.

[43] Avery, C.M., Walker, M.A. and Murphy, E.O. 2001. *Teamwork Is An Individual Skill: Getting Your Work Done When Sharing Responsibility.* San Francisco, CA:Berrett-Koehler.

[44] Blanchard, K., Randolph, A., and Grazier, P. *Go Team!: Take Your Team to the Next Level,* San Francisco, CA: Berrett-Koehler Publishers.

[45] Mersino, A. 2007. Emotional Intelligence for Project Managers. *American Management Association,* New York.

Adapting the Disciplinary Commons Model for High School Teachers: Improving Recruitment, Creating Community

Briana Morrison, Lijun Ni, Mark Guzdial
School of Interactive Computing
Georgia Institute of Technology
85 5th Street NW
Atlanta, GA, 30332-0760
bmorrison@gatech.edu, {lijun, guzdial} @cc.gatech.edu

ABSTRACT

The Disciplinary Commons (DC) is a model of teacher professional development that encourages members of the group to reflect upon their teaching practices, develop a community, and, more broadly, to become more scholarly about their teaching. The DC involves a series of monthly meetings where university faculty members examine their course in detail while producing a course portfolio. Evaluation of the early DC's suggests that they successfully created a sense of community and sharing among the participants. We have adapted the original model to a new audience, high school computing teachers. The adapted model maintains the key aspects of the original model while adding two new, important goals for this new audience: improving recruitment and creating community. The high school teacher audience particularly needed strategies for recruiting students and was in greater need of community. We present evaluation evidence suggesting that we achieved the design goals in a replicable model, including a substantial increase (over 300%) in recruiting students.

Categories and Subject Descriptors

K.3.2 [**Computers and Education**]: Computer and Information Science Education: computer science education, information systems education

General Terms

Measurement, Documentation, Design.

Keywords

Disciplinary Commons, K-12 computing teachers, community.

1. INTRODUCTION

A *Disciplinary Commons* (DC), developed by Tenenberg and Fincher ([1, 2]) involves a group of educators from diverse institutions who teach within the same subject area meeting monthly over an academic year. In monthly increments, the participants prepare a *course portfolio*. Unlike a *teaching portfolio* ([3, 4]), which provides a perspective on a teacher over time across a range of courses, the *course portfolio* [5] describes

the teaching of a single course during an academic term. At each meeting, participants focus on a separate aspect of teaching and learning, for example: situating the subject taught within an institutional and departmental context; examining the course content (via syllabus documents, or comparing textbooks chosen); considering the instructional design adopted and how it is appropriate for the content; sharing how material is assessed and how learning is evaluated. Artifacts that participants bring in from their own classrooms (for example, lesson plans, syllabi, assessments, examples of student work) anchor each of these discussions.

We called the Georgia version the *Disciplinary Commons for Computing Educators* (DCCE) which was funded through an NSF Grant. Our aim was to involve both college and high school educators, because we realized that there was interest in bridging the secondary/post-secondary school divide [6].

The high school teachers had a different set of needs than the higher education faculty. High school teachers have an increased need for community. They normally teach in isolation as the only computing teacher at their school [7]. In Georgia, as in most US states, high school computing teachers are placed in the business department [8]. This means that even when they attend department meetings they are grouped with business class educators (e.g., accounting and keyboarding). The lack of a community can reduce teacher confidence and performance.

High school teachers also have a greater need to recruit students for their computing classes. CS classes are electives for US high school students. There are no CS majors in high school. If enough students aren't recruited for the classes, the classes aren't scheduled and the teachers are then required to teach other, non-computing classes.

Because of the different needs of high school teachers, we adapted the original DC model. Our iterative approach and evaluation addressed the following research questions: Can the DC model be adapted to support high school CS teachers and still be successful? What components should be modified and what content should be added? Are the benefits to high school CS teachers the same as for college faculty?

The DCCE ran for three academic years with three separate cohorts. The first year took a different approach from the original DC as it used an action-research model, but we found that the model didn't work as well as we'd hoped. In the second year we implemented the traditional portfolio model. In the third year we again used the portfolio model, but in that year, the group of participants involved only high school educators, which allowed for greater adaptation.

The next section discusses the background of the DC including previous instantiations and findings. We present the implementation of the DCCE model in detail for years two and three and the corresponding evaluation results. We end with a discussion of the implications of our findings.

2. BACKGROUND
2.1 Defining a Disciplinary Commons
The Disciplinary Commons was created in 2005 by Fincher and Tenenberg [1, 2] who ran the first two instantiations in the UK and Washington, USA, respectively. The initial cohorts all involved members in higher education. The original goals of the DC were twofold:

1. To *document* and *share* knowledge about student learning in Computer Science classrooms.
2. To establish practices for the scholarship of teaching by making it *public*, *peer-reviewed*, and amenable for *future use and development* by other educators. [2]

The objectives were accomplished through the production of course portfolios by the participants. In the traditional DC model, participants meet once a month during the academic year to discuss teaching and assessment within their discipline, while participants construct a teaching portfolio. Each meeting is targeted on a specific piece of the course portfolio, as seen in Table 1 [2].

Table 1. Monthly Meeting Topics

Meeting	Month	Portfolio Section
1	September	Institutional Context & personal trajectory into teaching
2	October	Curricular Context
3	November	Course Content
4	January	Instructional Design
5	February	Student Assessment
6	March	Evaluation
7	April	Delivery (including debrief of peer observation)
8	May	Complete "first draft" overview
9	June	Portfolio Presentations

2.2 Evaluation Results
External evaluation of both of the original DC's used surveys and semi-structured interviews. In examining the evaluation results of the original DC goals, the first goal was met, but not the second [9]. The participants were overwhelmingly positive about the experience, agreed that it was a good use of their time, and would recommend it to colleagues. However the participants reported that they would use their portfolio for their own purposes as opposed to public dissemination [9]. The participants did make use of each others' content, suggesting a willingness to share and reuse [1].

Two additional outcomes were discovered through the evaluations. The first was the development of a strong and vibrant *community*, not an explicit original goal of the DC. A second outcome discovered was the *change of practice* as a result of participation. While neither of these outcomes may have been unexpected, perhaps the strength and amount of change could not have been predicted.

Analysis of surveys from participants after the original DC offerings revealed that 100% of the participants indicated that they reflected on their own teaching at least several times each term. 58.9% indicated a change in their teaching practices at least once per term based on these reflections. The participants indicated that the most valuable part of the DC experience was the community, the opportunity to share ideas, learn from each other, and become more connected to like-minded colleagues [10].

Evaluations were also completed on the 2009-2010 replications of the DC held in Illinois (Software Engineering centered) and the UK (Database centered), led by different facilitators. These realizations were true to the original model with the only changes being the discipline and the facilitators / leaders. These replications had similar results to the original DC offerings in that the participants enjoyed their experience and felt their decision to participate was a good one. However, these replications were not as successful in meeting the original first goal of the DC (only 35.3% completed their portfolio and 41.1% indicated their portfolio needed revision) [11]. The participants expressed concerns about sharing their portfolios, although 76.5% indicated they may share their portfolio with instructors from their own departments. (Only 47.1% of the participants indicated adopting practices from other participants.) The participants reported that the peer review process was difficult because participants were not always able to keep up with the proposed review schedule [11].

3. OUR MOTIVATION
Our original motivation in creating the Georgia DCCE was to promote the communication and community between high school and college teachers around teaching of introductory programming. We hoped to see teachers (1) creating community as in the original DCs (e.g., as evidenced by promoting the opportunity for future collaborations), and (2) sharing resources and knowledge of how things are taught in other contexts (e.g., as evidenced by change of practice). Later, we added a goal (3) of supporting student recruitment within the high school environment. Goals 1 and 3 are unique to DCCE. Goal 2 was our restatement of the original DC goals, yet we wanted to make explicit the desire for capturing and sharing of resources to make the teaching knowledge public and available for use by others.

4. IMPLEMENTATION
The DCCE was run three times in Georgia with participants from both college and high schools (Table 2). We found in our initial discussions with potential participants that there was interest on both sides in understanding and influencing the other side of the secondary/post-secondary school gap. High school teachers wanted to understand the context to which they were sending their students. The undergraduate teachers wanted to understand and improve high school computer science courses.

Table 2. DCCE Participants By Year

Year	High School Teachers	College Faculty
2008-2009	5	3
2009-2010	4	4
2010-2011	8	0

4.1 Year 1

The first year implementation was based on an action-research model rather than production of course portfolios. Based on survey evaluations from this first year of the DCCE, the action-research plan was not achieving our goals. The participants did not engage with the formation of research questions—that wasn't an activity common for high school teachers. We didn't see signs that the participants were forming a community, and we saw no signs of change of practice. Since the action-research model did not help us achieve our goals, the Georgia implementation model changed for the second year.

4.2 Year 2

During the second instantiation of the DCCE, both high school teachers and college faculty were recruited. We followed the design of Fincher and Tenenberg around a portfolio construction model. Recruiting started in August and the leaders of the Commons were a college instructor (first author) and a high school teacher who were participants in the Year 1 DCCE. The leaders borrowed meeting agendas and information from the previous Disciplinary Commons instantiations and adapted them for their participants.

Important changes made to the original DC model for our Year 2 implementation involved adapting the schedule and content of meetings. We added minor topics to each meeting specific for our Georgia participants, such as an overview of the Georgia university computing curricula, competitions available for high school students, and field trip possibilities in Georgia, among others. These topics became part of the working lunch at each meeting and served to build community among the participants. The main topics for each monthly meeting for the Year 2 DCCE can be seen in Table 3.

Table 3. DCCE Year 2 Monthly Meeting Topics

Meeting	Month	Portfolio Section
1	October	Personal trajectory into teaching
2	November	Institutional Context, Recruiting
3	December	Curricular Context, Course Content
4	January	Instructional Design
5	February	Teaching Philosophy, Reflection Log
6	March	Student Assessment, Grading Rubrics
7	April	Peer Observation Debrief
8	May	Student Feedback
9	June	Portfolio Presentations

A major adaptation to the original DC model was to combine course context and course content, as they were similar for both sub-groups of participants. All of the high school teachers were teaching, or planned to teach, AP CS. For the AP CS course, the curriculum is defined by the College Board, so the course content is the same for all of those teachers. For the college faculty, the introductory programming class is an entry level class at all of the institutions, thus their curricular context was similar. So we combined course context and course content into a single meeting concentrating more on the context piece.

The second major adaptation to the original model was adding a student recruiting module in November. We added the focus on student recruiting to support activities coinciding with the first National CS Education Week (CSEdWeek), held the first week of December. Recruitment is a more salient issue for high school teachers than college faculty. High school teachers typically teach more than just computer science [12]. The high school teachers see their potential students in their other classes or in the hallway. If they are successful in building up their enrollment, they get the reward of teaching more computer science and not splitting their time between multiple subjects. We used CSEdWeek as a natural opportunity to discuss what kind of outreach and recruiting strategies we could use during that week to raise the visibility of computer science at each institution. We discussed best practices of recruiting for courses, both at the high school and college level. Participants discussed strategies that worked for them and the group brainstormed additional methods of recruitment.

For the February meeting we added a component on teaching philosophy to encourage participants to explicitly state their beliefs and attitudes of the classroom environment and what they wanted their students to know or achieve upon completion of the course. This accompanied a reflection log homework assignment that required participants to document and reflect on a single teaching unit: their goals, instructional design, delivery, assessment, and reflection upon the overall success and failure of the unit and the individual pieces. Up until February, participants were finding it difficult to see the whole picture of the portfolio, just as participants in the original Disciplinary Commons expressed [9]. Participants felt they were lacking the "big picture" and were not connecting the pieces of the portfolio to the overall reflection practice. By making the reflection explicit in both the teaching philosophy and the reflection log they began to understand the connections.

Another adaptation came in the March meeting with a unit on grading rubrics. This occurred because of a request from the high school teachers for more information on how the AP CS test is graded (the free response questions) and how to incorporate that style of grading practice into their classroom. As one of the regional leaders was also a reader (grader) for the AP CS exam, an example grading rubric for a test question was presented. Participants were then asked to devise a grading rubric for a test question (student assessment mechanism) they had brought with them to the meeting. Discussion on assessment mechanisms, fitness of test questions, and grading schemes resulted. Adding the discussion on grading rubrics enhanced both the community and teacher reflection, specifically on assessment.

This led to the final adaptation of the meeting schedule, the Student Feedback meeting. An entire meeting was used to discuss formative versus summative feedback, wording of student feedback, useful examples of feedback, and ways to simplify the feedback process. Participants specifically requested more information related to assessment and feedback as their reflections led to questions about feedback on assessments. Discussions during the year revealed that the participants had a wide range of feedback practices which the participants wanted to hear more about and see examples. This served as another mechanism to build community and enhance the documentation of their teaching practices.

4.3 Year 3

In the final year of DCCE, we accepted only high school teacher participants and expanded beyond the state of Georgia. Not enough college faculty were recruited to have a balance of high school and higher education faculty as was originally planned for Year 3. During the previous year we found the high school teachers benefitted from the community building aspect of the DC more than the college faculty. We know that high school teachers often don't succeed without a community [13]. Without a community to identify with, they are less committed to teaching computing. In Year 3, eight high school computing teachers were recruited. They taught two different classes—6 of them taught AP CS and 2 taught introductory programming (a pre-AP CS programming course). The leaders were the same from Year 2.

We kept the same discussion topics from Year 2 as well as the content adaptations. In Year 3 there were eight meetings (Table 4). We removed one meeting by combining the Institutional and Curricular Context topics. Most of the high school teachers had very similar curricular context. Feedback from the participants in Year 2 indicated they felt these two topics should have been combined. The recruiting module was kept in November, again to tie into the upcoming National CS Education Week. Student Feedback and Peer Observation were switched only because of the timing of spring break so as to allow the participants ample time to schedule and complete their peer observation.

Table 4. DCCE Year 3 Monthly Meeting Topics

Meeting	Month	Portfolio Section
1	September	Personal trajectory into teaching, *Selection Structures*
2	October	Institutional & Curricular Context, *Repetition Structures*
3	November	Instructional Design, Recruiting, *Teaching Classes*
4	January	Teaching Philosophy, Reflection Log, *Arrays and Sorting*
5	February	Student Assessment, Grading Rubrics, *Recursion*
6	March	Student Feedback, *Inheritance / Polymorphism*
7	April	Peer Observation Debrief
8	May	Portfolio Presentations

There were three significant adaptations to the DC model added in Year 3. The first was an addition of a discipline specific content topic. In each month, a discipline specific content area was discussed (italicized in Table 4). For example, in November we discussed how each participant taught "objects" and "classes" to their students. The first topic area was picked by the leaders, but the remaining topics were nominated and selected by a vote of the participants. Each month the participants were asked to bring in an artifact or example of one piece of instruction for each content topic. Examples ranged from practice worksheets, test questions, and project assignments. These resources were all posted to the website to allow sharing among the participants. The purpose of this adaptation was twofold: 1) to increase the amount of resource sharing between participants and 2) to promote change of practice among the participants by providing them with easily adaptable, peer-reviewed resources.

The second adaptation in Year 3 was to the review process. Instead of asking participants to write one section of the portfolio and review two other participants' contributions, they were only asked to write (with an occasional outside reading) between meetings. The rest of the review was made part of the meetings. The first agenda item for each meeting was to review and discuss another's portfolio piece.

Reserving meeting time for the peer review of portfolio pieces yielded two benefits. First, it encouraged completion of the writing assignment by the participants. With less outside time required the assignments became more manageable. Also, to prevent embarrassment and appearing as a "slacker," participants were more likely to have completed their writing knowing that the first topic of the day was peer review. The second benefit of scheduling the peer review sessions during the meeting is that more in depth review and discussion occurred in the face-to-face reviews than occurred during the previous electronic based reviews. This improved the content of the portfolios and strengthened the sense of community as more participants had more in depth personal conversations with the other participants.

The final adaptation to the model in Year 3 was in holding two "mini-conferences" for the high school teacher participants combined with college faculty. College faculty are motivated by the presentation of scholarly work as this counts for yearly evaluation, promotion, and tenure. High school teachers want to attend conferences where scholarly work related to introductory computing classes is presented, but are often limited due to financial constraints. In order to encourage the cross-community building between college and high school teachers, we organized and held two mini-conferences, held in the afternoon of two regularly scheduled DCCE meetings to minimize travel for the high school teachers. College faculty and high school teachers were invited to submit proposals on topics that would be of interest to both subgroups of attendees. Presenters were both selected and recruited based on input from Year 2 and Year 3 participants. Invitations were issued to all Georgia college institutions and to high school computing teachers in the state.

5. METHOD

Year 2 and Year 3 of the DCCE collected similar data. Participants completed surveys before the first meeting and at the conclusion of the last meeting. These pre/post surveys were based on the original DC evaluation surveys.[1] We added questions to the surveys to allow us to derive a social network analysis. In addition, a feedback form was completed for each meeting discussing whether the goals for the meeting were met and eliciting suggestions for improvements in future meetings. All data was recorded and analyzed by an external evaluator, The Findings Group, who produced reports. The external evaluator also conducted phone interviews with participants from Year 2 and Year 3 for qualitative results. The Year 2 participants were invited back for a reunion meeting six months after the conclusion of their DCCE. Survey data on this meeting was collected also.

---

[1] Original DC pre and post surveys can be found at http://depts.washington.edu/comgrnd/leaders/DisciplinaryCommons_PrePostSurveys_R5.docx

The purpose of the survey questions was to determine if the goals for specific meetings were being met and if the adaptations made to the original DC model were effective. Survey results for the meetings and the overall effectiveness of the DCCE have been reported previously [6, 12, 13]. This paper reports on the results from Year 3 and the social network analysis of Year 2 and Year 3.

6. RESULTS

Overall approval of the DCCE experience was similar to the original DC's. On a 5 point Likert scale where 1 signifies "strongly disagree" and 5 signifies "strongly agree", Year 3 participants rated their overall DCCE experience a 4.75, while Year 2 participants rated their experience a 4.86. All participants indicated that they would recommend the DCCE to a colleague by responding either "definitely" (majority), "very probably" or "probably" (average of 5.25 on 6-point Likert scale where 1 signifies "Very probably not" and 6 signifies "definitely"). They also indicated that the DCCE was a good use of their time (88% agreed or strongly agreed with this statement).

In evaluating the goals for the DCCE, we examine our results based on the original goals defined for the DCCE.

6.1 Building Community (DCCE Goal 1)

The DCCE had two additional goals beyond those of the original DC: building community and encouraging student recruitment. While the original DC noted that the participants created and felt part of a community, it was not explicitly measured. For the DCCE, a social network analysis was completed for each cohort. Social Network Analysis (SNA) is a method for studying social relations among a set of participants. SNA is the mapping and measuring of these relationships among individuals.

Measurements include the **density** (a number between 0 and 1 indicating how inter-connected the nodes are in the network), **degree** (count of the number of edges or paths that are connected to a node), and **betweeness centrality** (quantitative value that identifies individuals who act as a bridge to the rest of the group) [14].

For Year 2 of the DCCE, the average participant did not know 95% of their DCCE peers prior to their participation in the program. By the conclusion of the DCCE, the average participant knew and had collaborated with 88% of their DCCE colleagues. Participants reported that they shared materials and ideas with 32% of their DCCE peers and formally worked on a at least one project with 34% of their DCCE peers.

Due to space limitations, only the sociogram from Year 3 is shown (Figure 1). The sociogram for Year 2 is similar. For Year 2, the sociogram representing the relationships prior to DCCE suggests a disconnected and clustered social network whereby high schools and college/universities were disconnected and isolated from one another. Also, the social network within the high school teachers has a hierarchical structure such that one or two individuals served as the primary communication hub.

After DCCE, the network of participants expanded and became more integrated; high schools and college/universities were more interconnected. The density of the network for Year 2 likewise grew by 100% (Before= 0.29, After=0.58; Scale= 0, low density to 1, high density) indicating a moderately interconnected community of computer science instructors.

It is important to note that despite the increase in density from pre to post, the social network structure upon completion of the DCCE program (post) for Year 2 revealed that one participant played an important role in bridging the group together. One

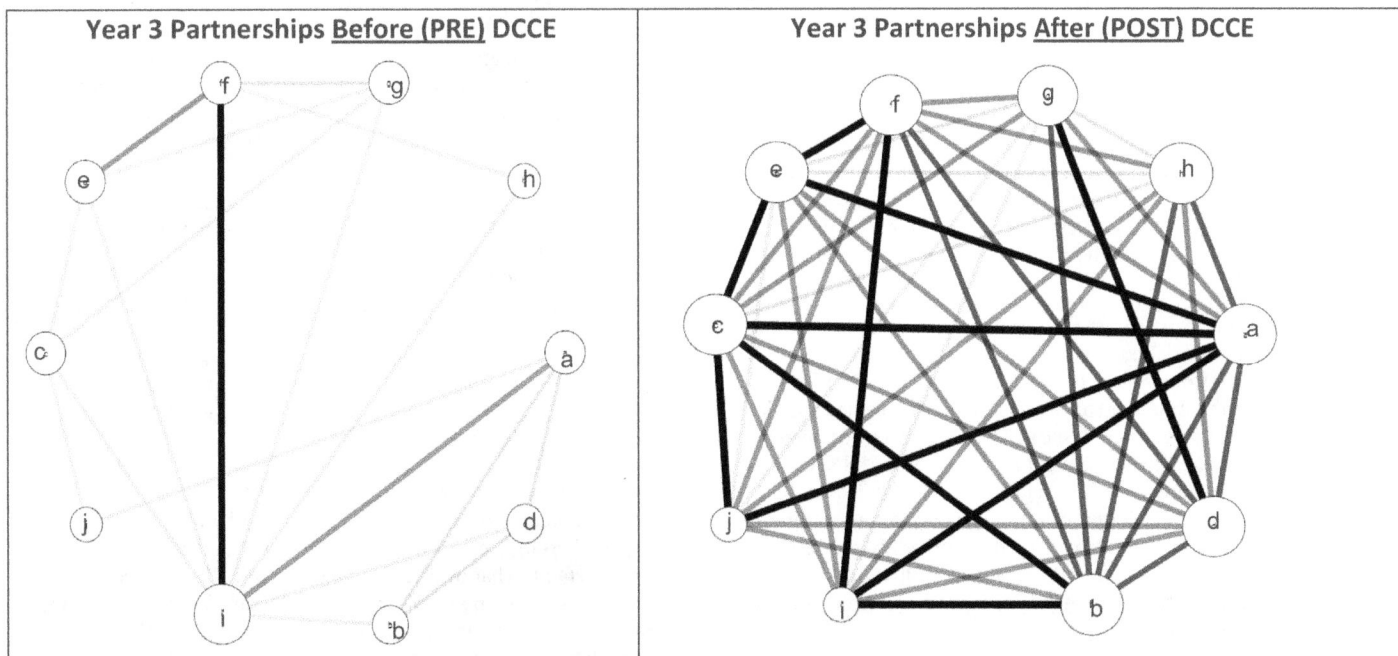

Figure 1. SNA Analysis For Year 3

Note. Omitted edges (paths) signify no interaction between participants ("*I did not know this person at all.*")

Key: Density and Opacity of edges (paths) signify type and/or quality of interaction between participants: **thin line/most transparent**= "*I knew this person but we have never collaborated*" **medium line/moderately opaque**="*We shared materials and ideas, but never formally worked on a project together*" **thick line/most opaque**= "*We formally worked together on at least one project.*" Size of node (participant) signifies degree of popularity (i.e. large circles= popular participants) participant had a betweeness centrality score of 14.867, suggesting that she was vital for assuring that information was communicated across the network. The other participants for Year 2 had betweeness centrality scores ranging from 0 to 8.367. Reducing the number of participants who serve as "bridges" or "connectors" will increase the density of the network and ensure that such individuals do not create a bottleneck effect in which the performance or capacity of an entire network is limited by these few individuals. This was accomplished in Year 3.

In Year 3 of DCCE the average participant did not know 67% of their DCCE peers prior to their participation in the program. As a result of their participation, the average participant reported that they had interacted with 100% of their DCCE peers. They had shared materials and ideas with 53% of their DCCE peers and formally worked on at least one project with 18% of their peers. The amount of collaboration increased as well. Participants reported that they collaborated with less than 3% of the organizations represented by their DCCE peers before their participation in the program. After DCCE, the average participant reported that they had received advice, materials, or other help from faculty at 50% of the organizations and worked on at least one project with 21% of the organizations represented.

The SNA for Year 3 is shown in Figure 1. The left side of Figure 1 suggests a hierarchical network structure whereby one individual served as the primary communication hub. Prior to DCCE, one participant ("i") played a critical role in bridging groups together; she served as the informal linkage between groups.

Figure 1 on the right illustrates a non-hierarchical network structure whereby all individuals play an equal role in transferring communication and materials across the network. A nonhierarchical network structure indicates 1) low key leadership - decision making is shared among cohort members, 2) community action among members - activities are orchestrated as a group, and 3) little conflict and informal communication – in general there is little conflict among the members of the network and most communication between members is informal in nature. According to previous research, this network structure is best for facilitating 1) common understanding, 2) a clearinghouse for information, and 3) a base of support [14].

After DCCE, the network of participants expanded and became more integrated. The number of connections in the network expanded 132% from before the DCCE to after the DCCE. This difference in the number of partnerships established before DCCE and after DCCE is statistically significant (p<.05 using a paired samples t-test), as measured through the SNA. The structure of the network also changed: All participants have merged into a single large community and a more tightly clustered community. The density of the network likewise grew by 265% (Before= .267, After=.977; Scale= 0, low density to 1, high density) indicating a highly interconnected community of computer science instructors.

6.1.1 Overcoming Isolation
Part of building community is to allow the high school teachers to reduce their feeling of isolation. The DCCE was especially effective at reducing their perception of isolation in their teaching. A Year 2 high school teacher commented:

I felt like I didn't belong to a community at all of CS teachers until DCCE. But now I have a lot of teachers that I would feel fine about either calling up or emailing. That did not exist before. That's one reason I think it's so important that we have things like DCCE, because CS teachers are usually pretty isolated in high schools. That has now been changed because now I know a lot of people that do what I do.

Another commented:
The [DCCE] group, for me, was so helpful in solidifying or making me want to continue to teach in Computer Science, because it was a group where I could share a Computer Science question, an issue and how did you deal with this. We're on islands.

A Year 3 participant commented:
Computer Science teachers don't have this opportunity to get together with other Computer Science teachers because we're the only one. I'm the only one in the county.

Another commented:
It's basically a way to create community, especially because most of us, I think pretty much all of us teach in a school where we are the only Computer Science teacher.

The key to this is that the participants report that the DCCE allowed them to obtain feedback in a safe, comfortable, and reassuring environment. They felt this support made them more accountable and motivated to be good teachers. The DCCE also allowed them to develop an awareness and appreciation for the diversity in their teaching environments. The awareness and appreciation of the diversity in teaching environments facilitated teachers' realization that the pedagogical practices that worked for one teacher within their own teaching context may not work for another teacher. This in turn, prompted teachers to reflect on their own teaching context and to objectively assess and select what worked for them the best.

6.2 Sharing Resources (DCCE Goal 2)
The original DC goals were to (1) document and share knowledge about student learning in CS classrooms and to (2) establish practices for the scholarship of teaching by making it public, peer-reviewed, and amenable for future use and development by other educators [2]. These were restated as goal 2 for the DCCE: sharing resources and knowledge of how things are taught in other contexts (e.g., as evidenced by change of practice)

6.2.1 Meeting Original DC Goals
Our adapted versions of the DC met both of the original DC goals. Through completion of their portfolios the participants documented what was occurring in their CS classrooms. All participants in both Year 2 and Year 3 completed their portfolios. In Year 3, less than half of the participants had completed a course portfolio prior to DCCE. After completing DCCE and their portfolio, most participants reported that they planned on reviewing and revising their portfolios in the future and using their portfolios to reflect and refine their teaching philosophies. By having their portfolios peer-reviewed during the DCCE and then published on the websites, we met the second original goal of the DC. In addition, of the Year 3

participants, 62.5% intended to share their course portfolios with instructors in their own or in other institutions.

The original DC measured success by improving the quality of teaching in Computer Science (CS). This is accomplished through a change in practice of the participants, both through self-reflection and transfer [1]. The DCCE was a success based on these measurements. We increased participant self-reflection and measured a change in practice. 63% of the Year 3 DCCE participants reported that they reflected on their teaching at least once a week after completing the experience. An additional 25% indicate they reflect at least once per term. 88% indicated that they document their reflections on their teaching at least once a term (only 51% reported documenting their teaching reflections prior to DCCE). Transfer is discussed under change of practice below.

6.2.2 More Reusable Resources
Specifically the addition of adding discipline specific content topics increased the number of shareable and reusable resources available from the DCCE. By providing an online repository for participants to upload their resources allowed access beyond the duration of the DCCE. This adaptation was also seen as beneficial by the participants:

> I felt like this [discipline specific content discussions] was probably one of the most helpful parts for me. It was basically because I got to see what other teachers were using in the classroom and what was successful for them. I think this is valuable for any teacher with anything that you're teaching. ... So, the DCCE allowed me the opportunity to meet with other teachers and go over things that worked out and things that didn't.

Another teacher commented:

> It was very helpful. That was the most helpful part. To me, that's what I went to immediately. You know, I talked earlier about getting tools to use in the classroom. That's where I got my tools was from the best practices. And I felt like if I could contribute a few decent things to that, I felt like I was making a contribution. But the more experienced teachers were the ones who really contributed to that, and I think the less experienced really drew upon that.

6.2.3 Change of Practice (DCCE Goal 2)
100% of Year 3 participants reported that they gained new ideas for teaching practices from the DCCE. 88% indicated they would definitely adopt a practice from the DCCE and 63% indicated they would make changes to other CS courses based on their DCCE experience.

A Year 2 participant commented:

> After seeing [another teacher] teach, I realized that there were definitely a lot of things I could do in my own teaching to improve. It really inspired me a lot and made me realize I've got a lot of room for improvement... I definitely have a lot of plans of how I will do things differently.

The most common change of practice that the teachers made in their class was in the area of assessment. One Year 3 teacher commented:

> Some of the things that I did, for example, were different ways of questioning. There was at least one month where we focused on how we ask questions and the types of questions. So, I really started to pay more attention to

> when I give assessments or testing quizzes, and making sure the questions are asking what I want them to ask, and that they're also modeling after the AP exams, since that is the test that the kids have to take at the end.

6.3 Improving Recruitment: Increasing the Number of Students (DCCE Goal 3)
One explicit adaptation of the DCCE from the original DC model was the inclusion of content related to student recruiting. This was measured by asking the high school teachers their current class numbers and the expected number of students for the following academic year. Because high school students register for next year's classes before the end of the current school year, the teachers had an initial idea of their class sizes before the conclusion of the DCCE. According these self reported numbers, the high school teacher participants increased the number of AP CS students in the year following their participation in the DCCE by 302%. During their year of participation in the DCCE the participants had a total of 122 students enrolled in their CS class. These same teachers had 491 students pre-registered for their CS classes for the year following their participation in DCCE. One teacher in Year 3 had a 700% increase in students in her AP CS class and attributed it to the recruiting help received from the DCCE, going from 3 students to 24.

Teachers felt that the DCCE had helped them with recruiting in two ways: 1) it provided them a platform to share their own recruitment ideas and also to obtain ideas from experts, and 2) it provided them with a sense of community where they were able to keep up each others' morale during their recruitment efforts. These were a result of the adaptations made in the DCCE of introducing a recruiting module and explicitly building community.

7. DISCUSSION
There were two additional goals measured for the DCCE beyond the original DC, that of building community and improving student recruitment. Community was built during the DCCE through a combination of the adaptations made. The quality of the partnerships also increased. Participants also reported a significant increase in the number of students registered for their classes the following year, in large part due to the recruiting module added. The addition of discussing rubrics and feedback to students resulted in the largest change of practice, as assessment was the most common area reported as changed by the participants. Additionally, the assessment and rubrics meeting was the highest ranked meeting among Year 3 participants.

One improvement to the original DC model was to alter the manner in which the peer reviews of the course portfolios are conducted. The original DC model involved a double review of each portfolio piece to be conducted before each meeting. In the original DC model and its replications, a common complaint among the participants was the amount of time involved in being a participant [10, 11]. By moving the peer reviews from before to during the meetings, we reduced the amount of time participants needed to dedicate to the DCCE. As a result, 75% of the Year 3 DCCE participants reported never missing a single homework assignment and the other 25% missed only one. The change to the peer review process had the additional benefit of improving the community aspect as the participants had the opportunity to have more in depth conversations for all participants throughout the experience.

An unexpected benefit of DCCE was an improvement of teacher confidence. A Year 2 teacher stated:

I think DCCE definitely did help [me feel more confident]. I think it was just being a part of a community of teachers that you can actually talk with about teaching. That gives you confidence when you don't teach it in a vacuum.

They also felt that the tasks of reading articles on pedagogy and writing their own teaching portfolios had introduced them to good pedagogical standards and to the value of following those standards in their classrooms. For instance, one teacher commented:

I was surprised, but I really enjoyed writing the course portfolio. I'm not a writer. I don't particularly like writing things. But writing the course portfolio, reading the pedagogy sort of assignments before we wrote the portfolio was really helpful and really made me feel more comfortable in the education environment I was before.

This increase in perception of their ability to teach may be evidenced in the participants' willingness to share their completed portfolios with others. This may illustrate confidence in their portfolio and its contents. A side effect of increased confidence may lead to solidification or a change in teacher identity [13]. This is especially important for high school teachers whose identity may be due to things outside of their control (e.g., area of certification, department, etc.).

8. CONCLUSION

The Disciplinary Commons for Computing Educators (DCCE) is an adaptation of the Disciplinary Commons. It achieved the original goals of the Commons and the additional goals of creating a statewide community of computing educators and increasing the number of students who enroll in computer science courses. It's important to note that Year 2's adaptations achieved our additional goals for the high school teachers, and Year 3 increased those outcomes. Thus, we see Year 3 as a positive refinement of Year 2's model. We are currently planning additional work with new high school disciplinary commons groups to demonstrate that our model is replicable.

9. ACKNOWLEDGMENTS

We would like to thank our co-leader, Ria Galanos, whose help and support were instrumental in making the DCCE a success. The Findings Group was the external evaluator for the DCCE and produced all the evaluation reports. Finally, we thank Josh Tenenberg and Sally Fincher for their continuing support in our adaptation of their work. This work is supported by the National Science Foundation CPATH program under Grant No. 0829601. Any opinions, findings, and conclusions or recommendations expressed in this material are those of the author(s) and do not necessarily reflect the views of the National Science Foundation.

10. REFERENCES

[1] Fincher, S. and Tenenberg, J. Warren's question. In *Proceedings of the third international workshop on Computing education research* (Atlanta, Georgia, USA, 2007). ACM, New York.

[2] Tenenberg, J. and Fincher, S. Opening the door of the computer science classroom: the *Disciplinary Commons*. *SIGCSE Bull.*, 39, 1 2007, 514-518.

[3] Seldin, P., Miller, J. E., Seldin, C. A. and McKeachie, W. *The teaching portfolio: A practical guide to improved performance and promotion/tenure decisions.* Jossey-Bass, 2010.

[4] Yellin, J. M., Huang, Y., Turns, J., & Tsuruda, C. *Teaching portfolios in academia: How are they used?*. Chicago, IL 2006.

[5] Hutchings, P. *The Course Portfolio: How Faculty Can Examine Their Teaching To Advance Practice and Improve Student Learning.* American Association for Higher Education, 1998.

[6] Ni, L., Guzdial, M., Tew, A. E., Morrison, B. and Galanos, R. Building a community to support HS CS teachers: the disciplinary commons for computing educators. In *Proceedings of the 42nd SIGCSE technical symposium on Computer science education* (Dallas, TX, USA, 2011). ACM.

[7] Ericson, B., Guzdial, M. and Biggers, M. Improving secondary CS education: progress and problems. In *Proceedings of the 38th SIGCSE technical symposium on Computer science education* (Covington, Kentucky, USA, 2007). ACM.

[8] Wilson, C., Sudol, L., Stephenson, C. and Stehlik, M. *Running on Empty: The Failure to Teach K–12 Computer Science in the Digital Age.* <http://www.acm.org/runningonempty/fullreport.pdf > Association for Computing Machinery & Computer Science Teachers Association, 2010.

[9] Davis-Unger, A. and Maring, B. L. Disciplinary Commons: Brief Summary. <http://depts.washington.edu/comgrnd/leaders/OEADiscCommonsEval09.docx> , University of Washington, 2009.

[10] Maring, B. L. and Davis-Unger, A. Disciplinary Commons Follow-Up Survey Evaluation Report. <http://depts.washington.edu/comgrnd/leaders/DiscCommons_FollowUpSurveyReport_FINAL.docx>, University of Washington, 2010.

[11] Davis-Unger, A. and Maring, B. L. Disciplinary Commons 2009-2010 Evaluation Report. <http://depts.washington.edu/comgrnd/leaders/DiscCommons_2011_EvalReport_R1.pdf >, University of Washington, 2011.

[12] Ni, L. Building professional identity as computer science teachers: supporting secondary computer science teachers through reflection and community building. In *Proceedings of the seventh international workshop on Computing education research* (Providence, Rhode Island, USA, 2011). ACM.

[13] Ni, L. and Guzdial, M. Who AM I?: understanding high school computer science teachers' professional identity. In *Proceedings of the 43rd ACM technical symposium on Computer Science Education* (Raleigh, North Carolina, USA, 2012). ACM.

[14] Cross, J. E., Dickmann, E., Newman-Gonchar, R. and Fagan, J. M. Using mixed-method design and network analysis to measure development of interagency collaboration. *American Journal of Evaluation*, 30, 3 2009, 310-329.

A Fast Measure for Identifying At-Risk Students in Computer Science

Nickolas J. G. Falkner
School of Computer Science
The University of Adelaide
Adelaide, South Australia, Australia 5005
nickolas.falkner@adelaide.edu.au

Katrina Falkner
School of Computer Science
The University of Adelaide
Adelaide, South Australia, Australia 5005
katrina.falkner@adelaide.edu.au

ABSTRACT

How do we identify students who are at risk of failing our courses? Waiting to accumulate sufficient assessed work incurs a substantial lag in identifying students who need assistance. We want to provide students with support and guidance as soon as possible to reduce the risk of failure or disengagement. In small classes we can monitor students more directly and mark graded assessments to provide feedback in a relatively short time but large class sizes, where it is most easy for students to disappear and ultimately drop out, pose a much greater challenge. We need reliable and scalable mechanisms for identifying at-risk students as quickly as possible, before they disengage, drop out or fail. The volumes of student information retained in data warehouse and business intelligence systems are often not available to lecturing staff, who can only observe the course-level marks for previous study and participation behaviour in the current course, based on attendance and assignment submission.

We have identified a measure of "at-risk" behaviour that depends upon the timeliness of initial submissions of any marked activity. By analysing four years of electronic submissions over our school's student body we have extracted over 220,000 individual records, spanning over 1900 students, to establish that early electronic submission behaviour provides can provide a reliable indicator of future behaviour. By measuring the impact on a student's Grade Point Average (GPA) we can show that knowledge of assignment submission and current course level provides a reliable guide to student performance.

Categories and Subject Descriptors

K.3 [**Computers and Education**]: Computers and Information Science Education

General Terms

Human factors, measurement

Keywords

Engagement, assessment

1. INTRODUCTION

Students engaged in tertiary studies have many potential issues that may negatively influence their studies [16]. While we can make some assessment of potential on entry to University, through the mechanisms used to determine eligibility [1], it is the faculty staff who are responsible for the continuing assessment and development throughout the student's academic career. Regular performance review of students by faculty members, to monitor student academic progress and the realisation of potential, allows Computer Science (CS) schools to focus their resources, assist struggling students and maintain quality levels. However, given that faculty load is already very high, our resources must be focussed in the most effective way and in the areas where the resources allocated will have the most impact.

During their tertiary studies, we expect students to move from requiring external regulation to self-sufficiency and self-regulation. Systematic adoption of strategies that will allow students to achieve their own goals is one of the key features of a self-regulated learner but the development of the "self-oriented feedback" loop that assists in the development of these structures can be disrupted while it is forming [19]. Students must be motivated to move to a self-regulated mode because to do so requires time, effort and preparation - they wish to be sure that their investment will reap reasonable rewards. However, while the reasons for a student to become self-regulating may vary, from operant models of punishment and reward to phenomenological models of self-esteem and self-actualisation, there is no doubt that the perception of achievement and success are crucial to students choosing to move to this mode[19]. Measurement of success, in academic terms, is heavily linked to performance of skill-based assignments, which requires more time, effort and preparation on the students' part. Thus, to perform well and to achieve measurable success, students not only require the *skill* to complete the assignment but the *will* to carry out the preparation, complete the assignment and then submit it in a timely fashion - the skill and the will are closely interlinked aspects of self-regulation[12].

Disengagement and, worse, silent disengagement where a student drops away from regular participation and attendance, is an obvious inhibitor to satisfactory progress. Where class sizes are small, and faculty can establish relationships with all of the students, this level of disengagement is harder to hide and easier to address. However, any estimate of social network formation limits the number of effective 'friendships' that any one academic can form, with the Dunbar limit[5] of 150-200 being easily exceeded by a number of colleges' freshmen' classes. Given that we cannot maintain a sufficient social relationship to notice when students are reducing their attendance and participation, we must use other mechanisms to identity this behaviour. Some measures of under-performance are easier to measure than others, and are far more timely. Poor assignment practices, such as incompletion or lateness, are early indicators of problems that may culminate in failure. These must be identified quickly and addressed before we risk producing sub-standard graduates - or allow students who would be successful, with intervention, to fall away. However, we must be sure of how to interpret these early indicators, to specifically focus on those who need assistance.

In this paper, we present a simple, low-faculty-load estimator for assessing the likelihood that a student will perform poorly in assignments. To show this, we present the analysis of a body of data that spans four years of collected student assignment submission data. This dataset contains over 220,000 individual records spanning an undergraduate Computer Science programme. The question that we ask is "Will assignment-related temporal metadata give us insight into the future behaviour of a student with any reliability?" As we will show, the answer appears to be "Yes". We can identify, quite clearly, a group of students who are less likely to submit their assignments on time and are three times as likely to submit late on average.

The assignment submission patterns that are being analysed are based on programming assignments, across our degree and ranging from introductory to advanced assignment work. These assignments are, in Bloom's revised taxonomy, at least at the Applying level and may, in later years, move all the way through to Creating. The assignments that we are measuring will assess both the application of a discipline-related skill and all require at least some thought and preparation time, which meets both of the will and skill requirements for activities that encourage the development of self-regulation. While we focus on Computer Science in this paper, these results are generalisable to similar assignment types across other disciplines.

The final measure that we produce allows faculty to quickly identify those students who are more likely to be at risk and allocate resources for assistance and mentoring appropriately. We do not underestimate the inherent load of such follow-up activities, but if we can reduce the at-risk group identification to a simple, low-load task, then our overall effort in tracking and contacting these students is reduced. Such contact may be as simple as e-mail, or messages to the class, or personal interaction.

In the final discussion, we shall identify the benefits of the identifying characteristic, and discuss why this mechanism is, ultimately, only part of a solution for improving student performance and retention.

2. RELATED WORK

A large body of work exists to describe how we assess CS students, why we assess CS students and the impact this assessment can have as it is correlated to future performance, as well as the level of knowledge in key skill areas [18, 11, 13]. There is a great deal of related discussion on the mechanisms that may be used to reduce the amount of faculty load required to carry out effective and timely assessment, with tools such as Learning Management Systems and Computer-Aided Assessment [3, 17]. Although there is discussion as to

what we even mean by the concepts of year level, for example where CS1 and CS2 actually sit [8], there is widespread agreement that early assessment and feedback is critical for the development of mature, aware students [15].

These studies frequently identify programming skill as the artefact that unifies Computer Science theory and practice: a skill that directly reflects the amount of effort expended in that practise [13, 10] where we seek to provide mechanisms to explain and demonstrate student progress by interpreting their assessment within a shared framework [6]. In the Mc-Cracken study[13], assessment took place as *charettes*, short lab-based assignment exercises with fixed time limits and post-hoc assessment, to determine the programming abilities of students who had completed first-year training and discovered that, of those who had passed, many were sub-standard by second-year perspectives. Rather than identifying students who are potentially at-risk, this identified students who were firmly entrenched in the at-risk group. However, enforced attendance and the use of an exemplar appeared to lead to improved performance in a exercise that was generally undertaken very poorly.

Follow-up studies identified other areas where students were deficient. Lister concluded that, rather than a lack of problem-solving, the students had a lack of the knowledge and skills that are a precursor to problem solving [11]. However, in this study, the students surveyed were both volunteers and those who had to perform the task as part of an assignment. The datasets were also capped so that only institutions who contributed 20 students were included and no volunteer, or compulsory component, participation rates were given. There is clear evidence that encouragement to participate, through teaching mechanisms or collaborative activities, is beneficial [14]. Whether we are developing skills or sharing knowledge, the research clearly indicates that attendance and participation are crucial to success.

Valid assessment must measure a range of indicators that strongly correlate with the desired set of final graduate attributes, and many approaches have been assessed from the early studies into traditional assessment activities such as programming assignments, to peer-based learning, game-based learning, measures of abstract thinking and even, to some extent, ability to interact with industry [4, 7]. Few, if any, of these additional measurements may be used without significant additional work in development and on-going monitoring by the coordinating staff. However, we return to the measurement of programming skill as a sound, repeatable and quantifiable assessment mechanism. But, we must recognise that the first step to performing well in any assignment is to participate - tardy or non-existent participation will undermine all of our attempts to teach.

Reading through the preceding studies, we often find reference to, effectively, minimum participation rates, or statements such as "Note that the quartiles are not adjusted for participation in each assignment, resulting in some variation in quartile sizes" [7, 14], where only institutions that could contribute more than 20 student data were included. We are well aware of the statistical burden that we are under, in our search for significance, but this also means that we are potentially ignoring a rich area of metadata, the influence of participation itself on future performance. Measurement of attendance is also a well-studied area, in both attempts to improve it through technology [2] and communities [9] with well-defined attendance policies, but it is rare to find studies that combine a study of participation, which is a very easy-to-obtain statistic, and correlate that with long term performance, as quantified in terms of future participation and academic performance.

Existing tools, such as the University of New England's Automated Wellness Engine (AWE)[1], developed over a year with a commercial partner, use a wide range of available metrics to identify at-risk students but have a significant cost and development lead time, as well as the requirement to completely unify student metrics - from performance in class to which residential college is occupied. While this is an ideal solution, and has led to a significant reduction of attrition rates, developing the systems and methods to track and integrate 34 variables per student is well beyond the scope of most institutions. In the absence of generic tools or a standardised tracking framework, we have to use the metrics that are available to all lecturers - participation in their classes that can be measured, as well as current year level and previous course activity.

3. METHODOLOGY

Our focus is on increasing the efficient utility of our staff resources without adding to workload. While we can increase our performance analysis of students by allocating more time to a given course or cohort, this is often time that faculty do not have. Delegating the work to other staff may not have the desired result as, even with the use of scalable assessment techniques, such as automated or peer-based marking, we may not provide the depth and quality of feedback and assessment that would occur if could do it ourselves, or using trained tutors [9]. This motivates us to seek an approach where the resources of the faculty may be directed to where they are most needed and act at a point where they can usefully assist students. We wish to maintain the same or a reduced performance management workload by reducing the misdirection of resources - thus we seek measures of student performance that have a short capture time and, preferably, are already being collected for other reasons. By overloading an existing piece of collected data, we also reduce the cognitive and kinaesthetic load on students incurred by requiring an additional collection point. Rather than force ourselves to introduce an assignment artefact that must be low-latency, at the possible risk of compromising quality, we look to other low-latency artefacts that allow us to increase our chances of detecting problem areas upon which we may concentrate. One of these is a measure of *timeliness*, as evidenced by the student's submissions for assessment. Can we tell anything from this very low-latency, easy to measure and already collected metric?

If every student submitted their work on time, we would have no strong partitioning of behaviour, but fortunately or not, students can be divided into two groups for each assignment – those who submit on-time and those who submit late. Regular unjustified lateness, for whatever reason, is a clear indicator that a student is not meeting course requirements – as the existence of a definition of lateness in a course indicates a requirement that has not been met. Our question now is whether this requirement can be correlated with other course requirements to the extent that the correlated behaviour is significant in determining the pass/fail outcome

of the course. We can assess the student's participation in terms of temporal metadata, as there is a large amount of temporal metadata that is associated with any assessment activity. Such metadata includes, but is not limited to:

1. Time when the activity is first viewed;

2. Time when the first steps are taken to undertake the activity, which may include, from a vast body of possibilities:

   (a) Writing a design document,

   (b) Obtaining any prerequisite code artefacts, or

   (c) Beginning a survey of techniques or methodologies.

3. Time of first submission for assessment (if multiple stages are allowed);

4. Time spent in review between early feedback, if available, and final submission; and

5. Time of final submission for assessment.

Modern learning management systems and web logging make obtaining this metadata easy [3]. Faculty can now tell how many students have reviewed the electronic specification of the work well before any lab sessions start, and will know on the final day of the assignment how many more students are left to submit, if they have not already done so. We can easily respond to a late student with a message saying "Do not be late again" but, if the assignments are few and marks are lost quickly for lateness, such admonishment borders on an empty gesture if there are insufficient opportunities for redemption.

To begin our search for temporal artefacts we turn to the most significant and consistently identified and retained source of data in our school, the repository of student assignment submission information.

3.1 The Dataset

We maintain a locally developed web-based submission system, the Web Submissions System (WSS), that, in conjunction with a Subversion (SVN) repository, provides a reliable version-control backend through which students can submit their work for automated and manual marking. We can track any submissions of any artefacts that are not on paper, which are the vast majority of submissions for all courses. WSS has been in operation since 2007 and now stores over 220,000 individual assignment submission events to the end of 2010, for more than 1900 students. The WSS dataset provides us with a clear measurement of the temporal metadata for items 3, 4 and 5 above.

The main dataset consists of a set of course-based assignment activities, where a marked activity has a *key* that clearly indicates the course, any specific course offering, the year, the semester or term and the assignment that it refers to. Each of these keys is associated with a due date, a maximum mark and an associated set of marking scripts that execute on submission. The keys, in turn, are associated with SVN repositories by a well-defined repository name so that the most recent SVN version is used for the submission. When a student wishes to submit an assignment, they must create the correctly named SVN repository, accept our submission conditions (including statements of the work being

[1]http://www.cio.com.au/mediareleases/12169/university-of-new-england-goes-live-with-altis/

their own and not copied or otherwise plagiarised) and then the repository is copied into the WSS storage space, the acceptance and marking scripts are run and feedback is given to the user. The student's feedback and their code copy is kept for each submission to the system – hundreds of thousands of user-generated assignment submission records that can be compared back to a well-known submission time and an equally well-established marking scheme, if automated marking is used.

To integrate this Computer Science-specific performance data with other measures of academic achievement we have used the list of student identification numbers for the students identified in the WSS capture window and obtained all student academic performance data as course and final mark for each completed course. This has been converted to Grade Point Average (GPA) data for both CS and non-CS courses. The Grade Point Average (GPA) measures that we use are based on a scale 0 to 7, where 0 corresponds to a late withdrawal and failure and 7 corresponds to "High Distinction". The intervening elements of the scale correspond to grade boundaries, not as a linear range from 100 to 0. A student who obtains passes, and only passes, in all courses would receive a GPA of 4 out of 7.

4. ANALYSIS

Our initial analysis sought to locate highly informative facets of the dataset, in order to draw conclusions about what constitutes "standard" student behaviour, in order to allow us to quickly categorise students in the future, based on student activity in the past.

4.1 Data Cleaning

As mentioned previously, the imposition of a charette as a compulsory activity does not match the type of participation we would see in an exercise carried out in the student's own time. We removed all charette data from the set, as the large amounts of set and supervised laboratory time, with or without assigned practical demonstrators, would conceivably mask a student's influence on their own behaviour. (Almost all charette activity had large amounts of in-lab interaction, leading to a level of interaction that would be missing in larger class groups or without high teacher-student ratios.) We also removed all records where the final assignment submission date was missing or invalid. After removing these, we retained 202,082 records of the original 220,613.

We then summarised these records to record the first assignment submission, the last assignment submission and the intermediate time. Where marking information had been calculated and was available, we recorded the final mark that would have been awarded (if on-time) and the final mark that was awarded (on-time or not). From this, we derived 27,939 summary records, spanning 710 individual assignments, 1,925 students and a total of 22 courses. We now had a large-scale collection of the temporal metadata for items 3, 4 and 5.

On inspecting the summary data, it was quickly apparent that the majority of activity takes place within +/- 120 hours of the final designated assignment submission date. Outside of these times, the distribution of activity is random. The data were limited to an initial assignment submission date of no earlier than 120 hours and a final assignment submission date no later than 120 hours - plus or minus 5

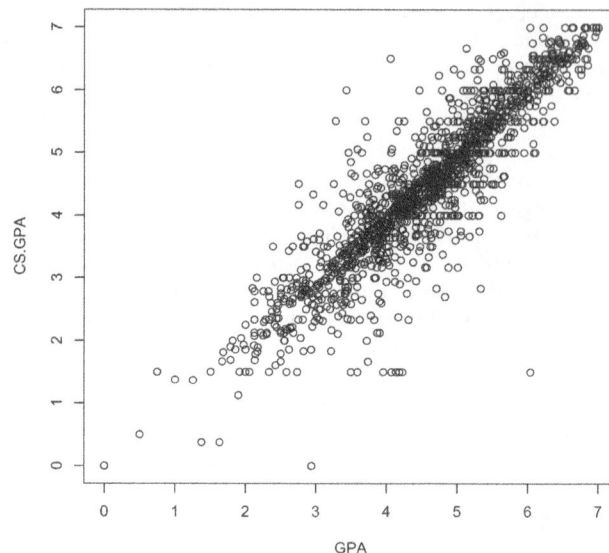

Figure 1: Scatter plot of CS.GPA versus GPA

days. This further reduced the dataset to 18,479 summary records.

4.2 Maintaining partial course attempts

The students that are most in need of early identification for intervention are those who appear once or twice in our submissions database and then discontinue their Computer Science studies. They are most in need of early identification because we have such a small window in which to act. While some of these students may simply have changed their mind, identifying them early and attempting to contact them will allow us to quickly establish if they are leaving because they have made a mistake in career choice or if they are leaving because they are in need of help which is not forthcoming. These students quite frequently do not complete any Computer Science courses and, as a result, have no CS-Specific GPA data. If we cannot find a measure of academic performance with which we can correlate their on-time or late behaviour, they must be excluded from our dataset.

We have obtained the GPA data for all students in the study, removed any with NULL entries (which indicate no completion of any courses in any sense and usually correspond to withdrawal prior to census and discontinuation) and have then produced two measures of GPA for the 1,555 students which remain. The first, GPA, is the GPA of all of their courses. The second, CS.GPA, is the GPA of only their Computer Science courses. Figure 1 shows the scatter plot of GPA versus CS.GPA, with a Pearson's R value of 0.9101 for the data and, for a linear model based on this data and sent through the origin, an R-squared value of 0.9866. The alternative hypothesis, that the data is correlated, is accepted with $p < 2.2*10^{-16}$, over 1553 degrees of freedom. This allows us to include those students who have even a single instance of submission behaviour, without a corresponding CS GPA, and provides us valuable extra elements in the dataset.

To verify this, we can now examine the performance of

Table 1: Comparative GPA between singleton and multiple-submission students

Multiple Submissions (89%)	%	GPA	CS GPA
On time	85.4	4.56	4.47
Late	14.6	4.25	4.1
Single Submission (11%)	%	GPA	CS GPA
On time	77.0	4.34	4.27
Late	23.0	4.09	4.00

these "singleton" students, compared to their peers, and the result is shown as Table 1. We would expect to see a corresponding performance difference between GPA and CS GPA for the on time and late behaviour in both groups. If the assignment submission behaviour is indicative of overall performance issues, we would also expect to see decreased GPA for both "Late submission" groups. As expected, we see precisely this behaviour - a clear separation between the GPA for On time and Late submission groups, as well as substantial depression of GPA in those students who only make a single submission in a CS course and then leave. Recall that a GPA of 4 indicates a bare pass grade on average - including these singleton students has now retained a group who barely scraping by and are those most at need of possible intervention, across all of their courses.

4.3 Overall student behaviour - all courses and year levels

While we are interested in *when* students start their activity, it is the final submission that carries the most weight. In our dataset, a student can submit an unlimited number of times, although with decreasing marks. For each student, course and assignment, we identify the last submission that they made for a given assignment. Thus, there will only be one of these per student, per course, per assignment where a student has made any submissions at all for that combination. The final submission time reflects the point at which the value of continuing has dropped below some defined value, or the student has completed the work. Figure 2 shows the histogram of these final submissions for the last five days before the deadline and the five days after deadline, with a per-hour breakdown over that time. As late submissions are measured in negative hours, the days preceding the deadline are found on the right-hand, x-positive, side of the y-axis. As can be seen, and is expected, activity builds until the final day, peaking in the hours before submission. The hour following the deadline has the 13th highest rate of final submission, on average.

4.4 Student behaviour - on-time and late

We can now clearly see that, unsurprisingly, the majority of students submit their work on time and, given the overall distribution and the known number of students and courses involved, we can make some assumptions that the majority of students not only submit on time but that they submit the majority of their work on time, or even early. By our earlier argument, if students are handing in their final work on-time, they have access to the majority of marks and it is only their own decision to submit at this point, with the work in a set state, that has an effect upon their received mark. Students who submit late, or submit the majority of their work late, have constraints upon them that com-

bine to increase their chances of losing marks. If they are constantly, and sufficiently, late, it becomes impossible for them to achieve a passing grade, unless a marking scheme is employed that awards no late penalties or allows truly open-ended submissions.

While it should be possible to derive a mechanism that uses measures of lateness to indicate a likelihood of potential problems, we must consider the utility of such a measure. A measure that says "All students may be at-risk" is useless, whether all are or not, but a measure that identifies the wrong group further misdirects our limited resources.

To this end, let us consider both the final submission date, and the initial submission date, to see how good an indicator the final submission is. 88% of students submit their initial attempt at a solution before the deadline and 83% of students submit their final submission attempt on time. It is more surprising that such a high percentage of the final late submissions must have been initially submitted late and, in fact, a large number of these consist of a single submission. However, in our system, students are not required to checkpoint their work regularly. Off-site development is both possible and encouraged, and a large amount of student development takes place on their own equipment, or remotely on local resources. The student will only update their work, or submit it, when they need to save a version or wish to check their work, or submit it as a final version. Thus, we cannot say what the student has actually done, although it is a reasonable conjecture that a student who had completed the work early would be more likely to submit on-time to maximise their potential for marks.

Of the dataset filtered to within +/- 120 hours, there are 18,479 records. A total of 3,333 recorded final submissions are late, with a total of 2,424 being late because their first recorded attempt was late. The number of submissions that were late given that they started on-time was 909. A staggering 72% of final submissions were late because the first attempt was late. 83% of all submissions are on-time or early. While this is an excellent abstract view of the data, we must tie this to student behavioural patterns.

4.5 Establishing lateness patterns

For a given course in a single semester, the number of submitted assignments varies from as low as three to an upper bound of twenty, if we include tutorial assignments and all other participatory activities. The number of final submissions measured through the WSS system is 14.5 for all students, rising to 17.8 for students who are undertaking third-year. While this includes students who have withdrawn early, or have enrolled late via cross-institutional or -degree transfer, this clearly shows that we have very little data to work with, as these total submissions are spread across every course that a student undertakes.

Rather than attempt to establish a more granular pattern, a student's timeline is defined based on the average of their submission activities, where an on-time final submission receives a mark of 1, and a late final submission receives a mark of -1. We take the approach that a student who is still handing work in after the due date does so in the expectation that this is not a valueless exercise - namely, that the work has sufficient worth to be considered for marking. We take the +/- 1 marks for each assignment, for each student, and average them by number of assignments to give a nor-

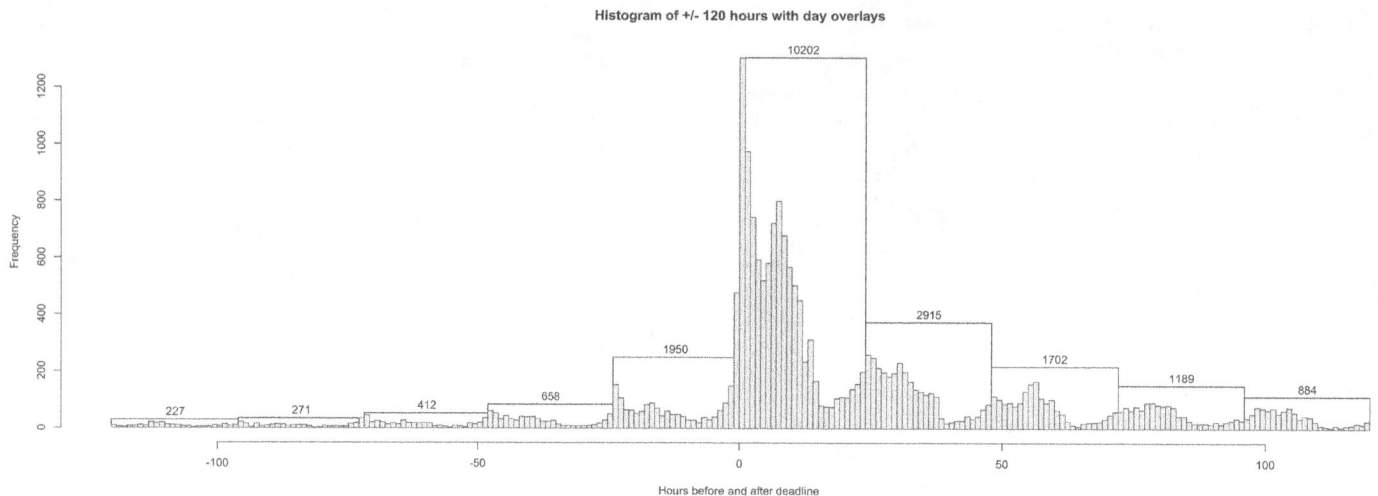

Figure 2: Student final submissions, -/+ 120 hours

malised weight indicating timeliness for each student. We refer to this as their *average timeliness*.

4.6 Predicting behaviour

Our first estimators are based on a simple idea: by looking at the first submission, is it a good estimator of what will come; and, looking at the last submission, is this predicted by the set of submissions that came before? If we consider a students set of submissions, across all course and assignments, across their career to be represented as a chain of submissions $S_{1..n}$, can we identify any of the S_i that will allow us to predict the overall pattern?

We identify those students who have $n : n > 1$ records for final submission and then divide their data into their submissions $S_{1..n}$ where S_1 is their first recorded submission and S_n is their most recently recorded submission. From their submission records, we now test two hypotheses. The first is that the most recently recorded submission is an estimator of the preceding average timeliness. The second is that the first recorded submission is a predictor of future average timeliness.

No obvious clustering or relationship is evident between S_n, the most recent record, and the average timeliness which preceded it: while students who perform well tend to have better more recent performance, there is no correlation between poorly performing students and their most recent performance and, given that we seek to identify at-risk students, this is of no use to us.

However, examining the relationship between S_1 and the average timeliness across $S_{2..n}$ gives a correlation for both highly performing students and poorly performing students. Eliminating those students who only have a single assignment, $n == 1$, we have a total of 1616 students, 1380 who handed in their first assignment on time, and 236 who handed in late. By comparing $S_{2..n} : (S_1 = 0)$ (Expected behaviour given the first submission recorded is late) and $S_{2..n} : (S_1 = 1)$ (Expected behaviour given that the first submission is on time) we can quickly see obvious differences. Table 2 shows the summary of our findings. The table shows the behaviour in the remaining set of submissions, $S_{2..n}$, and does not include the submission used to

Table 2: Summary of performance in remaining career for students who do and do not hand their first work up on time

Description	$S_1 = 0$	$S_1 = 1$
Chance of being late on average	16%	6%
On-time submissions (average)	78%	90%
Number of students with 100% on-time	30%	39%
Mean submission pattern score	0.45	0.66

assign group membership. It is, therefore, possible for a student to achieve a 100% on-time submission rate.

Students who submit their first piece of work, in any course from first-year onwards, in a way that the final submission is late are at substantially more risk of submitting late for the rest of their career. They have over twice the possibility of handing up the majority of their work late and a reduced possibility of handing up their remaining work on time. However, rather that immediately discounting all students who are initially late as 'lazy' or 'under-prepared', the majority of these students do manage, on average, to submit more work than they miss, and 30% of them then hand everything else in on-time. However, the mean submission pattern score indicates the clear difference in average performance - students who submit their first assignment late will submit an additional 10% of their assignments late for the rest of their career, compared to their peers. If we assume, reasonably, that late submission is likely to lead to reduced marks or cascading lateness, with the inherent risks of disengagement and failure, this one measure immediately identifies a group who will benefit from contact, follow-up or mentoring.

5. PREVIOUS ENROLMENT AND GPA

The two measures available to all lecturers are the student's performance in their course, as well as an indication of previous student activity, either through the existence of prerequisites or through explicit knowledge of a given student's academic performance prior to this course. We have analysed the data and separated the data by the factors *initial assignment submission on time* and *previous record*

Table 3: Student GPA for students categorised by timeliness of first assignment submission

Starting Course	Data	On-time	Late
1	Average GPA	4.59	4.26
	Submission Metric	0.70	0.56
2	Average GPA	4.30	4.24
	Submission Metric	0.62	0.46
3	Average GPA	4.13	NA
	Submission Metric	0.41	NA
HONS	Average GPA	6.68	No data
	Submission Metric	1.00	No data
PGCW	Average GPA	4.62	4.33
	Submission Metric	0.56	0.36

of CS courses. We have only shown students whose studies in Computer Science commenced from the cut-off date, Semester 1, 2007.

We can now more clearly separate the students in more closely aligned groupings for analysis. While commencing at Level I is the standard entry path, students who commenced their studies at Level 2, with no prior courses, are usually in other programs and articulating, while those who commence at Level 3, with no prior courses, are involved in post-graduate conversion or coursework masters programs. This simple separation allows us to quickly sift the students into groups based on similarity of experience.

The average GPA is the GPA for all courses and the Submission Metric value has a range of [-1,1], where each submission is given a + or -1 value, as earlier identified. The Submission Metric excludes the first assignment, to avoid double measurement. Quite clearly, late submission is having an impact on GPA across each year level, but there is a corresponding impact on submission patterns, which increases with year level.

The HONS row has a No Data entry in the Late column as no students entering the dataset at the HONS level had a first submission that was late, refers to fourth year coursework above a standard Bachelors course and requiring the successful completion of a Bachelors degree. The PGCW row contains data from all courses that are listed as elements of postgraduate coursework, including those with a research project component. There are very few students in Level 3 who submit their first piece of work late and thus there is insufficient data to provide a value due to extremely high variance over a small number of values. The absence of data here is quite telling: in a dataset of over 1500 students, the students who entered Level 3 in 2007, having previous study, were almost all handing in on time. Either almost all students who enter third year have developed such skills, maturity and professionalism that they all submit on time or the students who do not develop timeliness leave the course due to disengagement or failure. Disengagement and departure are, sadly, more likely.

Table 3 clearly shows that this simple separation supports our initial Submission Metric measure and provides evidence that this behaviour is correlated with GPA. As discussed earlier, we have now shown identified a low-latency easy to measure factor (timeliness) that may be correlated with measurable impact on a factor that has direct bearing on performance – GPA. The student who approaches GPA 4 is now very close to the pass/fail line. Compared to the

behaviour of the "first assignment on-time" students, these students are consistently under performing.

Again, this is one of the most naive separations that we can make across this data - we are not tracking individual students in any detail other than a raw aggregate measure of their timeliness in submission, their GPA data and their previous activity. Because of the very large number of samples, we would expect random influences to dominate if there was no strong and consistent message from the data. We can carry out far more detailed analyses but the overall message from this simplest of separations is clear: if we do not intervene to address the late first submission, the behaviour becomes steadily more destructive until, by third year, the student is at serious risk of never completing a degree.

6. FIRST IMPLEMENTATIONS

The recorded date of the first submission is a single measure that can be obtained for any class, at any time, in seconds and will identify a group where nearly 1 in 4 are at increased risk of failure and all of whom are in a group that is likely to miss 1 in 10 of their assignment deadlines. Combined with current year level and previous enrolment information, we gain an indication of the urgency of this intervention and can now clearly identify the need for early identification of poor submission behaviour in later years, as these students are most at risk of a sub-pass GPA. At the early stages of the course, we are attempting to build good habits and foster knowledge. Now we have sound statistics to back up our intuition that a student who has problems with the first assignment is more likely to repeat this behaviour - but we also have strong evidence that there is more than enough hope for a good, solid redemption, based on the number who become timely submitters. By measuring the first participation in a compulsory submitted exercise, we can immediately identify a group of students who are more likely to underperform and direct resources towards them.

From a program perspective, tracking a student's overall submission rate can establish a performance pattern for that student. Students who do not establish a sound submission pattern are at higher risk of poor participation. Tracking students in terms of 1,-1 values across their assignments is simple to implement and does not force academics to align their marking schemes, or grade ranking systems.

We have not solved all of our problems – 10% of those students who make their initial submission on time then underperform and we cannot detect them using this approach. However, by focusing on the developing timeliness of a student, as part of the overall framework of temporal metadata in Section 3, we can identify at-risk students across courses and programs, without having to align marking artefacts or discount any scaling or curve-fitting in grading.

We are already using this approach to immediately assign resources to contact students who have demonstrated this behaviour, as and when they enter new courses, in order to provide the best resources possible to try and reduce the impact of this systematic and highly self-destructive behaviour. We are providing students with a sound and demonstrable rationale to address their own behaviour.

7. CONCLUSIONS

Faculty need early indicators of potential student problems that do not add significant additional load. By identifying whether the first recorded completion of a student's assignment work was on time or late we can quickly identify the group of students who are already at risk of under performing in our class, due to factors that are affecting their time management and lowering their overall marks. One measurement of performance can potentially identify an entire cohort, before any marking has been completed.

We are currently investigating future work to determine the threshold at which students do give up, as a more detailed analysis of the original data, utilising the explicit linkage (by student ID) between records. We are also separating lateness classifications to more clearly show students who are slightly late from those who are very late. This is a very rich dataset and we are steadily adding dimensions from other student management systems in our quest to find useful, and usable, student performance assessment measures. As part of our work on extending the database, we are identifying and collecting data that will clearly indicate when a student activity is first viewed and the time when any first steps are taken, addressing the first two points in our earlier list of desirable metadata.

Our overarching goal is to provide a rich and shareable resource that allows us to clearly identify students who are at-risk, provide insight into student behaviour and that will be useful to other researchers.

8. REFERENCES

[1] S. Alexander, M. Clark, K. Loose, J. Amillo, M. Daniels, R. Boyle, C. Laxer, and D. Shinners-Kennedy. Case studies in admissions to and early performance in computer science degrees. *SIGCSE Bull.*, 35:137–147, June 2003.

[2] B. Burd, J. Goulden, B. Ladd, M. Rogers, and K. Stewart. Computer games in the classroom, or, how to get perfect attendance, even at 8 am. In *Proceedings of the 38th SIGCSE technical symposium on Computer science education*, SIGCSE '07, pages 496–496, New York, NY, USA, 2007. ACM.

[3] J. Carter, K. Ala-Mutka, U. Fuller, M. Dick, J. English, W. Fone, and J. Sheard. How shall we assess this? *SIGCSE Bull.*, 35:107–123, June 2003.

[4] D. Chinn. Peer assessment in the algorithms course. In *Proceedings of the 10th annual SIGCSE conference on Innovation and technology in computer science education*, ITiCSE '05, pages 69–73, New York, NY, USA, 2005. ACM.

[5] R. I. M. Dunbar. Neocortex size as a constraint on group size in primates. *Journal of Human Evolution*, 20:469–493, 1992.

[6] U. Fuller, C. G. Johnson, T. Ahoniemi, D. Cukierman, I. Hernán-Losada, J. Jackova, E. Lahtinen, T. L. Lewis, D. M. Thompson, C. Riedesel, and E. Thompson. Developing a computer science-specific learning taxonomy. In *Working group reports on ITiCSE on Innovation and technology in computer science education*, ITiCSE-WGR '07, pages 152–170, New York, NY, USA, 2007. ACM.

[7] J. Hamer, H. C. Purchase, P. Denny, and A. Luxton-Reilly. Quality of peer assessment in cs1. In *Proceedings of the fifth international workshop on Computing education research workshop*, ICER '09, pages 27–36, New York, NY, USA, 2009. ACM.

[8] M. Hertz. What do "CS1" and "CS2" mean?: investigating differences in the early courses. In *Proceedings of the 41st ACM technical symposium on Computer science education*, SIGCSE '10, pages 199–203, New York, NY, USA, 2010. ACM.

[9] T. Howles. Community and accountability in a first year programming sequence. *SIGCSE Bull.*, 37:99–102, June 2005.

[10] D. Janzen and H. Saiedian. Test-driven learning in early programming courses. In *Proceedings of the 39th SIGCSE technical symposium on Computer science education*, SIGCSE '08, pages 532–536, New York, NY, USA, 2008. ACM.

[11] R. Lister, E. S. Adams, S. Fitzgerald, W. Fone, J. Hamer, M. Lindholm, R. McCartney, J. E. Moström, K. Sanders, O. Seppälä, B. Simon, and L. Thomas. A multi-national study of reading and tracing skills in novice programmers. *SIGCSE Bull.*, 36:119–150, June 2004.

[12] B. L. McCombs and R. J. Marzano. Putting the Self in Self-Remulated Learning: The Sleft as Agent in Iintegrating Will and Skill. *Educational Psychologist*, 25:3–17, 1990.

[13] M. McCracken, V. Almstrum, D. Diaz, M. Guzdial, D. Hagan, Y. B.-D. Kolikant, C. Laxer, L. Thomas, I. Utting, and T. Wilusz. A multi-national, multi-institutional study of assessment of programming skills of first-year cs students. In *Working group reports from ITiCSE on Innovation and technology in computer science education*, ITiCSE-WGR '01, pages 125–180, New York, NY, USA, 2001. ACM.

[14] C. McDowell, L. Werner, H. Bullock, and J. Fernald. The effects of pair-programming on performance in an introductory programming course. In *Proceedings of the 33rd SIGCSE technical symposium on Computer science education*, SIGCSE '02, pages 38–42, New York, NY, USA, 2002. ACM.

[15] A. H. Miller, B. W. Imrie, and K. Cox. *Student Assessment in Higher Education: a Handbook for Assessing Performance*. Routledge, 1998.

[16] A. Moffat, B. Hughes, H. Søndergaard, and P. Gruba. Making connections: first year transition for computer science and software engineering students. In *Proceedings of the 7th Australasian conference on Computing education - Volume 42*, ACE '05, pages 229–238, Darlinghurst, Australia, Australia, 2005. Australian Computer Society, Inc.

[17] G. Rößling, M. Joy, A. Moreno, A. Radenski, L. Malmi, A. Kerren, T. Naps, R. J. Ross, M. Clancy, A. Korhonen, R. Oechsle, and J. A. V. Iturbide. Enhancing learning management systems to better support computer science education. *SIGCSE Bull.*, 40:142–166, November 2008.

[18] A. E. Tew and M. Guzdial. Developing a validated assessment of fundamental cs1 concepts. In *Proceedings of the 41st ACM technical symposium on Computer science education*, SIGCSE '10, pages 97–101, New York, NY, USA, 2010. ACM.

[19] B. J. Zimmerman. Self-regulated learning and academic achievement: An overview. *Educational Psychologist*, 25:3–17, 1990.

The Abstraction Transition Taxonomy:
Developing Desired Learning Outcomes through the Lens of Situated Cognition

Quintin Cutts
School of Computing Science
University of Glasgow
Glasgow, Scotland
+44 141 330 5619

Quintin.Cutts@glasgow.ac.uk

Sarah Esper, Marlena Fecho,
Stephen R. Foster, Beth Simon
Computer Science and Engineering Department
University of California, San Diego
La Jolla, CA 92093
{sesper, srfoster, mfecho, bsimon}@cs.ucsd.edu

ABSTRACT

We report on a post-hoc analysis of introductory programming lecture materials. The purpose of this analysis is to identify what knowledge and skills we are asking students to acquire, as situated in the activity, tools, and culture of what programmers do and how they think. The specific materials analyzed are the 133 Peer Instruction questions used in lecture to support cognitive apprenticeship – honoring the situated nature of knowledge. We propose an *Abstraction Transition Taxonomy* for classifying the kinds of knowing and practices we engage students in as we seek to apprentice them into the programming world. We find students are asked to answer questions expressed using three levels of abstraction: English, CS Speak, and Code. Moreover, many questions involve asking students to transition between levels of abstraction within the context of a computational problem. Finally, by applying our taxonomy in classifying a range of introductory programming exams, we find that summative assessments (including our own) tend to emphasize a small range of the skills fostered in students during the formative/apprenticeship phase.

Categories and Subject Descriptors

K.3.2 [Computer Science Education]

General Terms

Human Factors

Keywords

taxonomy, CS0, CS1, CS2, situated cognition, cognitive apprenticeship, deliberate practice

1. INTRODUCTION

Situated cognition is a learning theory in which learning is seen not from the isolated cognitive, conceptual, or abstract perspective of the individual learner, but rather as situated within "the activity, context, and culture in which it [learning] is developed and used." [1] This viewpoint would seem to resonate with the computing education community. We are a discipline with a strong professional focus, grounded in the development of a tool (i.e., the

computer) for use in solving problems for the benefit of society. As such, it is *implicit* in our curriculum that we seek to apprentice students in becoming (more) masterful computing professionals. Could instruction be improved by developing more *explicit* learning goals generated through the lens of situated cognition?

In this paper we consider the learning materials used in a pilot of the CS Principles course, under development in the United States. It provides an interesting case because of two factors:

1. The course sought to provide general education (not pre-professional) computational thinking skills. As developers of the course, we were vigilant in considering our target audience. Our mantra "if this is the last computing course a student ever takes, what do I want them to know" resulted in an emphasis on acculturating students into the ways computing professionals see, understand, and solve problems – because it is these ways of thinking that will serve them as they engage with computation throughout their lives. The ability to write programs was important primarily in service to the acculturation goal, not as a goal in its own right.

2. The course was highly successful in how it impacted students' perceptions of future computing use. In [2] we report on the ways students said they could solve problems better, transfer what they had learned to new situations, and more generally, how their confidence had increased and that they could now see technology in a new way.

Because of these factors, we have performed an analysis of the course learning materials to provide an explication of what it was that students were engaged in doing that might have contributed to these results. Using situated cognition theory in this analysis is appropriate because the course design centered on Peer Instruction – a pedagogy that supports cognitive apprenticeship in the classroom. The 133 clicker questions we analyzed were developed by the instructor through daily consideration of the programming concepts and constructs presented in the text-book in light of the following questions: "How can I get students to see this concept/construct the way I see it? To understand why I use it the way I do to analyze, solve, or debug problems?" Because clicker questions are presented as multiple-choice questions (MCQs), this required focusing on one small aspect of computing thinking at a time.

The *Abstraction Transition Taxonomy* resulting from our analysis forms a description framed by situated cognition: the amalgamation of activities, tools, and culture that the instructor felt would acculturate the students into the world of computing. We express our analysis in terms of a taxonomy because of the nature of the analyzed materials – a number of taxonomies exist to classify assessment questions. Taxonomies are useful because they afford communities a shared vocabulary for discussing learning. We propose that the categories of clicker questions define both a more explicit and more extensive set of learning goals, a set that we should adopt for introductory programming classes. Nonetheless, we find, through analysis of summative assessment items from 7 different introductory programming courses, that a much-restricted set of these learning goals are measured by final exams – including our own.

2. MOTIVATION

2.1 Expertise Development

The goal of any introductory-sequence programming course is not simply to create students who can generate working programs. Rather, more holistically, we want students to begin to see problems as programmers do and learn to apply programming concepts and constructs in the "right way" to solve computational problems. Perhaps because we are aware of our responsibility to produce computing *professionals*, compared to disciplines such as biology or math, our curriculum embraces the intertwining of theory and application and we start students immediately down the path of 10,000 hours of deliberate practice required to develop expertise [3]. That is, we start them solving problems by writing computer programs as they learn the vocabulary/language and concepts underpinning the discipline. We posit that our typical educational practices could be better informed by the literature on expertise development.

Let us consider a long-utilized method for developing expertise – the master-apprentice model. Consider an analogy: the apprenticeship of tailors.[1] Apprentice tailors work closely with their masters in two important ways we want to contrast to common models of programmer education:

1. *Scaffolding.* Tailors are scaffolded in the development and practice of their skills by the master – starting with tasks like ironing which engage them in legitimate peripheral participation (the opportunity to observe and acculturate while making a contribution) [4]. They are also set smaller, simpler tasks – they are not assigned to make an entire suit, they might be given various piecework a bit at a time; the button holes, cloth selection and preparation, fitting, etc.
2. *Process.* Tailors are not judged merely on the final outcome or garment. The master works in close proximity to the apprentice with the responsibility to observe critical professional skills: processes, analysis and decision-making, and intermediate results.

We propose that there is a lesson for us to learn from the master tailor. Computing instructors focus far too much on the final product – the small program/the simple garment. We do not provide enough direction in the preparatory steps – moreover, while we may "teach" students about various steps, we don't provide enough guidance on the specific masterful ways we approach the steps, the ways in which we evaluate our activities in the steps, and the considerations we take in deciding upon steps. We require our students to experience these for themselves through their experiences doing programming problems. We really only look at their finished products –we don't go through

---

[1] An example inspired by the work of Jean Lave, but expanded and interpreted by the authors.

the process with them and observe whether they are thinking and deciding as we would like – not just "doing" as we do.

2.2 Defining Learning Outcomes through Situated Cognition Theory

Situated cognition theory embraces the notion of learning and knowing as inseparable from the way in which that knowledge will be applied in real life. This stands in contrast to the individualistic view of learning, where learners can be taught conceptual knowledge abstracted from the situation in which it is learned and used [1]. Instead, situated cognition theory states that *knowledge is situated in a triad of activity, tools, and culture*: that it's not just what steps to take using what resources; a critical aspect comes from the context and culture in which that knowledge is to be exercised.

In the language of situated cognition theory, in computing education we engage students in *activities* using computing *tools*. What is missing is the *cultural* portion – the fact that our students are not doing real piecework that will contribute to a real suit for a real customer and, most importantly, under the auspices and detailed guidance of a master. To support development of expertise we need to consider all three components – activities, tools, and culture.

Figure 1 proposes some programming-specific interpretations of activity, tools, and culture. Culture is critically interdependent in this creation; it determines how and why practitioners choose the tools they do, what activities they engage in and how they know to make those choices. As stated in [1], "[t]he activities of many communities are unfathomable, unless they are viewed from within the culture." Perhaps this sheds light on bizarre programming behaviors, completely unexpected questions, and often intense frustration expressed by so many of our students.

Activity	Running a program, observing program behavior or output, inspecting code, making edits, compiling, hypothesizing
Tools	Programming constructs, programming concepts, IDEs
Culture	Knowing to match up runtime behavior with static codebase, knowing what variables to trace, knowing the right way to decompose a problem, knowing to look at a problem in light of what constructs are available to solve it.

Figure 1. The core components of situated cognition, using programming as an example.

To shed light on the difference between activity and culture as defined in Figure 1, consider the difference between novice and expert debugging. Instructors joke about stories of novices using the following activities: run program, observe output, note that it's not what was expected, make an edit at random, recompile, run again, and so on. This is a novice culture. The expert would: run the program, observe the output and note that it wasn't what was expected, examine the code and the problem statement or maybe add diagnostic print statements in order to develop a hypothesis as to the problem, run the program with particular test data to check the hypothesis, and so on. The individual activities are simple and should be relatively easy to enact. It is the choice of activities and the way the activities are combined that defines the difference between novice and expert, and hence the cultural aspect.

One of the primary manners of supporting learning within the lens of situated cognition is through the development and support of communities of practice [5]. A community of practice is made up of experts or practitioners who share a profession. Member development (from novice to more expert) is embedded within all of the shared information and activities of the community. Members' expertise is developed through interactions with others in the community, while working on real problems of community interest, expressed using the community's own vocabulary..

Communities of practice have inherent conflicts with traditional modes of academic instruction. Most critically, the members of the community (the students) are novices (or relative novices in the course in question). The expert is the lone instructor (who may or may not be involved in a professional community of practice in the subject area). Additionally, the customs of individual assessment often lie in conflict with authentic practice processes and problems.

Cognitive apprenticeship is a method developed by [4] seeking to "try to enculturate students into authentic practices through activity and social interaction in a way similar to that evident – and evidently successful – in craft apprenticeship" [1]. In this course, we employed Peer Instruction to support cognitive apprenticeship [6]. We deliberately and consciously developed clicker questions *not* with the goal of asking students to program, but asking them to perform various tasks and consider various analyses that the instructor felt would help them see how the computing community sees such things.

In this paper we discover how incorporating the consideration of culture helped generate a more specific and larger set of desired abilities and knowledge than are traditionally discussed in literature of desired competencies of introductory programming students (see related work). Since these competencies have mostly been studied within the realm of summative assessment (exam) classification and evaluation of student performance, this is not too surprising. However, we believe the community will benefit from consideration of this new approach and from comparison of these competencies with those previous discussed.

3. RELATED WORK

Learning Taxonomies. Learning taxonomies are important for computing education because they give the community a vocabulary to use when discussing student understanding and learning – and curriculum supporting it. Taxonomies should support educators in having conversations and in reporting on their courses and efforts to improve what goes on in them. Bloom's Taxonomy is a highly popular taxonomy. It consists of 6 levels to describe students' cognitive development. In 2001 Anderson produced a revision of Bloom's Taxonomy consisting of 24 categories within two dimensions. The Knowledge Dimension consists of Factual, Conceptual, Procedural and Metacognitive knowledge and the Cognitive Process Dimension consists of Remember, Understand, Apply, Analyze, Evaluate and Create. A more detailed description of each category can be found in [7] (pp 29-31).

The Revised Bloom's Taxonomy's value has been called into question in computer science [8] and has been modified to include "higher application" in order to make it relevant to the field [9]. Other taxonomies, such as SOLO [10] assess cognitive level through student response-type. Our work differs from these in that we move our focus beyond assessment of students' cognitive skill development to consideration of their development in the situated goal of coming to think like and perform the actions of a programmer. Most recently, work by Lister, et. al, has moved to consider desired programming skill development through Piagetian constructivist learning theory [11].

Apprenticeship and Deliberate Practice. Our clicker questions sought to support students during the apprenticeship phase of learning. Similarly, Faulkner created a more authentic experience for novices through *Worked Examples*: "These are designed to encompass the spectrum of the problem solving process:

• observing the application of programming concepts

• observing authentic problem solving

• cooperative problem solving" [12]

Furthermore, Faulkner asserts that the instructor must display the problem solving in the same environment that the students will be working. [12]

Bareiss takes an approach similar to *Worked Examples* where students are engaged in cognitive apprenticeship learning techniques through coaching. [13] More specifically, Bareiss defines five techniques needed to coach students: Modeling, Scaffolding and Fading, Articulation, Reflection and Exploration. Scaffolding and Fading is similar to *Worked Examples* in that it focuses on Task Design, Direct Guidance and Feedback.

Worked Examples and coaching are two ways to encourage deliberate practice [3] in novice programmers. As described by Ericsson:

"The theoretical framework of deliberate practice asserts that improvement in performance of aspiring experts does not happen automatically or casually as a function of further experience… The principal challenge to attaining expert level performance is to induce stable specific changes that allow the performance to be incrementally improved." [3]

Deliberate practice involves practicing with the goal of making small improvements at each step, and more importantly, getting feedback along the way to improve the practice when improvement attempts are unsuccessful.

Acculturation. There have been efforts to acculturate students in programming using professional-world approaches. Pair programming [14] is a technique where one student (the driver) works on the lower level parts of programming (e.g., coding) and the other student (the navigator) works at the higher-level (e.g., design and integration). The students switch over being driver and navigator throughout the assignment. Pair programming has been effectively used in the classroom [15] and is an effective way to encourage students to engage in confident practice while learning and consequently doing better in their programming. [16]

Coding Dojos [17] harken back to something like the master-apprentice model to support acculturation. Seemingly not formally studied, Coding Dojos are places where programmers can go and watch others program or be watched programming. The idea is if novices are watching experts they can see the choices experts make and if experts are watching novices they can guide them. Compared to pair programming this emphasizes the community and culture aspects of situated cognition.

4. CREATING THE AT TAXONOMY
4.1 Methodology
4.1.1 The Transition Levels
We developed the *Abstraction Transition (AT) Taxonomy* through analysis of learning materials from a CS0-type course teaching Alice serving ~570 students as a general education course at a large research-intensive institution in the US. The learning materials we analyzed were multiple-choice clicker

questions (MCQs) posed *during lecture* for students to answer and analyze in groups (via the Peer Instruction pedagogy [6]). These formative assessment questions sought to support learning through cognitive apprenticeship. However, most exam questions for this course were modeled very closely on these MCQs.

All but one author (Foster) was involved in the teaching and delivery of the course – creating questions and interacting with students discussing them during lecture. After the end of the term, Fecho reviewed the in-class clicker questions and generated categories stemming from her instructional experience with those questions. She identified three levels of abstraction in the questions: English, CS Speak, and Code.

The primary instructional team (Simon and Cutts) did not consciously consider "levels of abstraction" in clicker question development but, in retrospect, this focus was not surprising. On the second day of class, the instructor used Figure 2 as an overview to students of what they would be asked to do in the course.

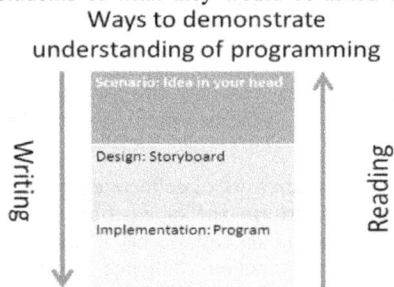

Figure 2. Slide presented in second lecture revealing (in hindsight) instructional focus.

In our analysis we refined Scenario to English, Design to CS Speak and Implementation to Code. We use English instead of specification to indicate that no specialized language is used describing the intended behavior. In Alice, an example of English would be "make a skater spin around 3 times". In CS Speak this might be "have the iceSkater turn 3 revolutions". In code this would be:

In Alice, for the simplest cases, English and CS Speak can be quite similar, and are differentiated by the specific methods and objects defined in Alice.

Through continued discussion we developed a taxonomy that describes those activities and tools, and ways of thinking about *using* those activities and tools, that the instructor felt students need to engage with in order to understand how computing and computing professionals work. A clear finding involved our emphasis on developing students' skills in *transitioning between levels of abstraction*. This was especially evident because of our use of MCQs – with their "stem" and "option" components. Figure 3 represents a transition from the CS Speak abstraction level to the Code abstraction level.

Figure 3. Example MCQ: Transition from CS Speak to Code.

To better clarify the difference between English and CS Speak, we also provide a question transitioning from English to CS Speak. This question is asked in English and the answer choices require the students to use their understanding of CS Speak:

> *Suppose there are customers waiting in line at the store. You want to serve each customer one at a time, so each one should walk to the counter one at a time. How could you do this? A. Use a DoTogether tile, B. Use a DoInOrder tile, C. Use a ForAllTogether tile, or D. Use a ForAllInOrder tile.*

After categorizing a few sample questions, we began to acknowledge that some question and answer sets remained within one level of abstraction, mainly CS Speak or Code. However, these non-transition questions still lie explicitly within an abstraction level and bring out interesting issues from the point of view of cognitive apprenticeship. CS Speak was especially interesting – as it represents the "lingo" of expert programmers. We found we asked two types of tasks with these questions. We term them: CS Speak Apply and CS Speak Define. That is to say, a CS Speak Apply question would engage students in identifying what CS Constructs/Concepts were involved in an algorithm or in deciding which/how CS Constructs/Concepts might solve a goal described by a CS Speak description. For example, CS Speak Apply would be:

> *If we write a method called drive, which would not makes sense as a parameter to control how drive occurs? A. Destination, B. How Fast, C. Which car, or D. Car color*

A CS Speak Define question, on the other hand, would engage a student in explicitly reflecting on what CS Construct/Concept does or what it is used for in the programming community. For example, a CS Speak Define question would be:

> *Which of the following is the best explanation of what makes a good parameter? A. It's something that supports common variation in how the method is done, B. It's got a meaningful name, C. It can be either an Object or a number, or D. It helps manage complexity in large programs*

Questions that remained in the Code abstraction level were code-tracing questions. Although this may not be a transition through abstraction levels, it represents a skill all experts have and sometimes employ in that it requires tracing of code without any analysis or deeper understanding past that of the logic required to solve the problem. For example, a question in this transition would be:

> *How far up will the bee move in the second instruction, given that the tulip is 0.3 meters high and our fly is 0.1 meters tall? A. 0.2 meters, B. 0.3 meters, C. 0.35 meters, D. It's not possible to tell, or E. I don't know*

Furthermore, we agreed that due to the nature of Alice, there might be questions that were unrelated to computing concepts and solely related to Alice-specific issues. These, we gave a classification of "other" and did not expect these types of questions to appear in other programming languages. We do not report on these here.

4.1.2 Different Types of Questions

While performing this analysis we noted an orthogonal question classification descriptor: rationale questions and mechanism or definition questions. We summarized these as *why questions* and *how questions* (respectively) and they are defined in Table 4. *How questions* are a norm in computing education. The *why questions* are a natural outgrowth of making explicit the need to rationalize, culturally, decisions of activity and tool use in programming problems. That is, rather than just *hoping* students internalize how programmers think, we use *why questions* to *explicitly* engage students in discussion and evaluation of various programmer rationales.

An example of a *why question*, with AT level 32, shows two code snippets that have the same outcome and then asks:

What is the BEST explanation of why one is better than the other? A. Option 1 is better because it is shorter, B. Option 1 is better because it does the least number of "checks" (or Boolean condition evaluations), C. Option 2 is better because it makes clear exactly what the "checks" (or Boolean condition evaluations) are, or D. Option 2 is better because it has a regular structure with empty "else" portions

On the other hand, Figure 4 is an example of a *how question*, with AT level 13 asking the student to choose code that would match the description.

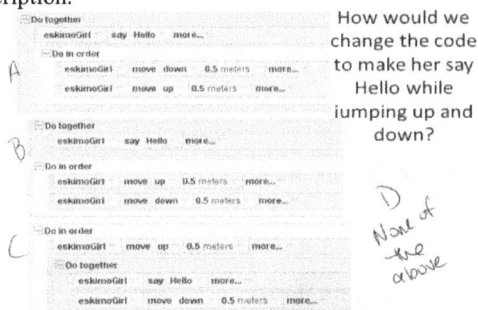

Figure 4. Example question showing a how-type question

To improve the clarity and support reproducibility of AT Taxonomy categorizations, we selected a random sample of 20% (27/133) of all the MCQs asked over the term and had two authors categorize and discuss them based on our taxonomy. From that the two authors iteratively refined the taxonomy. Once finalized, those two authors individually categorized a second random 20% (28/133) of the MCQs for both transition number and type. The authors reached an 87% inter-rater reliability (counting matches for agreement on transition number and agreement on type). Finally, one of the authors coded the remaining 60% of the MCQs from the CS0 course.

4.2 Results

The transition levels used to categorize questions are defined in Table 3. The types (why and how) used to further categorize questions are defined in Table 4. Together, Tables 3 and 4 define the Abstraction Transition Taxonomy. Table 1 below shows the final results of applying the classification scheme to our in-class Peer Instruction MCQs. Due to lack of space, we don't show the breakdown of how and why questions in each category, but overall 21% of questions were *why* and the rest were *how*.

Q/A	English: 1	CS Speak: 2	Code: 3
English: 1		6%	9%
CS Speak: 2	2%	8%(A) / 28%(D)	6%
Code: 3	12%	15%	9%

Table 1. CS0 in-class MCQ Distribution. Overall 21% were why questions

To read the chart, look in the row for the level of the question stem, and then move to the column that indicates the option level. This shows that 9% of the questions asked in lecture through MCQs had a question stem in English and the answers were in Code, making 9% of the questions an AT level 13. Similarly, 12% of questions were AT level 31, 6% were 23 and 15% 32.

5. APPLYING THE AT TAXONOMY
5.1 Methodology
Returning to our original goal, we used the AT Taxonomy to help both overview and tease out the manners in which this course sought to help students develop computational thinking practices – or to reach a basic level of understanding of the programming community. We noticed that our CS0 course was fairly distributed amongst all the transitions, with perhaps a surprising focus on use (2A) and understanding (2D) of CS Speak.

With this enlightened view of the course, we explored how our summative assessment (final exam) differed from or matched our formative assessment (in-class MCQs). We were also interested to explore other introductory CS courses' (CS0, CS1 and CS2) summative exams to see a) if our taxonomy would be applicable to others' assessments and b) if our course differed from theirs (as measured by summative assessment).

We analyzed 7 exam sets taken from 4 sources: recent assessment literature, a standardized exam from the Advanced Placement series in the US, a complete exam with 8 questions from a large mid-west US Institution found on the web, and our own CS0 exam. Of note, the CS2-DCER data represents 3 complete exams from the year 2009 (the most recent available) accessed through the DCER project [18]. Table 2 summarizes the datasets.

Dataset Name	Language	Number of Questions	Complete or partial set
CS0 - Our Exam	Alice	37	Complete
CS0 - Meerbaum-Salant	Scratch	5	Partial
CS1 - Lister	Java	12	Partial
CS1 - Lopez	Java	24	Complete
CS1 - APCS	Java	22	Partial
CS1 - R1	Java	8	Complete
CS2 - DCER	Java	143	Complete

Table 2. Summary of Datasets. The CS2 dataset is 3 exams.

5.2 Results
5.2.1 Transition Distribution
As noted in Section 4.1, the in-class clicker questions from our CS0 course are fairly distributed across the taxonomy categories. How were these skills reflected in summative assessments? Tables 5 through 11 show the AT Taxonomy applied to the exams.

CS0. It is thought provoking that our exam question distribution was not reflective of the kinds of questions asked in class. Rather, the exam is almost "all about code" – all but four (related) questions involve an AT level 3. This suggests that even if an educator is fully aware of the need for more diverse cognitive apprenticeship in programming culture and tasks, the norms of examinations may send a very different message to students about what is important.

Transition Level	Description
12	**English-CS Speak:** Given an English description of a scenario or goal, choose a technical description in "CS Speak" of the process to achieve the goal in the form of an algorithm or storyboard.
23	**CS Speak-Code:** Given a technical description (CS Speak) of how to achieve a goal, choose code that will accomplish that goal.
13	**English-Code:** Given an English description of a scenario or goal, choose the code that will accomplish that goal.
32	**Code-CS Speak:** Given code, choose either a description in CS Speak of the goal of the code, or choose which coding constructs are used within the code.
21	**CS Speak-English:** Given a description in CS Speak or a coding construct, choose an English description that describes what the CS Speak does or the goal that it accomplishes.
31	**Code-English:** Given some code, choose an English description that describes the goal of the code, not the step-by-step process, but the overall goal.
3 (Apply)	**Code:** Given code and conditions, choose a result from executing the code. This is "code tracing" and does not imply overall goal, but simply the execution of the code.
2 (Apply)	**CS Speak:** Given a CS Speak description, choose the coding constructs that are present (or vice versa).
2D (Define)	**CS Speak:** Provided coding constructs choose a technical description of their purpose or how they work.

Table 3. Definition of Transition Levels

The numerical coding in the leftmost column represents the particular transition where 1 is English, 2 is CS Speak and 3 is Code. Thus, an AT level 23 would be a transition from 2 (CS Speak) to 3 (Code). AT levels that do not follow this scheme are: CS Speak Apply (AT level 2), CS Speak Define (AT level 2D), and Code (AT level 3).

Type	Description
Why	Choose a **rationale** for why a statement or answer choice is correct or incorrect.
How	Choose an unambiguous answer that depends on **mechanism or definition**.

Table 4. Definition of Types

Q/A	English: 1	CS Speak: 2	Code: 3
English: 1		0%	27%
CS Speak: 2	0%	11%(A)/0%(D)	11%
Code: 3	8%	27%	16%

Table 5. CS0 Final Exam

Q/A	English: 1	CS Speak: 2	Code: 3
English: 1		5%	9%
CS Speak: 2	0%	0%(A)/0%(D)	14%
Code: 3	0%	23%	50%

Table 9. AP CS A

Q/A	English: 1	CS Speak: 2	Code: 3
English: 1		0%	0%
CS Speak: 2	0%	0%(A)/20%(D)	40%
Code: 3	20%	0%	20%

Table 6. Meerbaum-Salant

Q/A	English: 1	CS Speak: 2	Code: 3
English: 1		0%	13%
CS Speak: 2	0%	25%(A)/0%(D)	50%
Code: 3	0%	0%	13%

Table 10. Midwest R1 Institution

Q/A	English: 1	CS Speak: 2	Code: 3
English: 1		0%	0%
CS Speak: 2	0%	0%(A)/0%(D)	42%
Code: 3	0%	0%	58%

Table 7. Lister

Q/A	English: 1	CS Speak: 2	Code: 3
English: 1		2%	0%
CS Speak: 2	0%	46%(A)/29%(D)	3%
Code: 3	0%	5%	14%

Table 11. DCER

Q/A	English: 1	CS Speak: 2	Code: 3
English: 1		0%	13%
CS Speak: 2	4%	8%(A)/8%(D)	8%
Code: 3	13%	17%	29%

Table 8. Lopez

Of the set of assessment questions reported in Meerbaum-Salant's Scratch paper [19] 60% of them fall in the 23 or 3 AT level. The course is therefore assessing the students' coding ability – can students write or trace code, possibly given a storyboard or pseudocode description. The focus of the course is to introduce computing concepts, but it is clear that the assessments are also focused on code.

CS1. Both the Lister [20] and Lopez [21] datasets reflect efforts to study student abilities on commonly desired programming skills across institutions and countries. Lopez was a part of the

BRACElet [22] project where assessment of Lister's questions led to the development of Explain in Plain English (EiPE) questions. The Lopez dataset is the only set that reports assessment of a range of AT levels. This is likely because he sought to explore a new type of question within the framework of existing exam questions. Lopez's identified types of questions are: EiPE (AT31), Code Writing (AT13), Tracing 1 (AT3) and Tracing 2 (AT3).

Both the APCSA sample and the R1 exam show strong emphasis on level 3 activities. 50% of the sample questions for the APCSA exam are AT 3 level requiring code tracing with no abstraction transition and no engagement with contextualization of the problem. In the R1 exam, we also see the emphasis on transitions focusing on the code – 75% of questions fall into AT 13, 23, or 3.

CS2. Quite strikingly, different skills seem to be valued in CS2 exams. These exams represent 3 complete exams from the DCER international dataset. Nonetheless, we find a switch in emphasis from code (and transitions to/from it) to CS Speak; asking students to apply appropriate computing concepts or indicate understanding of the purpose of use of those concepts.

5.2.2 Type Distribution
Of the questions asked on our CS0 final exam, 11% of them were *why questions* (89% were *how questions*). Of these *why questions*, 75% of them were 32 and 25% of them were 23, meaning some kind of CS Speak was involved. Of the remaining sets, there are only three exams that have any *why questions*; CS1-Lopez, CS1-R1 and CS2-DCER. The distribution of *why questions* across these exams also never exceeds 15%. The remaining sets, CS0-Meerbaum-Salant, CS1-Lister and CS1-APCSA, have no *why questions* whatsoever. Although why questions might be considered challenging or subjective to grade, we hope instructors will consider the value of asking students to be able to explain their rationales and therefore situate their abilities and use of tools in the programming culture.

6. DISCUSSION

6.1 Culturally-Informed Learning Outcomes: *Why* Questions are Critical
Reflecting on the AT Taxonomy in light of situated cognition theory – the amalgamation of activities, tools and culture that define the programming community – we are struck by the relative scarcity of *why questions* among both our clicker and exam questions. Surely the integration of culture with activity and tools means that "just" being able to apply a tool or perform and activity is not sufficient. We wouldn't claim one was a vetted member of our community who couldn't explain *why* -- for any question in any of our 9 AT categories.

But *every clicker question is a why question* – regardless of whether the question's stem or options make that why explicit. It's inherent in the Peer Instruction pedagogy that questions are developed based on the kinds of discussions one wants the students to have (through the vote, discuss in small groups, revote procedure). Quite specifically, in Peer Instruction, the instructor frequently exhorts students to discuss not only why the right answers are right, but also why the wrong answers are wrong. Students aren't just "doing" an AT transition, but they are rationalizing their thought process and describing what they did and thought. In their groups, the class-wide discussion where they hear the explanations of other groups, and the instructor wrap-up, they are apprenticed in how programmers think about problems and rationalize actions.

We claim this means that we have identified 18 learning goals for development of programming students: All 9 categories have both how and why goals. So for example, by the end of the course students should be able to:

- In the context of a computational problem, read an English description and write code to solve the problem (13 how)
- In the context of a computational problem, read an English description and write code and describe why that code solves the problem in the English description. (13 why)

The truth is, as much as we do care about 13 how, in the absence of demonstrated 13 why ability, we cannot claim a student has, from a situated cognition perspective, become proficient as a practitioner in the community. Similarly though rarely a featured part of instruction, we need goals that students should be able to:

- Read code and give an English description of what it does (31 how)
- Read code and explain why their English description of what it does is correct (and possibly why another is not) (31 why)

These goals contribute to defining the community practitioner's ability to read the code of others, perhaps for code maintenance, modification, or debugging.

6.2 Can Summative Assessments Measure Computational Thinking?
We began this work with the goal of summarizing and elucidating our in-class learning materials. We hoped this would help us understand how a CS0 course which, at surface level, is focused on programming was achieving the positive changes in student confidence and abilities previous reported [2]. This paper has shown that a new view on how we want to think about, teach, and assess introductory programming courses can be found by stepping back and focusing on cognitive apprenticeship of computational thinking skills.

Interestingly, most of our identified 18 learning outcomes are not assessed on summative assessments – based on a sample selected primarily from recent research literature. Notably, *why questions* represent less that 15% of any exam – with three of the exams evidencing no *why* questions at all. Does this bother us as a community? We hope this work spurs discussion of that question.

Through our recent experiences in supporting high school teachers in the CS Principles project, the need to assess *why* ability has sharpened. We are beginning to explore multiple-choice questions (of the *how* variety) and asking students to explain in written English form how they analyzed it and why the wrong answers were wrong. These responses are more challenging to grade, but seem to be both more valuable and easier to create than multiple-choice *why questions* where the options are various explanations or rationalizations. In future work, we hope to further explore the potential and validity of these questions.

7. CONCLUSION
We propose that situated cognition theory, with its focus on learning for application in the "real world" and its focus on developing expertise within the context of a community is a useful lens for reconsidering programming instruction and perhaps computer science instruction more generally. A number of factors support this idea. First, our community has norms that seem particularly challenging for outsiders to understand. The common stereotype of a computer programmer makes it clear that we are to be considered other and our actions incomprehensible. It may be

that part of our collective recruitment and retention issues (at least in the US) stems from the lack of attention to acculturation of new members. The AT Taxonomy defines 18 learning outcomes that explicitly address the required culture, activity, and tools required for members of the programming community – which we believe needs to extend, at least minimally, to embrace everyone in modern, digital society.

8. ACKNOWLEDGMENTS

This work was supported in part by NSF CNS-0938336 and NSF CNS-1138512. Any opinions, findings, and conclusions or recommendations expressed in this material are those of the author(s) and do not necessarily reflect the views of the NSF.

9. REFERENCES

[1] Brown, J. S., Collins, A. and Duguid, P. (1989) Situated Cognition and the Culture of Learning. *Educational Researcher* , Vol. 18, No. 1 (Jan. - Feb., 1989), pp. 32-42

[2] Cutts, Q., Esper, S., and Simon, B. 2011. Computing as the 4th "R": a general education approach to computing education. ICER 2011. ACM, New York, NY, USA, 133-138. DOI=10.1145/2016911.2016938 http://doi.acm.org/10.1145/2016911.2016938

[3] Ericsson, K. A. (2006). The influence of experience and deliberate practice on the development of superior expert performance. In K. A. Ericsson, N. Charness, P. Feltovich, and R. R. Hoffman, R. R. (Eds.). *Cambridge handbook of expertise and expert performance* (pp. 685-706). Cambridge, UK: Cambridge University Press.

[4] Collins, A., Brown, J. S., & Newman, S. E. (1990). Cognitive apprenticeship: Teaching the crafts of reading, writing, and mathematics. In L. B. Resnick (Ed.), Knowing, learning, and instruction: Essays in honor of Robert Glaser (pp. 453-494). Hillsdale, NJ: Lawrence Erlbaum.

[5] Wenger, E. (1998). *Communities of practice. Learning, meaning and identity.* New York: Cambridge University Press.

[6] Mazur, Eric. (2009). Farewell, Lecture? *Science.* Vol 323 No. 5910, pp. 50-51.

[7] Anderson, L.W., Krathwohl, D.R., Airasian, P.W., Cruikshank, K.A., Mayer, R.E., Pintrich, P.R., Raths, J. and Wittrock, M.C. (eds.) (2001). A taxonomy for learning and teaching and assessing: A revision of Bloom's taxonomy of educational objectives. Addison Wesley Longman.

[8] Johnson, C. G. and Fuller, U. (2006). Is Bloom's taxonomy appropriate for computer science? *Baltic Sea 2006.* ACM, New York, NY, USA, 120-123. DOI=10.1145/1315803.1315825 http://doi.acm.org/10.1145/1315803.1315825

[9] Fuller, U., Johnson, C. G., Ahoniemi, T., Cukierman, D., Hernán-Losada, I., Jackova, J., Lahtinen, E., Lewis, T. L., Thompson, D., Riedesel, C. and Thompson, E. (2007). Developing a computer science-specific learning taxonomy. *SIGCSE Bull.* 39, 4 (December 2007), 152-170. DOI=10.1145/1345375.1345438 http://doi.acm.org/10.1145/1345375.1345438

[10] Biggs, J. B. & Collis, K. F. Evaluating the quality of learning: The SOLO taxonomy (Structure of the Observed Learning Outcome). New York, Academic Press, 1982.

[11] Corney, M. W., Teague, D. M., Ahadi, A., & Lister, R, (2012) Some empirical results for neo-Piagetian reasoning in novice programmers and the relationship to code explanation questions. In de Raadt, Michael & Carbone, Angela (Eds.) *CRPIT.* Australian Computer Society Inc, RMIT University, Melbourne, VIC. (In Press)

[12] Falkner, K. and Palmer, E. (2009). Developing authentic problem solving skills in introductory computing classes. *SIGCSE 2009.* ACM, New York, NY, USA, 4-8. DOI=10.1145/1508865.1508871 http://doi.acm.org/10.1145/1508865.1508871

[13] Bareiss, R. and Radley, M. (2010). Coaching via cognitive apprenticeship. *SIGCSE 2010.* ACM, New York, NY, USA, 162-166. DOI=10.1145/1734263.1734319 http://doi.acm.org/10.1145/1734263.1734319

[14] McDowell, C., Werner, L., Bullock, H. and Fernald, J. "The Impact of Pair Programming on Student Performance of Computer Science Related Majors". (2003). *ICSE 2003.* Portland, Oregon.

[15] Braught, G., Martin Eby, L. and Wahls, T. (2008). The effects of pair-programming on individual programming skill. *SIGCSE 2008.* ACM, New York, NY, USA, 200-204. DOI=10.1145/1352135.1352207 http://doi.acm.org/10.1145/1352135.1352207

[16] Braught, G., Wahls, T., and Martin Eby, L., 2011. The Case for Pair Programming in the Computer Science Classroom. *Trans. Comput. Educ.* 11, 1, Article 2 (February 2011), 21 pages. DOI=1921607.1921609 http://doi.acm.org/1921607.1921609

[17] Gaillot, E., Bache, E. *CodingDojo.* http://codingdojo.org.

[18] Sanders, K., Richards, B., Mostrom, J., Almstrum, V, Edwards, S., Fincher, S., Gunion, K., Hall, M., Hanks, B., Lonergan, S., McCartney, R., Morrison, B., Spacco, J. & Thomas, L. (2008). DCER: Sharing Empirical Computer Science Education Data. *ICER 2008.* Sydney, Australia. 137-148.

[19] Meerbaum-Salant, O., Armoni, M. & Ben-Ari, M. (2010). Learning Computer Science Concepts with Scratch. *ICER 2010.* Rhode Island, USA. 69-75.

[20] Lopez, M., Whalley, J., Robbins, P., and Lister, R. 2008. Relationships between reading, tracing and writing skills in introductory programming. *ICER 2008.* ACM, New York, NY, USA, 101-112. DOI=10.1145/1404520.1404531 http://doi.acm.org/10.1145/1404520.1404531

[21] Lister, R., Simon, B., Thompson, E., Whalley, J., and Prasad, C. 2006. Not seeing the forest for the trees: novice programmers and the SOLO taxonomy. *ITICSE 2006.* ACM, New York, NY, USA, 118-122. DOI=10.1145/1140124.1140157 http://doi.acm.org/10.1145/1140124.1140157

[22] Whalley, J. L. Lister, R. (2009). The BRACElet 2009.1 (Wellington) specification. *ACE 2009.* Margaret Hamilton and Tony Clear (Eds.), Vol. 95. Australian Computer Society, Inc., Darlinghurst, Australia, Australia, 9-18.

Subgoal-Labeled Instructional Material Improves Performance and Transfer in Learning to Develop Mobile Applications

Lauren Margulieux
Georgia Institute of Technology
School of Psychology
Atlanta, GA, 30332-0170, USA
1-404-894-7556

l.marg@gatech.edu

Mark Guzdial
Georgia Institute of Technology
School of Interactive Computing
Atlanta, GA, 30332-0760, USA
1-404-894-5618

guzdial@cc.gatech.edu

Richard Catrambone
Georgia Institute of Technology
School of Psychology
Atlanta, GA, 30332-0170, USA
1-404-894-2682

rc7@prism.gatech.edu

ABSTRACT

Mental models are mental representations of how an action changes a problem state. Creating a mental model early in the learning process is a strong predictor of success in computer science classes. One major problem in computer science education, however, is that novices have difficulty creating mental models perhaps because of the cognitive overload caused by traditional teaching methods. The present study employed subgoal-labeled instructional materials to promote the creation of mental models when teaching novices to program in Android App Inventor. Utilizing this and other well-established educational tools, such as scaffolding, to reduce cognitive load in computer science education improved the performance of participants on novel tasks when learning to develop mobile applications.

Categories and Subject Descriptors

K.3.2 [Computers and Education]: Computer and Information Science Education – *computer science education, information systems education.*

General Terms

Measurement, Performance, Experimentation, Human Factors, Languages, Theory.

Keywords

Subgoal learning; mental models; cognitive load, instructional text, educational videos

1. INTRODUCTION

As a domain that focuses on problem solving, CS is similar to other procedural domains, such as physics and mathematics, so many of the educational tools from these other domains can be applied to CS. The computational tools used to solve CS problems, however, are more complex than many of the computational tools used in other domains. For example, to solve physics problems, students mainly use computational tools with which they are already familiar, such as a calculator. To solve CS problems, on the other hand, CS students must learn how to use the computational tools (programming languages) needed to solve the problem and implement the solution. Though CS instructors can emulate the graduated learning that is used in other procedural domains with novice CS learners, the added cognitive load from using a novel programming language increases the demand on working memory and creates a barrier to learning CS and presents a major problem in CS education (Gray, Clair, James, & Mead, 2007). The present study explores techniques to reduce the cognitive load of novices learning to program.

1.1 Improving Mental Models

The present study defines mental models as a personal, cognitive representation of procedures and how actions will affect problem states. For example, when a carpenter builds a house frame, he or she has a mental model of the actions needed to complete the task. Similarly, a competent programmer will have a mental model of how to create a program. Mental models are important for reasoning in procedural domains because they enable learners to integrate simple skills to achieve a complex skill. Mental models help this process by allowing reasoners to hierarchically classify information and focus on high level problem solving without getting distracted by low level details (van Merriënboer, Clark, & de Croock, 2002). For example, mental models allow people to conceptualize how to achieve a higher function math skill, such as solving for a variable, without allocating attention to lower function math skills, such as addition (because those details are not needed for the higher level goal; Norman, 1983).

The problem, however, is that novice programmers have trouble creating mental models for programming knowledge. Therefore, organizing, interpreting, and remembering new information is more difficult and requires more cognitive load than if the learner had good mental models for the knowledge (Committee on Developments in the Science of Learning, 2000). For example, one problem that novices have is that they try to carry over syntax rules from other languages, such as English and algebra, which complicates learning programming syntax (Davis, Linn, Mann, & Clancy, 1993). Furthermore, novices' mental models emphasize different knowledge than CS experts' mental models (Brooks, 1990). Experts in CS focus on deeper structural aspects of problems because they have mental models to classify problems, whereas novices are misled by incidental features of the problem because they have mental models for syntax (Atkinson, Derry, Renkl, & Wortham, 2000). Therefore, novice solution structures tend to be bottom-up and details-first which often makes their solutions needlessly convoluted (Anderson, Farrell, & Sauers, 1984; Guzdial, 1995).

1.1.1 Creating Mental Models

CS education researchers recognize the need to help learners develop mental models (e.g., Caspersen, Larson, & Bennedsen, 2007). CS instruction, however, tends to emphasize the product of the design and development process, but does not emphasize the process itself, leading to students creating mental models of syntax rather than structure (Brooks, 1990). Moreover, teachers assign grades to the running code but not the process that produced it (Linn & Clancy, 1992). Davis et al. (1993) argue that to fix this problem, novices need more instruction in how to construct mental models for programming in general rather than more instruction in a specific programming language.

To help students create mental models, Kirschner, Sweller, and Clark (2006) advocate guided instruction over minimally guided instruction because guided instruction provides students with the instructor's mental model framework into which students can integrate new information. Providing a mental model framework reduces the cognitive load required to create mental models which leads to better long-term learning. In contrast, the problem-based approach, a type of minimally guided instruction, asks students to solve problems as a way of learning. Solving problems too early in the learning process, however, can overload working memory and inhibit the creation of mental models (Kirschner et al., 2006). The problem-based approach, however, is analogous to some methods used to introduce programming languages to novices.

Conventional methods of teaching computer science ask novices to solve problems using unfamiliar knowledge while applying novel code construction rules. These methods lead to poor performance on program-writing problems due to cognitive overload and lead to common complaints such as "I don't know where to start," or "You've taught me so many details, I don't know which ones to use," (Clancy & Linn, 1990). Possible solutions to this problem are to reduce the intrinsic cognitive load (cognitive load associated with the material being taught) or to reduce the extraneous cognitive load (cognitive load associated with **how** the material is being taught; Sweller, 2010).

1.2 Reducing Cognitive Load

The only way to decrease intrinsic cognitive load for novices is to reduce the amount of information being used to solve the problem (Sweller, 2010). To reduce the amount of information, components of programming can be isolated so that students are not trying to learn multiple aspects at once. Students can first be taught and tested on computational thinking without concerning themselves with syntax. Drag-and-drop programming languages, such as Android App Inventor and Scratch, replace writing code with dragging components from a menu; this approach reduces the cognitive load associated with syntax because users can easily understand it, which allows users to focus on conceptually solving a problem (Brennan, 2009). Drag-and-drop programming languages are also meant to be easy for users of all ages, backgrounds, and interests and to allow users to "tinker" with components, joining code commands together, similar to "Lego bricks" (p. 63; Resnick et al., 2009). This approach might also help novices create mental models focused on the structure of solutions rather than on syntax.

1.2.1 Worked Examples

To reduce extraneous cognitive load, the present study uses a few techniques; the first of which is worked examples. Anderson et al. (1984) argues that in CS, problem solving by novices is guided by making structural analogies to worked examples. Providing worked examples helps students learn more than instructional text does because worked examples provide information about the application of domain principles (Catrambone, 1996). Additionally, worked examples provide a solution for a learner to study before the student is able to solve problems independently (Atkinson et al., 2000). Worked examples are most effective when labeled subgoals are incorporated because this presentation emphasizes the conceptual structure of the problem solution being taught (Catrambone, 1996).

1.2.2 Subgoal Labels

The main technique that the present study used to reduce extraneous cognitive load is subgoal-labels. Subgoals are "task structures to be learned for solving problems in a domain," (Catrambone, 1994); subgoals are inherent in complex problem solutions. Illuminating the subgoals of a problem solution through subgoal-oriented worked examples have caused problem solving performance improvements in a number of procedural fields, such as statistics (e.g., Catrambone, 1998). Subgoal labels group steps of a worked example into a meaningful unit and help students identify the structural information from incidental information. Learning subgoals can also reduce cognitive load when problem solving because the student has fewer possible problem-solving steps on which to focus (i.e., subgoals [consisting of multiple steps] versus individual steps) similar to functional programming (Clancy & Linn, 1990). Furthermore, subgoal-labeled worked examples might provide students with mental model frameworks. Students who were given labels for subgoals used those labels when explaining how they solved a problem, suggesting that is how they mentally organized information (Catrambone, 1996).

Apprising learners of the underlying structure of the worked examples promotes self-explanation (Bielaczyc, Pirolli, & Brown, 1995; Renkl & Atkinson, 2002), and greater number of self-explanations are related to more successful learning. "Self-explanation directs cognitive resources to deal with relevant [information] and reduces the effect of extraneous cognitive load," (Sweller, 2010, p. 136). .

1.2.3 Beyond Worked Examples

Worked examples help reduce extraneous load, but learners' benefit from them is capped. The theory of knowledge compilation argues that learners need more than worked examples to learn to solve problems in a domain. It postulates that in order to fully develop problem-solving skills, learners need to solve problems because solving problems allows students to create rules from their knowledge. Trafton and Reiser (1993) similarly found that learners presented with interleaved examples and problems took less time on novel problems than learners presented with blocks of examples and problems. To reduce the demand on working memory when transitioning from worked examples to practice problems, one technique that can be used is scaffolding. Scaffolding can be used as an intermediate step between giving a learner worked examples and asking them to solve problems on their own; it gives the student a problem to solve and some of the components of the solution to guide his or her solution (Pea, 2004). This extra step between guided instruction and unguided instruction allows learners to develop problem-solving mental models for the domain (Kirschner et al., 2006).

1.3 Present Study

The present study employed subgoal labels, worked examples, and scaffolding to reduce intrinsic and extraneous cognitive load on novices learning to program. These techniques were expected to improve their performance on assessment tests and enable their development of mental models of program creation. To assess programming knowledge, students were asked to solve problems using a drag-and-drop programming language, so students did not need in-depth knowledge of the language to solve the problems. Because drag-and-drop programming involves selecting pieces of code instead of writing pieces of code, this approach might allow students to focus on making mental models of conceptual structures rather than language syntax.

The present studies manipulated the instructional material that learners received; that is, a participant either received conventional instructional material from the projects section of ICE Distance Education Portal (http://ice.cc.gatech.edu/dl/?q=node/641) created by Barbara Ericson, or he or she received instructional material adapted to include subgoal labels. The materials were identical except for the added subgoal labels (see Figure 1). During their two sessions, participants watched a video demonstration of an application (app) being created (worked example), created the app using a text guide (scaffolding), and modified components of or added components to their apps without guidance (practice problems).

To assess their knowledge, participants were asked to write the steps that they would take to program a feature (i.e., either a component or a block) for their app. Their answers were scored based on whether or not they attempted the subgoals required to program the feature and whether or not they completed the subgoal correctly.

Subgoal-Labeled Materials

Handle Events from My Blocks

1. Click on "My Blocks" to see the blocks for components you created.
2. Click on "clap" and drag out a *when clap.Touched* block

Set Output from My Blocks

3. Click on "clapSound" and drag out *call clapSound.Play* and connect it after *when clap.Touched*

Conventional Materials

1. Click on "My Blocks" to see the blocks for components you created.
2. Click on "clap" and drag out a *when clap.Touched* block
3. Click on "clapSound" and drag out *call clapSound.Play* and connect it after *when clap.Touched*

Figure 1. Sample Materials from Two Groups

1.3.1 Development of Instructional Materials

The present study used both video demonstrations of the task (i.e., a video of someone doing the task) and text instructions for how to complete the task. Palmiter and Elkerton (1993) found that video demonstrations can quickly and naturally show users how to learn a direct-manipulation interface, but they concluded that simply watching demonstrations might lead to superficial processing of a task. While participants who viewed the video demonstrations performed tasks on the immediate test more

quickly and accurately than participants who read text-only instructions, video-demonstration participants' performance on the delayed test, which was one week later, was much worse than text-only participants, whose speed and accuracy remained about the same (Palmiter & Elkerton, 1993; Palmiter, Elkerton, & Baggett, 1991). Given that video demonstrations are a useful aid in learning a complex task that uses an interface, that participants enjoy video demonstrations more than text instruction, and that text instruction leads to better transfer and retention, the present study used both methods of instruction (Palmiter & Elkerton, 1993).

For the subgoal condition, subgoal labels were incorporated into both the video demonstration and the text instruction. Given that participants in Palmiter's and Elkerton's (1993) video demonstration group reported that they felt like they were "'memorizing sequences of clicks'...without understanding the task" (p. 210), the subgoal callouts (see Figure 2 for an example) might help engage the subgoal participants during the video. The subgoal labels included in the materials were developed using the TAPS procedure (Catrambone, Gane, Adams, Bujak, Kline, and Eiriksdottir, 2012) in consultation with subject-matter experts, Mark Guzdial and Barbara Ericson (see Figure 3 for list of subgoal labels).

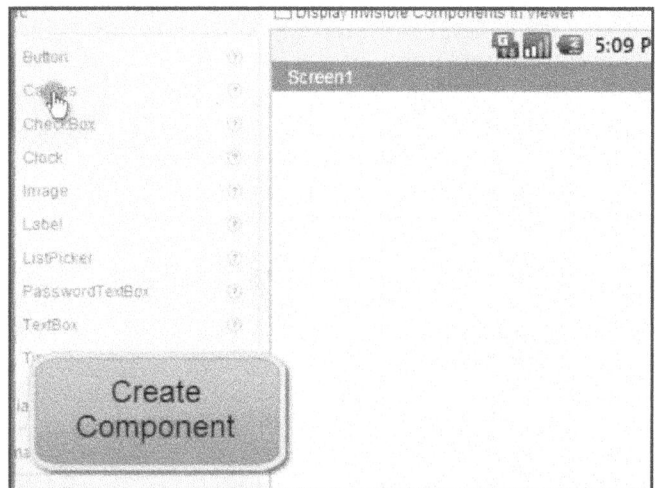

Figure 2. Sample of Subgoal Callout in Video Demonstration

Subgoals

- Create components
- Set properties
- Handle events from My Blocks
- Set outputs from My Blocks
- Define variable from Built-In
- Set conditions from Built-In
- Emulate app

Figure 3. Subgoals Used In Instructional Material

1.3.2 Development of Assessment Tasks

Assessment tasks were developed based on the material that participants were exposed to in the sessions (e.g., assessment one was based on the material taught in session one). During the assessment, participants were asked to write down the steps that they would take to create a feature (e.g., component or block) in App Inventor. Half of the assessment tasks were classified as "near transfer" tasks meaning that they followed an identical structure to tasks completed in the instructional period but substituted blocks, components, or properties of the **same** type. For example, the second task in assessment one asked participants to program the clap sound to play when the phone was tilted down. To complete this task, participants could follow the same steps that they used in the instructional period to program the drum sound to play when the phone was tilted to the right, but they had to replace the drum sound with the clap sound and the x-axis acceleration sensor with the y-axis acceleration sensor.

The other half of the assessment tasks were classified as "far transfer" tasks meaning that they followed the same general scheme as tasks completed in the instructional period but substituted blocks, components, or properties of a **different** type. For example, the third task in assessment one asked participants to program an ImageSprite to move 5 pixels to the right if touched. To complete this task, participants had to integrate steps from several tasks from the instructional period (e.g., using a "Math" block), but the subgoals that needed to be achieved to complete the assessment task were the same as the subgoals that needed to be achieved to complete tasks in the instructional period. There were no statistically significant performance differences between near and far transfer tasks either within participants or between groups.

Hints were given on assessment tasks that asked participants to use features that they had not used before. The hints directed participants to the correct feature but did not tell them how to use that feature (see Figure 4). Instructional material was not available to the participants during the assessment, but participants had access to the App Inventor interface and the apps that they had created during that session. Participants were allowed access to the apps that they had made, so the apps could serve as memory cues and reduce cognitive load.

1.5 Write the steps you would take to make the screen change colors depending on the orientation of the phone; specifically, the screen turns blue when the pitch is greater than 2 (hint: you'll need to make an orientation sensor and use blocks from "Screen 1" in My Blocks).

2.1 Write the steps you would take to add a tambourine to your Music Maker app (create the component only).

3.3 Write the steps you would take to create a list of colors and make the ball to change to a random color whenever it collided with something.

Figure 4. Sample of Assessment Tasks

2. EXPERIMENT ONE
2.1 Method
2.1.1 Participants
Participants were 40 students recruited from Georgia Institute of Technology. To participate in the experiment, students must have been at least 18 years of age, and they must not have completed more than one computer programming or computer science class. Experience with Android App Inventor disqualified students. Information about participant's age, gender, academic field of study, SAT scores, high school and college GPA, year in school, number of complete credits, computer science experience, primary language, number of math courses completed, subjective comfort with computers, and expected difficulty of learning a programming language were collected to be analyzed as possible predictors of performance (Rountree et al., 2004). None of these demographics correlated with performance except that expected difficulty of learning a programming language correlated positively with amount of time spent on assessment tasks, $r = .38$, $p = .02$. That is, the more difficult participants thought the task would be, the longer they spent on the task.

2.1.2 Procedure
The study consisted of two one-hour sessions which were one week apart and was conducted using a computer-based learning environment (i.e., all instructional material was presented to the participants through a personal computer). During the instructional period for the two sessions, students learned how to create two apps in Android App Inventor using various components such as animations, sounds, and accelerometer input. Android App Inventor was chosen because it is a drag-and-drop program language. By watching videos of an app being created, creating their own apps with guidance, and modifying and adding to their apps, participants learned how to create components in the App Inventor Designer then program the components in the App Inventor Blocks Editor.

In the first session, participants completed a demographic questionnaire, and then they had 40 minutes to study the first app's instructional material. Next, participants had 15 minutes to complete the first assessment task. In the second session, participants had 10 minutes to complete the second assessment task, which measured their retention. Then participants had 25 minutes to study the second app's instructional material followed by 25 minutes to complete the third assessment.

2.2 Results and Discussion
Each solution for the assessment tasks was deconstructed into the subgoals (i.e., components necessary to successfully complete the solution) that were inherent in the solution; participants were given a point for each subgoal that they attempted and each subgoal that they completed correctly. Attempting a subgoal was operationally defined as listing at least one of the steps required to complete the subgoal or listing a step that would achieve a similar function (e.g., for a "set properties" subgoal, listing a step to change a property regardless if it was the correct property). There were 46 subgoals across the assessment task solutions, so participants could get a maximum score of 46 for both the attempted and correct measurements. Interrater reliability was high with a one-way random model intraclass correlation coefficient of agreement (ICC(A)) of .97, Cronbach's alpha of .98, and $r = .96$, $p < .001$. Participants were also given a score for the number of questions that they attempted (operationally defined as writing something for an answer) to account for participants who did not complete the assessments in time. Additionally, the amount of time that participants took to complete each assessment was measured.

2.2.1 Attempted Subgoals
Participants in the subgoal group ($n = 20$) attempted more subgoals ($M = 34.70$, $SD = 6.12$) than the conventional group ($n = 20$, $M = 29.42$, $SD = 7.40$), $F (1, 38) = 5.91$, $MSE = 45.91$, $p = .02$, $\omega^2 = .14$, $f = .38$. Furthermore, though the number of

attempted questions was not correlated with group or correct subgoals, the number of attempted questions was correlated with attempted subgoals, $r = .52$, $p = .001$. Linear regression was used to test if number of attempted questions and instructional group accounted for different parts of the variance of number of attempted subgoals. In the linear regression both group and attempted questions are significant predictors of attempted subgoals, $\beta = .32$, $p = .047$, and $\beta = .38$, $p = .02$, respectively.

These statistics mean that the participant group is a significant predictor of attempted subgoals with other predictors held constant, and group uniquely accounts for 14% of the variance for attempted subgoals, which is a high percentage for research of this type with human subjects. Furthermore, the effect size, which represents the magnitude of the difference between the two groups in units of standard deviations, equates to subgoal participants attempting on average 2.57, or 6%, more subgoals than conventional participants. These results could mean that participants in the subgoal group can better identify the subgoals necessary to complete the solution whether or not they complete the solution correctly. If this is true, then being better able to identify the subgoals necessary for a solution could be explained by having a mental model for the computer programming information that was learned and how to solve problems in the domain. Subgoal labels can help learners create better mental models because subgoals can provide a mental model framework that could be used to organize new information more efficiently. Based on these results alone, inferences about participants' mental models cannot be made, but Experiment Two addresses this issue.

2.2.2 Correct Subgoals
Participants in the subgoal group completed more subgoals correctly ($M = 28.10$, $SD = 7.22$) than the conventional group ($M = 20.63$, $SD = 6.72$), $F (1, 38) = 11.16$, $MSE = 48.71$, $p = .002$, $\omega^2 = .23$, $f = .53$. These statistics mean that 23% of the variance for correct subgoals was accounted for by group, which is very high for research of this type with human subjects, and the effect size equates to subgoal participants answering on average 3.69, or 8%, more subgoals correctly than the conventional group. To put these results in context, if this study had been a class, the difference in grades between the groups would be nearly a whole letter grade. These results support the hypothesis that participants in the subgoal group would perform better on the assessment tasks than those in the conventional group. This difference could be due to the subgoal participants learning the subgoals better. As described earlier, learning subgoals can reduce extraneous cognitive load by highlighting the structure of examples, promoting self-explanation, creating mental models early in the learning process, and chunking problem-solving steps (Catrambone, 1998). If extraneous cognitive load was reduced, subgoal participants could have learned more effectively than conventional participants and performed better on the assessment tasks. Though cognitive load theory would predict these results, the present study does not directly measure cognitive load, so the theoretical mechanism underlying the results cannot be definitively determined.

2.2.3 Time on Task
The subgoal group finished the assessments faster (M = 40.64 min., SD = 7.48 min.) than the conventional group (M = 45.45 min., SD = 5.11 min.) as well, F (1, 38) = 5.48, MSE = 41.07, p = .03, ω^2 = .13, f = .37. Additionally, the correlation between time and number of correct subgoals was nonsignificant (r = .06, p > .05), which suggests that participants did not rush through the

assessments at the cost of accuracy. These statistics mean that 13% of the variance for time spent on tasks is attributable to instructional group, and the effect size translates into the subgoal group finishing the tasks on average 2 minutes and 18 seconds faster than the conventional group. This result could suggest that participants in the subgoal group learned the subgoals more effectively, which allowed them to transfer what they learned more easily than those in the conventional group.

2.2.4 Defining the Variable Problem
The third question of assessment three asked participants to create a list, which was similar to the list that they created during the instructional period in the second session (see Figure 5). An important part of completing this task is defining the variable that contains the list because, without defining the variable, the list cannot be used in the program (e.g., other parts of the program would not be able to reference the list); that the variable happens to be a list is an incidental feature of this app. For this reason, the subgoal label used for these steps of the instructional material was "define variable." Interestingly, though the groups performed similarly for creating the list, participants in the subgoal group were more likely to define the variable in this assessment task ($M = .55$, $SD = .51$) than the conventional group ($M = .05$, $SD = .23$), $F (1, 38) = 15.12$, $MSE = .16$, $p < .001$, $\omega^2 = .29$, $f = .61$.

Subgoal-Labeled Materials

Define Variables from Built-in

1. Click on "Built-In" and "Definition" and pull out a *def variable*.
2. Click on the "variable" and replace it with "fortuneList". This creates a variable called "fortuneList".
3. Click on "Lists" and drag out a *call make a list*
4. Click on "Text" and drag out a *text text* block and drop it next to "item". Click on the rightmost "text" and replace it with your first fortune.

Conventional Materials

5. Click on "Built-In" and "Definition" and pull out a *def variable*.
6. Click on the "variable" and replace it with "fortuneList". This creates a variable called "fortuneList".
7. Click on "Lists" and drag out a *call make a list*
8. Click on "Text" and drag out a *text text* block and drop it next to "item". Click on the rightmost "text" and replace it with your first fortune.

Assessment Task

Write the steps you would take to create a list of colors and make the ball to change to a random color whenever it collided with something.

Figure 5. Instructional Materials by Group and Assessment Task for which the Solution Includes Defining a Variable

These statistics mean that 29% of the variance for correct subgoals is attributable to group, and the effect size translates into 23% more of the subgoal group defined the variable than the conventional group. This result could mean that the subgoal label helped the subgoal participants to learn the subgoal and recognize the underlying structure of the example, which helped them transfer what they learned in the instructional period to the assessment task. That is, the subgoal label could have helped the subgoal participants recognize that defining the variable was an important task in creating the app. However, this result could also mean that the subgoal label "define variable" simply doubled the subgoal participants' exposure to the idea of defining a variable, and that the extra exposure helped them to remember those steps. That is, the subgoal label could have helped subgoal participants remember the steps to define a variable during the assessment without helping them to understand the structure of the task. Further probing of participants' problem solving strategy would be required to better determine the cause of this result.

2.2.5 Retention
To test retention of knowledge, participants took an assessment at the start of the second session, which was one week after the first session. During this assessment, they had access to the App Inventor website but not access to a previously created app like they did in the other assessments.Therefore, they did not have a memory cue for creating features of an app other than the website itself. There were a total of 11 subgoals in the correct solutions for this assessment. On this retention assessment, subgoal participants completed more subgoals correctly ($M = 5.95$, $SD = 2.61$) than conventional participants ($M = 4.05$, $SD = 1.75$), $F (1, 38) = 7.06$, $MSE = 4.97$, $p = .01$, $\omega^2 = .16$, $f = .42$. These statistics mean that 16% of the variance for correct subgoals is attributable to instructional group, and the effect size equates to the subgoal participants answering on average .92, or 8%, more subgoals correctly than the conventional participants. This result suggests that participants in the subgoal group retained knowledge about App Inventor better than those in the conventional group. Similar to previous results, this result suggests that subgoal participants learned the material better than conventional participants. This difference could be due to lower extraneous cognitive load while learning, which would allow more mental resources for germane cognitive load and long-term learning.

3. EXPERIMENT TWO
3.1 Method
3.1.1 Participants
Participants were 12 students recruited from Georgia Institute of Technology. Criteria for participation were the same as for Experiment One. The same demographic information about participants that was collected in Experiment One was collected in Experiment Two. None of these demographics correlated with performance.

3.1.2 Procedure
The procedure for Experiment Two was identical to Experiment One except that while participants completed the assessment tasks, they engaged in a talk-aloud protocol. The talk-aloud protocol asked participants to explain their goals or strategies for completing the assessment tasks and also to identify the features for which they searched while working on the tasks. Before starting assessment one, participants practiced the talk-aloud procedure by playing a game of tic-tac-toe with the experimenter. During the assessment tasks, the experimenter did not provide information about how to complete a task but did provide information or instruction about the protocol (e.g., the experimenter could encourage the participant to talk more). Assessments in Experiment Two were not timed due to the talk-aloud protocol. As a result, participants had as much time as they wanted to work on assessment tasks.

3.2 Results and Discussion
In addition to scoring participant responses for attempted and correct subgoals, participants were also scored on the number of subgoal labels they used when describing their strategies and goals when solving tasks and the number of blocks they dragged out while solving assessment tasks.

3.2.1 Attempted and Correct Subgoals
Due to the small number of participants in this experiment (N=12), there was not enough power in the null-hypothesis-significance-testing framework to achieve statistically significant results. The attempted and correct subgoals were still analyzed by effect size between groups. Similar to results from Experiment One, the effect size for attempted subgoals was .42, and the effect size for correct subgoals was .59. These effect sizes suggest that if the same number of people who participated in Experiment One had participated in this experiment, the same statistically significant difference in performance between groups that were observed in Experiment One would have been observed in this experiment. Besides replicating the results from the first experiment, these results mean that without time constraints during the assessments, subgoal participants again performed better than conventional participants. This conclusion suggests that subgoal participants learned the material better perhaps because the subgoal labels allowed them to learn the subgoals better. If they learned the subgoals better, they also might have created better mental models of the material, and they might have experienced less cognitive load while learning the material.

3.2.2 Subgoal Labels in Descriptions
Participants who had subgoal labels in their instructional materials used those labels when describing their strategies and goals while solving the assessment tasks ($M = 5.75$, $SD = 4.27$). That participants used these labels during the talk aloud protocol suggests that the information that they learned is mentally organized under these labels. Organizing information under subgoal labels might help participants create better mental models and perform better than participants in the conventional group.

3.2.3 Number of Blocks
Participants in the subgoal group were less likely to drag out blocks while working through assessment tasks ($M = 18.83$, $SD = 13.09$) than those in the conventional group ($M = 49.85$, $SD = 5.66$), $F (1, 10) = 9.84$, $MSE = 148.14$, $p = .02$, $\omega^2 = .62$, $f = .91$. These statistics mean that 62% of the variance for number of blocks was accounted for by group, and the effect size equates to subgoal participants dragging out 8.5 fewer blocks on average than the conventional group. Thus, another benefit to having their knowledge apparently organized by subgoals is that learners in the subgoal group were more efficient in their problem solving (i.e., dragging out fewer blocks).

These results could mean subgoal participants did not need as much external representation of the problem state to solve the problem suggesting that they represent the problem state more internally than the conventional group. If subgoal participants had better mental models than the conventional participants, they might have been better able to internally represent the problem state compared to the conventional participants.

3.2.4 Having Fun
A major challenges of teaching programming is that instruction and practice can often be frustrating for students, so motivating

students is difficult (Kinnunen & Simon, 2011). An exciting finding in this experiment is that four of the six participants in the subgoal group said that they enjoyed the experiment. After their last sessions ended, each said, completely unpromted, that they thought the sessions were interesting and that they had fun. Computing educators know that learning the basics of programming does not have to be a frustrating and difficult endeavor. In fact, in some circumstances, it can be fun and engaging. Computing educators have found a combination of conditions that has made computing education fun for the majority of their students. In this experiment, the conditions include being introduced to a programming language, Android App Inventor, that can be made easy to learn, whose purpose can be made easy to understand, and is supported by instructional materials that cover new knowledge but are not unreasonably demanding of the learner's cognitive resources. We believe that these conditions contributed to the sense of fun.

4. CONCLUSION

One well-established reason that novices struggle to learn programming is because of the cognitive overload that they experience (Gray et al., 2007). Cognitive overload not only prevents information from being stored in long-term memory, it also hinders the development of mental models (Kirschner et al., 2006). Mental models, however, help students organize, interpret, and remember new information (Committee on Developments in the Science of Learning, 2000). Furthermore, the stunted development of mental models compounds the difficulty of learning additional information about programming, so helping novices develop mental models from the beginning of instruction is crucial (Sweller et al., 2010). The purpose of the present study was to determine if techniques to reduce cognitive load and to promote the creation of mental models improved performance on assessments of programming knowledge.

The results of the present study could support that subgoal-labeled materials help novices learn subgoals, which reduces the extraneous cognitive load imposed on novices learning programming. Learning subgoals could have reduced extraneous cognitive load in a few ways. It could have reduced extraneous cognitive load by highlighting the essential features of worked examples, by chunking problem-solving steps, and by promoting self explanation (Catrambone, 1998; Sweller, 2010). This reduction in extraneous cognitive load might have allowed students to learn faster because more of their mental resources were available for germane cognitive load which is responsible for creating mental models and storing information in long-term memory (Kirschner et al., 2006). Furthermore, subgoals emphasize the structure of solutions, which aids the development of mental models (Atkinson et al., 2000).

The results could also support that the subgoal labels aided novices in developing mental models early in the learning process. In addition to reducing cognitive load, subgoal labels are a type of guided instruction that could give learners a framework for a rational mental model that they could have filled in with information (Kirschner et al., 2006). In turn, mental models reduce cognitive load required to process new information, which increases long-term learning, and long-term learning reduces the cognitive load required to process new information on the same topic (Kirschner et al., 2006). More research is still needed to understand the connection between subgoal-labeled materials and mental models in CS.

Due to the compounding effects of good mental models and reduced cognitive load on learning, if these groups were to continue learning about programming, the differences between the groups would be expected to get larger. Though the present study is too short to demonstrate divergence between the two groups, if the manipulation was implemented in an introductory CS class, the difference between groups by the end of course would likely be much larger than the difference demonstrated in this study. More research would be necessary to examine this prediction.

Many students view CS classes as difficult and frustrating, so they avoid taking them, even though the knowledge could be beneficial to them as the prevalence of technology increases (Clancy & Linn, 1990). A major goal for CS education researchers is to dispel this stigma associated with CS classes (Kolodner et al., 2008). The purpose of the present study was to develop materials that improved the performance and transfer of novices learning the basics of programming. It was a success.

A key idea in this paper is that *instructional design matters*. The two groups did not differ in the *content* of the instruction but in the *design* of that material (e.g., whether subgoals were made explicit). The two groups performed significantly differently, with the subgoal group performing better on several measures. We believe that CS learning was enhanced through the application of instructional design principles. Thus, instructional design principles can be useful in achieving our goals as CS education researchers and CS educators to help more students to gain knowledge about computing.

5. ACKNOWLEDGMENTS

Our thanks to the NSF for grant CNS-1138378 and to the GVU Center and IPaT for the grant that made this research possible. We thank Joe Dagosta, Hannah Fletcher, and Catherine Hwang for help collecting and scoring data.

6. REFERENCES

[1] Anderson, J. Farrell, R. & Sauers, R. 1984. Learning to program in LISP. *Cognitive Science, 8*(2), 87–129. DOI= 10.1207/s15516709cog0802_1

[2] Atkinson, R. K., & Derry, S. 2000. Computer-based Examples Designed to Encourage Optimal Example Processing: A Study Examining the Impact of Sequentially Presented, Subgoal-oriented Worked Examples. *Proceedings of ICLS 2000 International Conference of the Learning Sciences*, 132–133.

[3] Atkinson, R. K., Derry, S. J., Renkl, A., & Wortham, D. 2000. Learning from Examples: Instructional Principles from the Worked Examples Research. *Review of the Educational Research, 70*(2), 181-214. DOI= 10.3102/00346543070002181

[4] Bielaczyc, K., Pirolli, P., & Brown, A. L. 1995. Training in self-explanation and self-regulation strategies: Investigating the effects of knowledge acquisition activities on problem solving. *Cognition and Instruction, 13*, 221–252.

[5] Brennan, K. 2009. Scratch-Ed: an online community for scratch educators. In *Proceedings of the 9th international conference on Computer supported collaborative learning - Volume 2* (CSCL'09), Angelique Dimitracopoulou, Claire O'Malley, Daniel Suthers, and Peter Reimann (Eds.), Vol. 2. International Society of the Learning Sciences 76-78.

[6] Brooks, R. 1990. Categories of programming knowledge and their application. *Int. J. Man-Mach. Stud.* 33, 3 (August 1990), 241-246. DOI=10.1016/S0020-7373(05)80118-X http://dx.doi.org/10.1016/S0020-7373(05)80118-X.

[7] Caspersen, M., Larsen, K. D., & Bennedsen, J. 2007. Mental models and programming aptitude. In *Proceedings of the 12th annual SIGCSE conference on Innovation and technology in computer science education.* ACM, New York, NY, USA, 206-210. DOI=10.1145/1268784.1268845

[8] Catrambone, R. 1994. Improving examples to improve transfer to novel problems. *Memory and Cognition, 22,* 605–615.

[9] Catrambone, R. 1996. Generalizing solution procedures learned from examples. *Journal of Experimental Psychology: Learning, Memory, and Cognition, 22,* 1020-1031. DOI= 10.1037/0278-7393.22.4.1020

[10] Catrambone, R. 1998. The subgoal learning model: Creating better examples so that students can solve novel problems. *Journal of Experimental Psychology: General, 127,* 355-376. DOI= 10.1037/0096-3445.127.4.355

[11] Catrambone, R., Gane, B. D., Adams, A. E., Bujak, K. R., Kline, K. A., & Eiriksdottir, E. 2012. Task Analysis by Problem Solving (TAPS): A Method for Uncovering Expert Knowledge. Unpublished manuscript, School of Psychology, Georgia Institute of Technology, Atlanta, GA.

[12] Clancy, M.J., & Linn, M.C. 1990. Functional fun. In *Proceedings of the twenty-first SIGCSE technical symposium on Computer science education* (SIGCSE '90), James E. Miller and Daniel T. Joyce (Eds.). ACM, New York, NY, USA, 63-67. DOI=10.1145/323410.319085 http://doi.acm.org/10.1145/323410.319085

[13] Committee on Developments in the Science of Learning. 2000. *How people learn: Brain, mind, experience, and school: Expanded edition.* Retrieved from http://www.nap.edu/catalog.php?record_id=9853

[14] Davis, E., Linn, M., Mann, L., & Clancy, M. 1993. Mind your Ps and Qs: Using parentheses and quotes in LISP. In C. R. Cook, J. C. Scholtz, and J. C. Spohrer (Eds.), Empirical Studies of Programmers: Fifth Workshop, (pp. 62–85). Norwood, NJ: Ablex. 1993.

[15] Dehnadi, S., Bornat, R., & Adams, R. 2009. Meta-analysis of the effect of consistency on success in early learning of programming. *21st Annual Workshop of the Psychology of Programming Interest Group* (p.10pp)

[16] Gray, S., St. Clair, C., James, R., & Mead, J. 2007. Suggestions for graduated exposure to programming concepts using fading worked examples. In *Proceedings of the third international workshop on Computing education research* (ICER '07). ACM, New York, NY, USA, 99–110. DOI=10.1145/1288580.1288594

[17] Guzdial, M. 1995. Centralized mindset: a student problem with object-oriented programming. In *Proceedings of the twenty-sixth SIGCSE technical symposium on Computer science education* (SIGCSE '95), Curt M. White, James E. Miller, and Judy Gersting (Eds.). ACM, New York, NY, USA, 182-185. DOI=10.1145/199688.199772 http://doi.acm.org/10.1145/199688.199772

[18] Kinnunen, P., & Simon, B., 2011. CS majors' self-efficacy perceptions in CS1: results in light of social cognitive theory. In *Proceedings of the seventh international workshop on Computing education research* (ICER '11). ACM, New York, NY, USA, 19-26. DOI=10.1145/2016911.2016917

[19] Kirschner, P., Sweller, J., & Clark, R. 2006. Why minimal guidance during instruction does not work: An analysis of the failure of constructivist, discovery, problem-based, experiential, and inquiry-based teaching. *Educational Psychologist, 41*(2), 75-86. DOI= 10.1207/s15326985ep4102_1

[20] Linn, M., & Clancy, M. 1992. The case for case studies of programming problems. *Communications of the ACM, 35*(3), pp 121–132.

[21] Norman, D. A. (1983). Some observations on mental models. In D. Gentner & A. Stevens (Eds.), *Mental models* (pp. 7-14). Retrieved from http://books.google.com/

[22] Palmiter, S., Elkerton, J., & Baggett, P. 1993. Animated demonstrations versus written instructions for learning procedural tasks: A preliminary investigation. *International Journal of Man-Machine Studies, 34,* 687-701. DOI= 10.1016/0020-7373(91)90019-4

[23] Pea, R. 2004. The social and technological dimensions of scaffolding and related theoretical concepts for learning, education, and human activity. *Journal of the Learning Sciences, 13*(3), 423-451. DOI= 10.1207/s15327809jls1303_6

[24] Renkl, A., & Atkinson, R. K. 2002. Learning from examples: Fostering self-explanations in computer-based learning environments. *Interactive Learning Environments, 10*(2), 105–199.

[25] Resnick, M., Maloney, J., Monroy-Hernández, A., Rusk, N., Eastmond, E., Brennan, K., Millner, A., Rosenbaum, E., Silver, J., Silverman, B., & Kafai, Y. 2009. Scratch: programming for all. *Commun. ACM* 52, 11 (November 2009), 60-67. DOI=10.1145/1592761.1592779 http://doi.acm.org/10.1145/1592761.1592779

[26] Rountree, N., Rountree, J., Robins, A., & Hannah, R. 2004. Interacting factors that predict success and failure in a CS1 course. In *Working group reports from ITiCSE on Innovation and technology in computer science education* (ITiCSE-WGR '04). ACM, New York, NY, USA, 101–104. DOI=10.1145/1044550.1041669 http://doi.acm.org/10.1145/1044550.1041669

[27] Sweller, J. 2010. Element interactivity and intrinsic, extraneous, and germane cognitive load. *Educational Psychology Review, 22*(2), 123-138. DOI= 10.1007/s10648-010-9128-5

[28] Trafton, J. G., & Reiser, B. J. 1993. The contributions of studying examples and solving problems to skill acquisition. In *Proceedings of the Fifteenth Annual Conference of the Cognitive Science Society* (pp. 1017–1022). Boulder, CO.

[29] van Merriënboer, J., Clark, R., & de Croock, M. 2002. Blueprints for complex learning: The 4C/ID-model. *Educational Technology Research and Development, 50*(2), 39-61. DOI= 10.1.1.113.8484

Using Collaboration to Overcome Disparities in Java Experience

Colleen M. Lewis   Nathaniel Titterton   Michael Clancy

Computer Science Division, EECS
University of California, Berkeley
Berkeley, CA 94720

{colleenl, xtitter, clancy}@cs.berkeley.edu

ABSTRACT

The lower-division CS curriculum at the University of California, Berkeley includes a version of CS 2 that is intended to introduce students to Java as well as data structures and programming methodology. Some students in the course already have Java experience. In one course offering, students without previous Java experience received final grades that were 0.27 standard deviations below their peers who already had some Java experience (d=0.27, p<0.05). In a subsequent offering, the instructor adopted course policies and teaching strategies that made student collaboration more frequent in hopes that students without Java experience could learn from their peers with Java experience. In this highly-collaborative offering, there were no statistically significant differences in average final grades between students with and without Java experience (d=0.12, p>0.1). A smaller percentage of students dropped the highly-collaborative offering than the less-collaborative offering. This decrease in attrition was most notable for female students, from 37 percent to 5 percent.

Categories and Subject Descriptors

K.3 [Computers and Education]: General

Keywords

Collaboration, group work, pair programming, competition, gender, satisfaction, lab-centric instruction, CS 2, attrition, programming experience

1. INTRODUCTION

This research compared two offerings of CS2 to examine the extent to which course policies that require and support collaboration can provide opportunities for students without Java experience to learn from and catch up with students that already had Java experience.

This study presents a comparison between two offerings of a data structures and programming methodology course (CS2) at U.C. Berkeley. The first offering (N=166), in the spring of 2008, emphasized individual work on homework assignments and multi-week programming assignments (projects). The second offering (N=227), in the spring of 2010, emphasized group work: lab exercises were done with pair programming, all small

programming assignments could be completed with a partner, and all projects were completed in three- to four-person groups. We call this offering in 2010 the "highly-collaborative" offering. The first offering in 2008 where collaboration was less systematic will be referred to as the "less-collaborative" offering.

A direct comparison of learning outcomes between the two courses was not possible, because the two offerings did not use the same assessments. Instead we investigated our hypotheses using the relative performance of different groups across the two offerings and patterns of attrition between the two offerings.

In this study we compared the relative performance and attrition rates of three populations:
- students with and without Java experience,
- male and female students, and
- students who reported a preference for individual or collaborative work.

We found that differences in performance between students with and without Java experience were larger and were statistically significant in the less-collaborative offering. In the less-collaborative offering, students without previous Java experience received lower final grades than their peers who already knew some Java (d=0.27, p<0.05). In the highly-collaborative offering, there were no statistically significant differences in average final grades between students with and without Java experience (d=0.12, p>0.1). This suggests that prior experience with Java was less relevant to success in the highly-collaborative offering. We attribute this to the use of collaboration and believe it allowed students without Java experience to catch up with their peers with Java experience.

A smaller percentage of students dropped the highly-collaborative offering, but this drop in attrition was similar for students with and without Java experience.

Female students were overrepresented in the population of students without Java experience and on most assessments male students averaged a higher score than female students. However, there were no statistically significant differences in male and female students' final grades in either offering and differences in male and female students' scores were smaller in the highly-collaborative offering. The decrease in attrition was also most notable for female students, from 37 percent to 5 percent.

Although we expected differential benefits for students in the highly-collaborative offering who reported a preference for collaboration, we found no meaningful performance or attrition patterns for these populations between the two offerings.

2. PREVIOUS RESEARCH

There is a multitude of research investigating benefits of collaboration at both the college [4][13] and pre-college level [2]. For example, Springer, Stanne, and Donovan [13] report on a meta-analysis of studies of small-group learning in undergraduate STEM courses. They summarize studies of achievement, persistence, and attitudes with 3,417, 2,014, and 1,293 undergraduate students sampled in each. They report a positive effect of small-group learning on all three outcomes with an effect size of 0.51 on achievement, a reduction of attrition by 22%, and an effect size of 0.55 on students' attitudes. They report from their meta-analysis of these studies that "*all* average effect sizes are positive and only two… are not statistically significant."

This meta-analysis compared treatments with and without small-group learning, but both treatments in the current study include small-group learning opportunities. Springer *et al.* [13] call for development of a more unified theoretical base to explain the effects of small-group learning including studies that, like this one, compare various levels of small-group learning.

A collaborative environment may also support a less competitive or defensive community [5]. This may be particularly advantageous for female students, who research has found are less likely to prefer competitive environments [9]. Werner, Hanks, and McDowell [14] also discuss some of the benefits of pair programming for female students in dispelling beliefs that computer science is not collaborative and that it is socially isolating [11].

Pair programming has become a popular collaboration technique for research in computer science education and many studies have shown positive results (*e.g.*, [1][7][8][14]). Pair programming is the technique whereby two students work together, using a single computer. Typically the students take turns using the keyboard and mouse, but work collaboratively to create and debug programs.

It is hypothesized that the use of pair programming increases persistence among students who would have otherwise dropped the course, possibly through creating feelings of mutual dependence among collaborators [15]. The authors of [8] claim that a lack of significance between a pair-programming treatment and non-pair-programming control may be because pair programming allowed students to complete the course who would have otherwise dropped the course. They assume that these students contribute generally lower outcomes, lowering the average of the pair-programming condition.

A collaborative environment may also support a less competitive or defensive community [5]. This may be particularly advantageous for female students, who research has found are less likely to prefer competitive environments [9]. Werner, Hanks, and McDowell [14] also discuss some of the benefits of pair programming for female students in dispelling beliefs (described in [11]) that computer science is not collaborative and that it is socially isolating.

3. RESEARCH CONTEXT

This study considered two offerings of CS2 at U.C. Berkeley, one in the spring of 2008 and a second in the spring of 2010. The course is the second in the sequence for computer science majors at U. C. Berkeley and introduces Java, data structures, and programming methodology. Both offerings were taught by the same instructor, covered the same content, and used similar assessments; however, the second offering was modified to include additional opportunities for collaboration. The following sections describe the course format, the intervention, and differences that were independent of the intervention.

3.1 Course format: lab-centric instruction

Both offerings implemented an instructional approach called lab-centric instruction [10]. This approach trades lecture and discussion time for supervised closed-lab time. The format used in these offerings included one hour of lecture and six hours of scheduled lab sessions per week (two sessions of three hours each). Seven of the first eight lab sessions focused on Java constructs and programming techniques normally covered in an objects-early Java-based CS 1. Both offerings included three exams, three projects, three surveys, and numerous homework assignments and quizzes.

In lab-centric instruction, all lab activities are delivered online. They include conventional programming activities (*e.g.*, invention, modification, debugging, and testing) as well as collaborative activities and numerous embedded assessments. The lab instructor can monitor students' work as they proceed through the online activities, and can intervene immediately with targeted tutoring if a student is confused.

The lab-centric approach facilitates on- and off-line collaboration [10]. However, in the first offering considered in this research, off-line collaboration was not systematically encouraged.

3.2 Intervention: Increasing collaboration

The second offering of the course was intended to systematically increase opportunities for collaboration. Below, we discuss the elements of collaboration that were added in this highly-collaborative offering.

3.2.1.1 Group projects

There were three projects in both offerings of the course. In the less-collaborative offering, the first two projects were done individually and the third in a partnership of two. In contrast, students in the highly-collaborative offering worked in a static three- to four-person group on all projects.

In the highly-collaborative offering, project groups were formed in each lab section after six weeks of instruction. The teaching assistant (TA) was responsible for forming the groups, with the primary goal of creating heterogeneous groups, based upon scores on the first exam, and a secondary goal to avoid, when possible, isolating female students in a group with three male students. (These goals were recommended by [4] but other research [1] found that students from the lowest quartile were most successful if they pair-programmed with another student from the lowest quartile.)

TAs were charged with monitoring group dynamics. TAs had the opportunity to monitor group processing through observing group interactions during lab and meetings. The TAs met with each group before each project to discuss the team's technical and collaboration plans, which were determined by members of the group.

In the highly-collaborative offering, all group members confidentially rated their fellow group members' contribution to project. On projects 2 and 3, individuals that were identified by their teammates and TA as not contributing to the project received only a fraction of the team's project score. Similarly, a few individuals that contributed far beyond their share of the project received additional points above the score earned by their team's project. Ratings were combined into a percentage that was multiplied by the points for code and write-up to get the project grade, which are summarized in Table 1.

Table 1. Range of project score multipliers in the highly-collaborative offering determined by teammate and TA ratings

	Min %	*Max %*	*Median %*
Project 2	19%	110%	101%
Project 3	12%	110%	100.5%

The sum of all project scores, including these adjustments, is used as an outcome in the study and accounts for 20 percent of each student's final grade.

3.2.1.2 Pair programming
In lab-centric courses, students engage in on- and off-line whole class discussions or small group discussions with the TA. Although collaboration is a primary component of the lab-centric pedagogy [10], in the less-collaborative offering collaboration was typically *ad hoc*. The online lab curriculum frequently encouraged students to work with a partner, but it was relatively infrequent for students to engage in pair programming in the less-collaborative offering.

In the highly-collaborative offering, pair programming received significantly more emphasis. TAs were encouraged to help all students find a partner with whom to pair-program. After project groups were formed, students were encouraged to pair-program during lab with another member of their project group. If no other members of one's project group were present, a student could partner with another classmate or work individually.

3.2.1.3 Collaborative and individual assignments
In both offerings of CS2, lab exercises were not graded, but homework assignments were graded and accounted for 10 percent of a student's final grade. Homework assignments were completed individually in the less-collaborative offering, but could optionally be submitted with a partner in the highly-collaborative offering. Students submitting a homework assignment in partnership submitted only a single copy of the assignment and both partners received the same grade.

3.3 Differences independent of intervention
There were additional differences between the offerings that did not relate directly to collaboration.

The lab-centric curriculum evolves with each offering of the course. Between the less-collaborative offering and the highly-collaborative offering, changes were made to the curriculum by a second instructor. Additional modifications were made throughout the highly-collaborative offering. All modifications were intended to improve the clarity and quality of the lab curriculum and were not intended to modify the content of the course. We do not expect that these improvements to the curriculum differentially affect different populations in the course and as we are not directly comparing these two offerings this does not limit the findings of our study.

A characteristic of lab-centric instruction is that the majority of learning takes place in the weekly six hours of lab. Therefore TAs had the most direct contact and possibly the most influence on student learning. Both offerings were taught by the same

instructor, but none of the graduate and undergraduate teaching assistants (TAs) who led the lab sections were the same in the two offerings. Thus it was not possible to control for TAs between course offerings.

While the content covered in the course was the same between the two offerings, the individual assessment items differed to varying degrees. There were three exams in both offerings that were worth 12, 18, and 30 percent of students' grade. The exams given in each offering covered the same topics but had no overlapping questions. These exams were all completed individually.

In both offerings, individual quizzes were given in lab and were worth 10 percent of students' grade. To discourage academic dishonesty, students received all of the points for the quiz portion of their grade if they averaged 70 percent across these quizzes. Most students received full credit for the quiz portion of their grade and it is therefore not used as an outcome in our study.

There were three multi-week programming assignments (projects) in each offering. However, only the third project, the "Sliding Blocks Puzzle" from the Nifty Assignments archive [12], was used in both offerings. The first two projects in the less-collaborative offering (a number-line interval data type; simulation of a UNIX directory), where students worked individually, each required approximately 800 lines of code. In the highly-collaborative offering, where students worked in groups of 3 or 4, the first project (a variant of the "DNA Splicing" project in the Nifty Assignments archive [12]) required 350 lines of code and the second project (a proof checker for propositional logic) required 1700 lines of code.

4. METHODS
4.1 Outcome measurements
As outcome measurements we use students' scores on the three exams (exam 1, exam 2, and final), students' total adjusted scores on the projects, and students' course point total (grade). The exams between the two offerings were similar and were designed by an experienced instructor to test the same content.

There were no common assessments that could be used for direct measurements of differences in learning between the courses. Therefore we cannot simply compare students' performance on the exams between the two offerings. However, even if this were possible, other uncontrolled factors such as the refinement of the curriculum and the content of the projects may have affected total learning gains.

4.2 Survey data collection
The first lab's curriculum included a demographic survey. This survey was not anonymous and all questions on this survey were optional. Students' responses to the following three survey questions are featured in the analysis.

- "What is your gender?" Radio-button options: "male," "female," "I decline to state."

- "Do you prefer to work on large projects in a group or alone?" Radio-button options: "I prefer to work in a group," "I prefer to work alone." "I don't know/can't say."

- "In which of the following have you written programs?" Checkbox options: "C," "C++," "Java."

Some students did not answer all of the questions on the survey. The analysis of each research question includes the students with complete data related to that question.

4.3 Effect size

We calculated *Cohen's d* for each offering across each outcome, and will refer to this value as the *effect size*. The effect size is calculated by dividing the difference in population means by the standard deviation for the full sample (*e.g.* the standard deviation for exam 1 in the spring of 2008).

Consider a fictional case where the average score on exam 1 in one offering was 80 points for students with Java experience and 70 points for students without Java experience. The difference between these means is 10 points. If the standard deviation on this exam was 20 points, the effect size would be 10/20 or 0.5. This indicates that students with Java experience scored on average 0.5 standard deviations above students without Java experience.

4.4 Attrition

To test whether or not there were significant differences in attrition patterns across the two course offerings, we compared students who took the final exam with those that took the introductory survey, but did not take the final exam.

For these analyses, attrition serves as the outcome, and we predict it across offerings for each of the three survey questions discussed in section 4.2. Separate log-linear analyses were used for each of the survey questions, forming three 3-way contingency tables. For analyses of gender, for instance, the three-way table is formed with gender, offering, and attrition.

The sample for the attrition analyses is a superset of the sample used for the analyses for performance; the previous includes only students that did not drop the course.

5. RESEARCH QUESTIONS

5.1 Java experience

The majority of students took the Scheme-based CS1 course that introduced object-oriented programming, linked structures, and recursion. It is not expected that students know Java on entry, and approximately the first quarter of the course contains an introduction to loops, conditionals, objects, and arrays in Java (the content of a typical Java-based CS1).

However, some students have had experience with Java before the course, such as from high school. Java is the programming language tested on the Advanced Placement Computer Science (AP CS) Exam and is therefore frequently used in U.S. high schools. Although course time is dedicated to teaching Java, these students who already have experience with Java have an advantage because they are not simultaneously learning Java and the data structures content.

We hypothesized that students without prior Java experience might better be able to keep up with their peers in a collaborative environment where teammates with more advanced Java knowledge could support their learning of Java.

1. Do students with prior Java experience receive higher scores on exams, projects, and total course points?

2. Are differences in scores between students with and without prior Java experience reduced in the highly-collaborative offering?

3. Is attrition reduced among students without prior Java experience in the highly-collaborative offering?

5.2 Gender

A primary source of students' experience with Java before CS2 is a class to prepare for the AP CS exam. This exam has the lowest ratio of female to male test takers of any Advanced Placement exam [3]. In 2010, only 19.2 percent of AP CS test takers were female [3]. This pattern motivates a hypothesis that female students are less likely to have Java experience and as a result will be less successful in CS2.

1. Do male students (who are more likely to have taken AP CS) receive higher scores on exams, projects, and total course points? Are differences eliminated when controlling for prior Java experience?

2. Are differences in scores between male and female students reduced in the highly-collaborative offering?

3. Are patterns of attrition for male and female students different in the highly-collaborative offering?

5.3 Preference for group or individual work

We expected that students who prefer to work alone would perform better on individual assessments than students who preferred to work in a group. The inclusion of additional collaboration would likely favor students who reported a preference for group work and we were curious if this improved their relative scores or alternatively if it increased attrition among students who reported a preference for individual work.

1. Do students who report a preference for individual work score higher on exams?

2. Does the relationship between collaboration preference and exam scores change in the highly-collaborative offering?

3. Does the relationship between collaboration preference and attrition change in the highly-collaborative offering?

6. RESULTS

6.1 Java experience

Students with Java experience outperformed students without Java experience on all outcome measures in both offerings. We calculated the difference between these populations as the average score for students with Java experience minus the average score for students without Java experience. Therefore, this difference was a positive value for each assessment in each offering. Table 2 shows the number of students in each offering with and without Java experience.

Table 2. Sample size included in the analysis of students with and without Java experience. The number in parentheses is the percentage of students in that offering that selected that they did or did not have Java experience, respectively.

	Java experience	*No Java experience*
Less-collaborative offering	69 (43.9%)	88 (56.1%)
Highly-collaborative offering	121 (54.8%)	100 (45.2%)

Table 3 shows the effect size for each assessment in each offering. For each assessment in each offering, we also conducted a linear regression to see if the difference in scores between students' with and without Java experience was statistically significant. These effect sizes are also shown in Figure 1 with ** indicating p<0.01 and * indicating p<0.05.

Table 3. Differences between students' average performance for students with and without Java experience.

	Assessment	Effect size	Significance
Less-collaborative offering	Exam 1 Exam 2 Final Projects Grade	0.44 0.38 0.33 0.03 0.27	t=3.36, p < 0.001 t=2.79, p < 0.01 t=2.58 , p < 0.05 t=0.25 t=2.17, p < 0.05
Highly-collaborative offering	Exam 1 Exam 2 Final Projects Grade	0.28 0.14 0.13 0.09 0.12	t=2.74 ,p < 0.01 t=1.35 t=1.36 t=0.95 t=1.55

The largest differences between students with and without Java experience were seen on exam 1, which emphasized loops, conditionals, objects, arrays, and linked lists in Java. In both offerings, there was a statistically significant difference between the performance of students with and without Java experience on exam 1 (p<0.01). However, the difference between students with and without Java experience was greater in the less-collaborative offering where students without Java experience averaged scores that were 0.44 standard deviations below their peers as compared to 0.28 standard deviations in the highly-collaborative offering.

The differences in performance between students with and without Java experience were also reduced in the highly-collaborative offering on the other individual assessments. In the less-collaborative offering, the differences in performance between students with and without Java experience were statistically significant for exam 2, final exam, and course grade. On these same assessments, the differences in the highly-collaborative offering were smaller in magnitude and were not statistically significant (p>0.1). In the highly-collaborative offering, the difference between students with and without Java experience also decreased between each exam.

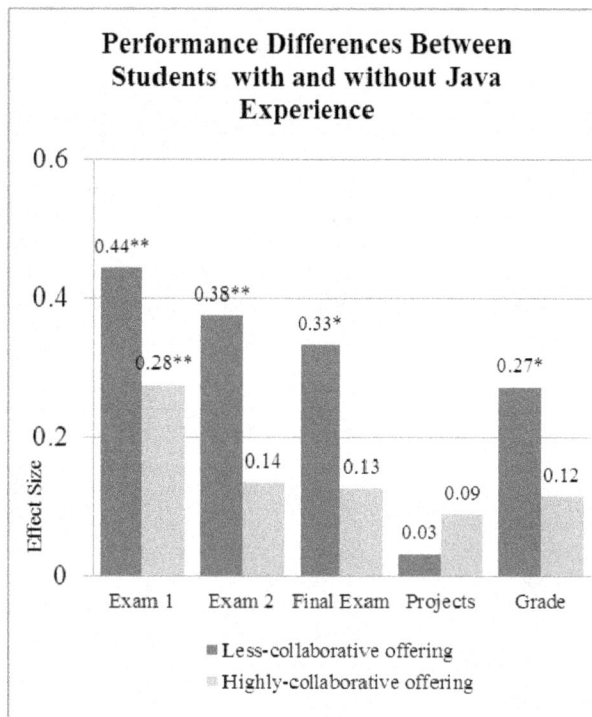

Figure 1. Effect size for difference between students with and without Java experience. ** indicates p<0.01 and * indicates p<0.05.

On the projects, the differences between students with and without Java experience were not statistically significant in either offering.

Table 4 shows the attrition rates for students with and without Java experience in each of the two offerings. Rates of attrition were lower in the highly-collaborative offering. The overall attrition rate in the less-collaborative offering was 18 percent and it was only 11 percent in the highly-collaborative offering.

We hypothesized that there would be a greater decrease in attrition between the offerings among students without Java experience, but observed the opposite: there was a greater decrease in the attrition among students who had Java experience. The interaction between offering and Java experience was not statistically significant (L^2=2.56, df=1, p>0.1), although the main effect of Java experience on attrition approached it (L^2=3.76, df=1, 0.1<p<0.05).

Table 4. Attrition rates for students with and without Java experience.

	Java Experience Attrition	No Java Experience Attrition
Less-collaborative offering	14/84 (17%)	20/108 (19%)
Highly-collaborative offering	8/129 (6%)	19/119 (16%)

6.2 Male and female students

Male students outperformed female students on all outcome measures except the projects outcome in the highly-collaborative offering. Across both offerings, a larger percentage of male students began the course with experience in Java. Fifty-five percent of male students had experience with Java while 43 percent of female students had experience with Java.

Table 5 shows the number of male and female students in each offering.

Table 5. Sample size included in the analysis of male and female students in each offering. The number in parentheses is the percentage of students in that offering that answered this question and selected male or female, respectively.

	Female	Male
Less-collaborative offering	11 (7.5%)	135 (92.5%)
Highly-collaborative offering	38 (18%)	171 (82%)

To calculate effect size we chose to represent the difference between male and female students' performance as average male performance minus average female performance. When male students had a higher average performance this difference would be positive, while when female students had a higher average performance this difference would be negative.

Table 6 shows the effect size for each assessment in each offering. For each assessment in each offering, we also conducted a linear regression to see if the difference between male and female student scores were statistically significant. These effect sizes are also shown in Figure 2 with ** indicating p<0.01 and * indicating p<0.05.

Table 6. Differences between male and female students' performance.

	Assessment	Effect size	Significance
Less-collaborative offering	Exam 1	0.34	t=−1.29
	Exam 2	0.33	t=−1.25
	Final	0.54	t=−2.12, p<0.05
	Projects	0.30	t=−1.32
	Grade	0.39	t=−1.62
Highly-collaborative offering	Exam 1	0.28	t=−2.10, p<0.05
	Exam 2	0.17	t=−1.30
	Final	0.24	t=−1.96
	Projects	−0.13	t=1.26
	Grade	0.10	t=1.02

Figure 2 shows a graphical representation of the differences in effect size between the less-collaborative and highly-collaborative offerings of the course, which shows a smaller difference in performance between male and female students in the highly-collaborative offering.

Of the ten significance tests that compared male and female students' performance, there were only two differences that were statistically significant. Female students in the less-collaborative offering had an average final score of 0.54 standard deviations below male students (p<0.5), which was still statistically significant when controlling for Java experience. Female students in the highly-collaborative offering had an average exam 1 score of 0.28 standard deviations below male students (p<0.5), but this

was not statistically significant when controlling for students' Java experience. Differences on the remaining outcomes were not statistically significant.

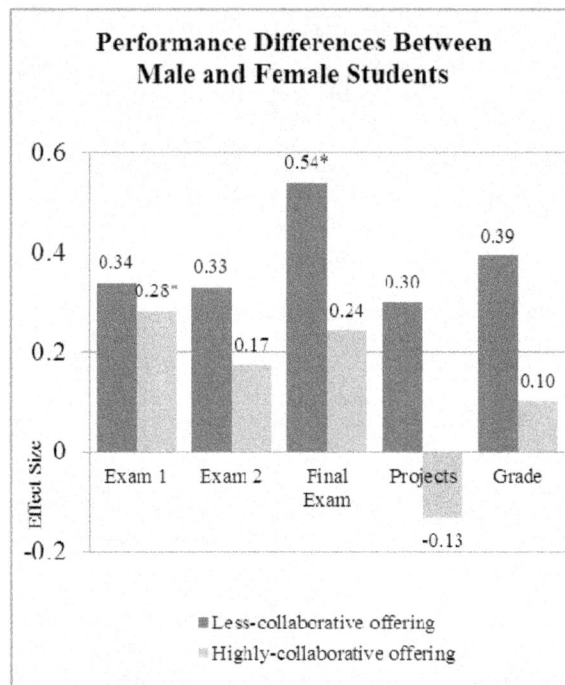

Figure 2. Effect size for difference between male and female students. ** indicates p<0.01 and * indicates p<0.05.

Table 7 shows the attrition rates for male and female students in each of the two offerings. A higher percentage of female students dropped the less-collaborative offering (37%) than dropped the highly-collaborative offering (5%). This difference approached significance, but was not statistically significant (L^2=3.45, df=1, 0.1>p>0.05). A lack of significance is not surprising given the small numbers of female students dropping the course.

Table 7. Attrition rates for male and female students.

	Female attrition	Male attrition
Less-collaborative offering	7/19 (37%)	20/155 (13%)
Highly-collaborative offering	2/40 (5%)	12/193 (7%)

6.3 Preference for group or individual work

There was not a clear pattern of elevated performance either for the students who reported a preference for group work or for the students who reported a preference for individual work. Table 8 shows the total size of each population in each offering.

Table 8. Sample size included in the analysis of students that prefer group and individual work. The number in parentheses is the percentage of students in that offering that answered this question and selected group or individual work, respectively.

	Prefer group work	*Prefer individual work*
Less-collaborative offering	72 (60%)	48 (40%)
Highly-collaborative offering	107 (68%)	50 (32%)

The only statistically significant difference between these populations was on exam 2 in the highly-collaborative offering where students who reported a preference for individual work scored higher than students who reported a preference for group work (d=0.37, p<0.05). All other p-values were above 0.2 and given the high number of tests performed in this analysis (ten), it is not appropriate to draw conclusions from a single test that shows significance. On projects, students who preferred group work outperformed students who preferred individual work, but only in the highly-collaborative offering were all projects completed in a group.

Given the lack of statistical significance found in differences between collaboration preference and exam scores, we omit the tabular and graphical representation of these data.

Table 9 shows attrition rates for students that reported that they prefer individual versus group work. In both offerings, more students dropped the course that reported a preference for individual work. There is no significant interaction between preference and offering on attrition, and no significant main effect of preference on attrition.

Table 9. Attrition rates for students reported that they prefer individual versus group work.

	Attrition when preferring group work	*Attrition when preferring individual work*
Less-collaborative offering	10/82 (12%)	10/58 (17%)
Highly-collaborative offering	6/113 (5%)	6/56 (11%)

7. DISCUSSION

7.1 Java Experience
We expected that students that did not have Java experience before taking CS2 would be at a disadvantage as they needed to learn both Java and the data structures content. On all assessments in both offerings, students with Java experience outperformed students without Java experience.

In both offerings, the largest difference between these groups appeared on exam 1. This exam was taken by students early in the semester after five weeks and covered loops, conditionals, objects, arrays, and linked lists in Java. We expected differences in Java experience would be pronounced on exam 1.

The differences in performance on exams between students with and without Java experience were greatest in the less-collaborative offering. These differences were statistically significant in the less-collaborative offering, but in the highly-collaborative offering only the differences on exam 1 were statistically significant.

The differences in scores on projects were not statistically significant in either the less-collaborative or highly-collaborative offering. It is reasonable to assume that the projects were less difficult for students fluent in Java, but regardless of students' comfort with Java it might have been possible to successfully complete the assigned task of each project.

In the highly-collaborative offering there were lower attrition rates, but there was not a significant change in the pattern of attrition for students with and without Java experience.

These data show that the increased collaboration may have allowed students without Java experience to catch up with their peers with Java experience. While students without Java experience had not caught up with their peers before the first exam, in the highly-collaborative offering differences in their later exam scores and final grades in the class were not statistically significant (p>0.1).

Educational research has documented a number of benefits of collaboration (see [13] for a review). However, if the highly-collaborative offering had a differentially negative effect on students with Java experience we could have observed the same patterns described above. It is possible that students that knew Java learned less because they spent time supporting students with less knowledge of Java. Research has shown a consistently positive benefit only for low-achievers working in heterogeneous groups and not medium- or high-achievers [2], but the collaboration tasks, such as explaining technical details to peers, may improve students' technical communication skills, which is perceived by the instructor as highly valuable. We did not have common assessments across the two offerings and therefore cannot investigate the hypothesis that the highly-collaborative offering had a differentially negative effect on students with Java experience.

7.2 Gender
There were notable differences between the attrition rates for female students between the less-collaborative and highly-collaborative offerings. In the less-collaborative offering 37 percent of female students dropped the course while in the highly-collaborative offering only 5 percent of female students dropped the course. There was also a reduction in attrition among male students from 13 percent in the less-collaborative offering to seven percent in the highly-collaborative offering. Given the small number of students that dropped the class these patterns were not statistically significant, but we believe warrant future research.

Our assumption is that students who drop the course are more likely to be struggling in the course. We expected that the higher attrition among female students in the less-collaborative offering would improve the relative performance of the female students in the course. Therefore in the highly-collaborative offering, when only 5 percent of female students dropped the course, we expected that the average performance of female students would drop in comparison to their male peers. This would predict a relative drop in performance for female students in the highly-collaborative offering, which was not observed.

Male students scored higher on all outcomes excluding the projects in the highly-collaborative offering. However, only two of these ten outcomes were statistically significant and only one was statistically significant when controlling for students' Java experience. We make no claims regarding the performance of male and female students or differential effects for female and male students resulting from collaboration, but remind the reader that the highly-collaborative offering may have included female students that would otherwise have dropped the course.

7.3 Preference for group or individual work
In both offerings, students who preferred collaboration performed slightly better on projects than students who reported a preference for individual work. However, there were no other noteworthy patterns in differences between these populations and the majority of the results were not statistically significant. In future work it may be possible to better triangulate students' collaboration preferences to investigate differential benefits.

8. CONCLUSION
In this paper we compared outcomes in two offerings of CS2. The offerings were taught by the same instructor and used similar assignments, but they differed in the level of collaboration. In the first offering, collaboration was mainly *ad hoc*, while in the second, the instructor adopted course policies and teaching strategies to make collaboration more frequent.

The effect of Java experience on a student's final grade differed between these offerings: in the less-collaborative offering, students with Java experience received final grades that were 0.27 standard deviations above their peers ($p<0.05$), while in the highly-collaborative offering there was no statistically significant difference. We believe that collaboration supported students without Java experience in catching up with their peers who knew Java. This would explain the pattern observed in the highly-collaborative offering that the difference between students with and without Java experience decreased between each exam.

Female students had lower rates of attrition and higher scores in the highly-collaborative offering, but these patterns were not statistically significant. We also did not find statistically significant patterns of performance or attrition for students who reported a preference for collaborative or individual work.

Although the course does not require Java as a prerequisite, students with Java experience performed better than their peers without Java on all outcome measures. We hope that these results encourage instructors to evaluate the accessibility of their courses for students that have only the experience specified in the official prerequisites for their courses.

We hope that this study will encourage other researchers to investigate the effect of collaboration on attrition patterns and will contribute to instructors' motivation to adopt collaborative techniques in their courses. The collaboration techniques in this study are not the only options available and research has shown similar benefits for alternatives to pair programming [6].

9. ACKNOWLEDGMENTS
Work described in this paper was supported by NSF grant DUE-1044106. Any opinions, findings, and conclusions or recommendations expressed in this paper are those of the authors and do not necessarily reflect the views of the National Science Foundation.

10. REFERENCES
[1] Braught, G., MacCormick, J., & Wahls, T. (2010). The benefits of pairing by ability. *Proceedings of the 41st ACM Technical Symposium on Computer Science Education,* 249–253.

[2] Cohen, E. (1994). Restructuring the classroom: Conditions for productive small groups. *Review of Educational Research. 64(1),* 1.

[3] College Board (2011). Retrieved April 1, 2012, from http://www.collegeboard.org

[4] Felder, R. M. and Brent, R. (1994). Cooperative learning in technical courses: procedures, pitfalls, and payoffs. ERIC Document Reproduction Service Report ED 377038.

[5] Garvin-Doxas, K. & Barker, L. J. (2004). Communication in computer science classrooms: Understanding defensive climates as a means of creating supportive behaviors. *Journal of Educational Research in Computing, 4(1)*, 1-18.

[6] Lewis, C. M. (2011). Is pair programming more effective than other forms of collaboration for young students? *Computer Science Education. 21(2).* 105-134

[7] McDowell, C., Werner, C., Bullock, H. E., Fernald, J. (2006). Pair programming improves student retention, confidence, and program quality. *Communications of the ACM.* 49, 90-95.

[8] Nagappan, N., Williams, L., Ferzil, M., Wiebe, E., Yang, K., Miller, C., & Balik, S. (2003) Improving the CS1 experience with pair programming. *Proceedings of the 41st ACM Technical Symposium on Computer Science Education,* 359-362.

[9] Niederle, M. & Vesterlund, L. (2007). Do women shy away from competition? Do men compete too much? *The Quarterly Journal of Economics. 122(3).* 1067-1107.

[10] Titterton, N., Lewis, C. M., & Clancy, M. (2010). Benefits of lab-centric instruction. *Computer Science Education* (Ed. Y. Ben-David Kolikant) *20(2).* 79-102. DOI: 10.1080/08993408.2010.486256

[11] Margolis, J., & Fisher, A. (2003). *Unlocking the clubhouse: Women in computing.* Cambridge, MA: The MIT Press.

[12] Parlante, N. Nifty Assignments. http://nifty.stanford.edu/

[13] Springer, L., Stanne, M. E., & Donovan, S. S. (1999). Effects of small-group learning on undergraduates in science, mathematics, engineering, and technology: A meta-analysis. *Review of Educational Research. 69(1).* 21-51.

[14] Werner, L. L, Hanks, B., & McDowell, C. (2005) Pair programming helps female computer science students. *Journal on Educational Resources in Computing. 4(1)* Article 3.

[15] Williams, L. & Kessler, R. R. (2000). The effects of "pair-pressure" and "pair-learning" on software engineering education, *Proceedings of the 13th Conference on Software Engineering Education & Training,* 59-65.

Improving Student Learning Outcomes with Pair Programming

Alex Radermacher, Gursimran Walia, and Richard Rummelt
Dept. of Computer Science, North Dakota State University
Fargo, ND
alex.radermacher@ndsu.edu, gursimran.walia@ndsu.edu,
richard.rummelt@ndsu.edu

ABSTRACT

This paper presents ongoing research into the use of mental model consistency (MMC) to produce more effective student programming pairs. Previous studies have found that pair programming is highly useful in improving students' enjoyment of programming as well as improving the retention rates of students enrolled in computer science programs. However, existing research provides little support that pair programming actually benefits student learning in terms of improved test or exam scores. This research focuses on evaluating the use of MMC-based student pairs to increase student performance in introductory programming courses. Empirical studies were conducted over two semesters to determine if pairings based on different levels of MMC produced more effective pairs. The results from this study indicate that MMC is a good predictor of success in a course when using pair programming and that students who migrate towards greater consistency tend to do better than those who do not migrate. However, the current results do not support that pairs based on any combination of mental models are more effective than others. Still, the authors of this paper feel that MMC is a valuable method and that if combined with other techniques to produce more compatible pairs, may yet produce substantial results. Other potential uses for MCC are also discussed.

Categories and Subject Descriptors

K.3.2 [**Computer and Information Science Education**]: Computer Science Education; D.2.9 [**Management**]: Programming Teams

General Terms

measurement, performance, experimentation, human factors

Keywords

pair programming, mental model consistency, compatibility

1. INTRODUCTION

Pair programming (PP) is a programming technique where two individuals work as a team to accomplish a programming task [1]. It has been shown to have numerous benefits when used in introductory computer science courses including increasing the retention rate of computer science students [6], improving enjoyment of programming [21], and producing more meaningful interactions between students and instructors [16]. However, many researchers have also concluded that pair programming does little to improve student learning and usually only in limited ways such as better grades on programming exercises [23] and generally does not extend to exams [15]. There are some notable exceptions such as a recent study by Braught, et al. that found pair programming improved scores on programming tests for students in the bottom quartile of the class [4].

Additionally, much recent research into pair programming has been targeted at improving pair compatibility [7, 12, 19, 20, 22]. Several researchers have investigated the effectiveness of using Myres Briggs personality types to form pairs [12, 22]. Generally, the results have not been overwhelmingly positive, but there was support to indicate that pairing students with dissimilarities in their perceiving-judging dichotomy produced more compatible pairs. Other research has indicated that pairing students of roughly similar abilities levels produces more compatible pairs [7]. Sfetsos, et al. evaluated the effects of personality type on pair programming and found that pairs with dissimilar temperaments resulted in pairs that produced higher quality work [19]. A similar study by Thomas, et al. found that pairing individuals based on confidence level also resulted in pairs that produced higher quality work [20].

This paper presents ongoing research into the use of mental model consistency (MMC) to form pairs. The original intent of this research was to evaluate pairing methods that lead to improved performance on exams and other non-programming assignments, rather than only improvements on programming exercises. Although not originally used in conjunction with pair programming, Dehnadi and other researchers found that the MMC test instrument was generally successful at predicting which students were more likely to succeed in an introductory programming course, even if they had no previous exposure to programming [3, 9, 8]. Because mental model consistency was easily testable and had a strong correlation with exam scores in some previous studies, it was considered as a possible pairing method.

This research presents the results of two empirical studies that were conducted to test the effectiveness of arranging programming pairs based on mental model consistency (as indicated by Dehnadi's test instrument) and their effect on student learning. At this point, there are several positive results to indicate that mental model consistency continues to be a good predictor of success, even when pair programming is used, but currently there is not evidence to support one particular pair arrangement being more effective than any other. However, it is believed that by incorporating other methods that have been shown to produce more compatible pairs, pairing based on mental model consistency may still lead to improvements in student learning.

2. BACKGROUND

Although this paper focuses on pair programming, the background section will focus almost entirely on mental models as it is necessary to have a better understanding of them and how they have been used in computer science education.

A mental model is a term used by cognitive scientists to describe an individual's cognitive representation of some system or other knowledge, which is used by individuals in order to reason [11]. When presented with information, an individual will begin to construct a mental model used to help explain or process that information. Once an individual has developed a mental model, it will be used to form assumptions which can be tested against reality and fed back into the development of their mental model. For example, an individual observing a busy intersection may develop a mental model that can be used to explain the flow of traffic through that intersection. Once that mental model has been developed, it can be used to make predictions about how traffic will proceed through the intersection and further adjustments to that mental model can be made as the observed predictions are either validated or fail to come true.

In the same fashion, novice programmers construct mental models that allow them to understand programming concepts such as variable assignment [13] or recursion [18]. When dealing with a variable assignment statement (e.g. x = y;) it is possible for a novice programmer to believe that assignment occurs left to right, right to left, or that the variables are swapped, among other possibilities. In this way it is possible that students who are new to programming will construct non-viable mental models that represented a flawed or incomplete understanding of a concept [10, 13].

The main focus of this research centers around research conducted by Dehnadi, et al. that focused on evaluating students' mental model consistency (i.e. the tendency to use the same mental model when solving a large number of similar problems) for variable assignment [9, 8]. Dehnadi devolved a simple test instrument consisting of twelve questions related to variable assignment. These questions had multiple choice answers corresponding to different possible mental models for variable assignment. The major findings from their study were that those students who exhibited greater mental model consistency (even if they did not use the correct mental model) tended to perform better in the course than those students who had inconsistently used several different approaches [9, 8]. Another important results was that the test was effective even though none of the students in the course had any previous programming experience.

After some initial success with the method, several follow-up studies were conducted and reported on by Bornat, et al. [3]. In several of these studies, the predictive ability of the mental model consistency test was not nearly as accurate as in the original study conducted by Dehnadi and Bornat [9]. The main factors contributing to those results were a tendency for the worst performing students to drop the course before the end, or for many students in the course to have previously taken a programming course. In the first case, this likely skewed the results, and in the second, it is likely that the test does not hold any predictive value for students who already understand variable assignment due to the nature of how the test is designed. For these reasons, it is likely that Dehnadi's method is still useful as a predictor of student success in a programming course.

Mental models have also been used to evaluate interactions and performance in groups and teams. Mathieu, et al. evaluated the difference between task and team mental models and determined that team members must have a shared understanding of the tasks that they will complete as well as a similar view of how the team should operate in order for that team to perform well [14]. Cannon-Bowers, et al. examined team decision making and how it was affected by shared mental models between team members [5].

3. STUDY DESIGN

The purpose of this research is to evaluate the effects of pair programming on student mental model migration and to determine if pair programming improves mental model migration and whether pairing students based on MMC is more effective than other pairing methods.

To answer these questions, two controlled empirical studies, using introductory computer programming students at NDSU, were carefully planned and executed. The experiments used in these studies followed a control-group design in which subjects were given a mental model test related to variable assignment at the beginning of the semester to evaluate their mental model consistency [9]. Afterwards, subjects were placed into different groups based on the section of the course in which they were enrolled:

A) A group where subjects completed all programming assignments using pair programming.

B) A group where subjects completed two programming assignments during the first half of the semester using pair programming and worked individually thereafter.

C) A group where subjects completed programming assignments individually during the first half of the semester and used pair programming on two programming assignments during the second half of the semester.

Subjects in groups A and B were then randomly placed into one of three groups based on their mental model consistency:

I-I A homogeneous group where both members exhibited mental model inconsistency.

C-C A homogeneous group where both members exhibited mental model consistency.

I-C A heterogeneous group where one member exhibited mental model consistency and the other member exhibited mental model inconsistency.

Next, subjects in groups A and B were randomly assigned a partner within that group. Subjects in group C were paired based on their performance in the course up to that point as this creates more effective pairs [4]. Subjects then completed programming assignments during the first four weeks either individually or in pairs based on their group. During and after this time, subjects were re-tested using the same mental-model test in order to evaluate changes in the consistency and viability of their mental model. The subjects were then evaluated on the laboratory assignments and the exams over the course of the semester. The details of the study are provided in the following sections.

3.1 Research Questions

The following research questions were investigated in these studies:

Research Question 1: Is mental model consistency a good predictor of performance when using pair programming?

Research Question 2: Does the use of pair programming influence mental model migration among students?

Research Question 3: Are certain mental mode consistency-based pairing arrangements more effective at migrating students towards greater mental model consistency than other consistency-based pairing arrangements?

3.2 Independent and Dependent Variables

The following independent variables were manipulated:

Mental Model Consistency: The tendency for a subject to use the same mental model to solve similar problems.

Pair Programming Usage: Whether or not and to what extent the subject used pair programming.

Pair Arrangement: The consistency-based pair group type, if any, that the subject was placed into.

Researchers measured the following dependent variables:

Letter Grade: The final letter grade (i.e. 'A', 'B', etc.) received by the subject.

Total Grade: The final grade received by the subject, including the grades on exams and programming exercises.

Exam Grades: The grades received on midterm and final exams.

Mental Model Migration: Whether or not a subject migrated towards a more consistent mental model.

3.3 Study Subjects and Course Assignments

Study 1: The participating subjects in this study were 83 students enrolled in CS1 – Introductory Computer Programming at NDSU in the fall 2010 semester. The subjects in this study worked in pairs and completed programming exercises related to variable assignment, evaluating conditions, string manipulation, looping, and other object oriented programming concepts during the semester.

Study 2: The participating subjects in this study were 99 students enrolled in the CS1 – Introductory Computer Programming at NDSU in the fall 2011 semester. Subjects in two sections of the course completed two programming exercises in pairs, whereas subjects in the remaining section of the course completed programming exercises individually. The assignments covered similar concepts to those used in the first study.

3.4 Study Procedure

Step 1: *Test Subjects for Mental Model Consistency*: In both studies on the first day of class, subjects were surveyed about their programming experience and were given the test devised by Dehnadi, et al. to evaluate their mental model consistency [9]. In the first study, 11 subjects (and 11 subjects in the second study) who had previously taken a college-level programming course were placed in a separate group (and excluded from analysis) because previous results suggest that the test is not effective when given to subjects with previous programming experience [3]. Table 1 lists the different levels of mental model consistency and the number of subjects belonging to each level for both studies based on the results of the initial MMC test. Subjects who used the correct mental model for all or almost all test questions were placed in the *Consistent Correct (CC)* group. Subjects who used an incorrect mental model on all or almost all test questions were placed in the *Consistent Incorrect (CI)* group. Subjects who used several different mental models on the test questions were placed in the *Inconsistent (I)* group. Subjects who left their answer sheet blank were treated as inconsistent for the purpose of group assignment.

Table 1: MMC Categories and Subject Distribution

Category	Study 1	Study 2
Consistent Correct (CC)	13	8
Consistent Incorrect (CI)	27	22
Inconsistent (I)	31	50

Step 2: *Pair Subjects Based on Mental Model Consistency*: Subjects in both studies were randomly paired within one of three groups. The first group included pairs where both subjects had an inconsistent mental model (I-I). The second group included pairs where the subjects had a consistent mental model (C-C). The third group included pairs where one of the subjects had a consistent mental model while the other subject had an inconsistent mental model (I-C).

Step 3: *Subjects Work on Programming Exercises*: In the first study, all subjects worked on programming exercises in their assigned pairs for the duration of the course. In the second study, two sections completed two programming exercises in pairs during the first half of the semester, whereas the remaining section completed two programming exercises during the second half the semester. This was done both to provide a control group, and to ensure that all subjects had the opportunity to use pair programming in the class.

Step 4: *Re-test subjects for Mental Model Consistency*: In both studies subjects were re-tested after approximately four weeks with the same test as in Step 1 to determine whether or not they had migrated towards greater mental model consistency. In the second study, subjects were given one additional re-test after a lecture period on variable assignment, but before they began working in pairs on a variable assignment programming exercise. This was done in order to help isolate whether or not mental model migration occurred due to the use of pair programming.

Step 5: *Evaluate Changes in Mental Model Consistency*: Subjects and pair groups were evaluated to determine if certain pairing arrangements resulted in a higher tendency to migrate subject towards mental model consistency. Two types of mental model migrations analyzed in this research include: the migration from an inconsistent to a consistent mental model, and the migration from a consistently incorrect mental model to consistently correct mental model.

These two migrations are analyzed as results from the original study indicated that students who migrated between these groups tended to perform better than those students who did not undergo migration between these groups [9].

Step 6: *Evaluate Performance of Subjects*: Subjects completed several programming exercises as well as a mid-term and final exam. Analysis was performed on the grade subjects received on their exam scores as well as the overall course grade. The letter grade that subjects received is also used for analysis in order to control for differences in programming exercises, and exams across the two studies.

3.5 Data Collection and Evaluation Criteria

Subject performances on lab assignments and tests (including mid-term and final examinations) were analyzed to study the effects of the MMC-based pairings on the subjects' performance and on the changes in their MMC.

4. RESULTS

This section reports the results from both studies along with statistical analysis. Statistical analysis was conducted using the Minitab statistical software tool. An alpha value of .05 is used for statistical significant in all cases. A subject's total grade was removed from analysis if the subject did not complete either the midterm or final exam in order to avoid skewing the results. However, the results of any completed test were included in the analysis even if the other test was not taken or they later dropped the class.

Table 2: Grades Across Mental Model Groups

Initial Consistency Test (Week 0)				
Category	Mid-term Exam		Total Grade	
	Study 1	Study 2	Study 1	Study 2
CC	70.8	75.5	77.4	79.84
CI	58.3	66.5	71.9	67.6
I	54.3	65.6	70.0	69.2

Final Consistency Test (Week 4)				
Category	Final Exam		Total Grade	
	Study 1	Study 2	Study 1	Study 2
CC	61.1	66.3	76.3	76.3
CI	48.9	64.1	69.1	72.4
I	35.7	47.8	66.6	58.3

Table 2 shows the mean mid-term exam scores and mean total course grade for subjects based on the results of the initial MMC test given at the beginning of the course. A two-sample t-test was performed to determine if the results from these groups different by a statistically significant amount. In the first study, subjects in the CC group performed significantly better on the mid-term exam (p = .005) but not on the final exam (p = .074) or overall course grade (p = .158). In the second study, subjects in the CC group had a significantly higher course grade (p = .021), but the differences between the scores on the mid-term and final exams were not quite statistically significant (p = .067 and p = .051, respectively). The CI group did not perform significantly better than the inconsistent group in either study based for the mid-term exam (p = .133 and p = .408) or overall course grade (p = .380). Similarly, the results from the second study were also not statistically significant. When analyzing the results using ANOVA, results from the first study were significant for both the mid-term and final tests (p = .002 and p= .030) but not for the total grade (p = .159). None of the results for the second study were significant.

When evaluating the differences in performance for the categories based on the results of the final MMC test taken at the beginning of the forth week of the course, subjects in the first study from the CC group performed significantly better than subjects in the CI group on both the mid-term exam (p = .001) and total course grade (p = .005). In the second study, only the results for the mid-term exam (p = .009) were statistically significant. When evaluating differences between the CI group and the I group, only the results for the final exam (p = .020) were statistically significant, but results for the second study were significant for both the final exam (p = .020) and total course grade (p = .046). ANOVA analysis showed that the results were significant for the mid-term exam, final exam, and total grade in both the first study (p <.000, p = .002, and p = .006) and the second study (p = .006, p = .039, and p = .016)

Table 3: Subject Letter Grades Across Both Studies

Category	C or Better	Below C
Consistent Correct (CC)	56	8
Consistent Incorrect (CI)	26	12
Inconsistent (I)	5	8

To further evaluate the effects of mental model consistency on grades, the subjects were also evaluated based on the letter grade that they received. Table 3 shows the number of subjects from both studies that passed the course with the grade of C or higher and those who received lower than a C based on the results of the final MMC test. This value was chosen as students majoring in computer science must pass the course with at least a C in order to receive credit for the course. The results of a chi-square test indicate that there is a significant difference between the CC and CI groups (p = .019), but that the different between the CI and I groups is not quite statistically significant (p = .056).

The effects of migrating between different mental model consistency categories between exams was also analyzed. In the first study, subjects who migrated from the I group to the C group performed better than those who did not. In

Table 4: Grades Based on Mental Model Migration

	Study 1			
	I to CI or CC		CI to CC	
	Migration	None	Migration	None
Mid-term	57.3	49.6	64.8	54.3
Final Exam	53.3	39.0	61.7	48.9
Course Grade	71.5	66.9	77.0	69.4
	Study 2			
	I to CI or CC		CI to CC	
	Migration	None	Migration	None
Mid-term	68.6	55.8	75.8	62.5
Final Exam	64.2	37.6	72.7	53.2
Course Grade	71.6	54.8	61.0	65.0

the first study, those who migrated performed better on the final exam (p = .003), but not on the mid-term (p = .075) or in terms of overall course grade (p = .102). In the second study, those who migrated performed better on the mid-term, final exam, and overall course grade (p = .013, p = .001, and p = .018, respectively).

Similarly, performance differences were evaluated between those who migrated from the CI category to the CC category. In the first study, subjects who migrated performed better on the mid-term (p = .041) and overall course grade (p = .022), but the results for the final exam (p = .058) were not quite statistically significant. In the second study, only the results for the mid-term (p = .008) were significant.

In the second study, subjects in one section of the course used pair programming during the second half of the semester. This enabled a comparison between those subjects who used pair programming in the first half of the semester. Table 5 shows results indicating the number of subjects who migrated from initially having mental model inconsistency to having consistency. Because subjects in the second study were given a second MMC test after learning about variable assignment, but prior to beginning to work in pairs, it was possible to determine if a shift in MMC was due to the use of pair programming, or due to other causes such as class lectures. Subjects in the first study did not take an intermediate test, so it is not possible to determine if the results were due to the use of pair programming or not.

Table 5: Migration Based on the Use of PP

Category	Migration	No Migration
Study 1 (Used PP)	22	5
Study 2 (Used PP)	12	2
Study 2 (No PP)	6	2

Due to the low number of data points, it was not possible to perform statistical analysis to determine if the use of pair programming was more effective at migrating subjects exhibiting mental model inconsistency towards consistency. Similarly, it was not possible to analyze whether any particular pair arrangement was more effective than others. Additionally, because subjects in the first study were not tested for MMC after learning about variable assignment, it is not possible to conclude to what extent the use of pair programming influenced any migration in MMC.

5. DISCUSSION

Based on the results from both studies, there is support to indicate that performance differs based on mental model consistency. This result indicates that the answer to the first research question (Is mental model consistency a good predictor of performance when using pair programming?) should be yes. However, at this point it is not possible to provide solid answers to the other two research questions. The second research question (Does the use of pair programming influence mental model migration among students?) has not been answered, although the results in 5 indicate that it may be a possibility. Further experimentation using control groups will be necessary. Similarly, due to a low number of data points, the third research question (Are certain mental mode consistency-based pairing arrangements more effective at migrating students towards greater men-

tal model consistency than other consistency-based pairing arrangements?) cannot be answered.

Moving forward, the authors of this paper feel that it may be necessary to incorporate other pairing strategies in order to maximize the effectiveness of mental model consistency based pairing. In the studies presented in this paper, subjects were not surveyed to determine if they felt as though their pair was effective or if they worked well with their partner. Because migration to greater consistency has been shown to correspond with an increase in subject performance (and not just for programming exercises), the next logical step is to find pairing strategies that serve as catalysts for such migrations. After looking at other studies related to group performance in computer science, the authors of this paper have a few potential leads.

The first is recent work done by Bender, et al. who examined the effects of pairing groups based on social sensitivity [2]. The researchers of that study found that groups with higher average social sensitivity scores performed better on a series of different assignments for a computer science ethics course. However, none of these assignments involved programming, but it is possible that pairs with higher social sensitivity will be more effective at communicating and transferring knowledge, leading to improved migration rates.

Another approach involves research published by Salleh, et al. who conducted a study investigating the effectiveness of pairing based on similarities in the Five-Factor personality model [17]. The results from their study indicate that pairing students with a high ratings in the openness to experience factor was correlated with improved performance on both the mid-term and final exams. This suggests that pairing two subjects with high openness to experience factors may also facilitate MMC migration in one of the students.

Even if mental model consistency does not prove to be useful in arranging pairs, Dehnadi's test may still be useful to educators. First, since it does appear to have a strong connection to success, it may help educators to identify students who are likely to struggle with the course long before they have completed several programming assignments or taken any tests. This would allow educators to recommend additional tutoring to certain students or take other measures to ensure that they are more likely to have a positive educational experience. Additionally, it may be useful in determining if a programming pair is ineffective. If one member of a pair possesses consistency and the other does not, it may indicate that the pair is not communicating effectively or that one member is doing the majority of the work. This would allow course instructors to rearrange the pair to ensure that both students are contributing and benefiting.

6. THREATS TO VALIDITY

In both studies, attendance was neither mandatory or recorded for the course, so it is possible whether or not subjected attended lectures may have had an effect on the tendency for subjects to migrate mental models that was not controlled for. Additionally, subjects who exhibited mental model inconsistency had a greater tendency to drop the course or did not take the final exam. This may skew the results, weaken the statistical analysis, or make it outright impossible. Also, in the first study, subjects were not re-tested immediately after learning about variable assignment. This was corrected in the second study by giving a second MMC test before subjects began working in pairs.

7. CONCLUSION AND FUTURE WORK

Mental model consistency has been shown to be a reasonable predictor of student success in an introductory programming course when pair programming is used. However, additional research is necessary in order to make the most use out of this method. There is sufficient evidence to suggest that future studies may produce valuable results, and there are several approaches that can be used in conjunction with Dehnadi's method to produce better results.

In addition to this, there are other avenues of mental model consistency that still remain to be explored such as producing consistency tests for other areas of introductory programming (e.g. iteration). Additionally, it would be worthwhile to investigate if a general mental model consistency test could be developed and applied to subjects who have previously taken a computer science course.

8. REFERENCES

[1] K. Beck. *Extereme Programming Explained: Embrace Change.* Addison-Wesley, Reading, Massachusetts, 2000.

[2] L. Bender, G. Walia, K. Kambhampaty, K. E. Nygard, and T. E. Nygard. Social sensitivity and classroom team projects: an empirical investigation. In *Proceedings of the 43rd ACM technical symposium on Computer Science Education*, SIGCSE '12, pages 403–408, New York, NY, USA, 2012. ACM.

[3] R. Bornat, S. Dehnadi, and Simon. Mental models, consistency and programming aptitude. In *Proceedings of the tenth conference on Australasian computing education - Volume 78*, ACE '08, pages 53–61, Darlinghurst, Australia, Australia, 2008. Australian Computer Society, Inc.

[4] G. Braught, J. MacCormick, and T. Wahls. The benefits of pairing by ability. In *SIGCSE '10: Proceedings of the 41st ACM technical symposium on Computer science education*, pages 249–253, New York, NY, USA, 2010. ACM.

[5] J. A. Cannon-Bowers, E. Salas, and S. Converse. Shared mental models in expert team decision making. In J. J. Castellan, editor, *Current issues in individual and group decision making*, pages 221–246+. Erlbaum, 1993.

[6] J. C. Carver, L. Henderson, L. He, J. Hodges, and D. Reese. Increased retention of early computer science and software engineering students using pair programming. In *IEEE-CS Conference on Software Engineering Education and Training (CSEE&T '07)*, pages 115–122. IEEE Computer Society, 2007.

[7] E. A. Chaparro, A. Yuksel, P. Romero, and S. Bryant. Factors affecting the perceived effectiveness of pair programming in higher education. In *Psychology of Programming Interest Group 17th Workshop*, pages 5–18, 2005.

[8] S. Dehnadi. Testing programming aptitude. In *Proceedings of the Psychology of Programming Interest Group 18th Annual Workshop*, pages 22–37, 2006.

[9] S. Dehnadi and R. Bornat. The camel has two humps. http://www.cs.mdx.ac.uk/research/PhDArea/saeed/, 2006.

[10] T. Götschi, I. Sanders, and V. Galpin. Mental models of recursion. *SIGCSE Bull.*, 35(1):346–350, Jan. 2003.

[11] P. Johnson-Laird. *Mental Models.* Cambridge University Press, Cambridge, MA, USA, 1983.

[12] N. Katira, L. Williams, E. Wiebe, C. Miller, S. Balik, and E. Gehringer. On understanding compatibility of student pair programmers. *SIGCSE Bull.*, 36(1):7–11, Mar. 2004.

[13] L. Ma, J. Ferguson, M. Roper, and M. Wood. Investigating the viability of mental models held by novice programmers. In *Proceedings of the 38th SIGCSE technical symposium on Computer science education*, SIGCSE '07, pages 499–503, New York, NY, USA, 2007. ACM.

[14] J. E. Mathieu, T. S. Heffner, G. F. Goodwin, E. Salas, and J. A. Cannon-Bowers. The influence of shared mental models on team process and performance. *Journal of Applied Psychology*, 83:273–283, 2000.

[15] C. McDowell, L. Werner, H. Bullock, and J. Fernald. The effects of pair-programming on performance in an introductory programming course. *SIGCSE Bull.*, 34(1):38–42, 2002.

[16] A. Radermacher and G. Walia. Investigating student-instructor interactions when using pair programming: An empirical study. In *IEEE-CS Conference on Software Engineering Education and Training (CSEE&T '11)*, CSEET '11, pages 41–50. IEEE Computer Society, 2011.

[17] N. Salleh, E. Mendes, and J. Grundy. The effects of openness to experience on pair programming in a higher education context. In *IEEE-CS Conference on Software Engineering Education and Training (CSEE&T '11)*, pages 149–158, may 2011.

[18] T. L. Scholtz and I. Sanders. Mental models of recursion: investigating students' understanding of recursion. In *Proceedings of the fifteenth annual conference on Innovation and technology in computer science education*, ITiCSE '10, pages 103–107, New York, NY, USA, 2010. ACM.

[19] P. Sfetsos, I. Stamelos, L. Angelis, and I. Deligiannis. An experimental investigation of personality types impact on pair effectiveness in pair programming. *Empirical Softw. Engg.*, 14(2):187–226, Apr. 2009.

[20] L. Thomas, M. Ratcliffe, and A. Robertson. Code warriors and code-a-phobes: a study in attitude and pair programming. *SIGCSE Bull.*, 35(1):363–367, Jan. 2003.

[21] L. Williams, R. R. Kessler, W. Cunningham, and R. Jeffries. Strengthening the case for pair programming. *IEEE Softw.*, 17(4):19–25, 2000.

[22] L. Williams, L. Layman, J. Osborne, and N. Katira. Examining the compatibility of student pair programmers. In *AGILE '06: Proceedings of the conference on AGILE 2006*, pages 411–420. IEEE Computer Society, 2006.

[23] L. Williams, E. Wiebe, K. Yang, M. Ferzli, and C. Miller. In support of pair programming in the introductory computer science course. In *ACM Conference on Object-Oriented Programming, Systems, Languages, and Applications (OOPSLA 2002*, pages 197–212, 2002.

Using Peer Review to Teach Software Testing

Joanna Smith
University of Texas at Austin
joanna.smith@utexas.edu

Joe Tessler
University of Texas at Austin
joe.r.tessler@utexas.edu

Elliot Kramer
University of Texas at Austin
ejameskramer@gmail.com

Calvin Lin
University of Texas at Austin
lin@cs.utexas.edu

ABSTRACT

This paper explains how peer review can be used to teach software testing, an important skill that is typically not carefully taught in most programming courses. The goals of such peer review are (1) to frame testing as a fun and competitive activity, (2) to allow students to learn from each other, (3) to demonstrate the importance of testing by uncovering latent bugs in the students' code, and (4) to provide a mechanism for evaluating testing skills. This paper explains how we added peer review to an honors data structure course without significantly reducing its heavy programming load. We evaluate our intervention by summarizing surveys of student attitudes taken throughout the course.

Categories and Subject Descriptors

D.2 [**Software Engineering**]: Testing and Debugging

General Terms

Human Factors

Keywords

Peer Review, Education, Software Testing

1. INTRODUCTION

Software testing is a crucial component of the software lifecycle. A 2002 study by the National Institute of Standards and Technology reports that software bugs cost the US economy an estimated $59.5 billion annually and that more than a third of this cost could be eliminated by improved software testing [17]. Bill Gates agrees with the importance of software testing, saying, "[At Microsoft,] we have as many testers as we have developers. And testers spend all their time testing, and developers spend half their time testing [8]."

Unfortunately, there are several reasons why it is difficult to teach software testing. First, most students are not enthusiastic about testing [4]. Second, in most programming courses, testing is not an important aspect of a student's grade, perhaps because testing is a complex process that can be time-consuming to grade. Third, there is a self-fulfilling aspect to the view that testing is unimportant: Students who do not value testing are likely to produce poor test cases, so they do not learn that testing can effectively reveal bugs. Finally, testing is difficult to teach through lectures or through mechanical procedures [12]; instead, "the challenge ... is to develop group activities that can foster insight—a level of abstract understanding that can apply from situation to situation—rather than emphasizing detailed procedural understanding [12]."

The situation is further complicated if we wish to teach white box testing of moderately large and complex programs. As opposed to black box testing, which focuses on a program's externally observable behavior, white box testing adds richness and complexity; for example, it allows testers to create custom test harnesses that stress specific internal interfaces.

Peer review, or peer testing, in which students attempt to break code written by their peers, has the potential to address all of these problems. Because it is competitive, it can be fun and exciting. Because the peer reviews are graded, they can be weighted heavily in the student's grade. Because peer testing often reveals bugs in a student's program, it can illustrate the benefits of good software testing. Finally, because the peer reviews describe the reviewer's testing methodology and because students receive multiple peer reviews, the process exposes students to a variety of testing ideas, allowing students to learn from their peers.

In this paper, we describe a novel approach of incorporating peer testing into a lower-division programming course, where the testing includes white box testing of moderately complex software. We also explain how we address a number of issues that arise from such an activity, including issues of fairness, anonymity, academic integrity, and the increased workload.

More specifically, we add a peer testing component to two of seven programming assignments in a freshman honors data structures course. For these two assignments, students work in pairs, first to produce their solution and then to review four other solutions. The reviews are double-blind, and the goal of each review is not simply to identify bugs, but to provide insights as to the possible causes of the bugs and to explain the reviewer's testing methodology. Finally, each team submits a peer testing report that summarizes what they've learned from the process and that evaluates the quality of the four reviews—and their underlying test methodologies—that they received.

We find that we are able to add these peer testing activities without reducing the heavy programming workload. We also find, through surveys taken throughout the course, that students enjoy peer testing, that students find peer testing valuable, and that peer testing increases their perceived ability to test software.

This paper is organized as follows. Section 2 places our work in the context of prior work, and Section 3 describes the setting for our experiment. Section 4 describes our peer testing intervention, and we evaluate the results in Section 5.

2. RELATED WORK

Peer review has been used in many teaching situations and has been found to have many benefits: It improves writing skills [14], develops critical thinking skills [5, 16], improves self-efficacy [2], and can provide detailed and careful feedback [16, 15]. In the context of software development, peer review has been used to critically comment on code quality [4] and to evaluate homework solutions using a web-based system [13]. Clark describes how interactive peer testing can be used to effectively review code in a third year capstone course: Peer teams are given 35 minutes to conduct both usability testing and code review, followed by 5 minutes to discuss their findings with one of the code's authors [4]. By contrast, our study explores the use of anonymous and more involved peer review, as students are given three days to write reviews and to describe their test methodology.

Peer review bears some similarities to collaborative learning methods, in the sense that both attempt to engage students to participate actively in the educational process. For example, in JavaFest [11], groups of students compete to design the optimal solution for a provided programming problem. With respect to software testing, most prior work on collaborative learning focuses on test input generation, which applies to black box testing but does not extend to richer forms of white box testing. For example, Carrington [3] describes exercises in which students generate test inputs for various software specifications, and Goldwasser [9] describes an approach in which students competitively submit test cases to break each others' code. However, Goldwasser's approach focuses on black-box testing methods, where students explore testing through small-scale programming exercises, such as merging two sorted linked lists. By contrast, our approach allows students to explore both white-box and black-box testing.

Testing has also been taught in the context of test-driven development, an entire software development methodology in which test cases are written first [6, 7]. Our work instead teaches software testing without asking students to adopt any specific software development methodology.

Finally, testing has been the subject of entire courses. Harrison [10] describes an upper-division software testing course that emphasizes two disparate testing roles—that of the developer and that of the tester. Thus, students serve as developers of one project and testers of a different project. In their role as testers, student perform peer review, but the emphasis of the course is on the importance of distinguishing between these two testing roles.

Not competent	13
Probably not competent	13
Probably competent	17
Competent	8

Table 2: Pre-course Survey: "Are you competent at software testing?"

3. BACKGROUND

The setting for our intervention is the Fall 2011 offering of CS314H, an honors data structure course at The University of Texas at Austin. The students in this course are predominantly freshmen honors students who are talented and highly motivated. Nevertheless, the instructor, who has taught this course for ten years, has been largely dissatisfied with his students' ability to acquire software testing skills, despite his efforts to stress the importance of testing, to introduce various testing ideas during lectures, to mandate that students explain how they have tested their programs, and to devote time in discussion sections (led by the teaching assistant) to share ideas about how the programs could be tested.

This course has a heavy programming workload. There are seven Java programming assignments. The assignments start small but quickly grow in both scope and complexity. Table 1 summarizes these assignments, showing those for which they should do Pair Programming, and showing the alloted time for each assignment.[1] (The alloted time for Assignment 7 includes the Thanksgiving holiday.)

The Fall 2011 instance of this course had 51 students, 1 TA, and 1 undergraduate grader who worked 20 hours per week. On the first day of class, students were given an anonymous survey which asked various questions about their background. Included in the survey was one open-ended question, "Are you competent at software testing?" We classified their responses into four categories, and the results are shown in Table 2; we conclude that students enter the course largely unsure of whether they are competent software testers.

4. OUR SOLUTION

Our solution has three main goals. First, we want to make testing fun and competitive so that students will put effort into testing. Second, we want students to learn from each other, so that they can see how others approach the same problem, perhaps with a greater degree of creativity than they have. And third, we wish to illustrate the tangible benefits of good software testing by uncovering latent bugs in their code.

4.1 The Process

Before describing our peer review process, we first specify five requirements for our solution.

1. The process should be double-blind, which removes bias and allows reviewers to be honest in their analysis and feedback without the fear of offending a friend.

---

[1] Pair programming is a software development methodology in which two students share a computer to collaborate on all aspects of the assignment.

Assignment	Name	Description	Pairs?	Alloted Time
1	Image Manipulation	Manipulate digital images	No	7 days
2	Random Writer	Use Markov process to generate text that is similar to some corpus of text	No	9 days
3	Critters	Write interpreter for simulate creatures	Yes	14 days
4	Tetris	Implement Tetris game	Yes	14 days
5	Boggle	Implement Boggle game	No	14 days
6	Treaps	Implement Treaps data structure	Yes	9 days
7	Web Crawler	Implement web crawler and search engine	No	21 days

Table 1: The seven programming assignments in previous versions of CS314H.

2. The process should encourage students to take the peer review process seriously, which will increase the chance that students will learn from each other.

3. The process should be fair in its assignment of reviewers to reviewees. Each team should get to review a representative cross section of the class's solutions, as opposed to, for example, only testing the best solutions and finding very few bugs. Similarly, each team should see reviews from a representative cross section of the teams, so that they are more likely to receive some reviews that use good test methodologies.

4. The process should preserve academic integrity by not allowing students to read or copy each other's code.

5. The process should allow rich test methodologies beyond black-box testing, including the ability to do unit testing and to create custom test harnesses.

Our peer review process can now be described in terms of three deadlines that the student teams must meet.

1. At the first deadline, teams submit their solutions to the assignment. The solutions are then anonymized and obfuscated. Four reviewers are then assigned to each team's solution.

2. At the second deadline, teams submit their peer reviews, which include a description of their test methodology and of their findings. These reviews are then anonymized and distributed to the reviewees.

3. At the third deadline, teams submit their Peer Testing Reports, which describes what they learned in this process and also evaluates the peer reviews that they have received. At this point, teams may also submit revised solutions that fix bugs that have been pointed out by peer reviews.

We can now provide details about how our process meets our stated requirements.

To implement a double-blind review process, we use a one-way mapping from a student's ID to a number. These numbers serve as identifiers, ensuring that the students are not aware of who they are interacting with in the process. By giving reviewers obfuscated byte code, reviewers are shielded from any identifying comments or tell-tale stylistic quirks.

To encourage students to think about the quality of the various peer reviews and to encourage students to write good reviews, each reviewee grades each review. The instructional staff also grades each review. In sum, the peer review represents 50% of the grade for Assignments 5 and 6.

To ensure a fair assignment of reviewers, we first place the teams into quartiles based on each team's performance thus far in the course, and we then randomly assign reviewers from each quartile so that each team's solution is reviewed by one team from each quartile. In our case, our 26 teams did not divide 4 evenly, so our process could only guarantee that each team was reviewed by teams from at least three different quartiles.

We preserve academic integrity and anonymity by obfuscating the code before compiling it into bytecode. Only the bytecode is distributed, and if a student does reverse the compilation, the code is extremely difficult to read and easily identifiable as obfuscated code. We employ a Java obfuscator called Smokescreen [1] for this purpose.

We encourage rich testing methodologies by giving students access to byte code with well defined interfaces, which allows them to create test harnesses and to perform unit testing on individual methods of well-defined interfaces. In addition, because the students are creating peer reviews of the same projects that they themselves are asked to complete, the same test harness that they use for peer testing can be directly applied to their own code.

4.2 The Reviews

Each review has two components. The first is an evaluation of the reviewee's code for bugs, and the second is a description of the testing methodology. The first component is further subdivided into two categories, namely, a summary of the most important findings and detailed comments that describe specific test cases and bugs. The second component helps the students learn from good reviewers. It also helps the reviewees understand the bugs that were identified in the peer reviews, and it helps the reviewee in evaluating the peer reviews.

By having the students grade each other's reviews, we hope to to make them accountable to their peers. We also hope to encourage their natural competitiveness, as teams will want to find more bugs than the other reviewers of the same code.

4.3 The Choice of Programming Assignments

Assuming that peer testing is not incorporated into every programming assignment, there are two factors to consider in deciding where it should be incorporated: (1) the timing of the assignment within the semester and (2) the suitability of the assignment for peer review.

The issue of timing is not clear cut. On the one hand, if

peer testing is introduced early in the course, it may provide lasting benefits for the remainder of the course. On the other hand, if too many students have poor testing skills, then peer review may not be fruitful, so it may be useful to delay peer review until students have learned some basic concepts, terminology, and techniques as applied to some early, simpler programming assignments.

The issue of suitability is more clear cut. An ideal candidate for peer review is a programming assignment with a well-defined interface with plenty of freedom in the implementation. The well-defined interface ensures that students will be able to access important methods, allowing for deeper testing beyond black-box testing of the overall program. The freedom of implementation encourages a variety of development and testing strategies.

4.4 Challenges

Our peer testing activities introduces two challenges with respect to workload.

First, peer testing increases the student workload. They are being asked to do more testing, more writing, and more critical thinking. In particular, the students need to write the actual peer reviews, along with two additional reports for each peer-tested assignment.

Second, peer testing as we have defined it introduces strict deadlines, where each tight deadline builds upon the previous one. The process fails if large numbers of students do not meet their deadlines. For example, if a team does not submit their solution on time, their peers may not have sufficient time to conduct their reviews. Worse, if a team submits code that does not compile or is badly dysfunctional, then their peers cannot meaningfully test it. Similar issues arise from missing the second deadline.

4.5 Implementation Details

Choice of Assignments.

We add peer testing to Assignments 5 and 6, which occur late in the course. We do not introduce peer review earlier because we first use lectures, discussion sections, and the early assignments to teach the students various testing concepts, such as black-box testing, white-box testing, unit testing, and the notion of a test harness, as they apply these concepts to simpler programs.

In addition, both Assignment 5 and 6 are ideal for peer testing because they give students great freedom in implementing well-defined interfaces and they provide testing challenges. In particular, the solutions to Assignment 5 typically make heavy use of recursion, which is a confusing topic for many students. Assignment 6 requires students to use randomization to produce balanced trees, and the random behavior introduces testing challenges.

We choose to not add peer testing to Assignment 7 because it is designed to evaluate all of the skills that each student has acquired over the course of the semester. Thus, this assignment is completed individually. In addition, this assignment is the most challenging and open-ended of the assignments, which makes it a poor candidate for peer testing, because the behavior and interfaces are not well defined.

Pair Programming.

We allow students to work in pairs on these assignments both because it reduces the increased workload and because it is often helpful to be able to discuss ideas with a partner, particularly when developing relatively new skills.

Changes to the Schedule.

To preserve the number of programming assignments in our course, we add peer testing to Assignment 5 while retaining the 14 days that are allocated for this assignment. (See Figure 1.) Thus, the additional five days of peer testing shrinks the amount of time that students have to complete the assignment. To mitigate the effects of this shrinkage, we allow students to work in pairs, whereas students in previous classes worked individually (see Table 1).

Because Assignment 6 is one that has always been done in pairs, we simply add 5 days for peer testing to the end of the original schedule. As a result, the deadlines for Assignment 6 are identical to those for Assignment 5, ie, there are 9 days until the first deadline, then 3 days until the second deadline, and then 2 days for the final deadline. To preserve the overall course schedule, we remove a five day gap that formerly existed between in the schedule between Assignments 4 and 5.

Submission Logistics.

The entire peer testing process is made easy by the existence of Google Docs—specifically Google Forms. With basic scripting, we easily map the students to a number and distribute the bytecode via email. All reviews are then submitted online via forms generated by another script that automatically fills in the proper reviewer and reviewee ID number. The student grades for a review are submitted in a different form with the same scripting algorithm. By using Google Forms, the instructor can easily evaluate all reviews and grades in a single spreadsheet.

5. EVALUATION

5.1 Methodology

There are several possible methods of evaluating our peer review intervention. One is to split the class in half, so that one group acts as a control group against the peer testing group. We discard this approach as being potentially unfair, since one group could gain an advantage that could impact their final grade. Another option is to split the class in half and alternate their use of peer testing, but this approach runs the risk of a spillover effect, where those who do peer review earlier may perform better on the next assignment even without peer review. Another method is to use two classes with similar populations where one is the control, but in our case, it was difficult to find two such courses.

We choose instead to introduce peer review to one entire class at the same time and to focus on observing changes in student attitudes over the course of the semester. To track the students' attitudes and self-perceptions, we conduct surveys at the end of each assignment. The questions remain constant throughout the semester, and are brief, simple statements with which students can Strongly Disagree, Disagree, Agree, or Strongly Agree. Each survey also includes an open text box that allows students to provide arbitrary comments.

5.2 Survey Results

We observe that early in the semester, students believe that they are good testers (See Figure 2). These results

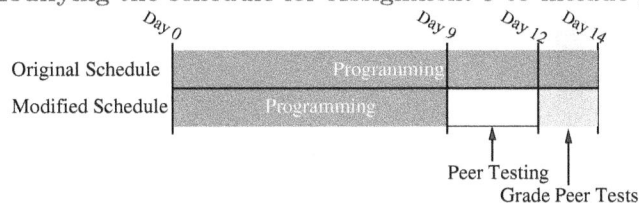

Figure 1: Modifying the schedule for Assignment 5 to include peer testing.

differ from the pre-course survey, where students express skepticism in their testing abilities, and we conjecture that because the surveys are taken immediately after students submit their programs, these confident responses refer to the students' perceived ability to test the just-submitted assignments.

As the semester progresses, we see that student confidence drops. Here, we believe that as the assignments become more difficult and as students receive low testing scores on previous assignments, students begin to understand the limits of their abilities.

Beginning with Assignment 4, testing confidence begins to rise, and confidence rises further after Assignments 5 and 6, which incorporate peer testing. These changes in attitude suggest that peer testing has been successful.

Over the course of the semester, we see similar trends for the question "I like testing software" (see Figure 3).

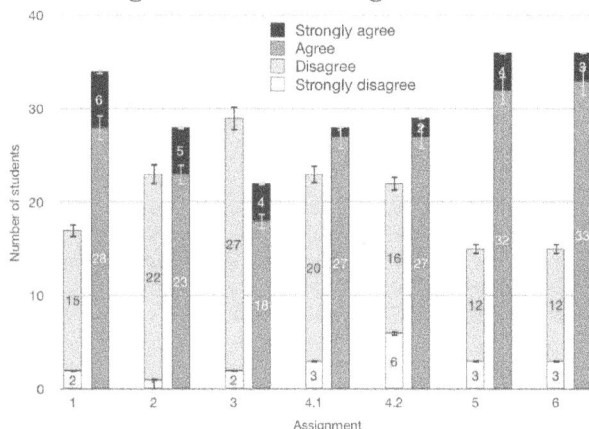

Figure 2: I'm good at testing software.

Error bars are represented by the vertical lines overlapping each bar.

We also observe that the students both like and believe that they learned from peer review, as is shown in Figures 4 and 5. These results show that the students believe that peer review is an effective use of their time and that it engages them in the process of learning to test software.

One common comment is: "It was fun to try to break other people's code." Another common comment is something akin to "they definitely helped us catch some good bugs that we missed." On the negative side, students often complain that peer review would be easier if each reviewee's assumptions were clearly stated, and if output was standardized.

Finally, several students indicate that they wanted to do peer review for all of their remaining assignments.

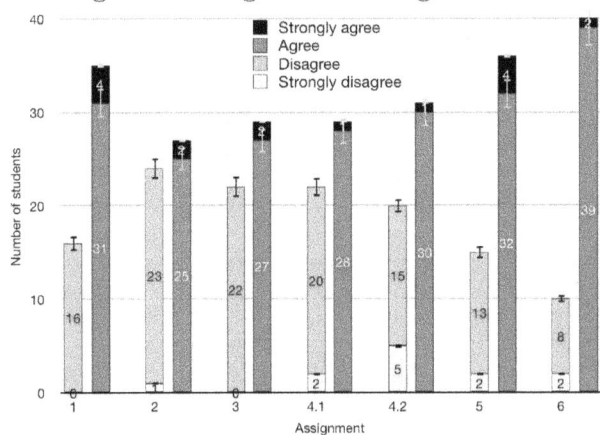

Figure 3: I like testing software.

Error bars are represented by the vertical lines overlapping each bar.

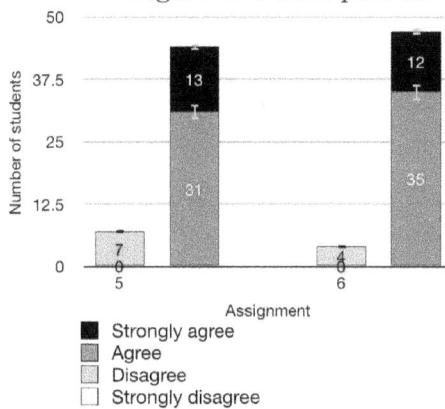

Figure 4: I liked peer review.

Error bars are represented by the vertical lines overlapping each bar.

5.3 Other Results

With a decade of experience, we believe that the heavy workload in this course causes some students to miss deadlines, particularly late in the semester.[2] Hence, the need to adhere to strict deadlines for our peer review activities was an early concern. However, in this case study, only two teams submitted late solutions for Assignment 5. In one case, the delay was minimal, a matter of hours, and they were able to fully participate in the remaining peer review. In the other case, the team was a day late and received no

_____
[2]Unfortunately, we do not have the detailed historical records needed to definitively support this claim.

Figure 5: I learned something through peer review.

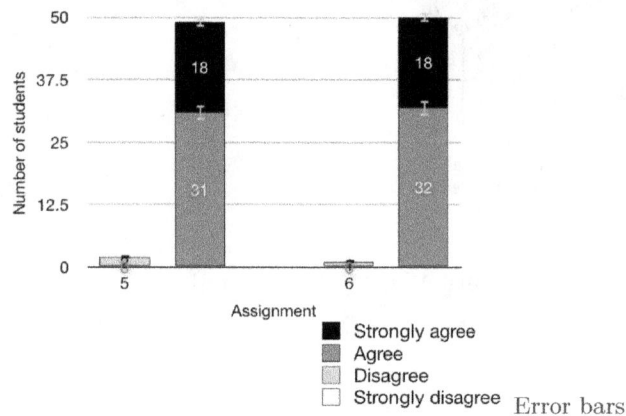

Error bars are represented by the vertical lines overlapping each bar.

peer review. Remarkably, for Assignment 6, all deadlines were met. For Assignment 7, which did not include peer review, one student submitted an assignment one day late, while another submitted an assignment two days late. We conjecture that the power of peer pressure helps students meet deadlines, a point that has been observed elsewhere [4], but our main observation here is that we were able add both extra work and additional deadlines without creating additional missed deadlines.

6. CONCLUSIONS

Software testing is a subject that can be difficult to teach, perhaps because it relies heavily on experiential learning; at the same time, because it is an activity that most students do not enjoy, students tend to expend minimal effort on testing. In this paper, we have described our experience in incorporating peer testing into a course with a heavy programming component and a tight schedule. We were able to do so without removing or significantly simplifying any of the programming assignments. Our results show that despite the extra work, the vast majority of students enjoyed peer testing and found it worthwhile, and many students expressed an interest in doing additional peer testing. The larger point, of course, is that students are often willing to do more work if the extra effort comes in the form of enjoyable activities that show tangible benefits.

Peer testing as we have described it imposes additional burdens on the student. In our experience with honors students, the students welcomed these additional burdens, but it would be interesting to see if peer testing would achieve similar results with a more general student population.

With our encouraging results, we would like to see further study in the use of peer testing in introductory programming classes, ideally studies that use a properly selected control group. Another avenue for future work is to explore the conjecture that with improved ability to test software, students produce software with fewer defects.

7. ACKNOWLEDGMENTS

We thank George Veletsianos and Bill Press for their valuable comments on this work. This work funded in part by NSF grant CNS-1138506.

8. REFERENCES

[1] Smokescreen. *http://www.leesw.com/smokescreen/*.

[2] K. Anewalt. Using peer review as a vehicle for communication skill development an active learning. *J. Comput. Small Coll.*, 21(2):148–155, 2005.

[3] D. Carrington. Teaching software testing. In *ACSE '97, the 2nd Australasian Conference on Computer Science Education*, pages 59–64. ACE, 1997.

[4] N. Clark. Peer testing in software engineering projects. In *ACE '04, the 6th Australasian Conf. on Computing Education*, volume 30, pages 41–48. ACE, 2004.

[5] R. Davies and T. Berrow. An evaluation of the use of computer peer review for developing higher-level skills. *Computers in Education*, 30(1):111, 1998.

[6] C. Desai, D. Janzen, and K. Savage. A survey of evidence for test-driven development in academia. *ACM SIGCSE Bulletin*, 40(2):97–101, June 2008.

[7] S. H. Edwards. Teaching software testing: Automatic grading meets test-first coding. In *OOPSLA '03, the 18th annual ACM SIGPLAN conference on Object-oriented Programming, Systems, Languages, and Applications*, pages 318–319. SPLASH, 2003.

[8] J. Foley and C. Murphy. Q&A: Bill Gates On Trustworthy Computing. *Information Week*, May 2002.

[9] M. H. Goldwasser. A gimmick to integrate software testing through curriculum. In *SIGCSE '02, the 33rd SIGCSE Technical Symposium on Computer Science Education*, pages 271–275. CSE, 2002.

[10] N. B. Harrison. Teaching software testing from two viewpoints. *Journal of Computing Sciences in Colleges*, 26(2):55–62, December 2010.

[11] M. Hauswirth, D. Zaparanuks, A. Malekpour, and M. Keikha. The javafest: A collaborative learning technique for java programming courses. In *PPPJ '08, the 6th Int'l. Symposium on Principles and Practice of Programming in Java*, pages 3–12. PPPJ, 2008.

[12] C. Kaner and S. Padmanabhan. Practice and transfer of learning in the teaching of software testing. In *CSEET '07, the 20th Conf. on Software Engineering Education & Training*, pages 157–166, 2007.

[13] E. Z.-F. Liu, S. S. J. Lin, C.-H. Chiu, and S.-M. Yuan. Web-based peer review: The learner as both adapter and reviewer. *IEEE Transactions on Education*, 44(3):246–251, August 2001.

[14] J. Liu, D. T. Pysarchik, and W. W. Taylor. Peer review in the classroom. *Bioscience*, 52(9):824–829, September 2002.

[15] E. Silva and D. Moriera. Webcom: a tool to use peer review to improve student interaction. *J. Educ. Resour. Comput.*, 3(1):1–14, 2003.

[16] W. J. Wolfe. Online student peer reviews. In *Proceedings of the 5th Conference on Information Technology Education*. ACM Press, 2004.

[17] W. E. Wong. Teaching software testing: Experiences, lessons learned and the path forward. In *24th Conf. on Software Engineering Education and Training (CSEE&T), 2011*, pages 530–534. IEEE, 2011.

Is Iteration Really Easier to Learn than Recursion for CS1 Students?

Claudio Mirolo

Dept. of Mathematics and Computer Science – University of Udine
via delle Scienze, 206 – 33100 Udine, Italy
claudio.mirolo@uniud.it

ABSTRACT

There is general consensus that recursion is difficult to learn, which may be meant to imply that novice students are more at ease with iteration — probably a widespread perception of students themselves. However, three years of investigation in a context where recursion is introduced earlier than iteration, as well as *control* experiments for a standard *imperative-first* introduction to programming, have provided no evidence that students make more progress with iteration than they do with recursion. More specifically, by means of a pair of questionnaires devised for this purpose, two research questions have been addressed. First, do the students who learned recursion before iteration actually exhibit a stronger ability to deal with the latter? Second, do the students of the *imperative-first* path master iteration better than those of the *recursion-earlier* path?

Categories and Subject Descriptors

K.3.2 [**Computers and Education**]: Computer and Information Science Education — computer science education

General Terms: Human Factors

Keywords:
programming learning, recursion, iteration, CS1, novices.

1. INTRODUCTION

It is accepted as common sense that students face difficulties to understand recursion [11, 13, 15, 22, 27]. This may seem to imply that they achieve better results with iterative programs. One purpose of educational research is to subject to critical scrutiny similar beliefs, that are someway cursorily "taken for granted". However, there have been only few attempts to compare learners' ability to deal with recursion and with iteration. Among these, Bhuiyan et al. [2] point out the influence of a "looping" mental model on the understanding of recursive computations. Kessler & Anderson [16], and in a weaker sense Wiedenbeck [27], infer from their analysis

that iteration should be taught before recursion in order to facilitate the development of a computation model. Turbak et al. [25] have instead observed an improvement of students' performance in the exams after changing the course structure and teaching loops as a special case of *tail-recursion*. Moreover, according to Benander et al. [1], recursive code does not seem to impair program comprehension.

Here we will discuss the results of a thorough departmental investigation addressing two related research questions. The first one arises in the context of a CS1 course based on a *functional-first* approach [6], where the imperative paradigm is introduced only after a great deal of work with recursive procedures. In this respect we will try to understand if the students following such a path are nonetheless more at ease with iteration. Were this not the case, however, it may still be due to the course structure; perhaps, as suggested in [16], teaching recursion earlier may hinder the learning of iteration. This motivates our interest in a second question: whether the students who attend a standard *imperative-first* introduction to programming master iteration better than those of the *recursion-earlier* path.

Before proceeding, we have to be more specific about what we mean by "learning iteration/recursion". To some extent it can be helpful to address students' grasp of the computation model as in [10, 16, 21], but relying only on this information would be misleading because it tells us little about planning and problem-solving abilities, which are our major concern. More broadly, students' achievements can be analyzed under a variety of *learning dimensions*, such as:

i. Learning the formalization medium (language *notation*);
ii. Understanding the underlying computation model (mechanics of the *notional machine*);
iii. Reasoning and establishing relations with the problem domain (basic problem solving skills);
iv. Interpreting and exploiting the program *structures* (basic organizational skills);
v. Conceiving and building abstractions (higher-level organizational skills, management of complexity).

The competence areas (i, ii, iv) were recognized in [9], to account for some difficulties of novice programmers. The prominence of higher-level abilities like (iii, v) is pointed up, e.g., in [3, 11, 19, 22], whereas in [5, 23] it is suggested that much emphasis should be placed on design issues relating the program structure (iv) to the pursued goals (iii). Other useful frameworks to analyze the learning outcomes have been proposed by Linn & Dalbey [17], who identify three broad levels of cognitive accomplishments: language features, design skills, and general problem-solving skills; by

Permission to make digital or hard copies of all or part of this work for personal or classroom use is granted without fee provided that copies are not made or distributed for profit or commercial advantage and that copies bear this notice and the full citation on the first page. To copy otherwise, to republish, to post on servers or to redistribute to lists, requires prior specific permission and/or a fee.
ICER'12, September 9–11, 2012, Auckland, New Zealand.
Copyright 2012 ACM 978-1-4503-1604-0/12/09 ...$15.00.

Lister, Whalley and colleagues [18, 26], who exploit Bloom's and the SOLO pedagogical taxonomies.

The scope of the present study includes dimensions (ii–iv), and marginally (v). Most data are collected through two questionnaires: a *recursion test* and an *iteration test* with a similar underlying structure relating to Bloom's and the SOLO taxonomies. Both questionnaires have been administered for three years to students following the *functional-first* course. Moreover, the iteration test has also been assigned to two *control* cohorts who attended the *imperative-first* course. Since the students of the different paths appear to be heterogeneous with respect to each other, for the sake of comparison they have been "filtered" into more balanced subgroups, based on the statistical distribution of a measure of "aptitude" for study. In essence, as a result of these two lines of investigation on different kinds of achievements relevant to programming, we found no evidence that students make more progress with iteration than they do with recursion.

The rest of the paper is organized as follows. Sect. 2 outlines the questionnaires and explains the rationale behind them. Sect. 3 describes the implementation of the experiments. Sect. 4 is about the methodology of analysis. Finally, the main findings are summarized and discussed in sect. 5.

2. INSTRUMENTS

The principal instruments are open-answer questionnaires with a main focus on the learning dimensions (ii, iii, iv).

2.1 Recursion Test

The questionnaire on recursion consists of seven items, labeled R1–R7. Items R1–2 pertain dimension (ii); R3–5 dimension (iii) and, marginally, (v); R6–7 address dimension (iv). The language used is *Scheme*. Here is a brief summary.

The first two items test the understanding of the "mechanics" of recursive computations as suggested in [12]. Students have to trace the key steps of a procedure application, including *all* recursive calls. The procedure in R1 computes the (integer) power function; that in R2 is tree-recursive and solves a problem related to the longest common subsequence. In both cases there are two recursive branches with different operations in the backward (return) chain of computation.

Questions R3–5 address the recursive relations between different instances of a problem. After introducing the problems, all these questions follow a common pattern: "[...] Someone has already defined for you a procedure p that solves the problem at hand. Given the arguments x, y ..., you are required to promptly determine the value returned by p. However, you are playing a game and you are not allowed to enter directly the expression $(p\ x\ y\ ...)$; you can use p, provided you change the value of at least one of the arguments. Which Scheme expression would you enter to answer the query?" The proposed problems are co-primality test (R3), palindromicity test (R4), and length of a b-ary integer representation (R5); some restrictions on the arguments are assumed to avoid the treatment of base cases.

Item R6 asks to describe the recursive structure of a Sierpinski's triangle drawn in a picture. In particular, students have to say how the base case looks and which operations can be applied to increase by 1 the recursion depth. Finally, to answer question R7 students have to define a recursive procedure that checks if a given input string consists of a sequence of open parentheses followed by an equal number of close parentheses.

Figure 1: Drawings of items I6 (left) and I7 (right).

2.2 Iteration Test

This questionnaire consists of seven items, I1 through I7, which are outlined below. The structure is the same as before: items I1–2, I3–5 and I6–7 refer to learning dimensions (ii), (iii), (v) and (iv), respectively. The language used is *Java*.

The first items are about the computation model. Students are asked to trace the salient steps of an iterative program and to report the final result. The code provided in I1 is an iterative version of the "power" procedure of R1, based on a *while* loop with a nested *if*. The program in I2 sorts a given array and prints its (sorted) components. The core of the code implements an insertion-sort scheme with two nested loops: a *while* within a *for*.

To answer questions I3 and I4, students have to explain in words the purpose of the previous code, i.e. the function computed by the method in I1 and the problem solved by the program in I2, respectively. Item I5 asks for the definition of an iterative method that computes the degree of a given prime in the factorization of a given integer.

The purpose of item I6 is to characterize in terms of iteration the tessellation shown on the left in fig. 1. Students have to choose a basic pattern and answer a few specific questions, namely, which operations are executed on the pattern at each iteration step, whether there are steps that need some special treatment, what changes if either the width or the height of the rectangular region increases by one unit. Lastly, item I7 asks students to write a Java program that assigns a sequence of integers to a matrix in "diagonal order", as suggested by the drawing on the right in fig. 1.

2.3 Rationale

The questionnaires have been devised to pursue, as far as possible, a twofold aim: to discriminate between different learning dimensions on the one hand, and to compare the results of corresponding items on the other. In the latter respect, a parallel between them can be schematized as follows:

recursion test		iteration test	
dimension (ii) – computation model (tracing code)			
R1:	linear recursion	I1:	simple iteration
R2:	tree recursion	I2:	nested iteration
dimensions (iii–v) – relations & functional abstraction			
R3–5:	relations between problem instances	I3–4:	program purpose
		I5:	simple method
dimension (iv) – program structures & planning			
R6:	structure analysis	I6:	structure analysis
R7:	structure synthesis	I7:	structure synthesis

In order to reduce students' tendency to rely on stereotypical patterns, most of the proposed questions are *unusual* in the light of their coursework experience, including their knowledge of past exam questions. The scope of each item can also be interpreted in terms of Bloom's and SOLO taxonomies of learning achievements. In particular, dimension

(ii) pertains the intermediate *application* level of Bloom's scale; items I3–4, R6 and I6 the *analysis* level; items R3–5, I5, R7 and I7 the *synthesis* level. From a SOLO viewpoint, on the other hand, the assessment of the answers to R1–2 and I1–2 are limited to the *multistructural* level, whereas the other questions address the *relational* level by testing either the ability to bridge the gap with the problem domain (iii) or to combine plans (iv). See, for instance, [24, 19] for related applications of these taxonomies.

3. EXPERIMENT

The investigation has been conducted at the University of Udine, that offers two computing curricula with alternative approaches to the teaching of programming: a general computer science (CS) curriculum and one oriented to web technologies (WT), a mix of the CS and IT models in [7]. Accordingly, two main groups of students took part in the experiment. The first group is composed of the CS students who engaged in the tests in the a.y. 2008-09, 2009-10 and 2010-11, when they were all attending the introductory programming course. We will refer to them as the *focus group*: 84 subjects participated in both the recursion and the iteration tests, 10 more only in the latter. The second, *control group* is composed of 95 WT students who attended introductory programming in the a.y. 2010-11 and 2011-12.

3.1 Context

The undergraduate programs in CS and WT have similar structures in the first year. Essentially, the main difference is that WT students follow a course on web technologies, whereas CS students have to take a course in physics. Introductory programming is worth the same number of credits (12/60) for both paths, but it is taught very differently. For CS, the course takes as a model Hailperin's et al. [14] functional-first approach. The students learn the basics of *procedural* and *data abstraction* in a purely functional style through Scheme. Then, in the second half of the course, they move to the imperative paradigm in Java and see the rudiments of object-oriented programming. On the other hand, introductory programming for WT follows a standard imperative-first approach, placing a little more emphasis on laboratory work. The students start with the main control-flow constructs and data structures in Java and, later, they learn some basic concepts of the object-oriented paradigm. In this course recursion is not treated in depth.

3.2 Implementation

The questionnaires have been administered to the CS cohorts toward the end of the first (recursion) and second (iteration) semesters. In order to ensure as fair a comparison as possible with the CS group, a first option was to assign the iteration test to WT students having completed the program of the first year to reach an equivalent level of general knowledge. A different choice was to administer the test a short time after the relevant material was covered in the course. Both options have been considered: the iteration test was given at the beginning of the second year, in the object-oriented programming class, for the 2010-11 WT cohort; at the end of the first semester for the 2011-12 cohort. (As we will see, however, the results of the two cohorts turned out to be similar.) Each test was taken in a two-hour session in a controlled situation. It is also worth noting that the students were not advised of the types of questions in it.

4. ANALYSIS

Before presenting the results of the investigation, in this section we summarize the methodology to assess students' answers and to sample the (focus and control) groups to be compared in order to limit some possible causes of bias.

4.1 Assessment

To reduce the arbitrariness inherent in fine-grained ratings, all the answers have been classified into three categories, where the specific categories depend on the item.

Items R1–2, I1–2. The computation traces have been assessed as *adequate*, *flat*, or *inadequate*. The answers in the first category are accurate enough to be assigned to the *multistructural* SOLO level. Flat traces correspond to *unistructural* answers in the SOLO taxonomy, where either the backward (*passive* [10, 12]) flow of recursive invocations or the steps of a construct nested in a loop are not treated appropriately. Other traces, which are either flawed by serious misconceptions or null, may indicate a *prestructural* level. To further simplify the analysis, here we will consider each pair of traces together (for recursion and for iteration) and see if they are *both adequate*, *uneven* (only one, usually the simpler trace is accurate) or both *inadequate*.

Items R3–5, I3–4, I5. These questions are less homogeneous, but all pertain the *relational* SOLO level and require to deal with functional abstractions. Of the three categories of answers relative to R3–5 and I5, two correspond to *adequate* solutions, which may be either *neat* or simply *acceptable*; the lowest to *inadequate* or null solutions. The answers to I3 and I4, on the other hand, may just be *adequate* or not. For the sake of the present analysis, the data of R3–5 and I5 will be aggregated with those of R7 and I7 in broader sets of "program synthesis" items (Bloom's *synthesis* level).

Items R6–7, I6–7. Also dealing with structures entails competences at the *relational* SOLO level, and specifically the ability to combine plans to achieve more complex behaviors. Two categories of *adequate* answers and one of *inadequate* or null answers are used as above. Cumbersome or partly ambiguous characterizations of the structures presented in R6 and I6, as well as unnecessarily cumbersome solutions of R7 and I7 are considered adequate, but not *neat* answers. For simplicity, in sect. 5.1 we will report the proportions of adequate answers to *both* questions R6 and R7 (respectively, I6 and I7), only to the *synthesis* question R7 (I7), or only to the *analysis* question R6 (I6). Cumbersome, stereotypical answers to items R6–7, I6–7 may indicate that the learning achievements have made little progress beyond the *multistructural* level of the SOLO taxonomy.

4.2 Dealing with Heterogeneity

The first step of this work is to compare students' ability to deal with recursion vs. iteration. This is meant to be achieved by analyzing the answers of the *focus group* to the two questionnaires. On the other hand, we may suspect that the results with iteration are affected by the functional-first approach. To investigate this hypothesis, it is interesting to identify a suitable *control group* with a different experience of introductory programming. A natural choice was to form a control group of WT students, who attended a course taught in a standard *imperative-first* way. These students come from the same area, have similar high-school backgrounds and most of the first year program is essentially the same as for CS: in particular, the courses of *calculus* and

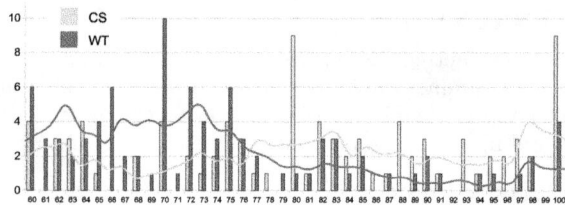

Figure 2: Histograms and estimated "smooth" distributions of the chosen measure of aptitude.

computer architecture are in common. We have to be careful, however, since the CS and WT "populations" are likely to be heterogeneous in some relevant aspects.

In order to compare two student samples as homogeneous as possible in terms of aptitude for scientific/technological study, we can rely on some reasonably fair measure of this feature. For students at the beginning of their career, one such measure is the score of secondary school diploma, ranging between 60 and 100. As we can see from the histograms in fig. 2 (number of students per score), the distributions of this measure are different for the CS and the WT groups.

For a clearer appraisal of these patterns, the histograms should be thought of as the contingent manifestations of underlying "smoother" distributions (related to probability densities), one for each group. We can estimate such underlying distributions by averaging the occurrences on score windows, say of width 7, and by doing some further adjustment to account for the "saturation" phenomena near the range bounds. In essence, this corresponds to applying a kernel density estimator with bandwidth 7. The result are the smooth lines in fig. 2. Now the idea is to filter two more homogeneous CS and WT subgroups by randomly sampling the subjects in such a way as to compensate for the unbalance of the smoothed distributions in a neighborhood of the respective measure. More specifically, a subject whose associated measure is m will be selected with probability 1 if the density of her group is less at m; with probability given by the ratio between the density of the other group and that of her group at m otherwise. The rationale of this procedure is to produce smaller samples with almost overlapping (smooth) distributions of the measure. The expected sizes of the resulting subgroups in our case are 62.0 and 61.1.

Another reasonable measure of aptitude can be introduced by adding up the final grades attained in the exams of the two common courses, retrieved after the end of the a.y. when the tests were taken. As far as available, we can refer to such information in order to further appraise the degree of balance (in terms of aptitude for study) between the samples under comparison.

5. RESULTS

In this section we outline the main findings of the investigation. We will first compare the answers of the *focus group* in the recursion and iteration tests. Then, we will consider the feedback from the *control group* in the iteration test.

5.1 Iteration vs. Recursion

Before presenting the results relating to the first research question, we mention a few figures that can help to understand the scope of the analysis. To begin with, we can observe that the 84 subjects of the *focus group* who took part in both tests amount to more than half of the students who

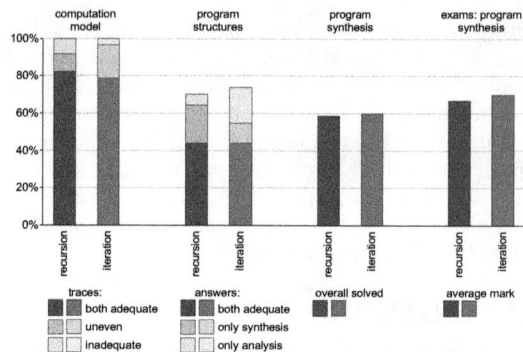

Figure 3: Comparative summary of the answers to the recursion and iteration tests (focus group).

engaged in the introductory programming exam. Moreover, students' behavior seems to be quite stable in time. We may also want to be a little more formal in this respect, and carry out a *homogeneity test* to explore the hypothesis that the three CS cohorts show similar patterns of performance. To this aim, we can build a contingency table of the numbers of students whose performance fall into a few broad categories (*broad* enough to guarantee that the outcome has statistical significance for the given figures).

In particular, we can put together the items pertaining to each of the three learning areas addressed by the questionnaires, and say that performance is *good* when: relative to the computation model area, all the traces required by R1–2 and I1–2 are adequate; relative to the relationships and functional abstraction area, at least 4 of the answers to R3–5, I3–5 are adequate; relative to the structures, at least 3 of the answers to R6–7, I6–7 are adequate. Then, we can introduce the categories of subjects with a *good* performance in all three areas (a), in two of them (b), or in less than two (c). The corresponding figures are: 11 (a), 7 (b), 10 (c) for the cohort '08-09; 12 (a), 5 (b), 10 (c) for the cohort '09-10; 13 (a), 6 (b), 10 (c) for the cohort '10-11. Now, $\chi^2 = 0.43$ for this contingency table with 4 degrees of freedom, which means probability $p = 0.98$ that $\chi^2 > 0.43$ if the homogeneity hypothesis is true. Thus, we have definitely no reason to reject it. What emerges is not simply the sum of sporadic phenomena, but the manifestation of recurrent patterns.

Let us also consider the correlations between answers to pairs of items. By following Cohen's interpretation guidelines [8], only the correlations R1–R2 (0.63) and I2–I4 (0.61) are strong, whereas all the other pairs are either weakly (< 0.3: more than half of the cases) or moderately (< 0.5) correlated. This suggests that the items are not too "redundant", but actually test features which are at least partly independent of each other.

Now we come to the main results of the first line of investigation, which are summarized in tab. 1 and in fig. 3. Overall, it appears that students' ability to master recursion and iteration is comparable. In particular, relative to the *synthesis* items, i.e. R3–5, R7, I5 and I7, where the students have to *write* appropriate code, we get a similar percentage of adequate solutions: 59% for recursion and 60% for iteration. This is in accordance with the feedback of the exams, which confirms that recursion and iteration are equally difficult to deal with: the average mark achieved in the exercises that require to write recursive code is 67% for the focus group and 61% for all CS students; for iterative code the corresponding figures are 70% and 61%, respectively.

focus group: 84 subjects	_recursion_	_iteration_
computation model	**R1–2**	**I1–2**
adequate traces	82%	79%
uneven traces	10%	18%
program structures	**R6–7**	**I6–7**
analysis and synthesis	44%	44%
only synthesis	20%	11%
only analysis	6%	19%
program synthesis	**R3–5, R7**	**I5, I7**
adequate solutions	59%	60%

Table 1: Results of the recursion and iteration tests.

Since the focus group includes several brilliant students, we can try to consider the "weaker" half of it (38 subjects), based on the final grades in the introductory programming exams. As expected, the results are uniformly worse, but we can explore the balance between performance in related sections of the recursion and iteration tests. What emerges is that the balance changes very slightly in favor of iteration for the (easier) items R1–5 vs. I1–5, whereas it remains essentially the same for R6–7 vs. I6–7. On the other hand, if we aggregate the synthesis items, we find that the worsening is comparatively more prominent for iterative code writing.

Another interesting question is if recursion or iteration may better match specific cognitive styles. Of course, individual inclinations play a role, but the correlation between overall performance in the two tests, measured as sum of adequate answers, is large (0.68), and indicates that students tend to be equally able to deal with recursion and iteration.

5.2 Focus vs. Control Group

In this section by _focus_, respectively _control_ group, we refer to the smaller samples produced by the procedure discussed in sect. 4.2. The "filtered" focus group consists of 62 out of the 94 CS students who took part in the iteration test. Their average score of secondary school diploma is 77.5, with standard deviation 12.0. The filtered control group is composed of 61 over 95 WT students, with average diploma score 77.1 and standard deviation 12.2. Also the distribution w.r.t. upper secondary education is similar for the two groups. 25 subjects of the CS sample come from some technological school (13 with a computing curriculum), 22 from a scientific school and 15 have a different specialization. For WT the corresponding figures are 24 (technology; 12 in computing), 20 (science) and 17 (other).

To present the core results of the second line of investigation, it is convenient to aggregate the items as in tab. 2 and fig. 4. As we can see, the answers of the control group are much poorer when planning and programming capabilities are implied (items I5–7). In particular, relative to item I7, that can be solved neatly by combining iterative constructs in a non-stereotypical way, the percentage of success of the control group is only 15% against 45% of the focus group.

The disparity in programming performance between the two groups cannot be explained in terms of previous experience in school. On the other hand, it can neither be explained by the alternative "fair" measure of aptitude for study mentioned at the end of sect. 4.2 (total score in the common exams), whose averages are 39.8 for the CS sample and 41.8 for that of WT. We may perhaps conjecture that WT students are generally less enthusiastic about program-

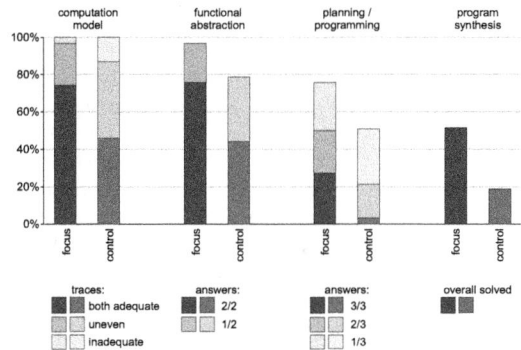

Figure 4: Comparative summary of the answers of the focus and control groups (iteration test).

iteration test	_focus group_	_control group_	
computation model: I1–2			
adequate traces	74%	46%	(76%)
uneven traces	23%	41%	(24%)
functional abstraction: I3–4			
2 adequate answers	76%	44%	(62%)
1 adequate answer	21%	34%	(31%)
planning/programming: I5–7			
3 adequate answers	27%	3%	(0%)
2 adequate answers	23%	18%	(17%)
1 adequate answer	26%	30%	(28%)

Table 2: Results for the focus and control groups.

ming than their CS peers. In this respect, we can try to explore the answers of the subjects with a final grade in introductory programming in the upper half (i.e. 24–30), who should conceivably be more skilled in programming. This subgroup consists of 29 students of the '10-11 cohort. The corresponding figures are reported in parentheses in tab. 2: the percentages of success for items I1–4 are closer to those of the focus group, but there is no improvement for items I5–7. Again, we observe a marked gap in favor of the focus group when higher-level competences are implied. The data of the '11-12 exams are not yet available, but we may expect that they will be similar to the above ones, since the performance in the test of the two WT cohorts are homogeneous. By applying the same categories as in sect. 5.1, the contingency table is now: 5 (a), 9 (b), 35 (c) ['10-11]; 5 (a), 7 (b), 34 (c) ['11-12]. Hence, $\chi^2 = 0.17$ and probability $p = 0.92$ that $\chi^2 > 0.17$ if the homogeneity hypothesis is true.

5.3 Discussion

This work has tried to investigate the first steps toward the achievement of high-level competences in introductory programming. Some of the proposed questions are then slightly more challenging than in related studies of novices, e.g. [1, 20, 21]. Here is a brief summary of the results.

Computation model. Most students have a basic understanding of the computation models, though the control group appears to be weaker with nested loops. The level of accuracy to trace recursive vs. iterative code is essentially the same for the subjects of the functional-first path.

Relations and functional abstraction. The gap between the focus and control groups rises as we move from the multistructural to the relational SOLO level. Although not in the same proportion for the two groups, however, a large part of the students who have successfully traced some code are also able to infer the purpose of that code.

Structures. The focus group's ability to deal with recursive vs. iterative structures is comparable. The answers of the control group are instead poorer and, surprisingly, very few subjects were able to write a program as required in I7.

Code writing. The focus group's ability to write recursive vs. iterative code is very balanced. On the other hand, the performance of the control group in these tasks pertaining Bloom's synthesis level is markedly poorer.

Based on the above results, it may be tempting to conclude that teaching recursion before iteration leads to deeper learning. Although the findings suggest that this hypothesis should be subjected to further specific investigation, we have to be cautious in drawing such a strong conclusion, since it is conceivable that other elusive (motivational?) factors may affect the outcome. What seems to emerge quite convincingly, is that iteration should *not* be thought of as being easier to use appropriately than recursion in an introductory course. At least in the considered context, all the collected data give a different indication: neither the assumption that students are better able to exploit iteration than recursion, nor that iteration is best learned with an imperative-first approach are supported by the analysis.

6. CONCLUSIONS

Despite a general consensus on the difficulties faced by novices to master recursion, the investigation discussed in this paper does not corroborate the hypothesis that students are more at ease with iteration than they are with recursion. Rather, the quality of students' response is to be related to the "learning dimensions" implied by the task, independent of the programming paradigm, and, from a teacher's perspective, more effort should be spent to foster problem-solving, plan-composition and abstraction skills [11, 22].

We conclude with some possible directions of future work. First of all, it would be interesting to widen the research scope by carrying out similar investigations in different contexts. Then, the feedback from the control group's subjects with higher grades in introductory programming (sect. 5.2) suggests to put under scrutiny the hypothesis that *iteration-first* approaches may induce the students to rely too much on the computation model, at the expense of more valuable abilities. Moreover, as remarked in sect. 5.3, it can be worth investigating if teaching recursion before iteration may help to develop high-level competences earlier. Related phenomena in this respect have been observed by Turbak et al. [25] (see sect. 1) and, from an object-oriented viewpoint, by Bruce et al. [4]; incidentally, the larger correlation (0.52) between performance in some specific test section and final grade in object-oriented programming (second-year) is attained for the items addressing recursive structures (R6–7).

7. REFERENCES

[1] A. Benander, B. Benander, and H. Pu. Recursion vs. iteration: An empirical study of comprehension. *J. of Systems and Software*, 32(1):73–82, 1996.

[2] S. Bhuiyan, J. E. Greer, and G. I. Mccalla. Supporting the learning of recursive problem solving. *Interactive Learning Environments*, 4(2):115–139, 1994.

[3] R. Brooks. Towards a theory of the comprehension of computer programs. *International Journal of Man-Machine Studies*, 18(6):543–554, 1983.

[4] K. B. Bruce, A. Danyluk, and T. Murtagh. Why structural recursion should be taught before arrays in CS1. In *Proc. 36th SIGCSE*, pages 246–250, 2005.

[5] P. Byckling and J. Sajaniemi. A role-based analysis model for the evaluation of novices' programming knowledge dev. In *Proc. 2nd ICER*, pages 85–96, 2006.

[6] CC2001 Joint Task Force. Computing Curricula 2001: Computer Science. ACM and IEEE-CS, Dec. 2001.

[7] CC2005 Joint Task Force. Computing Curricula 2005: The overview report. ACM and IEEE-CS, Sept. 2005.

[8] J. Cohen. *Statistical power analysis for the behavioral sciences*. Lawrence Erlbaum, 1988.

[9] B. du Boulay. Some difficulties of learning to program. *J. of Educational Comput. Research*, 2(1):57–73, 1986.

[10] C. E. George. Using visualization to aid program construction tasks. In *Proc. 33rd SIGCSE*, 2002.

[11] D. Ginat and E. Shifroni. Teaching recursion in a procedural environment—how much should we...? In *Proc. 30th SIGCSE*, pages 127–131, 1999.

[12] T. Götschi, I. Sanders, and V. Galpin. Mental models of recursion. In *Proc. 34th SIGCSE*, 2003.

[13] B. Haberman and H. Averbuch. The case of base cases: Why are they so difficult to recognize? In *Proc. 7th ITiCSE*, pages 84–88, 2002.

[14] M. Hailperin, B. Kaiser, and K. Knight. *Concrete Abstractions*. Brooks/Cole, 1999.

[15] H. Kahney. What do novice programmers know about recursion. In *Proc. of SIGCHI*, pages 235–239, 1983.

[16] C. M. Kessler and J. R. Anderson. Learning flow of control: recursive and iterative procedures. *Human-Computer Interaction*, 2(2):135–166, 1986.

[17] M. C. Linn and J. Dalbey. Cognitive consequences of programming instruction: Instruction, access, and ability. *Educational Psychologist*, 20(4):191–206, 1985.

[18] R. Lister. Concrete and other neo-piagetian forms of reasoning in the novice programmer. In *Proc. 13th ACE*, pages 9–18, 2011.

[19] R. Lister et al. Not seeing the forest for the trees: novice programmers and the SOLO taxonomy. In *Proc. 11th ITiCSE*, pages 118–122. ACM, 2006.

[20] M. Lopez et al. Relationships between reading, tracing and writing skills in introductory programming. In *Proc. of the 4th ICER*, pages 101–112, 2008.

[21] I. Sanders, V. Galpin, and T. Götschi. Mental models of recursion revisited. In *Proc. 11th ITICSE*, 2006.

[22] R. Sooriamurthi. Problems in comprehending recursion and suggested solutions. In *Proc. 6th ITiCSE*, pages 25–28, 2001.

[23] J. C. Spohrer and E. Soloway. Novice mistakes: are the folk wisdoms correct? *CACM*, 29(7):624–632, 1986.

[24] C. W. Starr, B. Manaris, and R. H. Stalvey. Bloom's taxonomy revisited: specifying assessable learning... In *Proc. 39th SIGCSE*, pages 261–265, 2008.

[25] F. Turbak, C. Royden, J. Stephan, and J. Herbst. Teaching recursion before loops in CS1. *J. Computing in Small Colleges*, 14(4):86–101, 1999.

[26] J. Whalley and R. Lister. The BRACElet 2009.1 specification. In *Proc. 11th ACE*, pages 9–18, 2009.

[27] S. Wiedenbeck. Learning recursion as a concept and as a programming technique. In *Proc. 19th SIGCSE*, pages 275–278. ACM, 1988.

Exploratory Homeworks:
An Active Learning Tool for Textbook Reading

Sarah Esper, Beth Simon
Computer Science and Engineering Department
University of California, San Diego
La Jolla, CA 92093
{sesper, bsimon}@cs.ucsd.edu

Quintin Cutts
School of Computing Science
University of Glasgow
Glasgow, Scotland
Quintin.Cutts@glasgow.ac.uk

ABSTRACT

Constructivist learning theory suggests that learners must construct their own understandings, rather than have understanding passively dumped into their brains. These findings support the US National Research Council's recommendations for the adoption of active learning pedagogies in the classroom. However, the "classroom lecture" is only one of the resources students commonly have for learning in higher education. In this paper, we present *exploratory homeworks* -- a tool to support active learning for teaching programming languages. By leveraging the opportunity for the student to interact with the computer/compiler, we seek to provide a model for students of how to explore and understand programming language constructs and concepts. We report on the use of 15 exploratory homework assignments used in a CS0 course with 440 students in Winter 2011. We provide a model and advice for others wishing to develop exploratory homeworks for their programming courses and present quantitative and qualitative evidence regarding students' positive valuation of the homeworks.

Categories and Subject Descriptors

K.3.2 [**Computer Science Education**]

Keywords

CS0, active learning, constructivism, kolb learning cycle, cognitive apprenticeship

1. INTRODUCTION

Active learning is known to be a best practice in classroom pedagogy. Research shows that people don't learn very effectively from being "told" what to do. They gain a much deeper and meaningful understanding by constructing their own learning through engaging with a concrete problem [1]. Various classroom techniques such as Peer Instruction, POGIL (Process Oriented, Guided Inquiry Learning), PLTL (Peer Led Team Learning), studio-based instruction and lab-centric instruction replace or significantly augment lecture in order to accomplish this [2,3,4]. However, the classroom is only one learning resource common to undergraduate education.

The next most obvious resource (at least to students, since they pay for it) is the textbook. Textbooks are generally expository in nature and textbook reading by students is often very passive. A report from a genetics course finds students' attitudes and

descriptions of how they read textbooks to be quite novice – very much out of line with how faculty would want them to read it [5].

Teaching a programming language has a unique aspect that we seek to take advantage of – one can interact with the computer to get feedback on behavior of programming constructs. In fact, anecdotally, we posit that experts rarely learn a new programming language by sitting with a static, passive, textual or expository resource. Instead they combine explanatory sources with guided or self-defined micro-experimentation – isolating a specific construct or concept of interest and developing the simplest possible code to enable them to explore its behavior.

In this discussion paper we introduce a new "active learning" tool for supporting students in successful, and more expert-like, engagement with a traditionally passive resource – the textbook. *Exploratory homeworks* are written guides that engage students in their first exposure to and experimentation with a programming construct. In our experience, they augment the textbook by outlining small learning goals (at the subsection level or smaller), and provide specific guidance on how to use the book.

First, students are asked to both open the textbook and launch their programming language development environment. They are then asked to "follow along" building up an example code, and are stopped frequently and confronted with questions to pose to themselves, experiments in modifying the code, and explanations of what they should have just experienced. Afterwards students are provided with example questions that indicate the level of understanding they should have achieved by doing the homework.

In our context (and what we recommend), this homework is done individually by students before each lecture period, covering introductory material for that lecture. Students are encouraged to do the homework, which is not itself graded, by a 3-4 question quiz for credit given at the beginning of every lecture. This both supports and flows naturally into a lecture that also utilizes an active learning-based pedagogy. In such lectures, since students are involved in constructing their own understanding, not just listening, there is usually less time for standard expository lecture. Exploratory homeworks provide students the opportunity to become familiar with basic material before class, allowing the instructor to spend their valuable time with students working with more advanced, nuanced, and/or in-depth applications and explanations of the material.

Next we provide background and related work for the theoretical underpinnings supporting the efficacy of exploratory homeworks. In Section 3 we describe the setting of the course and in Section 4 we outline the flowchart guiding design of exploratory homework and provide an example from a section on looping. In Section 5 we provide qualitative and quantitative data on students' experiences with and perceptions of the value of the homeworks. In Section 6 we discuss our experiences and provide recommendations for instructors seeking to develop exploratory homeworks in their programming courses.

2. RELATED WORK

Lecture. Various forms of active learning are much studied both in STEM higher education and in computing education. Lab-centric instruction replaces all or most of lecture with extensive guided lab work, featuring frequent opportunities for feedback – something designed to help improve students' self-assessment skills [6]. Peer Instruction, POGIL, PLTL, and studio-based instruction all fall into the realm of collaborative pedagogies, and are designed for lecture or discussion section-type settings [2,3,4]. Modifying the lecture period to be more engaging and collaborative is an important pedagogical change to help students learn, but the lecture period is typically only a couple hours a week. Students spend the majority of their time outside of lecture, where they often do not have access to an expert (the lecturer) to clarify or ask questions.

Closed-Labs. Frequently computer science lectures are accompanied with a lab-section. This provides students with an additional few hours a week where they have access to an expert to help guide them or explain complex concepts. Lab manuals and tutorials [7] offer students guidance when in closed-lab settings, though they are still distinct from exploratory homeworks in that 1) The environment in which they are used is a completely guided, "safe" environment and 2) The goal of a lab manual or tutorial is typically to help the students understand a concept and actually write a program. Though exploratory homeworks guide students through complex concepts and writing programs, they are also focused around teaching students *how* to read a computer science textbook or text resource. Lab manuals or tutorials are separate from traditional textbooks or online resources in that they are completely contained. Exploratory homeworks ask students to go outside of the homework to seek information in order to progress (which is what is typically done when experts are learning a new language or concept).

Worked Examples. Casperson also realized that the textbook is a relatively mal-used resource in computer science education. He understood "A static program example presented in a textbook reveals nothing about the process of developing the program."[8] Casperson therefore developed Worked Examples in computing; problems that actively engage the students in a step-by-step process of learning the concept while attempting to minimize cognitive load. This was significant (though perhaps still in need of development) because it encouraged educators to engage their students in process rather than just results. Exploratory homeworks also focus the student on process. However, we specifically focus on directing students in understanding more "standard" static computing instructional text and translating it into problem solving and programs.

Our Work. Exploratory homeworks are uniquely designed to enhance at-home textbook reading. This setting is very different from both lecture and closed-lab. Typically reading is a sedentary action students engage in because "they are required to". Though almost every university has some form of student academic support unit that recommends various approaches for effective textbook reading, they are typically not discipline specific [9]. And we believe many of these suggestions do not encourage computing students to engage in thinking through problems and following or analyzing code. Kolb [10] describes a learning process (the Kolb Learning Cycle) that involves combinations of perceiving and processing information. The Kolb Learning Cycle involves four learning styles: *concrete experience, reflective observation, abstract conceptualization* and *active experimentation*. Typically, educators apply the Kolb Learning Cycle to a lecture or lab component. Exploratory homeworks seek to bring Kolb-like styles to the less-structured reading experience.

Finally, the efficacy of exploratory homework can be argued from another aspect of social constructivist theory – authentic practice. In [11] they argue that all too often "school-based" instruction ignores the situated nature of knowledge and suggest that development of expertise be guided through cognitive apprenticeship. That is, we must engage students not just in abstracted conceptual knowledge, but also in the authentic practices that experts in the practice use. We must engage students in "doing as we do" and support them in developing the ability to "think as we think".

3. SETTING

3.1 The Course

Exploratory homeworks were introduced in a CS0 course that was taught using the active learning pedagogy Peer Instruction (PI) [2]. The course taught 440 mostly non-major, undergraduate students at a large R1 institution in the western USA. Students learned the Alice programming language and Excel. The course was designed to help students develop a general understanding of computing concepts and constructs.

3.2 Incorporation of Exploratory Homeworks

Exploratory homeworks were incorporated into the course to enhance pre-lecture reading. The course structure was as follows:

- Students were assigned pre-lecture exploratory homeworks.
- At the beginning of the 90-minute lecture, a quiz was given to assess what students should have learned from the homeworks. A subset of the quiz questions came from questions provided in the homework.
- Lecture then continued in a typical PI fashion. Furthermore, the instructor could delve deeper into a problem by extending examples from the homework.
- The exploratory homework, quiz and lecture cycle took place twice per week.
- The week following both lectures, students were required to demonstrate understanding through a directed, closed lab involving code writing.
- Midterm and final exams also included questions of the style introduced in the exploratory homeworks.

Students were able to spend as much or as little time as they wanted or could manage on the exploratory homeworks. The homeworks were not graded, but every lecture students were directly rewarded for completing the homeworks via a quiz. Additionally, the homeworks served to help students engage in the kind of analysis processes they would be called to perform during peer discussions during lecture.

4. EXAMPLE HOMEWORKS

The course used the book "Learning to Program with Alice" [12]. This book is written in a fashion that easily supports active learning. Each chapter is divided into sections that ask the student to create (or use an existing) Alice program and then enhance or modify it based on instruction and guidance from the book. The exploratory homeworks were developed to focus on the led examples in the book, enhancing them with details and encouraging the students to further explore the code, make predictions and "play around". Homeworks were typically broken up into 3-4 sections. Figure 1 shows the structure of the exploratory homeworks.

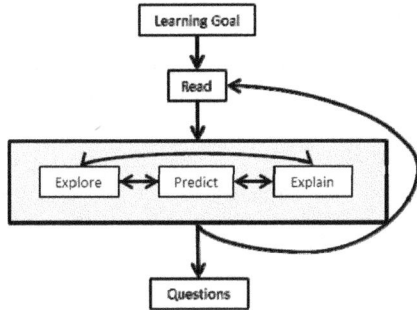

Figure 1: Exploratory Homework Structure

The purpose of this structure is to actively engage students in learning the basics of concepts and constructs.

- **Learning Goal** – One sentence description that tells students what they will learn and serves as a reference for study.
- **Read** – Asks students to read (and follow along coding) a specific section of the book.
- **Predict** – Focuses students on understanding a misconception through code changes, predictions, tests and reflections.
- **Explore** – Allows the students to gain confidence in manipulating, predicting and reflecting on changes in code.
- **Explain** – Points out common misconceptions or validates students' learning through logical reasoning.
- **Repeat** – The students will do the above four sections until the required reading is complete (order can vary).
- **Questions** – Allows students to self-assess their understanding and repeat sections if they find they are confused.

Figure 2 provides an example of one section of an exploratory homework, as well as the questions asked of them to check their understanding.

LEARNING GOAL 1: Reading and Predicting What Loops Do

Start Alice and open your book to section 7.1.

Load up the world called HW9_bunnyWorld that can be found here. **When you download it, make sure it's not saving as zip.**

Follow the book to page 211 and fill in the method myFirstMethod, but using the world we have provided for you, **not** the one in the textbook folder of Alice. (If you are confused on how to write the method with the loop, please be sure to seek help from a tutor.)

The section ends with a suggestion that you can have more complicated statements within the loop body. Let's try to make this bunny a little more interesting.

- In the HW9_bunnyWorld that is provided to you for this assignment, there is a bunny.dance method. Read this method, try modifying it to make him do a specialized dance, not just the generic one everyone is doing. After you have played with the bunny.dance method and made your bunny do an awesome dance, go back to your myFirstMethod.
- We want to make the bunny do a "hop-once-dance-once" combo, which he then repeats maybe 10 times. Add a DoInOrder inside of the loop. Put the call to bunny.hop followed by a call to bunny.dance inside of the DoInOrder.
- How many times will the bunny hop? How many times will the bunny dance? Is it 10 hops followed by 10 dances?
- Now Press Play. Did it do what you thought it would?

One of the most common problem people have with loops is knowing what goes "inside" the loop tile and what goes "outside" (before or after) the loop tile. Let's try moving instructions around in and out of the loop and predicting what it does:

- Drag the call to the hop method out of the loop tile to just above the blue loop tile. What will your world look like when you hit play? **PREDICT FOR YOURSELF** (because something like this would be a great exam question). Play and see if you are right.
- Next Drag the hop tile from before the loop to AFTER (below) the blue loop tile. What will happen this time? Try it out.
- Try copying the hop method call (right click on the tile, select copy) and paste a copy of it ABOVE the loop as well. (There should now be 2 tiles with a hop call on them). Predict...

Delete the hop tile before the loop. Drag the hop tile from below the loop back into the loop, but put it below the dance method call in the DoTogether tile. How will this be different that the first one we started with? When you are done, drag the dance tile below hop to get back where you started.

It makes more sense that when a bunny hops closer to the camera, it should get bigger. So inside the DoInOrder (still inside the loop) add a DoTogether and move the bunny.hop call into the DoTogether followed by a bunny.resize(1.05). Leave the bunny.dance in the DoInOrder, right after the DoTogether.

Press Play, did the bunny get bigger every time it hopped closer to the camera? How many times did the bunny hop, get bigger and dance?

Now try dragging other methods/actions into and around the loop to do a more complex dance routine. Any old bunny can hop then dance then hop then dance...make your bunny do something special. Maybe have him hop-dance-spin, or have a "grand finale" that only happens once after he hops-dances.

Questions:

1. Suppose I have a program that makes a guy wave after he walks up to a girl. How would you change it to make the guy wave repeatedly AS he walks up to the girl?

2. Which loop construct(s) is(are) incorrect?, Why?

- Loop 5 times
  Do Nothing
- Loop Infinity times
  Do Nothing
- Loop Alice.DistranceTo(Rabbit) times
  Do Nothing
- Loop Alive.MoveTo(Rabbit) time
  Do Nothing

Note: Original Exploratory Homework includes screenshots from Alice.

3. Why is Loop also called "Counted Loop"

Figure 2: Example Section from Exploratory Homeworks

The full texts of all 15 homeworks are available at http://peerinstruction4cs.org under CS Principles.

4.1 Learning Goal and Reading

Referring to Figure 2, the first step is a high-level learning goal:

Reading and Predicting What Loops Do

The explicit goal gives students context for the homework and the chance to find examples quickly in the future.

The first two paragraphs then ask the student to read and follow along in the book until a certain point. This step involves Kolb's *concrete experience* and *reflective observation* because students are asked to program what is in the book (passive) but also to ensure understanding (review). Students are discouraged from reading the entire text before attempting to follow the guided examples. Instead, they read small portions and then stop to reflect, predict and "play around" with the code to satisfy their own interests and curiosities. This encourages the students to work with small, doable goals versus large, daunting problems.

4.2 Explore

We choose to stop student reading where the book suggests that the student "try something different" for the bunny's dance. We enhance the book with some guidance for this task. The first bullet says:

- In the HW9_bunnyWorld that is provided to you for this assignment, there is a bunny.dance method. Read this method, try modifying it to make him do a specialized dance, not just the generic one everyone is doing. After you have played with the bunny.dance method and made your bunny do an awesome dance, go back to your myFirstMethod.

This bullet emphasizes to the student how to actively engage in learning a new programming language using three techniques: 1) Understand the current implementation, 2) Modify the code, 3) Test to make sure the result is what was expected. This step is Kolb's *active experimentation and abstract conceptualization*. This also encourages students to read more authentically (Kolb's *concrete experience*).

4.3 Predict

Next, we ask them to follow instructions on creating code, but before running it, to predict what will happen based on the code changes. This step is a form of *reflective observation* in the Kolb Cycle. This active learning skill is especially useful in debugging and will help students recognize errors based on prediction and reflection about code changes. If the prediction does not match, it can either be an error in the code change, or an error in their prediction, but either way the student gains more insight into the problem.

- We want to make the bunny do a "hop-once-dance-once" combo, which he then repeats maybe 10 times. Add a DoInOrder inside of the loop. Put the call to bunny.hop followed by a call to bunny.dance inside of the DoInOrder.

- How many times will the bunny hop? How many times will the bunny dance? Is it 10 hops followed by 10 dances?

- Now Press Play. Did it do what you thought it would?

These steps walk the students through the process:

Code change -> Predict -> Test

They also encourage them to re-visit the code and their hypothesis should there be a discrepancy.

4.4 Explain

The next section points out a common mistake made by novices:

One of the most common problems people have with loops is knowing what goes "inside" the loop tile and what goes "outside" (before or after) the loop tile. Let's try moving instructions around in and out of the loop and predicting what it does:

By pointing out the struggles novice programmers have with nested loops, the student is able to focus their attention on the intricacies of the loops that they will be working with in the next **Predict** section. Students engage in Kolb's *abstract conceptualization* and *active experimentation*. By presenting a difficult concept, the students gain confidence when they know that they are progressing and are prepared for lecture.

4.5 Questions

At the end of the entire exploratory homework there are 3-5 conceptual questions that the students should be prepared to answer. This is Kolb's *reflective experience*. The goal is to support students coming in to lecture prepared so the instructor can delve into more complex concepts.

1. Suppose I have a program that makes a guy wave after he walks up to a girl. How would you change it to make the guy wave repeatedly AS he walks up to the girl?

This is asking them to essentially do **Explore** and **Predict**, where they have to explore what already exists, then predict the outcome of changes they would make and then test to make sure the actual outcome matches the scenario, or expected outcome.

The questions in this section are not meant to be tested in the Alice programming environment; rather the students are expected to be able to do them on paper. At the beginning of lecture, the instructor will give a quiz as described in section 3.2. The students will not have access to any computer or notes; therefore it would behoove them to practice the questions in a similar environment.

5. STUDENT EXPERIENCE

From both an optional midterm survey (N=156) and a required end of term reflection[1] we can provide information on the experiences students had with exploratory homeworks[2].

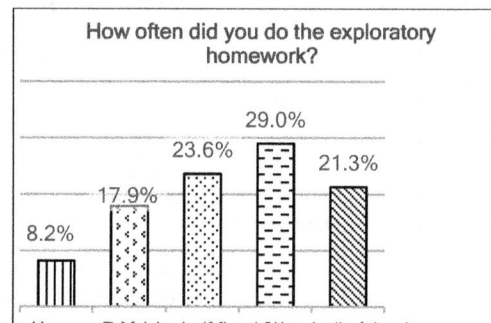

Figure 3: Student Survey Results for "How Often"

5.1 Usage

Although we assigned exploratory homeworks for every lecture and had a quiz covering the material at the beginning of each lecture, we're not so naïve as to think students always did the

---

[1] All data is from the end-of-term survey unless otherwise noted.

[2] Students were told "effortful and honest answers, both positive and negative, will receive full credit."

homework, or did it in the manner we asked them to. When we asked students how often they did the exploratory homework, we were pleased that just over 50% answered most or all of the time. Additionally only ¼ of the class said they rarely or never did it. Why is this pleasing? We also asked students about their homework habits in other classes. 45% stated that they almost never do non-required homework in their other classes (though 26% thought they should, 19% said they didn't need to). Since our homeworks weren't physically turned in, but motivated by a quiz, we were comparatively pleased.

We also asked students to indicate an approach that most correctly described the approach they took to their homework. Table 1 shows that only 30% of students followed the core portion of our approach: to work with the textbook and program simultaneously.

Approach (recommended approach in italics)	%
Read the textbook but don't do the code in Alice	33%
Create the code in Alice as I read the textbook	30%
Just create the code in Alice, skimming the textbook	15%
Create the code in Alice after reading the textbook	9%
Just read over the homework	8%

Table 1: Students Approach to HW.
(5% of students did not do the homework at all)

Perhaps to be expected, the largest number of students said they only read the textbook – negating our true intent (though we don't know if they also read the homework prompts (prediction prompts, explanations) as well). Based on student open-ended comments we expect that lack of easy access to a computer with Alice installed is a key factor. Traditional study locations in the dorm or library would be a barrier unless the student had their own laptop with Alice installed. In doing a post-hoc analysis of grades we were pleased to discover that students who created the code in Alice both in following the exploratory homework correctly and incorrectly (e.g. reading the textbook first or skimming it) did do significantly better (4.6 points) in the course than those who did not do the exploratory homeworks.

Finally, 76% students reported spending between 30 minutes and 2 hours on exploratory homework per week (averaging 40 minutes per homework). 10% reported spending more than 2 hours per week. We were expecting students to spend a somewhat greater amount of time on the exploratory homeworks. However a) 33% weren't actually doing the coding and b) student self-report of study time is a <100% reliable measure. On the other hand, the fact that most students *reported* spending less than 2 hours a week is positive (from the strategic view of teaching evaluations for a non-majors course). If they really spent more time, but did not realize it, that's educationally desirable.

5.2 Valuation

During week 5 of 10 in the quarter, we asked the students to take an *optional*, anonymous survey asking 3 questions:

1. Has the homework helped you understand lecture?
2. Has the homework helped you with labs?
3. Explain how the homework as helped you or why it has not helped you.

On questions 1 and 2 students choose between **Always**, **Sometimes**, and **Never**. Question 3 was open ended.

	Always	Sometimes	Never	Total
Lecture	58%	41%	1%	156
Labs	42%	54%	4%	156

Table 2: Homework Survey Results

There were five main points students brought up in their open-ended responses (all grammar and typing is original):

- **Step-by-step guidance** allowed them to understand the material easier and learn **skills and techniques**.
  Sometimes it is not clear which examples will help us with the lab, since the instructions depend on us to understand exactly how to utilize what we learned through the homework and lectures. Most times it helps because it teaches us techniques and skills.

- Gave them **prior-knowledge** and therefore **confidence** in lecture and lab to discuss and ask questions because they felt they knew what was going on.
  I feel like I can help myself get ahead by doing homeworks before class. I don't have to depend on my team mates to have the answers and I get to voice my opinion if I think they're wrong.

- Gave them a chance to **practice** more than once, which helped them **clarify confusions** they had the first time through.
  The hw allowed me to experiment and try out new things on my own. If there were any difficult concepts, it would stick a lot better if I struggled and learned it on my own rather just have someone tell me.

- Showed them **new ways** of accomplishing what they want to do and to be more **inventive**.
  The homework gives me an idea of how to do new things. I get to experiment with the ideas before doing the labs for them and that's good preparation.

- Pointed out **debugging mistakes** that they could make and give them a **reference** when they make similar mistakes in lab.
  Every homework assignment has helped me by explaining all the coding and understanding what the program does. It's really helpful and I advise on people to do the homework because it gives a better understanding when we have to solve our debugging mistakes.

One student in particular summed up his view of the role of exploratory homeworks in reference to the rest of the course:
  Homework teaches me the basics, class teaches me the details of how it works, and lab allows me to apply what I've learned to real situations.

This student has identified that the homeworks have allowed him to gain a familiarity with the concepts, more so than passively reading the text. Since the course was taught using the PI pedagogy, students were actively learning in lecture as well. The fact that the student was able to continue learning more complex concepts during lecture reinforces that they were ready to move on having done the exploratory homework. Finally, the fact that after two homeworks and two lectures the student was able to apply what they learned in a "real situation" (lab) indicates that the student had enough experience via similar problems to be able to tackle new, complex problems on their own.

At the end of the term we asked students, retrospectively, if the times they didn't (or couldn't) take the exploratory homework seriously had an impact on their learning in class. 62% said that it did hinder their learning in some way. 11% said it absolutely hindered their learning. 51% said it sometimes did, it depended on the material. The others claimed that they could usually figure out the material in class.

Finally, we wondered if the "spirit" of the homework would infect the students. That is, we were modeling for students the kinds of activities that "real programmers" do, and encouraging them to think about and explore concepts in the way we do. We asked:

How often did the exploratory homework prompt you to further experiment with Alice? - e.g. by writing and testing fragments of code not explicitly asked for in the homework, just to see what they would do?

24% of students said they did this all or most of the time and 34% did it "once or twice". To the extent that this informed "playing" somewhat reflects computational thinking, this is pleasing.

6. DISCUSSION

The role of the exploratory homeworks was to introduce and model for students "active learning", authentic approaches by which they can explore computing concepts and constructs and therefore acculturate themselves in technical reading. We have also explored how the components of exploratory homeworks can be assessed via the Kolb Learning Cycle – hopefully engaging students in an effective learning process. We hope both the methods and confidence (through practice) that students gained will serve them as citizens who will continue to learn and engage with new software and technologies throughout their lives.

Most notably, exploratory homeworks are a low fidelity way of introducing students to technical reading strategies employed by experts in the field. They are designed such that the students never get stuck and therefore can engage in authentic practice without an expert present (outside of lecture or lab). Students are taught to read technical material with their programming environment open, this is typical with experts in computing, but is discipline specific. Students learning physics do not typically read a section on gravity and then throw a watermelon off the roof to test the theories in the text. As described above, programming involves a very unique experience in that students can interact with the computer directly, getting feedback on behaviors and concepts they are learning. Exploratory homeworks engage students in cognitive apprenticeship without requiring in-person expert guidance.

7. FUTURE WORK

Having developed the structure of the exploratory homeworks and seen indications of students improved textbook reading habits and increased learning, we plan to develop more exploratory homeworks for CS1 courses. During this second phase we will explore the effectiveness of using the Kolb Learning Cycle as we do now (not necessarily in order) against a more rigid structure.

We also plan to observe some students completing the exploratory homeworks and ask them questions about their normal study habits as they compare to using exploratory homeworks. Finally, we plan to follow up with students who have been working through exploratory homeworks and see if they have transferred the textbook reading skills outside of the CS0 course.

We are eager to have a discussion with the community on how we might improve exploratory homeworks, what other educators would need to support them in creation of their own exploratory homeworks and advice they might have on measuring the effectiveness of exploratory homeworks when they are often coupled with effective pedagogies in lecture and tutorials in labs.

8. CONCLUSION

Exploratory homeworks are tools that encourage students to actively engage in pre-lecture reading; this includes writing and debugging code as well as learning how to read technical, static texts. Active learning is a technique that is often successfully used in lecture and lab based settings, but rarely are students asked to actively learn on their own, before lecture. Exploratory homeworks can enhance already active textbooks, like the Alice textbook used here, as well as more expository textbooks. The biggest benefit from students actively reading before lecture is they are able to come to lecture prepared to learn more complex concepts and constructs – enabling instructors to delve more deeply in lecture. Students are also developing authentic computing habits by actively participating in trial and error, predictions and reflections when learning a new programming language. We encourage the community to create exploratory homeworks for CS0 and CS1 courses using a variety of textbooks and report back on both effectiveness and challenges.

9. ACKNOWLEDGMENTS

This work was supported by the NSF CNS-0938336 and UK's HEA–ICS. We thank Spencer Bagley for quantitative analysis support.

10. REFERENCES

[1] Bransford, J. D. etc al eds. NRC. 2000. How People Learn: Brain, Mind, Experience, and School, Expanded Edition. Academy Press.

[2] Mazur, E. 2009. Farewell, Lecture? *Science.* Vol 323 No. 5910, pp. 50-51.

[3] Eberlein, T., Kampmeier, J., Minderhout, V., Moog, R. S., Platt, T., Varma-Nelson, P. and White, H. B. 2008. Pedagogies of engagement in science. *Biochemistry and Molecular Biology Education,* 36: 262–273.

[4] Hundhausen, C.D., Narayanan, N.H., & Crosby, M.E. 2008. Exploring studio-based instructional models for computing education. In SIGCSE '08, pp. 392-396.

[5] Bonner, J., Holliday, W. 2006. How College Science Students Engage in Note-Taking Strategies. *J. of Research in Science Teaching* 43, 8, pp. 786-818.

[6] Lewis, C., Titterton, N., Clancy, M. 2011. Developing students' self-assessment skills using lab-centric instruction. *J. Comput. Sci. Coll.* 26, 4, pp. 173-180.

[7] Waller, W. A. 1994. A framework for CS1 and CS2 laboratories. *SIGCSE 1994.* ACM, New York, NY, USA, 198-202. DOI=10.1145/191029.191107 http://doi.acm.org/10.1145/191029.191107

[8] Bennedsen, J., Caspersen, M. E., and Kölling, M. (Eds.). 2008. *Reflections on the Teaching of Programming: Methods and Implementations.* Springer-Verlag, Berlin, Heidelberg.

[9] Lorch, R. Jr., Pugzles Lorch, E., Klusewitz, M. 2009. College Students' Conditional Knowledge About Reading. *J of Educational Psychology.* Vol 85(2) pp. 239-252.

[10] Kolb, D. 1984. Experiential learning: experience as the source of learning and development. Englewood Cliffs, N.J.: Prentice Hall.

[11] Brown, J. S., Collins, A., and Duguid, P. 1989. *Educational Researcher,* Situated Cognition and the Culture of Learning. Vol. 18, No. 1. pp. 32-42.

[12] Dann, W. P., Cooper, S., Pausch, R. 2009. Learning to Program with Alice. New Jersey: Prentice Hall.

Ability to 'Explain in Plain English' Linked to Proficiency in Computer-based Programming

Laurie Murphy
Pacific Lutheran University
Tacoma, WA USA
lmurphy@plu.edu

Sue Fitzgerald
Metropolitan State University
St. Paul, MN USA
sue.fitzgerald@metrostate.edu

Raymond Lister
University of Technology
Sydney AUSTRALIA
Raymond.Lister@uts.edu.au

Renée McCauley
College of Charleston
Charleston, SC USA
mccauleyr@cofc.edu

ABSTRACT

This study investigates the relationship between novice programmers' ability to explain code segments and their ability to write code. Results show a strong correlation between ability to correctly answer 'explain in plain English' (EiPE) questions and ability to write code indicating that there are aspects of reasoning about code that are common to both writing code and explaining code. Student explanations were categorized using the Structure of the Observed Learning Outcome (SOLO) taxonomy. The better programmers were more likely to articulate relational aspects of the algorithms. While earlier work also found such a link, the code writing in those earlier studies was done on paper. This is the first such result where the writing component was done with 'hands on' a computer. Our results add further evidence for the existence of an aspect of reasoning about code that is common to both explaining code and writing code, which in turn suggests that a judicious mix of teaching both code skills and code explaining skills may lead to a more effective process by which novices learn to reason about code.

Categories and Subject Descriptors

K.3.2 [**Computing Milieux**]: Computers and Education - Computer and Information Science Education

General Terms

Human Factors

Keywords

Computer science education research, qualitative research methods, mixed methods, explain in plain English, SOLO, novice programmers

1. INTRODUCTION

Several recent studies have explored the relationship between the ability of novice programmers to read and explain code and their ability to write code. Whalley et al. (2006) [10] reported on a study in which students in an end–of–semester exam were given a question that began "In plain English, explain what the following segment of Java code does". They found that the better a student performed on other programming–related tasks in that same exam, the more likely the student was to provide a correct summary of the overall computation performed by the code in that explain in plain English (EiPE) question. As a result, they hypothesized that "a vital step toward being able to write programs is the capacity to read a piece of code and describe [its function]."

This result is interesting because it suggests that there may be other ways to teach programming, beyond writing lots of code. It is clear that some students pick up on programming quickly, while others struggle. In addition to writing code, is there another way to assist students in developing programming skills and perhaps reach students who struggle when taught only through coding?

Whalley et al. (2006) [10] analyzed student responses to EiPE questions using the Structure of the Observed Learning Outcome (SOLO) taxonomy [1]. There are five SOLO reasoning categories, roughly based on Piaget's stages of development, which describe how students understand problems in increasingly abstract ways. Four of the five SOLO reasoning categories are described in Table 1 (adapted from [10]). The fifth level, *extended abstract*, is not relevant to their work or our work, and so it is not discussed here. The highest level of reasoning shown in Table 1, *relational* reasoning, occurs when a student can describe the purpose of a code segment, with minimal or no reference to specific details of the code. Table 1 provides examples of each of these SOLO categories. The examples are excerpts from actual student descriptions of a code segment which sums all the positive numbers stored in an array (see problem iv in Section 2.3).

Lopez et al. (2008) [5] built upon the work of Whalley et al., using stepwise regression to analyze student responses to an end–of–semester exam. They found that, when combined with student performance on code tracing questions, the ability to provide a correct relational response to an EiPE question accounted for almost half the variance in a code writing question in that same paper-based exam. Venables, Tan and Lister (2009) [9] also found a strong relationship between student performance on tracing questions, EiPE questions, and code writing questions in a paper-based exam. Lister, Fidge and Teague (2009) [4] performed a non-parametric analysis of similar data, collected in a paper-based exam, and reported similar findings.

The above studies have clearly demonstrated a relationship between EiPE questions and code writing in paper-based exams. However, the question remains as to whether asking students to write code on paper is a valid indication of their code writing ability. Prior to taking these paper-based end-of-semester exams, the novices involved would have written most of their code 'hands on' (i.e., on a computer). While some computing educators might argue that having novices write code on paper has its virtues (as Edsger Dijkstra did), it remains a fact that doing so was probably a relatively unfamiliar process for these novices. Could that unfamiliarity have affected their performance?

Apart from familiarity, writing code 'hands on' allows the novice to run and test their code. By doing so, a novice might detect logical errors that would otherwise go undetected on paper. Could these novices have lost points on the paper-based test that they would not have lost had the test been computer-based?

Like the earlier studies cited above, this paper reports on a study of the relationship between introductory students' ability to explain code and to write code at the end of their first programming course. However, unlike the earlier studies, this paper reports on a final exam regime in which the students first completed the EiPE questions on paper and then immediately afterwards completed the computer-based code writing questions.

We believe that there is an underlying skill set common to both reading and writing code. Thus this study investigates whether the relationship between EiPE questions and code writing found in earlier studies was merely an artifact of having students write code on paper. The hypothesis for this study is that the relationship between EiPE questions and code writing also exists when the code writing is done on a computer.

This paper is organized as follows: Section 2 describes the study methodology. The results are presented in Section 3 and discussed in Section 4. Finally, Section 5 presents ideas for future work.

2. METHODOLOGY

2.1 Participants

Participants were 107 undergraduate students (34 female, 73 male) enrolled in six sections of a traditional "objects later" introductory Java programming course, offered over four semesters (Spring 2010 through Fall 2011). All sections of the class were taught by one instructor using very similar course materials. Students who took the class in Spring and Fall 2010 were not exposed to EiPE questions prior to the final exam, while those in Spring and Fall 2011 were given several EiPE questions on quizzes and tests throughout the term. The instructor also reviewed and emphasized the EiPE responses with the 2011 students when the graded tests were returned. (See [6] for details.)

2.2 Data Collection

All data were collected during a two-part final exam. Both the written part (worth 55 points) and programming part (worth 45 points, plus 5 bonus points) were administered in a computer classroom during a one hour and 50 minute final exam period. Students were encouraged to complete the written exam during the first hour to allow enough time to complete the programming part. Final exams are not returned to the students, so identical or nearly identical questions were used every semester.

2.3 Written Test Instrument

The written exams were closed book and closed notes. The EiPE questions were worth three points each (12 points total) out of 55 points for the written exam. The students were required to provide an explanation for four separate pieces of code (see i-iv below), which were preceded by the following instruction:

For each of these sections of code, explain in plain English what it does. For example, "It displays the sum of the two integers" or "It returns the last value in the array." Don't describe the code line-by-line; state what it does overall.

i. (Nested ifs) Assume a, b and c are all int variables that have been declared and initialized.

```
if ( a < b)
    if ( b < c)
        System.out.println( c );
    else
        System.out.println( b );
else if ( a < c)
        System.out.println( c );
else
        System.out.println( a );
```

Note: The code above displays the largest of the three values stored in variables a, b and c. Some students in our data sample were presented with a version that printed the smallest value. For either version, student responses were graded appropriately.

Table1. SOLO Categories

Category	Description	Examples for a method that sums the positive elements in an array
Relational	Provides a summary of what the code does in terms of the code's purpose	"adds up all values in the array that are positive and returns them"
Multistructural	A line-by-line description is provided of most of the code	"For integer i = 0 and 1 less than the amount of numbers in the array [numbers,] add 1 to i and if the array numbers is greater than zero add i to the num, return the num at the end."
Unistructural	Provides a description for only a small portion of the code	"Returns the value of num"
Prestructural	The answer demonstrates no relevant knowledge or is unrelated to the question	"This will return how many letters there are in statement"

ii. (Longest String) Consider the following method that is passed an array of strings:

```java
public String methodC(String[] word)
{
    String strOne = word[0];

    for (int i = 1; i <  word.length; i++)
    {
      if (word[i].length()>strOne.length())
        strOne = word[i];
    }
      return strOne;
}
```

iii. (Linear Search) Consider the following method that searches an array:

```java
public int methodB(int data[], int x )
{
    int found = -1;

    for (int i=0; i < data.length; i++ )
    {
        if( data[i] == x )
            found = i;
    }
      return found;
}
```

iv. (Sum of Positives) Consider the following method that is passed an array of doubles:

```java
public double methodA( double[] numbers )
{
    double num = 0;

    for(int i=0; i < numbers.length; i++ )
    {
      if ( numbers[i] > 0 )
        num += numbers[i];
    }
      return num;
}
```

2.4 Computer-based Instrument

Once students finished the written final, they were given a programming exam that required them to complete a set of short Java programs by adding basic constructs and simple object-oriented code. Students were provided with three syntax reference sheets during the programming exam, but were not allowed to use other references. To prevent access to lab and homework solutions, students were assigned temporary accounts that only included the exam source files. Their machines were also monitored using classroom management software. The programming exam counted for 45 of the 100 exam points with an opportunity to earn 5 extra credit points. Table 2 describes the programming questions.

Table 2: Computer-based Programming Exam Questions

	Problem Description
1	Prompt the user to enter a series of integers (-99 to signal the end of the series) and then display the largest and smallest numbers entered.
2	Prompt the user for an integer and display an upside down triangle with that number of rows. For example, for the input of 5: * * * * * * * * * * * * * * *
3	Prompt the user to enter a string and a character and return the number of times the specified character appears in the string.
4	Write a constructor for a class "Car".
5	Write a method that returns the miles per gallon performance of an instance of class Car.
6	Instantiate an object of the class Car.
7	Declare and instantiate an array of 20 integers.
8	Write a loop to fill the array from the previous task with random numbers from 1 to 100.
9	Calculate the average of all the values in the above array.
10	Declare an array to hold 5 Strings. Prompt the user for their five favorite leisure activities, read them into the array, then call a method to return the alphabetically first element in the array.

2.5 Data Coding

For grading purposes, the EiPE questions were marked along with all other questions on the final exam and they received partial credit in some cases. Points awarded during the marking were used for analysis purposes. These marks were then used in the analysis to examine correlations between performance on the explanation questions and the programming exam. These results are discussed in section 4.

To facilitate analysis, students were placed in "buckets" according to their test scores on the computer-based programming exam. The students were divided roughly into four quartiles. The quartiles were 0–30 points (28 students), 31–42 points (28 students), 43–49 points (27 students) and 50 points (24 students).

We also conducted analyses of the answers to the explanation questions using the SOLO taxonomy (see Table 1). Responses were categorized independently by two researchers who then argued to consensus on the appropriate categorization of 97.2% of the responses.

3. RESULTS

In this section we present an analysis of our results. Section 3.1 describes overall student performance. Sections 3.2-3.5 focus on each of the EiPE questions. The EiPE questions are presented in order from easiest to most difficult.

While our research hypothesis is that there exists a relationship between EiPE questions and code writing, we make no hypothesis about the exact nature of that relationship (e.g. a linear relationship). Consequently, we took a non-parametric approach to the analysis. As noted in section 2.5, the students were divided into quartiles based on their performance on the hands on code writing exam. In sections 3.2-3.5, the quartiles are compared via a close examination of the students' responses to the EiPE questions using a $\chi 2$ test. A statistically significant difference in performance between any two quartiles reveals a relationship between ability to describe algorithms relationally and ability to program. This analytic approach was also used in previous work by Lister, Fidge and Teague [4].

3.1 Overall Statistics

With four semesters of data involving 107 participants, we considered scores on the EiPE questions and results on the programming portion of the final. The EiPE question scores, out of a total of 12 points, had a range of 0-12, a mean of 8.65 and a standard deviation of 3.27. The final programming exam scores, out of a total of 50 points, had a range of 0-50, a mean of 36.83, and a standard deviation of 14.2. Our data was not normally-distributed, so a Spearman's correlation was used to show that the points on the EiPE questions and the computer-based programming instrument are highly correlated; Spearman's rho is .687, with $p < .001$. This is highly significant and indicates that it is extremely unlikely that this relationship occurred by chance.

We compared the EiPE question scores for students in Spring and Fall 2010 to those of students in Spring and Fall 2011. Students in Spring and Fall 2011 received extra instruction in how to explain code segments. We found no significant differences between the scores on EiPE questions between the two groups; the 2011 students' prior experience with EiPE questions did not appear to affect ability to answer explaining questions correctly.

An examination of the SOLO categorization of student explanations showed that students were more likely to express themselves relationally than any other way (see Table 3). For the most difficult question (summing positive numbers, question iv), approximately 40% of the students either identified only one element of the problem (unistructural) or answered meaninglessly (prestructural) but for the simplest problem (display the largest number, question i), 79% of the students were able to answer relationally.

Table 3. SOLO Categorization of Answers

	(i) Nested ifs	(ii) Longest String	(iii) Linear Search	(iv) Sum of Positives
Relational	79%	70%	54%	49%
Multi-structural	9%	5%	24%	11%
Unistructural	7%	9%	13%	27%
Prestructural	4%	16%	8%	13%

* Results may not sum to 100% due to round off error

The following sections focus upon how the performance on EiPE questions differs between buckets.

3.2 The Nested ifs

Student performance on the nested if EiPE question is summarized in column (i) of Table 4. Of the entire sample of 107

students, 79% provided a suitable answer (i.e., a SOLO relational response, indicating that the code printed the largest/smallest value, depending upon which version of the code the student was given). This 79% is the highest percentage of relational answers for the four explanation questions, which is perhaps not surprising, given that this code was the only code that did not contain a loop.

Almost two-thirds (64%) of the bottom quartile provided a suitable answer to this question, as did 71% of the second quartile. A $\chi 2$ test failed to establish a statistically significant difference in the percentages of these two quartiles ($p = 0.57$, as shown in Table 4, in column (i), row 3, the row between the 64% and 71% performance figures of these two quartiles). While 89% of the third quartile students answered the question correctly, that percentage is not statistically significantly different from the 71% percentage for the second quartile ($\chi 2$ test, p=0.11, as shown in column (i) row 5 of Table 4). Also, the 96% performance of the top quartile is not significantly different from the 89% performance of the third quartile ($\chi 2$ test, p=0.36, as shown in row 7 of Table 4).

Common sense suggests that we should not expect much difference between two students whose respective scores on the computer-based programming test differ by only 2 points out of 50. It follows that we should not expect much difference between students who scored 1 mark below a quartile boundary and students who scored 1 mark above that same quartile boundary. Thus, our use of the traditional statistical p=0.05 criterion is a tough standard to apply to adjacent quartile buckets. Table 5 summarizes $\chi 2$ tests on the non-adjacent second and top quartiles. The performance difference between these two quartiles does meet the traditional p=0.05 criterion on this explanation question and on all the other explanation questions.

In summary, the nested if problem was an easy explanation question for this sample of 107 students, as many students who performed in the bottom quartile of the computer-based programming test could answer this question. The most useful aspect of this question is that it serves to demonstrate that at least 79% of the entire sample of 107 students had a good understanding of what was required of them when answering this explanation question. It follows that those 79% of students also had a good understanding of what was expected when answering the other three explanation questions.

3.3 Longest String

The performance of the students on the longest string explanation question is summarized in column (ii) of Table 4. Of the entire sample of 107 students, 70% provided a SOLO relational response.

Less than one third (29%) of the bottom quartile provided a suitable answer to this question, compared with more than two thirds (68%) of the second quartile. A $\chi 2$ test established a statistically significant difference in these percentages ($p = 0.003$). This cell and some other cells in Table 4 are shaded to highlight statistically significant differences between quartiles. The "ES = 4" in that cell shows the effect size, as measured by the odds ratio. The 4 means that the odds a student in the second quartile gave a relational response are four times higher than for a student in the bottom quartile. Rosenthal (1996) [7] classified effect sizes measured by odds ratios as follows: an odds ratio in the range

Table 4. Comparing Quartile Performance on Computer-based Programming Exam (* indicates p ≤ 0.05, ** indicates p ≤ 0.01)

Row	Description	n	Explain in Plain English Questions (i) to (iv)			
			(i) Nested ifs	(ii) Longest String	(iii) Linear Search	(iv) Sum of Positives
1	Whole sample	107	79%	70%	54%	49%
2	Bottom Quartile , 0–30 points	28	64%	29%	18%	11%
3	χ^2 test		p = 0.57	p = 0.003** ES = 4	p = 0.02* ES = 4	p < 0.01** ES = 5
4	Second Quartile, 31–42 points	28	71%	68%	46%	39%
5	χ^2 test		p = 0.11	p = 0.12	p = 0.07 (1 in 14)	p = 0.04* ES = 3
6	Third Quartile, 43–49 points	27	89%	93%	70%	67%
7	χ^2 test		p = 0.36	p = 0.40	p = 0.14	p = 0.17
8	Top Quartile , 50 points	24	96%	96%	88%	83%

1–1.5 is small, 1.5–2.5 is medium, around 4 is large, and around 10 is "very large". Thus the effect size "ES = 4" in that cell is large.

While there is not a statistically significant difference between the second and third quartiles, or the third and top quartiles, Table 5 shows that there is a statistically significant difference between the second and top quartiles (as is the case with all four explanation questions). Furthermore, the effect size between the second and top quartiles is 11 – the odds that a student in the top quartile gave a relational response are eleven times higher than for a student in the second quartile. Such an effect size is very large.

3.4 Linear Search

The performance of the students on the linear search explanation question is summarized in column (iii) of Table 4. Of the entire sample of 107 students, just over half (54%) provided a response in which they mentioned that the code performed a search and returned a position in the array.

While there is not a statistically significant difference between the second and third quartiles, or the third and top quartiles, Table 5 shows that there is a statistically significant difference between the second and top quartiles with a large effect size of 8.

As discussed in the subsection on the nested if explanation question, the traditional statistical p=0.05 criterion is a tough standard to apply to adjacent quartile buckets. Thus, the p = 0.07 value for the difference between the second and third quartiles is weakly suggestive evidence that there is a performance difference, particularly as p=0.07 can be interpreted as indicating that there is only a 1 in 14 chance of the difference being a sampling fluke, compared to the 1 in 20 chance of the traditional p=0.05. The cell containing this p=0.07 value is more lightly shaded than other shaded cells, to indicate that it is weakly suggestive but not statistically significant.

Table 6 provides more detailed statistics on this Linear Search explanation question. The column headed "Notion of Searching" records the percentage of students, both as a whole sample and in each quartile, who indicated that the code was performing some form of search. Only 79% of the entire sample did so, which we regard as surprising since searching is mentioned in the preamble to the code ("Consider the following method that searches an array"). A mere 43% of the bottom quartile indicated that the code was performing some form of search, which is significantly lower than the 82% of the second quartile. Table 7 shows that there is not a statistically significant difference between the 82% of second and the 96% of the top quartile.

Only 31% of the entire sample mentioned that -1 is returned if the search value is not found. In fact, only 58% of the top quartile mentioned this aspect of the code, but the data in Table 7 indicates that the top quartile performed significantly better than the second quartile, and the data in Table 6 is weakly suggestive of a performance difference between the third and top quartiles.

The final column in Table 6 presents data on a subtle aspect of this piece of code – what happens when the search value occurs more than once in the array? Among the 56 students in the lowest two quartiles, only one student raised this issue in their answer. The percentage of students in the highest two quartiles who raised this issue is not high, but it is significantly different than the performance of the lowest two quartiles, with a large effect size.

In summary, the better performers on the computer-based programming test (students in the higher quartiles) were more likely to articulate aspects of the algorithm beyond simply that it performs a search. Note that we are not claiming that a student who did not mention aspects of the algorithm, such as for example returning -1 when the search value is not found, is incapable of understanding that aspect of the code. All we claim is that students who performed better on the computer-based programming test were more likely to make note of such details in their answers. We speculate that good programming students are also more likely to spontaneously think about contingencies when writing code.

3.5 Sum of Positive Numbers

The students performed surprisingly poorly on explaining the code that sums the positive elements of an array. As indicated in column (iv) of Table 4, only 49% of the entire sample of 107 students provided a suitable response. The performance of the bottom quartile was particularly poor (11%), and significantly worse than the performance of the second quartile, even though only 39% of the second quartile students answered appropriately.

Even in the third quartile, only two-thirds of the students answered appropriately.

An examination of student answers reveals that a common mistake was to respond that the code summed all the elements of the array. In making that mistake, students ignored the "if" statement within the loop – to do so is an egregious error. Table 8 summarizes statistics on the students who made this error. The percentages are calculated from the subset of 72 students who either articulated that the code summed the positive elements, or that it summed all elements. Only 8 students in the bottom quartile gave either type of answer, but 5 of those 8 (63%) ignored the "if" statement and wrote that the code summed all elements of the array. The performance of students improves with each higher quartile, with only 1 of the 21 students (5%) in the top quartile making the mistake of ignoring the "if" statement. While none of the percentage differences shown in Table 8 between the adjacent quartiles meet the strict p = 0.05 criteria, a χ2 test (not shown in Table 8) did find a statistically significant difference between the

45% of the second quartile and the 5% of the top quartile (p = 0.003), with a very large effect size of 16.

This error of ignoring the "if" statement is of a different class than, for example, not mentioning that the linear search returns -1 when the search value was not found. The "if" statement within the loop checking for positive values is written there in plain sight on the page in front of the student – how can a student possibly ignore it? The theory of cognitive load [8] provides one possible explanation. When the working memory of any person is overwhelmed, important information may be ignored. In the specific case of this code explanation question, a student who is struggling to cope with the details of this code may note the occurrence of a "for" loop controlled by a variable "i", and then focus upon the line "num += numbers[i]". Such an explanation is also consistent with the behavior of pre-operational novices as defined within the Neo-Piagetian view of the novice programmer [3].

Table 5. Comparing Performance of Second and Top Quartiles (* indicates p ≤ 0.05 and ** indicates p ≤ 0.01)

Row	Description	n	Explain in Plain English Questions (i) to (iv)			
			(i) Nested ifs	(ii) Longest String	(iii) Linear Search	(iv) Sum of Positives
4	Second Quartile, 31–42 points	28	64%	68%	46%	39%
	χ² test		p = 0.02* ES = 9	p = 0.01* ES = 11	p = 0.002** ES = 8	p = 0.001** ES = 8
8	Top Quartile , 50 points	24	96%	96%	88%	83%

Table 6. Comparing Performance on Linear Search by Quartile (* indicates p ≤ 0.05 and ** indicates p ≤ 0.01)

Row	Description	N	Explain in Plain English Question (iii), Linear Search			
			Notion of Searching	Returns position	Returns -1 when not found	Returns position of last found
1	Whole sample	107	79%	57%	31%	15%
2	Bottom Quartile , 0–30 points	28	43%	18%	11%	0%
3	χ² test		p = 0.002** ES = 6	p = 0.002** ES = 6	p = 0.17	p = 0.31
4	Second Quartile, 31–42 points	28	82%	57%	25%	4%
5	χ² test		p = 0.09 (1 in 11)	p = 0.49	p = 0.50	p = 0.04* ES = 8
6	Third Quartile, 43–49 points	27	96%	70%	33%	22%
7	χ² test		p = 0.93	p = 0.14	p = 0.07 (1 in 14)	p = 0.23
8	Top Quartile , 50 points	24	96%	88%	58%	38%

Table 7. Comparing Performance of Second and Top Quartiles for Linear Search Question (* for p ≤ 0.05, ** for p ≤ 0.01)

Row	Description	N	Explain in Plain English Question (iii), Linear Search			
			Notion of Searching	Returns position	Returns -1 when not found	Returns position of last found
1	Second Quartile, 31–42 points	28	82%	57%	25%	4%
2	χ² test		p = 0.12	p = 0.02* ES = 5	p = 0.02* ES = 4	p = 0.002** ES = 16
3	Top Quartile , 50 points	24	96%	88%	58%	38%

Table 8. The Percentage of Students Responding that the Sum of Positives Code Returned the Sum of All Elements

Description	N	Percentage of Sum of All Responses
Whole sample	72	28%
Bottom Quartile	8	63%
		χ^2 test, p = 0.4
Second Quartile	20	45%
		χ^2 test, p = 0.10 (1 in 10)
Third Quartile	23	22%
		χ^2 test, p = 0.10 (1 in 10)
Top Quartile	21	5%

4. DISCUSSION

Our results (and earlier results by others) indicate that there are aspects of reasoning about code that are common to both writing code and explaining code. Our use of a computer-based test of code writing ability establishes that the results of earlier studies were not an artifact of having students write code on paper.

There are probably reasoning abilities specific to writing code and abilities specific to explaining code. However, our results suggest the possibility that the reasoning abilities common to both writing code and explaining code are non-trivial, given the clear statistical relationships we have found between performance on our code explanation questions and our computer-based code writing questions. This result suggests that there may be other ways to teach and learn programming, beyond writing lots of code – ways that focus on the elements common to reading, writing and explaining code.

It could be asserted that our results are unsurprising, as "*better students tend to be better at everything*". However, this assertion contains a mix of implicit assumptions about innate abilities versus acquired abilities, and also near transfer versus far transfer in learning. These assumptions have implications for the interpretation of our results, which we discuss in the remainder of this section.

In future experiments, building on these results, it would be interesting to include a non-programming task, and attempt to factor out general ability from the analysis of the programming tasks, as Lopez et al. did in their study [5]. However, it is unlikely that general ability would account for most of the variance across quartiles that we see in our data, since it is known that grades for introductory programming courses do not correlate well with grades in general [2]. Perhaps a more accurate assertion would be "*better programming students are better at every aspect of programming*", as there is some evidence for that [2]. While we would not go so far as to say that better programming students do better on every aspect of programming, our results show that writing code and explaining code correlate. The crucial issue is whether this correlation is because (1) the ability to explain code is dependent on the

ability to write code, or (2) the opposite causal relationship (i.e. the ability to write code is dependent on the ability to explain code), or (3) the ability to write code and read code are both dependent on a common set of underlying skills. While our experimental results cannot choose among these three possibilities, our intuition is that the latter is the most likely possibility.

A further question is whether the ability that is common to both writing and explaining is innate or is acquired through learning. While there may be a component to programming ability that is innate, our intuition is that programming ability is largely acquired, at least at the CS1 level, but our results neither prove nor disprove our intuition.

5. FUTURE DIRECTIONS

Our results add further evidence for the existence of an aspect of reasoning about code that is common to both explaining code and writing code which in turn suggests that a near-complete pedagogical emphasis on writing code is too great, as writing code is a slow, tedious process, especially for novices. A more judicious mix of tracing code, reading code (e.g. by explaining it) and writing code may lead to a more effective and efficient process by which many novices would learn to reason about code.

Although proficiency at code explaining and code writing are linked, we can report that mere exposure to code explanation tasks does not appear to improve code writing ability. Across the four semesters in which we collected data, the students in the two early semesters were not shown any code explanation questions prior to the final exam, whereas the students in the two later semesters were given code explanation questions as part of their learning throughout the semester. We saw no statistical difference in code explaining performance of students in the first two semesters from those in the later semesters. The lack of such a difference is not evidence against placing a greater pedagogical emphasis on code explaining. While the students in the later two semesters were given some code explanation questions throughout semester, and the answers for these questions were discussed by the teacher in the classroom, the addition of these questions fell well short of being a systematic pedagogical intervention. Just as some students need a great deal of help to learn how to write code, some students will need a well developed pedagogical approach if they are to learn how to explain code. The development of pedagogical approaches that mix tracing, describing, and writing code is an area requiring substantial future work.

6. ACKNOWLEDGEMENTS

We thank Brian Hanks for his invaluable assistance with our statistical analysis.

7. REFERENCES

[1] Biggs, J. & Collis, K. 1982. Evaluating the Quality of Learning: The SOLO Taxonomy (Structure of the Observed Learning Outcome). Academic Press, New York, NY.

[2] Gomes, A. J. and Mendes, A. J.. 2010. A study on student performance in first year CS courses. In Proceedings of the fifteenth annual conference on Innovation and technology in computer science education (ITiCSE '10). 113-117.

[3] Lister, R. Concrete and other neo-Piagetian forms of reasoning in the novice programmer. 2011. In Proceedings of the 13th Australasian Computing Education Conference (ACE 2011). Australasian Computing Society.

[4] Lister, R., Fidge C. & Teague, D. 2009. Further evidence of a relationship between explaining, tracing and writing skills in introductory programming. In Proceedings of the14th Annual Conference on Innovation and Technology in Computer Science Education (ITiCSE '09), 161-165.

[5] Lopez, M., Whalley, J., Robbins, P. & Lister, R. 2008. Relationships between reading, tracing and writing skills in introductory programming, In Proceedings of the 4th International Computing Education Research Workshop (ICER'08), 101-112.

[6] Murphy, L., McCauley, R. & Fitzgerald, S. 2012. 'Explain in plain English' questions: implications for teaching. In Proceedings of the 43rd ACM Technical Symposium on Computer Science Education (SIGCSE 2012), 385-390.

[7] Rosenthal, J. 1996. Qualitative descriptors of strength of association and effect size, Journal of Social Service Research 21, 4, 37-59.

[8] Sweller, J., Ayres, P., and Kalyuga, S. 2011. Cognitive Load Theory. Springer, New York, NY.

[9] Venables, A., Tan, G., & Lister, R. 2009. A closer look at tracing, explaining and code writing skills in the novice programmer. In Proceedings of the International Computing Education Research Workshop (ICER'09), 117-128.

[10] Whalley, J., Lister, R., Thompson, E., Clear, T., Robbins, P., Kumar, P. & Prasard, C. 2006. An Australasian study of reading and comprehension skills in novice programmers, using the Bloom and SOLO taxonomies. In Proceedings of the 8th Australasian Computing Education Conference Conference (ACE'06), 243-252.

How Do Students Solve Parsons Programming Problems?
— An Analysis of Interaction Traces

Juha Helminen[*], Petri Ihantola, Ville Karavirta, and Lauri Malmi
Department of Computer Science and Engineering
Aalto University
Finland
firstname.lastname@aalto.fi

ABSTRACT

The process of solving a programming assignment is generally invisible to the teacher. We only see the end result and maybe a few snapshots along the way. In order to investigate this process with regard to Parsons problems, we used an online environment for Parsons problems in Python to record a detailed trace of all the interaction during the solving session. In these assignments, learners are to correctly order and indent a given set of code fragments in order to build a functioning program that meets the set requirements. We collected data from students of two programming courses and among other analyses present a visualization of the solution path as an interactive graph that can be used to explore such patterns and anomalies as backtracking and loops in the solution. The results provide insights into students' solving process for these types of problems and ideas on how to improve the assignment environment and its use in programming education.

Categories and Subject Descriptors

K.3.2 [**Computers and Education**]: Computer and Information Science Education—*Computer science education*

General Terms

Human Factors

Keywords

Parsons Puzzles, Problem Solving Process, Python

1. INTRODUCTION

Programming is inherently a complex mental process where a programmer solves a domain problem, transforms the solution into an algorithmic form coding it using a programming language, designs an appropriate structure for the program,

---

[*]Corresponding author.

and finally implements, tests, and debugs the program in an iterative process. In programming education, we train this process heavily by requiring our students to solve many programming assignments. However, the experience has widely been that the results are unsatisfactory and a large number of students have serious difficulties in learning programming [8, 12].

A great challenge in teaching programming is that the whole process of solving a programming task is mostly invisible to teachers because there is no possibility to monitor all students' working and give guidance and feedback for them when they face problems. Even in closed labs with a few dozen students and a tutor, the tutor mostly sees only snapshots of students' work. This has obvious drawbacks. First, we cannot give students enough adequate feedback and guidance when they would need it; even in closed labs they often need to wait a considerable time, until the tutor is available for them, not to mention open labs. Second, as we at best only see a few snapshots, which often have problems or errors, we have a hard time concluding how students ended up with these solutions. Students may also develop bad practices, such as using automatic assessment tools as testers. Poor development habits and misconceptions about programming constructs and concepts acquired early on the introductory programming courses can easily stick. Therefore, we should seek to identify and correct unsound practices and flawed understanding as early as possible.

In this study, we have analyzed how students solve *Parsons programming puzzles*. These are a type of scaffolded program construction tasks where the learner is given a set of code fragments, blocks of a single or multiple lines of code, and the task is to piece together a program from these [13]. We have used a Parsons assignment environment for Python, called js-parsons [5], where learners not only select and order but also indent code fragments. These are called two-dimensional (2D) Parsons problems for the two degrees of freedom. In Python, code indentation has a semantic meaning, as an indented statement falls into the surrounding control structure, which has lower indentation. That is, code blocks are defined by indentation instead of start and end symbols like curly braces (see Tables 3–5 for examples). Compared to the basic Parsons problems, indentation makes such problems better resemble actual programming tasks.

The research reported in this paper has two aims. First, we study methods to visualize and analyze the process of constructing a program. To this end, we have built a tool which performs analyses and allows interactive investigation of Parsons problems' solution paths. Second, by means of the different analyses and visualizations, we study students' problem solving process in 2D Parsons problems. Students solve Parsons assignments in an environment that gives automatic feedback and guides them towards a solution. In addition, the system logs all student interaction, i.e., all re-orderings of the code fragments, as well as, feedback requests. Using this kind of data we can explore many interesting questions, such as:

- How do they arrive at the solution? Can we observe common solving patterns in an assignment or across assignments? How similar or different are the solution paths across students? What types of ineffective solving patterns do students exhibit? Do students' solution paths share common incorrect states, where the rows are ordered or indented incorrectly? How can these states be characterized?

- Do students backtrack or go in circles in their solution paths, i.e., do the solution paths have loops where students return to an earlier state in their solution path? How can these loops be characterized?

- How do students use automatic feedback? When and how often do they ask for feedback? How can the situations when they use feedback be characterized?

2. RELATED WORK

2.1 Parsons Programming Puzzles

Originally, Parsons problems were conceived to provide an engaging learning environment with immediate feedback that allows focused rote learning of syntax without being sidetracked by complex program logic [13]. In addition to online learning environments (e.g. Cort [4], ViLLE [17], and js-parsons [5]), they can be used in traditional pen-and-paper exams where actual programming, i.e., straightforward writing of code from scratch, is problematic [2, 11]. There are many variants and flavours of Parsons problems [5]:

Extra code fragments that are not part of the correct solution can be used to make the problems more challenging. These *distractors* are often modified from a correct line with the aim of revealing misconceptions related to the syntax [13].

A context can be provided by having fixed lines of code before, in the middle, and after the code fragments to be rearranged [4]. This allows making the programs larger and, thus, more concrete and meaningful.

User-defined blocks raise complexity and emphasize problem solving and program logic in the problems. This can be realized by letting learners insert code block delimiters, such as, curly braces in Java.

As discussed in Section 1, the js-parsons tool implements a Python-specific variant of users defining blocks where code fragments must be both re-ordered and indented correctly [5]. The tool is further described in Subsection 3.1.

An interesting question is which types of skills Parsons problems test and how they relate to the commonly assigned tasks of tracing, explaining, and writing code. Initially, it was postulated that Parsons problems lie somewhere between tracing and writing code [21]. Denny et al. found a notable correlation between Parsons scores and code writing scores but a low correlation between tracing and writing, and Parsons problems and tracing [2]. This suggests that tracing and writing require different skills and that Parsons problems are similar to writing code. Whereas, Lopez et al. found strong correlation between tracing and writing, and reading and writing code [11]. Moreover, they found evidence of the existence of a hierarchy of programming-related skills and indications that Parsons problems might be a lower skill than tracing or writing code. However, they note that the difficulty of a task may also be a function of its size and the programming constructs involved than merely the task type. Indeed, as they also note, the one and only Parsons problem they used was rather simple and could mostly have been solved using shallow heuristics, especially, since the code blocks were predetermined with curly braces. Further studies have found more evidence of a hierarchy where some skill in tracing precedes explaining and some skill in these two precede writing code while all are still believed to develop in parallel reinforcing each other [9, 10, 20]. Nevertheless, Venables et al. do note that the strength of the relationships varies considerably according to the nature of the task [20]. Finally, Lister et al. give some results of a found correlation between the scores of a Parsons problem and scores in tracing and writing in an exam [9]. Overall, the topic warrants some more studies with clearer focus on Parsons problems and a clear separation of the different types and mediums of Parsons problems which may have very different characteristics in relation to the skills being practiced.

2.2 Programming Assignment Trace Analysis

There is a growing body of research into programming behavior analysis based on recorded interaction traces. Blikstein has logged students' actions in the NetLogo programming environment [1]. In the modeling assignments, he identified such behaviors as copy-pasters who would switch away from the environment for long periods of time and then suddenly the code would grow notably. Kiesmüller et al. have studied students' problem solving strategies in the finite state machine -based visual programming environment Kara [7]. They have built a real-time identifier for previously observed problem solving approaches based on methods from speech recognition. Jadud, Rodrigo, Tabanao et al. have studied novice compilation behavior within the BlueJ programming environment [6, 19]. They have presented a visualization for a programming session recorded at compilation events and quantified how much a student struggles in a session based on compilation events. They have shown that this measure correlates negatively with the exam score. Recently, Piech et al. logged compilation events in Eclipse and modeled programming assignment development paths using machine learning [15]. The different groups of development paths correlated with students' performance and their predictive power was stronger than that of the assignment scores. At a larger granularity, analyzing submissions of an automatic assessment system, Edwards et al. have found quantitative evidence, e.g., that starting early relates to better performance [3]. Spacco et al. have presented a schema for representing program evolution with data captured from Marmoset [18] which captures program code at every save. Poncin et al. have applied process mining techniques from business process analysis to investigate software repositories of students' capstone projects [16].

With regard to Parsons problems, in the original paper, the authors suggest that in future versions of the tool they would like to be able to record learners' interaction with the tool in order to analyze their patterns of error [13]. Subsequently, the js-parsons tool has implemented this and the authors intend this feature to allow analysis of how the assignments are solved [5]. However, we are not aware of any previous work that has performed these analyses, or with regard to Python, of anything similar.

3. DATA COLLECTION

3.1 Method and Tool

The js-parsons tool provides a web environment for solving 2D Parsons problems in Python as described in Section 1. In this study, we used a mode where the input, i.e., the building blocks for the code, is given in random order on the left and the learner is to construct the solution on the right by drag-and-dropping code fragments to their place. Code fragments can be freely inserted in the solution between other fragments, moved around, indented, and also removed from the code back to the input area (see Figure 1).

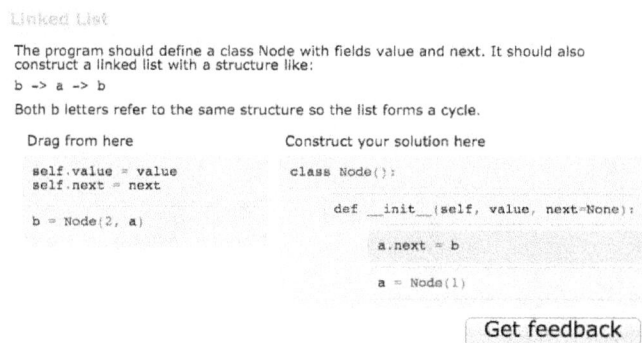

Figure 1: Parsons problem in js-parsons. Student has requested feedback, and the line in incorrect position is highlighted in red.

Feedback can be requested at any time and an unlimited number of times. There are three types of feedback: 1) there are too few lines, 2) the order or 3) the indentation is incorrect. The first two feedback types can occur simultaneously but feedback on indentation is given only after all the right fragments have been added and are in correct order. Previously, js-parsons would give feedback on ordering by highlighting in red the first incorrect fragment counting from the top [5]. However, we felt that this type of feedback would encourage adding lines linearly from top to bottom with a trial-and-error strategy of using repeated feedback requests to select the fragments. Thus, in this study, we modified the feedback so that we highlight a minimal set of fragments that need to be moved to fix the order, and the learner is informed that these fragments are in wrong positions relative to the others (see Figure 1). Incorrect indentation is pointed out by highlighting in red the start of the first incorrectly indented fragment. The size of whitespace used for indentation in Python can vary. For the feedback, indentation is normalized and any particular absolute indentation is not forced but feedback is given on the relative correctness of indentation in the learner's code. In addition to the use of color to highlight errors, a message window pops up. It is important to note that for this type of detailed feedback to be possible, the problem must be puzzle-like in the sense that there is a single correct combination, ordering, and indentation of code fragments, a unique solution.

The tool records a full trace of the learner's interactions during the problem solving session. Any changes in the input, solution, and all feedback requests are recorded with time stamps. We used this trace as the basis of our analyses.

As discussed in Section 2.1, the research is inconclusive on the skills needed to solve Parsons problems. However, we argue that it is not clear that 2D Parsons problems, as described here, are so simple that solving them lies beneath actual programming tasks such as tracing, explaining, and writing code. We argue that, depending on the exact task, they require similar skills and will invoke similar solving patterns and difficulties, and are thus an interesting, while simplified, data source to learn about the program construction process.

3.2 Assignments and Learners

We collected data on the solving of five different problems from students of two different programming courses at Aalto University, Finland. The problems are described below. In some problems, lines of code have been placed together as a fragment in order to force a unique solution. None of the problems included distractors. A student was able to advance to the next problem only after solving the current one.

P1: Find max (8 lines in 7 code fragments): Construct a function that finds the maximum value in a list.

P2: Draw triangle 1 (3 lines): Construct a function that prints a text triangle.

P3: Linked list (7 lines in 6 code fragments): Construct a program that defines a `Node` class and creates two objects to form a linked list with a cycle. See Figure 1 and Table 3.

P4: Draw triangle 2 (6 lines): Construct a function that prints an upside-down triangle. See Table 4.

P5: Sublist test (7 lines): Construct a function that tests whether a list is a sublist of the other. See Table 5.

In Fall 2011, these assignments were used on a Web Software Development (WSD) course. They were part of a compulsory exercise round on Python but students could pass this round without solving these assignments. Still, almost all students solved all of them. The assignments were given in the order described above.

In Spring 2012, the assignments were used on a CS2 course taught with Python. On that course, the assignments were optional, additional exercises. For this course, we switched the order of the first two assignments.

Before solving the assignments, students were asked two questions: *Have you programmed with Python before (yes/no)* and *How much have you programmed before (Python or some other programming language)*. The results of this background survey are summarized in Table 1. Based on the survey, 44% of the students on the WSD course had no previous Python experience whereas for CS2 this was only 11%. Parsons problems have not been used at Aalto University before so it is unlikely that students had previously been exposed to the concept.

Table 1: Learners' background on WSD and CS2 courses as evaluated by themselves. Programming experience choices were: 1) I am new to programming or have done very little programming. 2) I know basic programming. I have taken basic courses in programming and/or learned similar skills in my work or hobbies. 3) I have experience in programming. I have taken several courses in programming on various topics and/or have learned similar skills in my work or hobbies. 4) I am an experienced programmer with much practical experience. Programming is my profession or a hobby I am passionate about.

familiar with python	programming experience	WSD	CS2
no	1	4 (7.3%)	1 (25%)
	2	13 (23.6%)	1 (25%)
	3	23 (41.8%)	-
	4	12 (21.8%)	2 (50%)
yes	1	-	2 (6.1%)
	2	22 (31.0%)	12 (36.4%)
	3	35 (49.3%)	16 (48.5%)
	4	14 (19.7%)	3 (9.1%)

4. ANALYSIS AND RESULTS

The recorded interaction traces comprise a lot of data. To aid our analyses, we implemented a tool that does pre-processing and provides different quantitative measures and visualizations of the data. We conceptualized a solution as a graph where the nodes are different states of the code on the right as in Figure 1 and edges are transitions from a state to another invoked with the different possible operations: inserting a code fragment to the (partial) solution on the right, moving a code fragment within the solution and thus changing the order or indentation, and removing a code fragment from the solution. Each successfully completed solving session is thus a path from a state of empty code to a state with the correct solution, and the number of steps in the solution path is the number of edges traversed. The minimum is the number of code fragments in the solution which is reached when they are all added directly to their correct place. In addition, at each state along the path the student may have requested feedback. Code can also be rearranged in the input area but students were instructed to build the solution on the right and, looking from data, code reordering in the input area was relatively rare and code cannot be indented there, so we chose to focus only on the solution area.

Because the assignments were optional and not rewarded on the CS2 course, the number of students solving the assignments was quite low. Thus, we chose to focus our analysis efforts on the WSD course only. However, we have used the data from CS2 to validate some of our observations as discussed in Section 5. Furthermore, at first on the WSD course, P1 had an error in that the solution was not unique but that it was possible to build two different solutions with the given code fragments but still only one was accepted. Therefore, we had to omit a large portion of this data. It is also worth noting that P2 was a trivial problem with only three code fragments. So we have focused on P3, P4, and P5 in our analyses. Table 2 gives a summary of the general nature of the data collected as medians and their median absolute de-

viations (MAD). The table indicates that P4 and P5 were likely the most difficult assignments for the students.

Table 2: Average steps taken and time spent in solving the assignments. P1, P2, P3, P4, and P5 had 7, 3, 6, 6, and 7 code fragments, respectively.

course	assign.	n	steps		time (sec)		time/steps	
			med	mad	med	mad	med	mad
WSD	P1	73	13	4	185	76.0	13.9	5.3
	P2	142	3	0	26	8	8.3	2.3
	P3	140	10	4	142.5	58	12.4	4.7
	P4	137	9	3	219	98	19	7.6
	P5	136	10	3	247	109.5	19.1	8.0
CS2	P1	29	10	3	116	44	9	3
	P2	31	3	0	37	13	11	3.0
	P3	27	9	3	87	16	9.8	2.8
	P4	20	7.5	1	145	64	20.9	5.7
	P5	17	7	0	177	72	19	7.4

4.1 Use of Automatic Feedback

In general, automatic feedback was used sparingly in solving the assignments. The median of how many times a student asked for feedback in a solution ranged from 1 to 3 in the different assignments and there was little variance. Indeed, the median absolute deviation ranged from 0 to 2. Except for the trivial P2, 35-53% of the students were able complete the assignment on their first feedback request and, thus, most requested feedback more than once. Some few individuals requested feedback dozens of times, up to 62 times in a solution. On closer inspection, these students exhibited trial-and-error-like behavior where the student would request feedback after almost every modification they made and they took little time to think about their next move.

In all the assignments, in over 90% of the solutions, students asked for feedback for the first time only after all the lines belonging to the solution had been added. In most cases (54.8% of all solutions for P1, 90.8% for P2, 82.1% for P3, 78.8% for P4, and 82.4% for P5), this was *immediately* after adding the last line of code. The number is significantly lower for P1. We think this is on the one hand because students may not have at this point yet fully realized that feedback could be requested at any time and an unlimited number of times and on the other hand because an approach where code was indented only after all of it having been added was common as described in the next subsection.

Investigation into the states where feedback was requested reveals that the correct, complete answer is unsurprisingly the most common such state. In the last three assignments, the other most common feedback states were the same as the most common incorrect states described in Subsection 4.3.

4.2 Common Patterns

Overall, the variance of the solution paths across students was notable. As a quantitative measure of this, the solution paths in P3, P4, and P5 had in total 453, 444, and 781 different states, respectively. P5 had a higher count because it had 7 draggable code fragments compared to the 6 for the other two. The number of states that were included in many solution paths is quite low: for P3, P4, and P5 there were only 24, 22, and 14 states that appeared in at least every tenth solution, respectively. Worth noting is that the few low-performing students clicking through with a trial-and-error attitude grow the set of different states with nonsensical states not visited by others.

We examined whether any common patterns emerge across solutions by constructing an aggregate graph of all the solution paths for each assignment (see Figure 2). Each node represents one state and its size is relative to the number of solutions that have it. Start node is labeled with the number of solution paths the graph is built from and a solution is labeled with an *F*. Node outlines are colored according to the state correctness: black for correctly ordered, red for wrong order, and magenta for states with all code fragments in the correct order but incorrectly indented. Nodes themselves are colored from white to black to indicate the number of solution paths where feedback has been requested in that state. Each edge represents a transition from a state to another in response to changing the code in the solution area by, e.g., moving a code fragment. The width of the edge is relative to the number of solutions that have this transition. Edges are also labeled with this number. Edges are colored according to which drag-and-drop operation they represent: black for adding code, red for changing order, magenta for increasing indentation, pink for decreasing indentation, and brown for removing code. We implemented a tool to interactively browse these graphs that additionally shows the code corresponding to the state when hovering over nodes. To identify common patterns, we focused on transitions performed by most students by filtering out edges with weights less than some varying threshold value, and examining paths that were left.

For all the assignments we could see one primary overall pattern which was the simple add all the code fragments linearly, that is, in top-down order directly to their correct place. In the first assignment, P1, it was also quite common to first add the code fragments with no indentation and then do the indentation separately. This was less common in subsequent assignments and may be due to the students being inexperienced with the interface for solving the exercises. Also, we did not see this with the CS2 course. Because the assignments studied were rather simple and had few lines of code, it is not surprising that we see the pattern mentioned above. However, the variations to this are interesting. Indeed, we can see that many students preferred to first add code fragments that defined a block or control structure such as the `for` loop statement or the `if` branching statement. This is most evident in P5 (aggregate graph in Figure 2) whose solution included two `if` statements and one `for` statement. Students much preferred starting to construct the program with adding the `for` and `if` statements before the others. This is a clear deviation from the straightforward linear approach (the left path in the figure) and an indicator of some structured control flow- or block-driven thinking when constructing the program.

Another way to look at the pattern in which students solve the problems is shown in Tables 3–5. The tables show in which order the code fragments were added to the solution. For example, Table 4 informs us that after the first step, 98.5% of the solutions had the `def`-statement. After adding another line, all of the solutions contained this function signature and most solutions, 73.7%, also had the `for`-line. These tables illustrate the same pattern of preferring to add control structures before other statements.

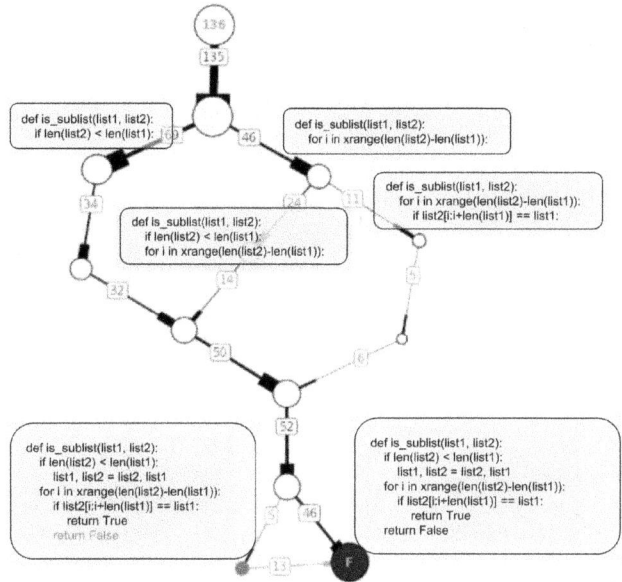

Figure 2: Solution strategies of P5 filtered so that transitions performed by less than five students not visualized. The resulted graph covers 29 % of transitions of all students and 27% of all solution paths.

Table 3: Lines added in P3 on the WSD course.

Code	S1	S2	S3
class Node():	64.3	88.6	97.1
def __init__(self, value, next=None):	35.0	88.6	95.7
self.value = value self.next = next	0.0	12.9	68.6
a = Node(1)	0.7	5.0	11.4
b = Node(2, a)	0.0	0.0	3.6
a.next = b	0.0	0.0	0.0

Table 4: Lines added in P4 on the WSD course.

Code	S1	S2	S3
def draw_triangle(h):	98.5	100.0	100.0
stars = (2*h-1)*'*'	0.0	17.5	41.6
for n in xrange(h):	0.7	73.7	94.2
spaces = n	0.0	5.8	40.9
print spaces * ' ' + stars	0.0	0.7	16.1
stars = stars[2:]	0.7	2.2	7.3

Table 5: Lines added in P5 on the WSD course.

Code	S1	S2	S3	S4
def is_sublist(list1, list2):	99.3	100.0	100.0	100.0
if len(list2) < len(list1):	0.7	53.7	77.9	86.8
list1, list2 = list2, list1	0.0	4.4	36.0	60.3
for i in xrange(len(list2)-len(list1)):	0.0	35.3	55.1	87.5
if list2[i:i+len(list1)] == list1:	0.0	4.4	14.0	33.8
return True	0.0	1.5	1.5	6.6
return False	0.0	0.7	14.0	19.9

123

4.3 Common Difficulties

Common difficulties can be observed by examining the most common[1] incorrect states for each assignment. The most interesting such observations are in P3 (see Table 3 for the code). The object instantiation code was commonly indented inside a wrong block: the same level as the code inside the constructor (in 39% of solutions), the same level as the constructor definition (33%), and one step deeper than code inside the constructor (11%). Particularly interesting is the last one where the code really makes no sense since the code is indented even though there is no surrounding control structure. It seems these students were just trying to get through with no consideration of whether it made sense.

In assignment P5, there was only one common incorrect state. In that state, the `for`-loop and code inside it was indented one step too deep and thus contained within the wrong block.

Assignment P4 was difficult, and the incorrect states included almost all permutations of the code fragments. Table 6 illustrates this. It shows the positions of code fragments in states where students had requested feedback and all the lines had been added but were ordered incorrectly. From the table we can see, for example, that a common mistake was to have the `print` statement as the last line (69.9% of times, column 6 in the table) while it's correct position was second to last. The values are normalized so that every student's solution regardless of its length or number of feedback requests has equal weight.

Table 6: Positions of code fragments in students' solutions when feedback was requested and the order was incorrect. From each line of the table, one can read the percentage of solutions where the code fragment was in the 1st, 2nd, etc position. For example, 0.2% of solutions had the `def` line as the 3rd line.

Line of Code	1	2	3	4	5	6
def draw_triangle(h):	99	0.7	0.2	0	0	0
stars = (2*h-1)*'*'	0	45	16.4	22.4	9.3	6.9
for n in xrange(h):	0	43.8	44.7	7.4	3.6	0.4
spaces = n	0.8	4.9	29.8	35	28.5	1
print spaces * ' ' + stars	0	0	1.3	7.3	21.8	69.6
stars = stars[2:]	0.2	5.6	7.6	27.9	36.7	22

4.4 Loops and Backtracking

Using the graph visualization introduced in Subsection 4.2, we also examined individual solution paths in addition to the aggregate graphs. Compared to the aggregate graphs, the node size and the edge width have no meaning in these, the start node is labeled with an *S*, and edges are labeled with the time in seconds between the transition from the state to the next and low values are greyed out to highlight longer pauses (see Figure 3). This state-centric view of the student's solution allowed us to spot the quite common ineffective behavior of revisiting states. Table 7 shows data on how many of the solution paths visited states earlier visited in the same path, that is, the solution paths had loops. Clearly, loops were most common in P4. This is not surprising, since it was also the assignment where students had many common incorrect states.

[1] We considered states present in at least 10% of the solutions to be common.

Table 7: Solutions with loops. Count is the number of solutions with at least one state revisit. Length of a loop gives the median and median absolute deviation of the number of steps between state revisits.

Assignment	Count	%	Length of a loop	
			med	mad
P1	19	26.0%	4	3
P2	1	0.7%	3	0
P3	29	20.7%	5	4
P4	45	32.8%	3	2
P5	28	20.6%	3	2

To better understand the student behavior in these loops, we examined and categorized all the solution paths with loops.

Backtracking happens when the student reverts to an earlier state by undoing the operations exactly in the reverse order. One might assume that in these cases returning to the earlier state was intentional.

Circular loop(s) occurs when the student visits multiple states and then returns to an earlier state via different intermediate states. In these cases it is difficult to say if the student returned to the earlier state intentionally or by accident.

Let us call the shortest path from start to the solution state within a solution path the *trunk*. Combinations of the two types of loops above are possible and can be further categorized based on how they are related to each other and the trunk.

Separate sidetrack(s) , where loops originating from the trunk do not start from the same or consecutive states along the trunk, are illustrated in Figure 3.

Concentrated sidetracks where many loops originate from a smaller number of states in the trunk are illustrated in Figure 3. We call these states concentration points.

Jumbled combinations where the number of concentration points is extremely high, there are nested loops, and the loops are lengthy are illustrated in Figure 4. In some cases drawing the line between this category and *concentrated sidetracks* is difficult.

5. DISCUSSION

The overall aim in our research is to build a tool that would allow us to monitor students' programming process, collect data about the problems they face in the process, and give tailored feedback to them. Though it is technically possible to log all students' interaction when they are using some programming environment, the problem is to get data that has adequate granularity. Automatic assessment tools, such as Web-CAT [3], provide only the submissions. Logging all editing data, on the other hand, would provide us with lots of too detailed data, like writing code sentences, misspellings and correcting them, most of which is not relevant to us. What we would need is data which includes all changes students make in the level of inserting, removing, and reordering syntactically correct statements, expressions, methods and other

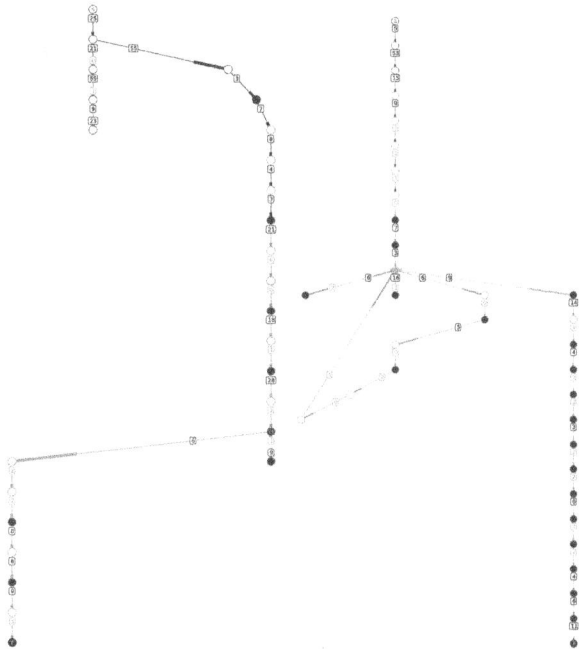

Figure 3: Separate sidetracks on the left and concentrated sidetracks on the right.

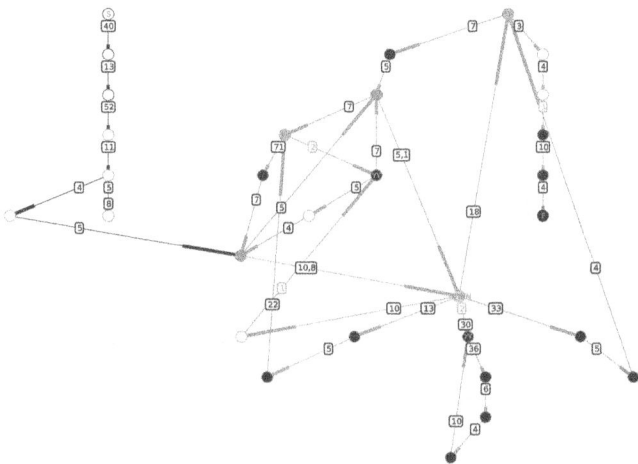

Figure 4: A jumbled combination of loops.

maining lines [5]. As discussed in Subsection 4.2, we found that some students did indeed follow this pattern while others did not. It would be interesting to further analyze whether they did not use the structured approach because they already had the full or partial solution figured out. Nonetheless, even though we can observe the tendency of using this approach, there are a lot of small variations in the solution paths and some guesswork must be present.

To validate the common solving strategies identified on the WSD course, we briefly checked the data collected on the CS2 course. It seems the same patterns were there, but since we only have little data from that course, we cannot definitely say that they were exactly the same. In the future, we need to collect more data and analyze patterns more thoroughly from multiple courses.

In Subsection 4.4, we examined loops in students' solution paths. Having no loops in a solution does not guarantee that the learner was always moving towards the solution, but loops clearly indicate that the strategy was not optimal. We assume that separate sidetracks could be slips or at least something where the learner realized a problem but was able to proceed immediately after returning to the previous state. It is, however, difficult to evaluate what the learners with jumbled state graphs were thinking while solving the assignment. Concentrated sidetracks are more interesting because it looks like a learner got somewhat stuck to the states from where multiple loops originate. In future, we could provide automated feedback when such behavior is identified. This could further be combined with feedback given when we identify *extreme movers*, that is, students who ignore the given feedback or do not use it effectively [14]. This would hopefully guide students away from falling into these ineffective patterns.

As is typical when new educational tools are introduced, we also collected comments on the assignments from students. The opinions of Parsons problems were quite varied ranging from boring to fun. The only emerging theme was that students see these kinds of assignments good for teaching novel solutions to (algorithmic) coding tasks.

We recognize that the current assignments we have, are in many sense artificial compared with actual programming tasks. We therefore direct our future work to extend the analysis to cases, which allow more realistic programming, such as allowing distractors, i.e., code fragments not part of the solution, allowing students to copy lines instead of restricting the number to one, and to construct expressions. We argue that most of the analysis methods we have used, would be readily available for such enhanced assignments. Essentially, this would move the assignments towards visual programming. and thus allow us to investigate closely how students solve programming tasks, what kind of strategies they have, what kind of errors they make and how do they cope with the errors. Another, interesting direction for research would be implementing automatic feedback on observations made from recorded interactions. Finally, one weakness with the analyses in this study is that we can see anomalies and common mistakes in the solutions but we can only speculate where they stem from. Indeed, in further research, we also need to gather data on what students are thinking, what are their reasons for doing what they did using methods such as simulated recall or talk aloud protocols in order to augment our analysis results.

larger programming concepts, as well as all interaction they have when compiling, testing, and debugging their problems. Here, we have studied Parsons problems in the js-parsons environment. This has enabled us to examine this type of data in terms of puzzle-like program construction sessions.

Nearly all students were able to solve all our Parsons problems. However, how they solved them varied. Thus, if these Parsons problems were used to assess some programming skills, we assume that assessing solving strategies is more meaningful than merely checking the final state. In our previous work, we observed how four experts solved algorithmic 2D Parsons puzzles. They seemed to follow a top-down strategy where they first added the function signature to the solution, then added loops and ordered them correctly if needed, then added the **if**-statements, and finally the re-

6. CONCLUSIONS

In this paper, we have demonstrated the use of various methods to extract meaningful information from Parsons problems' solving sessions based on a novel data source of automatically recorded detailed interaction traces. We have shown how to visualize the process of solving these problems as an interactive graph that can be used to explore patterns and anomalies in the solving process. By analyzing empirical data collected from students of two programming courses, we have identified some elements of poorly proceeding solutions, such as, loops in the solution paths. In future work, we plan to experiment with giving automatic feedback on these types of episodes whose recognition requires knowledge of the whole solution path and not just the current state. Moreover, we plan to extend the tool for more realistic programming tasks, collect data from this, and perform similar analyses.

7. REFERENCES

[1] P. Blikstein. Using Learning Analytics to Assess Students' Behavior in Open-Ended Programming Tasks. In *Proceedings of the 1st International Conference on Learning Analytics and Knowledge*, pages 110–116, 2011.

[2] P. Denny, A. Luxton-Reilly, and B. Simon. Evaluating a New Exam Question: Parsons Problems. In *Proceedings of the Fourth international Workshop on Computing Education Research*, pages 113–124, 2008.

[3] S. Edwards, J. Snyder, M. Pérez-Quiñones, A. Allevato, D. Kim, and B. Tretola. Comparing Effective and Ineffective Behaviors of Student Programmers. In *Proceedings of the fifth international workshop on Computing education research*, pages 3–14, 2009.

[4] S. Garner. An Exploration of How a Technology-Facilitated Part-Complete Solution Method Supports the Learning of Computer Programming. *Journal of Issues in Informing Science and Information Technology*, 4:491–501, 2007.

[5] P. Ihantola and V. Karavirta. Two-Dimensional Parson's Puzzles: The Concept, Tools, and First Observations. *Journal of Information Technology Education: Innovations in Practice*, 10:1–14, 2011.

[6] M. Jadud. Methods and Tools for Exploring Novice Compilation Behaviour. In *Proceedings of the Second International Workshop on Computing Education Research*, pages 73–84, 2006.

[7] U. Kiesmüller, S. Sossalla, T. Brinda, and K. Riedhammer. Online Identification of Learner Problem Solving Strategies Using Pattern Recognition Methods. In *Proceedings of the fifteenth annual conference on Innovation and technology in computer science education*, pages 274–278, 2010.

[8] R. Lister, E. S. Adams, S. Fitzgerald, W. Fone, J. Hamer, M. Lindholm, R. McCartney, J. E. Moström, K. Sanders, O. Seppälä, B. Simon, and L. Thomas. A Multi-National Study of Reading and Rracing Skills in Novice Programmers. *ACM SIGCSE Bulletin*, 36(4):119–150, 2004.

[9] R. Lister, T. Clear, D. Bouvier, P. Carter, A. Eckerdal, J. Jacková, M. Lopez, R. McCartney, P. Robbins, O. Seppälä, et al. Naturally Occurring Data as Research Instrument: Analyzing Examination Responses to Study the Novice Programmer. *ACM SIGCSE Bulletin*, 41(4):156–173, 2010.

[10] R. Lister, C. Fidge, and D. Teague. Further Evidence of a Relationship between Explaining, Tracing and Writing Skills in Introductory Programming. *ACM SIGCSE Bulletin*, 41(3):161–165, 2009.

[11] M. Lopez, J. Whalley, P. Robbins, and R. Lister. Relationships between Reading, Tracing and Writing Skills in Introductory Programming. In *Proceedings of the Fourth international Workshop on Computing Education Research*, pages 101–112, 2008.

[12] M. McCracken, V. Almstrum, D. Diaz, M. Guzdial, D. Hagan, Y. B.-D. Kolikant, C. Laxer, L. Thomas, I. Utting, and T. Wilusz. A Multi-National, Multi-Institutional Study of Assessment of Programming Skills of First-Year CS Students. *ACM SIGCSE Bulletin*, 33(4):125–180, 2001.

[13] D. Parsons and P. Haden. Parson's Programming Puzzles: a Fun and Effective Learning Tool for First Programming Courses. In *Proceedings of the 8th Australasian Conference on Computing Education*, pages 157–163, 2006.

[14] D. N. Perkins, S. Schwartz, and R. Simmons. Instructional Strategies for the Problems of Novice Programmers. *Teaching and Learning Computer Programming: Multiple Research Perspectives*, 1990.

[15] C. Piech, M. Sahami, D. Koller, S. Cooper, and P. Blikstein. Modeling How Students Learn to Program. In *Proceedings of the 43rd ACM technical symposium on Computer Science Education*, pages 153–160, 2012.

[16] W. Poncin, A. Serebrenik, and M. van den Brand. Mining Student Capstone Projects with FRASR and ProM. In *Proceedings of the ACM international conference companion on Object oriented programming systems languages and applications companion*, pages 87–96, 2011.

[17] T. Rajala, M.-J. Laakso, E. Kaila, and T. Salakoski. VILLE — a Language-Independent Program Visualization Tool. In *Seventh Baltic Sea Conference on Computing Education Research*, pages 151–159, 2007.

[18] J. Spacco, J. Strecker, D. Hovemeyer, and W. Pugh. Software Repository Mining with Marmoset: An Automated Programming Project Snapshot and Testing System. *ACM SIGSOFT Software Engineering Notes*, 30(4):1–5, 2005.

[19] E. Tabanao, M. Rodrigo, and M. Jadud. Predicting At-Risk Novice Java Programmers Through the Analysis of Online Protocols. In *Proceedings of the seventh international workshop on Computing education research*, pages 85–92, 2011.

[20] A. Venables, G. Tan, and R. Lister. A Closer Look at Tracing, Explaining and Code Writing Skills in the Novice Programmer. In *Proceedings of the fifth international workshop on Computing education research workshop*, pages 117–128, 2009.

[21] J. Whalley and P. Robbins. Report on the Fourth BRACElet Workshop. *Bulletin of Applied Computing and Information Technology*, 5(1), 2007.

The Importance of Students' Attention to Program State: A Case Study of Debugging Behavior

Colleen M. Lewis
Graduate School of Education
University of California, Berkeley
Berkeley, CA 94720
001-510-388-7215

ABSTRACT

To develop a model of students' debugging processes, I conducted a qualitative analysis of young students engaged in debugging computer programs they had written in the programming language Scratch. I present a microgenetic analysis that tracks how one student's attention to elements of computer program state shifted during his debugging process. I present evidence that this student had relevant domain knowledge and claim that his changing attention within the problem, and not his domain knowledge, mediated his debugging process. I hypothesize that a key competence in debugging is learning to identify what elements of program state are important to pay attention to and that this attention, and not only domain knowledge, mediates the debugging process. This hypothesis is consistent with a model of physics reasoning and learning from the Knowledge in Pieces theoretical framework and in this research I build upon education research outside of computer science. The case study analyzes the debugging process of a student entering the sixth grade, but I document an isomorphic case from a pair of college students to show that this pattern extends beyond this age.

Categories and Subject Descriptors

K.3 [Computers and Education]: General

General Terms

Human factors

Keywords

Debugging, programming state, Scratch, case study

1. INTRODUCTION

There are decades of research investigating difficulties experienced by novice programmers [2, 12, 21, 27]. While computer science education research typically identifies learning difficulties at the grain size of individual misconceptions [2, 16, 17, 27], I observed that difficulties with state and state change operations underlie many of the difficulties experienced by middle-school students engaged in programming and debugging.

State represents the idea, present in all programming environments, of a set of temporary or permanent variables that completely describe the current environment on which a program can act. This includes programmer-defined variables as well as other aspects of the runtime environment such as the current stack frame. Program commands change aspects of the computer program's state and the process of writing programs involves developing sequences of state change operations to achieve a particular goal. How a program changes state can be seen as a more formal definition of the broad notion of what a program "does." It is therefore essential that students recognize how state-change operations may act on a hypothetical state and that students have knowledge and techniques with which to track the current computer program's state.

I present a case study [29] from a qualitative study of students' debugging behavior from a summer enrichment program for students entering the sixth grade. This case study is used to illustrate the hypothesis that a key competence in debugging is learning to identify what elements of program state are important to pay attention to and that this attention, and not only domain knowledge, mediates the debugging process.

In this case study, a student experienced difficulty debugging a programming that involved angles and position in the programming language Scratch. However, once he attended to the relevant element of state, he demonstrated his competence with angles and positions and quickly rewrote his program to modify state correctly. His competence with angles and position challenges the alternative hypothesis that he had insufficient knowledge or a specific misconception regarding angles [14]. I explain his difficulties as a lack of attention to relevant elements of state and not simply a lack of knowledge.

Extrapolating the pattern from the case study, I propose a model of student debugging that depends upon the student's attention within the problem as the determining factor in the debugging process. This model is consistent with a model of physics reasoning and learning from the Knowledge in Pieces theoretical framework. The case study is intended to illustrate details of this model, but is not intended to establish the prevalence of this pattern. However, to show that the pattern from the case study is not unique to young students, I provide an example of a bug encountered by college students that is isomorphic to the bug the student addressed in the case study.

This paper has three primary contributions. First, this paper provides a microgenetic analysis [28] of naturally occurring debugging behavior. The second contribution is the proposed model of debugging behavior as mediated by students' attention to program state. The third contribution is that this model, which focuses on students' attention, creates a connection between computer science education and education research within the Knowledge in Pieces theoretical framework.

2. PREVIOUS RESEARCH

Based upon the framing of programming as developing sequences of state change operations, an understanding of state and state change operations is essential to successful programming. du Boulay and his colleagues [11, 12] developed this claim through a focus on what they call the notional machine, which is essentially a functional description of how program state can be changed. du Boulay and his colleagues argue that students need a firm understanding of these properties of the machine to be successful writing programs and that these properties should be made explicit to students. More recently, Ben-Ari [1] reiterated the importance of students' understanding of the notional machine and critiqued object-oriented programming languages for obscuring aspects of the machine.

The researchers involved in the design and evaluation of the Alice programming language also emphasize the importance of program state, particularly for understanding and debugging code [4, 6, 22]. "We believe the source of confusion in figuring out what went wrong, in all but the most trivial code, is an inadequate understanding of the program's state." [4, p. 109].

Sajaniemi and Kuittinen [23] have attempted to help students recognize common patterns of state change operations. Their work highlights the roles of variables in programs. They claim that 10 roles account for 99% of all variable roles used in introductory programming texts. In a later study [24], they asked students to represent the state of an object-oriented program at a moment in time. In this work they focus on students' perception of what is relevant to state and how students' perception changes during a programming course. They use what details a student represents as an indication of what aspects of state that student believes to be important. They track how the details that a student represents changes during a programming course.

3. THEORETICAL FRAMEWORK

I preface the analysis with a brief overview of the Knowledge in Pieces theoretical framework [7, 8, 9]. This overview serves to articulate assumptions about the nature of knowledge that guide the research methods and analysis.

Research that adopts the Knowledge in Pieces theoretical framework attempts to build and refine models of knowledge that describe the dynamic process of human reasoning. For example, researchers have developed models of a type of intuitive knowledge [7] as well as types of conceptual knowledge and how individuals apply them [8, 9].

Instead of assuming that individuals have rigid mental models, the Knowledge in Pieces theoretical framework models a student's use of knowledge as a complex emergent process. In a given situation, students' are assumed to make use of a subset of their potentially relevant knowledge, shaped by their perception of what knowledge is relevant and their attention within the context. An assumed challenge of learning is to consistently use the most appropriate knowledge in a given context [8, 9].

The Knowledge in Pieces theoretical framework specifies that a wide variety of subtle changes in a problem may change what an individual attends to within a problem and what knowledge an individual applies in that context [8, 9]. What an individual attends to within a context is both shaped by the individual's knowledge and mediates what knowledge that individual uses.

4. RESEARCH QUESTION

In this study, I address the following research question: How does a student's knowledge and changing attention within a problem shape the process of debugging?

5. METHODS

There are a number of challenges in studying students' debugging behavior. Observing students debugging their own buggy code does not provide any consistency across research participants because the bugs they identify and fix will be unique. However, observing students debugging uniform bugs in code they did not write may be an unfamiliar experience for students and not representative of their behavior debugging their own code. The methods used in this study prioritized observing natural debugging behavior rather than documenting behavior that could easily be compared across research participants.

Data was collected and analyzed using methods of microgenetic analysis [28] and informed by other qualitative methods [7, 8, 9, 13, 15, 25] described below, which are commonly used in conjunction with the Knowledge in Pieces theoretical framework.

5.1 Research Context

With students' and parents' consent, data was collected from two computer programming courses in a summer enrichment program for students entering the sixth grade. There were 50 students in total, all of whom had been accepted to the enrichment program designed for academically advanced children. Few of the students had any computer programming experience, but no other information was collected regarding students' academic background.

During the thirty-six hour course, students used pair programming [3] and learned to program in Logo and Scratch. Related studies have extensively documented this context [18, 19, 20] and therefore additional details are omitted here.

5.2 Data Collection

The data collection was designed to capture the behavior of students engaged in programming and debugging in Logo and Scratch. During class, the computers used by the students recorded a video of the computer screen and audio from a microphone attached to the computer. These recordings could be replayed for analysis and showed students' actions in the programming environment and simultaneous discussion. Three classroom video cameras could be used to disambiguate which student was acting as the driver and navigator within each pair.

Methods of data collection in the Knowledge in Pieces line of work consistently focus on gathering this type of process data frequently involving think-aloud protocols [26] or clinical interviews [10]. In the current study, conversations between pairs served a similar function as clinical interviews, encouraging students to elaborate and discuss their thinking.

5.3 Case Selection

The goal of the study was to examine individual cases of students engaged in debugging. With approximately 900 hours of screen recording data, the analysis began by narrowing consideration to a particularly challenging element of the curriculum, described in Section 5.4. I watched these videos and developed brief, time-stamped summaries of a selection of the video data, which are referred to as content logs [13]. From these content logs I identified recurring patterns of student behavior in the video data. I selected a particular case that was similar to the other cases in many ways except that the student spoke more frequently while he worked.

This case was also selected because the student acknowledged a discrepancy between the behavior of the program and the intended behavior of the program. There were many other instances in which the researcher identified a student as engaged in debugging. However, many of these cases were ambiguous because it was not clear if the student recognized the discrepancy or was taking actions to resolve the discrepancy. In the selected case I could more accurately characterize the student's behavior as debugging because he made reference to the discrepancy and was attempting to find a solution.

5.4 Data Analysis

Conducting qualitative research requires sensitivity to the data and does not typically follow a linear path of data analysis [5]. The analysis involved a grounded approach [5] to develop hypotheses about the students' patterns of debugging. After the case was selected, the video was transcribed and watched and re-watched. From segments of this video, I developed hypotheses about his debugging behavior and sought to generalize and validate the hypotheses by considering the full case [13]. This was an iterative process where hypotheses continued to be refined. The video and my formative hypotheses were presented on multiple occasions to groups of educational researchers who critiqued these hypotheses and offered alternative interpretations.

In the analysis I attempt to provide a systematic account of the student's debugging behavior. Building upon the Knowledge in Pieces theoretical framework [7, 8, 9], I focus on students' attention across the evolving context of the interview and students' resulting patterns of reasoning.

In the analysis of this individual case I used analysis methods from the Knowledge in Pieces theoretical framework [7, 8, 9], which are akin to methods of microgenetic analysis [28] and other detailed studies of learning [25]. In presenting these data I attempted to provide the reader with enough data to evaluate the analysis and hypotheses presented.

Case studies like this one are not intended to prove that a particular pattern of behavior exists within a population. Instead, the data serve to inform and exemplify hypotheses regarding features of learning within a domain.

5.5 Problem Description and Solution

The case study is taken from a video of a student debugging a program written in the programming language Scratch. Scratch, the problem, and a description of a solution to the problem are provided as necessary background for the case study.

In the programming language Scratch, students can modify state by moving a character around a 2D screen. For example, the Scratch command "move 10 steps" will move the character 10 pixels in the direction that it is currently facing. This effectively modifies the x- and/or y-location aspect of the character's state. Other commands in Scratch modify the current state relating to whether the character draws a line tracing its path when it moves. This aspect of state is determined by whether the commands "pen down" or "pen up" have been executed.

Students can use these commands to draw complex images in Scratch. For example, in the case study students were attempting to draw the image shown in Figure 1.

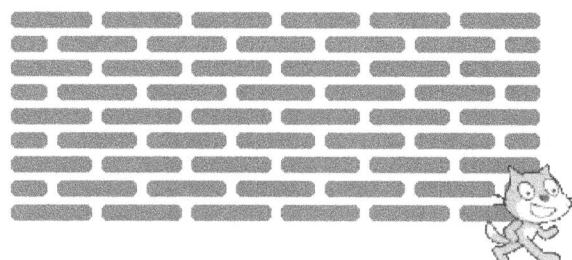

Figure 1: Representation of the goal of the program.

The bricks are created by moving the character forward while the pen is down. The spaces between the bricks are created by moving the character while the pen is up. For example, the script in Figure 2 shows how to draw two bricks that are forty pixels wide, separated by a fifteen pixel space.

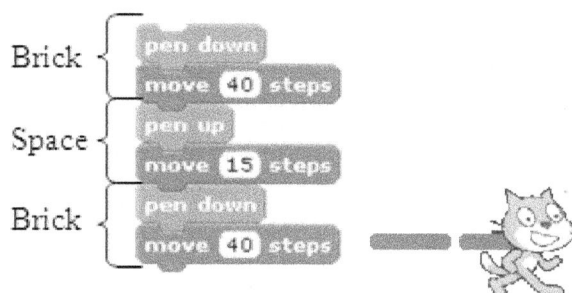

Figure 2 – Script to draw two bricks (left) and the resulting bricks and position of the character (right)

Drawing the entire brick wall involves creating scripts that draw each of the distinct rows. The first row and all odd numbered rows contain six full bricks (Figure 3). All even numbered rows contain five full bricks and a half brick on each end (Figure 4).

Figure 3: Pattern of bricks for all odd numbered rows

Figure 4: Pattern of bricks for all even numbered rows

To draw an entire brick wall, the student must direct the character to navigate between each row. For example, assuming that the character begins at the top left, the program begins by drawing the top row from left to right. The student must then direct the character to turn and move to a lower y-position to draw the second row. The script shown on the top-right of Figure 5 shows the process of turning right, moving down and turning right again to begin the second row, which also moves from an odd numbered row to an even numbered row. Once the character traces the second row, they must turn left, move down and turn left again to begin the third row. The script shown on the bottom-left of Figure 5 shows this process of turning between the 2nd and 3rd rows, which also moves from an even numbered row to an odd numbered row.

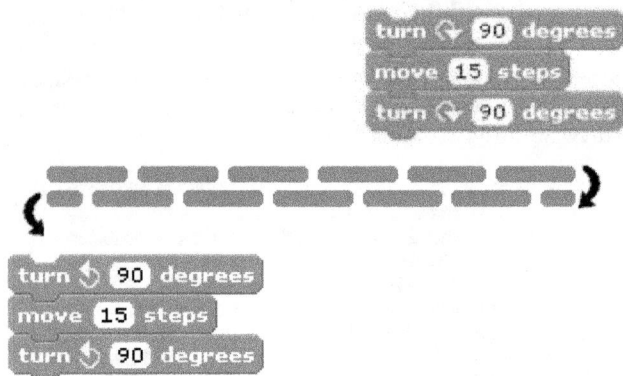

Figure 5 - Script to move from an odd numbered row to an even numbered row (shown on the top-right) and the script to move from an even numbered row to an odd numbered row (shown on the bottom-left) with arrows indicating the direction to turn between rows of bricks

This process of drawing the first two rows of bricks is repeated for each subsequent pair of rows to draw the entire wall.

6. CASE STUDY

The data and analysis are divided into four sequential episodes. Each episode is prefaced with a summary of the episode and followed by an analysis of the episode. In the analysis, I track the students' attention within the programming environment. His actions cause changes in what visual information is available and thereby changes what he pays attention to.

6.1 Excerpt One

6.1.1 Summary

The case study begins after two students had created programs to draw two distinct patterns for the rows of bricks. However, they were unsuccessful at drawing a brick wall because they did not have a way to move between rows such as with the method outlined in Section 5.4. They eventually created the script shown in Figure 6, which can move their character from the first row to the second row, but they incorrectly assumed that it could also move the character from the second to the third row.

Figure 5 shows arrows indicating the correct direction of movement to navigate between rows: turning right after the first row and left after the second row. However, the students used the script shown in Figure 6 to turn right after both the first and second rows. Therefore when they attempted to draw the third row, it retraced over the top row. The result of this is shown in Figure 7.

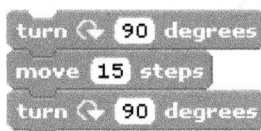

Figure 6 – Students' script to turn between two rows of the brick wall

Figure 7 – Two rows of bricks with arrows indicating the incorrect character movement between rows

While the students were working in pairs, the excerpt below features only one student. The classroom video indicates that during this time his partner was not paying attention to the work he was doing within Scratch. In the excerpt below, one of the students, Kevin (a pseudonym), had just finished adjusting the vertical distance between the rows of bricks specified by the number of steps moved in the script in Figure 6. He began with 10, then tried 20, and finally in the beginning of the transcript shown below, settled on 15. In the following transcript, Kevin traced the top row 3 times and did not show any indication that he observed the retracing of the first row or had identified why a third line was not drawn.

The following convention is used in the transcripts:

- "executed odd row" means that the script to draw the pattern of bricks for odd numbered rows was executed

- "executed even row" means that the script to draw pattern of bricks for even numbered rows was executed

- "executed turn" means that the script shown in Figure 6 to turn right between the rows was executed

6.1.2 Data

01   Kevin: Fifteen (Modified the move in Figure 6 to be 15 steps) I think I've got it.

02   Kevin: (Executed odd row, executes turn, executes even row, executed turn, executed odd row, which retraced the top row)

03   Kevin: What? Wait. (Cleared the screen)

04   Kevin: Okay (Executed odd row) – that (executed turn), that (executed even row), that (executed turn), that (executed odd row, which retraced the top row)

05   Kevin: (Cleared the screen)

06   Kevin: (Without speaking, executed odd row, executed turn, executed even row, executed turn, executed odd row, which retraced the top row.)

07   Kevin: Oh my god (Cleared the screen)

08   Kevin: Seventeen. (Modified the steps in Figure 6 to be 17 instead of 15.)

6.1.3 Analysis

Kevin retraced the top row three times and appeared unsure why a third line was not drawn. From a purely perceptual stand point, it is possible on the screen to observe the character's vertical location as on the top row. This problem could have been identified by Kevin by attending to the y-position of the character before beginning the second turn.

It appears from his statements of "What? Wait." (line 03) and "Oh my god" (line 07) that he had identified a discrepancy between what he wanted to happen and the actual result of the code, but without attending to the position of the character he seemed to identify only that a third row was not drawn, but not that the first row was retraced.

The modification Kevin made on line 08 was to change the spacing between the rows. Based upon his earlier seemingly purposeful tinkering with the spacing between the rows, I hypothesize that he did not believe this would solve the problem. However, it is ambiguous what motivated his action in line 08.

Kevin had the perceptual skills to identify the position of the character and later it will be apparent that Kevin had the required skills within Scratch to create the script to move the character to the correct orientation and position. The issue is therefore a matter of attention and needing to refine his knowledge for the purpose of paying attention to the correct variables of state in this context.

In summary, I hypothesize that Kevin was not able to isolate the discrepancy in the first excerpt because he paid insufficient perceptual attention to the position and direction of the character.

6.2 Excerpt Two

6.2.1 Summary

In excerpt two, Kevin accidentally drew a solid second row, as shown in Figure 8, which resulted from superimposing an odd and even row. Kevin had drawn row one and row two, leaving the cat facing left at the far left side of the bottom row. By turning the character right 90 degrees 6 times, the character turned 180 degrees to face right on the second row. When he then executed the script for the odd row it created a solid line.

6.2.2 Data

09   Kevin: (Without speaking executed odd row, executed turn, executed even row, and then separated the turning script from Figure 6. He executed a turn right 90 degrees command 6 times, which turned the cat to face back to the right on the second row. Next he executed odd row, which created the image shown in Figure 8 by retracing the second row with the odd row script)

10   Kevin: What? Oh my god – why isn't it working? (Cleared the screen and reconstructed the turn script shown in Figure 6)

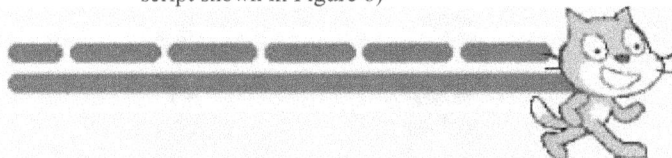

Figure 8 - Result of tracing over the second line with the script to draw the top line

6.2.3 Analysis

In excerpt two, Kevin retraced the second row with the odd row script. By experimenting with the rotation of the character, he appeared to be appropriately attending to the direction of the character. However, for a complete understanding of the bug he also needed to attend to the position of the character.

From Kevin's statements "why isn't it working?" (line 10) I assume that he identified a problem, but had not identified the cause. Kevin had the perceptual skills and experience in Scratch to identify that the vertical position of the character is unchanged by turning the character right 90 degrees 6 times; he was simply not attending to the y-position of the character at this time so as to identify the y-position before he executed the turn blocks.

While attending to the relevant program, the turn script (shown in Figure 6), Kevin had not begun to identify the cause of why the third row was not drawn nor the cause of the discrepancy shown in Figure 8. This is evidence of inappropriate attention to the state

of the character. As a possible example of the context dependent nature of knowledge, Kevin had relevant knowledge that he appeared to not apply in this context.

6.3 Excerpt Three

6.3.1 Summary

In excerpt three, Kevin executed the script to draw the first two rows and retraced the first and second row before accidentally tracing over the first row with a copy of the second row.

6.3.2 Data

11   Kevin: (Executed odd row, executed turn, executed even row) It works there.

12   Kevin: (Executed turn, executed odd row, which retraced the top row. Executed turn, executed even row, which retraced the second row. Executed turn, executed even row, which traced over row 1 with

13   row 2)

        Kevin: Oh. (Cleared the screen)

Figure 9 - Result of tracing over the row 1 with row 2

6.3.3 Analysis

The previous times that Kevin retraced the top row (lines 01 to 08); it appeared simply as if nothing was drawn. In those cases, he could have analyzed the script or attended to the character's position and direction to infer that the character retraced the top row. The fact that Kevin did not appear to have recognized that he was retracing the top row in those instances suggests that he was not attending to the relevant aspect of state, the character's location and direction.

By tracing over the top row with the even row script, Kevin created a solid line. There was then an indication that he has traced over the top row, present in this visual discrepancy shown in Figure 9. It is from this discrepancy that he appeared to orient to the relevant state and ultimately create the necessary program.

In summary, the visual discrepancy presumably made Kevin pay attention to the final location of the character, which indicated that the top line had just been retraced. This redirection of his attention shifted what knowledge he applied, which was ultimately productive as shown in the next excerpt.

6.4 Excerpt Four

6.4.1 Summary

In excerpt four, immediately after responding to the discrepancy with "oh", Kevin redrew rows 1 and 2 and executed the turn script from Figure 6 twice. From there he quickly constructed the opposite turn script to turn the character between even and odd numbered rows.

6.4.2 Data

14   Kevin: (Executed odd row, executed turn, executed even row, executed turn, and executed turn a second time. This left the cat in the same position as immediately following row 2.)

15   Kevin: Oh I see now. (Cleared the screen. Constructed a new turn script that mimics the current turn script from Figure 6, turning left as opposed to right.)

6.4.3 Analysis

In this excerpt Kevin drew the first two rows and then ran the turn script twice. Based upon his previous use of the program, he might have believed that executing the script twice would cause the character to move lower on the screen. However, executing the turn script twice appeared to highlight the location of the character for Kevin. After this change in attention, Kevin created the relevant script to turn left between rows and was able to navigate between the rows in the brick wall to draw a series of rows.

Kevin's facile creation of the second turn script suggests a level of competence in manipulating state that was not demonstrated by his difficulty in identifying the problem. While it may be possible to classify Kevin's previous actions as evidence of a misconception, such as a misunderstanding of turns [14], I argue that Kevin was developing his concept of state within the programming context by learning to pay attention to the appropriate variables of state.

7. EXTENSIBILITY TO COLLEGE STUDENTS

An example of a similar problem was experienced by a pair of students working on a final project in Scratch at the University of California, Berkeley. The students emailed me regarding a problem they were having. The bug was from within their final project after roughly 50 hours of programming experience in Scratch.

This example is not analyzed in depth because the data available was email correspondence and not process data. However this example demonstrates that problems of attention to state are not limited to a single age group.

In the students' email they described a problem that if they stopped the execution of their program in the middle of drawing and started it again from the beginning, that it did not draw in the same spot. This happened because their program only set the position of the character and not the orientation. Therefore, when the program was run with a different initial orientation, it drew in a different location. The students believed this to be a problem in Scratch, and not their code. They wrote: "If you run him again he will draw in a slightly different location, despite the fact he is being sent to coordinates in theory."

The program shown in Figure 10 draws a column of 7 circles. This is a slightly modified version of the students' original program, so as to more clearly demonstrate the problem with state. The original program changed the pen color to draw two-toned circles and the code for this was removed.

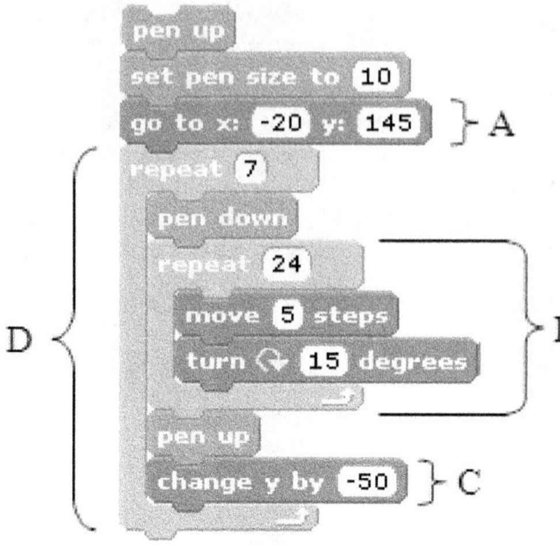

Figure 10 - Code to draw 7 circles (A) Specifies the start location (B) Draws a single circle (C) Lowers the y-position for the next circle and (D) Draws 7 copies of the circle each spaced 50 pixels apart.

The left of Figure 11 shows an incomplete execution of the code where it is stopped before it completed the 3rd circle. The image on the right in Figure 11 shows a subsequent execution of the code, with the pen color changed to make each execution more visible. From this image we can verify the issue described by the students, that a subsequent execution draws the circles in a different location.

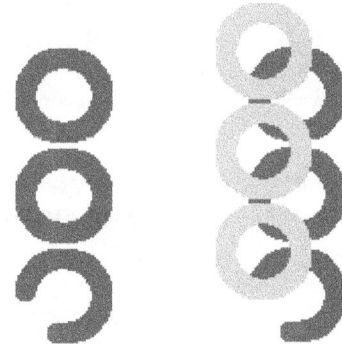

Figure 11 - A partially executed version of the code (left) followed by a second execution of the code that causes the circles to be misaligned (right)

The students here were not considering that an essential element of the position of the circle was not only the starting x- and y-position but also the direction of the character. For example, in Figure 12 we show the result of drawing two copies of a circle starting from the same x- and y-position. The first circle, in blue, began tracing the circle with the character facing the right, shown by the red arrow. The second circle, in green, began tracing the circle with the character facing left, shown by the yellow arrow. Both circles began at the same coordinate position, denoted with an X, however the character's direction before drawing the circle caused the positions of each circle to be different. When the students would stop their script before it had completed, the character would remain with its previous heading/direction. Therefore, the resulting circles would not match the previous execution because the initial state of the character was different before the two executions.

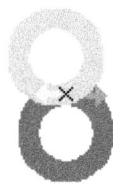

Figure 12 - Annotated image of drawing multiple circles starting with different initial directions

The students assumed that this was a problem with Scratch rather than their program. They came to this conclusion because they were not attending to the relevant variable of state. The students appear sensitive to state to some extent by resetting the position of state (the x and y location) within the program. However they failed to identify all variables of state that were necessary to initialize to ensure consistent behavior.

The direction that the character is facing is by default represented visually by the character. However, they had selected an option to not display the direction of the character on the screen, which made this state less apparent.

When the students realized the problem of the direction of the character they reported feeling "sheepish". This example highlights an anecdotally observed pattern of reaction to identifying the relevant aspect of state. After attending to the appropriate aspect of state, the solution appears obvious. Unfortunately, it would be easy for an instructor or student to dismiss this as a simple "mistake." However, this "mistake" may better be classified as a problem of state.

This anecdote suggests that problems of state can extend across age groups and shows a second example where students' inattention to particular elements of state and not their content knowledge of the state change operations determined their success debugging. Given that the data contained limited information regarding the students' thinking, a full analysis using rigorous methods, such as in the case study presented, was not conducted.

8. CONCLUSIONS

This work sits within a larger agenda of connecting educational research and educational theory from science and mathematics to understand the learning of computer science. In this work I attempt to strengthen ties between computer science education and science education research by applying the Knowledge in Pieces theoretical framework. This framework provided epistemological and methodological assumptions that guided the data collection and analysis.

This case study was unique in documenting a student's natural debugging behavior because for comparability many studies instead provide specific, artificial bugs for students to find and fix. Students' debugging behavior when working with these artificial bugs may be different because they did not write the buggy code and they may be less motivated to find and fix the artificial bug.

The particular case study showed the importance of what the student attended to within the problem to his process of debugging. The case study tracked how Kevin's tinkering within Scratch made particular features of state salient and how his

attention to these features allowed him to identify and eliminate the bug in his program.

Directed and systematic attention to the relevant features of state may develop after students develop competence with the functionality of relevant state change operations. When Kevin eventually attended to the relevant features of state, his identification and elimination of the bug were almost immediate. His facile creation of the second turn script showed remarkable competence in modifying the state of the character's position and rotation in Scratch. This competence was not apparent during much of his debugging process where he was inattentive to the y-position of the character.

Kevin's attention within the problem limited his debugging process despite ample relevant knowledge. I hypothesize that the development of debugging competence involves refining what features of state are relevant to attend to. Developing appropriate attention within a problem is learning challenge identified in mathematics and physics [7, 8, 9], which I believe is applicable to computer science education.

9. ACKNOWLEDGEMENTS

Work described in this paper was partially supported by NSF grant DUE-1044106. Any opinions, findings, and conclusions or recommendations expressed in this paper are those of the author's and do not necessarily reflect the views of the National Science Foundation. Reviews by Andrea diSessa, Michael Clancy, Katherine Lewis, and anonymous reviewers have improved the clarity and quality of this work.

10. REFERENCES

[1] Ben-Ari, M. (2001). Constructivism in Computer Science Education. *Journal of Computers in Mathematics and Science Teaching*, 20(1), 45–73.

[2] Clancy, M. (2004). Misconceptions and Attitudes that Interfere with Learning to Program. In Fincher, S. & Petre, M. (Eds.), *Computer Science Education Research* (pp. 85-100). New York: Taylor & Francis.

[3] Cockburn, A. & Williams, L. (2001). The costs and benefits of pair programming. *In Extreme programming examined.* Addison-Wesley Longman Publishing Co., Inc. Boston, MA. 223-243.

[4] Cooper, S., Dann, W., & Pausch, R. (2000). Alice: a 3-D tool for introductory programming concepts. *The journal of computing in small colleges.* ACM. 107-116.

[5] Corbin, J. M., & Strauss, A. C. (2008). *Basics of Qualitative Research.* Thousand Oaks, CA: SAGE Publications.

[6] Dann, W., Dragon, T., Cooper, S., Dietzler, K., Ryan, K., & Pausch, R. (2003) Objects: visualization of behavior and state. *Proceedings of the 8th annual conference on Innovation and technology in computer science education, ITiCSE.* Thessaloniki, Greece, 84-88.

[7] diSessa, A. A. (1993). Toward an epistemology of physics. *Cognition and Instruction, 10* (2-3), 105-225.

[8] diSessa, A. A., & Sherin, B. L. (1998). What changes in conceptual change? *International Journal of Science Education, 20*(10), 1135-1191.

[9] diSessa, A. A., & Wagner, J. F. (2005). What coordination has to say about transfer. In J. Mestre (ed.), *Transfer of learning from a modern multi-disciplinary perspective* (pp. 121-154). Greenwich, CT: Information Age Publishing.

[10] diSessa, A. A. (2007). An interactional analysis of clinical interviewing. *Cognition and Instruction. 25(4)*, 523-565.

[11] du Boulay, B., O'Shea, T. & Monk, J. (1989). The black box inside the glass box: Presenting computing concepts to novices, in Studying the Novice Programmer (E. Soloway & J.C. Spohrer, Eds.) Hillsdale, New Jersey: Lawrence Erlbaum Associates Inc., 431-446.

[12] du Boulay, B. (1989). Some difficulties learning to program, in Studying the Novice Programmer (E. Soloway & J.C. Spohrer, Eds.). Hillsdale, New Jersey: Lawrence Erlbaum Associates Inc., 283-299.

[13] Engle, R. A., Conant, F. R. & Greeno, J. G. (2007). Progressive refinement of hypotheses in video-supported research. In R. Goldman, R. Pea, B. J. Barron & S. Derry (Eds.), *Video research in the learning sciences* (pp. 239-254). Mahwah, NJ: Erlbaum.

[14] Fay, A. L., & Mayer, R. E., (1988). Learning LOGO: A cognitive analysis, in Teaching and learning computer programming: multiple research perspectives (R. E. Mayer, Ed.). Hillsdale, New Jersey: Lawrence Erlbaum Associates Inc., 55-74.

[15] Hammer, D. (2000). Student resources for learning introductory physics. American Journal of Physics. 68(1), 52-59.

[16] Kahney, H. (1989). What do novice programmers know about recursion? in Studying the Novice Programmer (E. Soloway & J.C. Spohrer, Eds.) Hillsdale, New Jersey: Lawrence Erlbaum Associates Inc., 209-228.

[17] Kurland, D. M., & Pea, R. D., (1989). Children's mental models of recursive logo programs. *Studying the Novice Programmer (E. Soloway & J.C. Spohrer, Eds.)* Hillsdale, New Jersey: Lawrence Erlbaum Associates Inc., 315-323.

[18] Lewis, C. M. (2011). Is pair programming more effective than other forms of collaboration for young students? *Computer Science Education. 21(2).* 105-134.

[19] Lewis, C. M. (2010). How programming environment shapes perception, learning and goals: Logo vs. Scratch, *ACM SIGCSE Bulletin. 41(1)*, 346-350.

[20] Lewis, C. M. & Shah, N. (2012). Building Upon and Enriching Grade Four Mathematics Standards with Programming Curriculum. *ACM SIGCSE Bulletin. 43(1).* 57-62.

[21] Lopez, M., Whalley, J., Robbins, P., & Lister, R. (2008) Relationship between reading, tracing and writing skills in introductory programming. Proceedings of the fourth International Workshop on Computing Education Research.

[22] Powers, K., Ecott, S., and Hirshfield, L. M. (2007). Through the looking glass; teaching CS0 with Alice. *Proceedings of the 39th SIGCSE Technical Symposium on Computer Science Education*, Covington, KY, 213-217.

[23] Sajaniemi, J. & Kuittinen, M. (2005) An Experiment on Using Roles of Variables in Teaching Introductory Programming. *Computer Science Education*, 15(1), 59 - 82.

[24] Sajaniemi, J., Kuittinen, M., & Tikansalo, T. (2008) A study of the development of students' visualizations of program state during an elementary object-oriented programming course. Journal on Educational Resources in Computing. 7(4) 1-31.

[25] Schoenfeld, A. H. (2007). Reflections on an assessment interview: What a close look at student understanding can reveal. In A. H. Schoenfeld (Eds.) *Assessing Mathematical Proficiency* (pp. 267-280). Cambridge: Cambridge University Press.

[26] Schoenfeld, A. H. (1985). Making sense of "out loud" problem-solving protocols. *The Journal of Mathematical Behavior,* 4. 171-191.

[27] Soloway, E. & Spohrer, J. C. (1989). Studying the Novice Programmer. Hillsdale, New Jersey: Lawrence Erlbaum Associates Inc.

[28] Siegler, R. S. (2006). Microgenetic analyses of learning. In W. Damon & R. M. Lerner (Series Eds.) & D. Kuhn & R. S. Siegler (Vol. Eds.), *Handbook of child psychology: Vol. 2: Cognition, Perception and Language.* (6th ed) Hoboken, NJ: Wiley, 464–510.

[29] Yin, R. K. (1989). Case Study Research: Design and Methods. Sage Publications, Inc. Thousand Oaks, CA.

Toward a Validated Computing Attitudes Survey

Allison Elliott Tew
University of British Columbia
2366 Main Mall
Vancouver, BC V6T 1Z4
aetew@acm.org

Brian Dorn
University of Hartford
200 Bloomfield Ave
West Hartford, CT 06117
bdorn@hartford.edu

Oliver Schneider
University of British Columbia
2366 Main Mall
Vancouver, BC V6T 1Z4
oschneid@cs.ubc.ca

ABSTRACT

The Computing Attitudes Survey (CAS) is a newly designed instrument, adapted from the Colorado Learning Attitudes about Science Survey (CLASS), for measuring novice to expert-like perceptions about computer science. In this paper we outline the iterative design process used for the adaptation and present our progress toward establishing the instrument's validity. We present results of think-aloud interviews and discuss procedures used to determine expert consensus for CAS items. We also detail results of a pilot of the instrument with 447 introductory students in Fall 2011 along with a preliminary factor analysis of this data. Findings to date show consistent interpretation of statements by faculty and students, establish expert consensus of opinion and identify eight candidate factors for further analysis.

Categories and Subject Descriptors

K.3.2 [**Computers and Education**]: Computer and Information Science Education—*computer science education*

General Terms

Design, Human Factors

Keywords

Assessment, surveys, attitudes

1. INTRODUCTION

With significant curricular innovations in computer science education, particularly at the introductory level, there is a recognized need to evaluate the impact of these changes on learning outcomes as well as students' beliefs about the field. Concerns about negative perceptions of computing and hostile classroom and work environments have become pervasive [3, 17]. A recent study by Lewis et al. links students' self-assessment of ability to their decision to major in computer science [16]. If we want to be sure our interventions have a positive influence on both learning and per-

ceptions, it is critical to be able to accurately and reliably measure students' attitudes and beliefs about the discipline.

Further, researchers across various STEM disciplines have found evidence of a relationship between student perceptions and learning outcomes within an academic discipline.[1] Studies by House have demonstrated that students' achievement expectations and self-concept were better predictors of success in chemistry and mathematics courses than previous mathematics or science instruction [14, 15]. Robins proposed a model of *learning edge momentum* to explain how the effects of learning in CS1, whether successful or unsuccessful, become reinforcing over time [21]. Student beliefs affect how they learn new information, and student experiences both inside and outside of the classroom can shape their beliefs [5, 23]. Thus, it is imperative that we understand how our educational practices impact the underlying perceptions students have about computer science.

Hammer [12] proposed a framework for examining distinctions in how novices and experts view a discipline along three different dimensions. *Content and Structure of Knowledge:* Experts believe knowledge is organized in a coherent framework of concepts, while novices often view knowledge as isolated collections of facts. *Source of Knowledge:* Novices believe that knowledge comes from an authority figure and rarely see the connection to the real world or their ability to help co-create new knowledge. Experts believe that knowledge is constructed from a set of working theories that are continually being re-tested and refined. *Problem Solving:* Experts rely on strategies that embody underlying conceptual principles applicable across a variety of contexts, whereas novices often rely on pattern-matching to a small set of memorized solutions and focus only on surface features of the current problem.

Our research examines how students perceive the field of computer science by employing this novice-to-expert continuum framework. The Colorado Learning Attitudes about Science Survey (CLASS) is a validated attitudes survey designed to measure student perceptions of physics according to this framework [1]. It has been successfully used to demonstrate the link between educational practices in introductory courses and student perceptions. Further, its ability to identify students who enter university with more expert-like perceptions is being used to actively recruit and retain students as majors [18]. The CLASS has been successfully adapted in both chemistry [2] and biology [22] with similar results. This paper describes the process of adapting the CLASS to computer science to build the Computing Atti-

---

[1]See [25] for a meta-analysis of the relationship between student self-beliefs and achievement.

tudes Survey (CAS). We discuss the process used to validate the instrument and our initial results of piloting the instrument in introductory computer science classrooms.

1.1 Related Work

Many surveys probe various aspects of student attitudes about science (e.g., [11, 20]). Two have been designed specifically for computer science. The Computer Science Attitudes Survey [26] was derived from a mathematics attitudes scale developed in the late 1970s [10], but the validity of the instrument was never established. Focused on the issue of declining enrollments, Moskal et al. developed a validated instrument for measuring the attitudes of non-majors about computer science, particularly those associated with negative stereotypes [13]. Both of these instruments focus on high level perceptions of the field with constructs such as gender, or "maleness" of the discipline, and usefulness of computing knowledge and programming skills. In contrast, instruments like the CLASS and CAS are designed to investigate how students view knowledge in computing and how that knowledge is constructed.

This type of attitudinal information also contrasts with two other types of investigation: self-efficacy and learning styles. Wiedenbeck's previous work [19] addresses students' self-efficacy about learning how to program, not their attitudes about the discipline of computer science itself. The Bigg's Revised Study Process Questionnaire [4] is an instrument used to measure student approaches to learning in general, independent of a particular discipline. While some of the items on the Bigg's instrument do require reflection on the problem solving or studying process, these items by design do not isolate the content or structure of knowledge in computing or the nature of solving problems specific to CS.

Overall, there are four key decisions that differentiate the design of the CAS instrument presented in this paper. First, CAS statements are designed to elicit attitudes about knowledge and problem solving in the CS discipline. Second, while attitude surveys are often given in an introductory course, CAS statements are written to measure attitudes about CS in general and are not restricted to attitudes about a specific course. Third, CAS items have been carefully selected and tested to provide clear and concise statements with a single interpretation. And finally, our work seeks to establish categories of attitudes based on an empirical analysis of the student responses themselves rather than determining categories a priori using the researchers' areas of interest.

1.2 Overview of the Iterative Method

The CAS was created following the same procedures used to adapt the CLASS for chemistry [2] and biology [22]. Original CLASS statements were modified, added, or removed based on faculty discussions and interviews. After the initial version of the instrument was developed, we conducted think-aloud interviews with both faculty experts and students to establish response validity and ensure consistent interpretation. We then solicited numerous responses from faculty to establish the expert consensus opinion for each survey item. Determining expert agreement is a key step in the analysis given our goal is to construct an instrument that distinguishes between novice and expert attitudes about knowledge in the discipline [12]. Expert opinions are subsequently used to used to score and interpret the student responses.

We gave a pilot version of the CAS at the end of the Fall 2011 term in both major and non-major introductory CS

1. Examined CLASS-Physics, -Bio, and -Chem instruments for survey items applicable to CS.
2. Interviewed CS faculty to generate additional discipline-specific CS items for initial instrument.
3. Conducted think-aloud interviews with faculty and modified questions based on responses.
4. Conducted think-aloud interviews with students and modified items accordingly.
5. Surveyed faculty to determine expert opinion (Fall 2011).
6. Piloted instrument with undergraduate students completing CS1 (Fall 2011), scored responses based on expert opinion, and conducted initial factor analysis.
7. Revise and repeat pre-post assessment with instrument (Spring 2012) to evaluate robustness of factors identified.
8. Revise items based on above results and additional faculty and student interviews as needed.
9. Administer survey again in pre-post format, conduct independent factor analysis, and finalize category robustness.

Figure 1: Summary of Iterative Method

courses at a large research university and a medium-sized teaching institution. We conducted an exploratory factor analysis to determine a set of candidate *components*, meaningfully interpretable groupings of individual statements, to be used in subsequent analyses. The results of our pilot test and analysis was used to revise the statements, and a full pre-/post-term deployment is currently underway during the Spring 2012 term. Analysis and development on the CAS will continue in an iterative fashion—revising statements, soliciting additional feedback from faculty experts, conducting additional student interviews, and repeating the survey—until we are able to fully validate the CAS for use in measuring student attitudes and beliefs about the nature of computer science at the university level. A summary of these procedures is outlined in Figure 1; steps 1–6 are discussed in this paper, while steps 7–9 remain as future work.

In the remainder of this paper, we discuss our process and progress towards building the Computing Attitudes Survey. Section 2 explains how the first version of CAS was developed by modifying the CLASS. The next sections describe our efforts at beginning to establish response validity through think-aloud interviews and establishing expert consensus in Sections 3 & 5 respectively. We provide a brief overview of the research method in Section 4 and present the initial results from our pilot study in Section 6. Since development of the CAS instrument is ongoing, we conclude with a discussion of implications and future work.

2. INITIAL ADAPTATION FROM CLASS

Following Hammer's theoretical framework for investigating novice-to-expert differences [12], CAS statements were designed to probe a range of student attitudes and beliefs about computing, focused in the following areas: 1) learning computer science, 2) problem solving in computer science, and 3) the connection of computer science to the real world.

Many items ($n = 29$) in the CAS were able to be directly replicated from the CLASS survey as is, simply changing the word "physics" to "computer science." For example:

Q1 After I study a topic in computer science and feel that I understand it, I have difficulty solving problems on the same topic.

Q3 I cannot learn computer science if the teacher does not explain things well.

A few statements ($n = 4$) in the CAS were able to be adapted by using terms more appropriate to the discipline. For example, substituting the notion of algorithms for equations or formulas. Examples of these modifications follow.

Q38 When I am working on a computer science program, I try to decide what reasonable output values would be.

Q47 Spending a lot of time understanding where algorithms come from is a waste of time.

Other statements were not applicable to computing and were replaced by new discipline-specific statements ($n = 26$). Ideas for the CS specific topics were generated by the researchers, interviews with expert faculty, and references to the literature on the misconceptions and challenges faced by our discipline (e.g., [17, 27]). These additional computer science topics focused on notions of abstraction, data representation and scalability, errors and testing, and problem solving strategies. For example:

Q9 When working on a complex computer science problem, I have to understand all of the details of the program implementation before I am able to make progress on a solution.

Q18 I am confident my solution to a computer science problem is correct when the output matches the sample output provided in the problem set.

Items in three additional areas (personal interest/motivation, real world connections, and sense of belonging) were added to address the societal impacts of computing. These address the broader notions of seeing connections and relevance of computing concepts and their role in society, as well as whether students can see themselves as producers and not just consumers of technology. Examples are below.

Q21 Tools and techniques from computer science can be useful in the study of other academic disciplines (e.g., biology, art, business).

Q29 I find the challenge of solving computer science problems motivating.

After all of the revisions and adaptations, the initial draft of the CAS contained 58 statements designed to be be used in a wide range of undergraduate computer science courses, for both majors and non-majors alike.

3. THINK-ALOUD INTERVIEWS

Following the development of the initial survey draft, we conducted think-aloud interviews with both faculty members and students. The primary purpose of these interviews was to verify the interpretability of the survey prompts.

3.1 Faculty Interviews

In the fall of 2011, faculty members were recruited for the think-aloud study from a wide range of colleges and universities in North America. Faculty members from both research intensive and teaching intensive institutions were included to ensure the data reflected a broad range of expert opinions. In total, we interviewed 11 faculty members from 8 distinct institutions.

We collected data with a series of background questions to characterize each participant's number of years of teaching experience, the typical courses he or she teaches, and how much experience he or she has with teaching CS1. Participants completed the draft version of the CAS and were then asked to go back through each question explaining how they personally interpreted each question and reached a rating. We also requested feedback about which questions they felt students would have difficulty understanding and inquired about any common misconceptions not covered on the current version of the survey.

On average, these participants had 23 years ($\sigma = 9.4$) of experience teaching computer science and all participants indicated that they had significant experience with teaching introductory computer science courses. They also regularly taught a broad range of courses beyond CS1.

Overall, feedback from faculty about the survey was positive and few potential problems were noted. We re-evaluated each item on the survey based on the feedback from faculty members. In the resulting revised survey, 52 items remained the same, and 6 were reworded to clarify potentially confusing language. At the suggestion of one faculty participant, we also added a new question "I am interested in learning more about computer science" as a complement to other items measuring personal interest in the field.

3.2 Student Interviews

In order to confirm that the revised questions were consistently and correctly interpreted by novices, we then conducted think-aloud interviews with students who were near the end of their first post-secondary computer science course. We interviewed 9 students who were recruited from both a large research institution and a medium-sized teaching institution. Participants were recruited from various introductory courses including those intended for non-majors, though we note that a majority had already decided to major in computer science.

Participants were asked background questions regarding their year of study, courses they were taking alongside CS, general study habits in STEM courses, and long term career goals. They completed the CAS and were then asked to verbalize how they interpreted each question to arrive at their personal response. This data was used to verify that novices were able to interpret items in the manner intended.

In general, novices interpreted items consistently and in the same manner as our faculty experts, though as expected their responses did not always match those of experts. Students occasionally had difficulty understanding items that dealt with computing outside their current university environment. For example, some students expressed that they did not know what the phrases "the real world" or "everyday life" mean in the context of items like "The subject of computer science has little relation to what I experience in the real world." Because such issues were isolated and the majority of questions were unaffected, we determined that the items in the revised draft were sufficiently unambiguous to proceed with the next phase of the validation process.

4. ADMINISTRATION & SCORING

Upon completion of the revisions based on think-aloud interviews, the updated survey draft was entered into a Web-based surveying tool for use in the next phases of validation. This version of the survey was used both to determine expert consensus for each item and to pilot the instrument as an end-of-term survey in introductory computing courses. As administered, this version of the survey consisted of 59 items. It is important to keep in mind that at this stage of the validation process, the instrument contains more candidate questions than will appear on the final version. One purpose of the pilot procedures described in the next two sections is to further eliminate questions which do not score consistently or reliably in large-scale distribution.

Participant responses on each survey item were recorded using a 5-point Likert scale from Strongly Disagree to Strongly Agree. Individual items which are skipped by a participant are treated as though they did not exist for that particular participant. In fact, survey instructions indicated that an item was to be skipped if the participant did not understand the statement. This was done to ensure that a response of "neutral" truly expressed that the participant had no opinion. However, in practice, only a small number of items were skipped by either experts or novices.

As an additional precaution to eliminate noise in the data caused by students completing the survey without actually reading the prompts (e.g., choosing neutral for every question simply in order to earn extra credit), item 49 read: "We use this statement to discard the surveys of people who are not reading the questions. Please select 'Agree' for this question to preserve your answers." Participants indicating a response other than "agree" were removed prior to analysis.

During analysis of both expert and novice data, we collapsed the range of Likert values from a 5-point to a 3-point scale indicating only disagreement, neutrality, or agreement with a statement. Compression of the value range is appropriate in situations where Likert data is treated as an ordinal scale and it is not likely that participants will maintain a consistent interpretation of the distance between a response of strongly agree and agree (see, e.g., [11, 1]). Further, this procedure mirrors that used in the prior validation of the CLASS-Physics [1], -Chem [2], and -Bio [22] instruments.

The two sections that follow outline specific details related to using the survey in determining expert agreement and piloting the scoring procedure with students.

5. ESTABLISHING EXPERT CONSENSUS

To determine expert consensus for each of the items on the survey we recruited faculty members primarily via email distribution lists. We explicitly chose to recruit experts from mailing lists that focused on computing education research, as it was likely that such individuals had considerable experience with teaching introductory courses and represented a wide range of institutions. We also distributed email recruitment materials to faculty at the authors' institutions.

In total, 37 experts completed the survey, and their responses are used to establish expert agreement for each item on the survey. A question was considered to achieve consensus if 66% of the faculty members had the same answer on the three-point scale, and such items were used in scoring student responses (described in Section 6). All items for which consensus was reached explicitly expressed an opinion (i.e., "neutral" was never the expressed expert opinion). The following questions did not achieve consensus, and were excluded from our subsequent analysis: 2, 3, 8, 12, 13, 15, 17, 26, 28, 31, 32, 36, 39, 44.[2] These questions were also considered for elimination in the next iteration of the survey. Of the 44 items remaining, experts exhibited an average of 87.1% agreement ($\sigma = 9.7$).

Comparable data from the physics and chemistry validation procedures is not available, but our results are similar

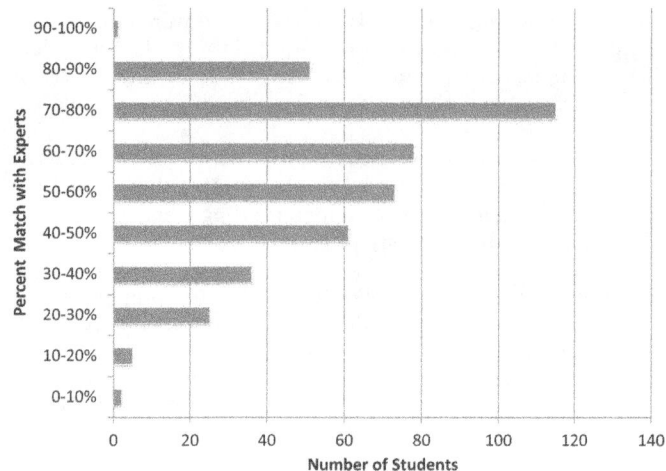

Figure 2: Student Agreement with Expert Opinion

to those noted in the biology validation process where a minimum expert agreement of 70% was required to achieve consensus [22]. We also note that the overall average expert agreement on scored questions is undifferentiated between the computer science, chemistry, and biology instruments (87.1%, 89.2%, and 90%, respectively).

6. PILOT STUDENT SURVEY RESULTS

Students were recruited for the survey at the end of the Fall 2011 academic term through email to class lists. Recruitment information was distributed to students in introductory courses for both CS majors and non-majors at the authors' institutions. After filtering student responses based on correctly answering Q49, we were left with 447 valid responses. These responses were then scored as described below and subjected to an exploratory factor analysis.

6.1 Scoring the Student Responses

As mentioned above, the first part of the analysis process involved collapsing the 5-point scale to a 3-point scale indicating simple agreement or disagreement for each item. Responses to individual items were then scored with respect to whether they matched expert opinion or not. A score of 1 was given for a student who agreed with the faculty consensus on that particular question, -1 if the student opposed the expert viewpoint, and 0 if the student responded neutrally. These scored values for each item were used in the subsequent factor analysis, rather than the raw opinion.

To better understand how student views matched those of experts in this version of the survey we also computed the average rate of agreement with expert opinion for each student. This is the total number of questions on which he/she was given a score of 1 divided by 44, the number of scored questions. Thus, a student who expressed expert opinions for all scored questions would receive an aggregate score of 44 and show 100% agreement. As seen in Figure 2, only one student showed greater than 90% agreement following the first semester of instruction, a plurality agreed with experts between 70% and 80% of the time, and the majority fell somewhere between 40% and 70% agreement. This result is encouraging in that it shows that the survey would be a useful longitudinal measure of growth toward expert-like opinion because, as one would expect, some student misconceptions persist beyond the first course.

---

[2]Q49 was also excluded in further analysis as it is only used to eliminate meaningless responses.

6.2 Exploratory Factor Analysis

To categorize responses to individual questions, we then conducted an exploratory factor analysis. The goal of such an analysis is to statistically identify coherent and relatively independent subsets of statements on the CAS based on correlations within the observed variables. These statement groups, known as *components*, provide an indication of underlying latent relationships within the data [24]. Each component is theorized to represent a single conceptual facet. It is then up to the researcher to interpret the meaning of each component and assign it a name that captures the collective essence of its items. For our purposes, factor analysis is a key element in characterizing the different aspects of novice thought processes about computer science.

Prior to performing the factor analysis we first removed "expert-like" students, those that agreed with experts on 80% or more of the questions. As our intent was to understand the underlying facets of novice opinions, data points too closely mirroring expert-like opinions would have skewed the final factor groupings [24]. Of the 447 valid student responses, 52 were removed for being too expert-like, leaving 395 responses for the exploratory factor analysis.

There are numerous procedural decisions to make when conducting an exploratory factor analysis that may ultimately impact the final categories identified [7, 9, 24]. We chose to primarily replicate the procedures used in the CLASS-Physics/Chem/Bio validation studies for consistency across the instruments [1, 2, 22]. We conducted a principle component extraction using the direct oblimin rotation method. This rotation method allows for potentially correlated (i.e., partially overlapping) components and is appropriate here given that it would be unreasonable to assume that attitudes and beliefs cluster in mutually exclusive categories. As input to the method, student responses were first correlated using Pearson's correlation coefficient on scored data. Missing data was deleted pairwise, as less than 0.387% of all data points were missing.

We extracted eight components during analysis based on Scree plots and overall interpretability [7, 24]. All items surpassed the recommended 0.5 minimum for the individual Kaiser-Meyer-Olkin (KMO) measure of sampling adequacy. We iteratively removed questions that demonstrated a low communality—contributed minimally to the explanation of covariance—(Q10, 16, 18, 20, 23, 27, 45, 46) along with those that showed complex structure by loading heavily on too many components (Q19) [24]. The factor analysis was run iteratively after each set of questions was dropped.

Final results from this process are shown in Table 1. The overall KMO measure was 0.866, and Bartlett's test of sphericity was significant ($\chi^2(595) = 3359.49$, $p < 0.001$). All communalities were above 0.4. Finally, statements were included in a component if their loading value in the final iteration was ≥ 0.32 according to established guidelines. The greater the loading value for an individual item, the more it represents a pure measure of the component [24].

Below we discuss each of the eight extracted components, present our interpretation of their underlying meaning, and highlight their relation to components identified on the CLASS instruments from other disciplines.

6.2.1 C1: Problem Solving—Transfer

This component contained six items relating to students' ability to see and/or apply connections between concepts and ideas in order to solve problems. Thus, we interpreted

this category as capturing notions of knowledge transfer [5]. Example items included:

Q5 If I want to apply a method used for solving one computer science problem to another problem, the problems must involve very similar situations.

Q11 Knowledge in computer science consists of many disconnected topics.

Five of the six items in this component originated on the CLASS-Physics exam, and our interpretation of the items appears closely related to the "Conceptual Connections" and "Applied Conceptual Understanding" components identified in the validation studies from Physics [1] and the other disciplines.

6.2.2 C2: Problem Solving—Strategies

The four items in this component related to classic problem solving strategies in computer science including topics of practice, problem decomposition, code commenting, and planning prior to writing code. Three of the four items had component loading values over 0.63, which is regarded as very good [6]. Example items include:

Q7 When I solve a computer science problem, I break it into smaller parts and solve them one at a time.

Q22 When working on a computer science problem I find it useful to brainstorm about solution strategies before writing code.

While the "Problem Solving Strategies" component also emerged on other CLASS instruments, we note that all four statements here are new discipline-specific items.

6.2.3 C3: Problem Solving—Fixed Mindset

This component contained 10 items closely related to a student's belief of predetermined fate or learned helplessness within the discipline—i.e., either I'll understand it right away or I won't have a chance. Thus, we interpreted this category as related to Dweck's notion of the fixed or malleable mindset [8], specifically towards the field of computing. Particular survey statements in this component included:

Q52 Understanding computer science basically means being able to recall something you've read or been shown.

Q54 If I get stuck on a computer science problem, there is no chance I'll figure it out on my own.

Q56 There is usually only one correct approach to solving a computer science problem.

All 10 items loaded on this component with a value above 0.4, and a majority exceeded 0.5. The large size of this component and relatively high loading values is an indication of this component's overall robustness [7]. However, only 4 of the 10 items came from the original CLASS instrument. While issues of memorization and recall have appeared in various factors on other CLASS surveys, this component of the CAS appears to group together statements in a unique way that expresses a negative attitude about the discipline and problem solving therein. It is notable that this component is also negatively correlated with the component involving personal interest and motivation (see Table 2).

6.2.4 C4: Real World Connections

This component contained six items exhibiting moderate loadings between 0.33 and 0.59. Items in this category

Component	Questions	Explained Variance	Cumulative Explained Variance
C1: Problem Solving–Transfer	**1**, 4, **5**, **6**, **11**, **14**	18.720%	18.720%
C2: Problem Solving–Strategies	7, 22, 40, 53	9.247%	27.967%
C3: Problem Solving–Fixed Mindset	**11**, 41, **42**, **47**, **48**, 52, 54, 56, 57, 58	5.247%	33.214%
C4: Real World Connections	21, **34**, 37, **51**, **52**, **55**	4.095%	37.309%
C5: Problem Solving–Confidence	24, 25, 51	3.984%	41.293%
C6: Problem Solving–Sense Making	**35**, **38**, 43	3.588%	44.881%
C7: Abstraction	9, **35**, **50**	3.413%	48.294%
C8: Personal Interest & Enjoyment	**1**, **6**, 29, **30**, **33**, **34**, **38**, 40, **54**, 59	3.287%	51.581%

Scored, but uncategorized questions: **10**, **16**, 18, **19**, 20, 23, 27, **45**, 46
*Questions in bold were adapted from CLASS-physics

clearly dealt with the relationship between the "real world" and the computer science discipline, though each addressed a different angle of that broader notion. Items included:

Q21 Tools and techniques from computer science can be useful in the study of other disciplines (e.g., biology, art, business).

Q55 The subject of computer science has little relation to what I experience in the real world.

In studies of the CLASS from all other disciplines, "Real World Connections" was consistently a component that emerged in factor analysis. In part, this is likely due to the fact that some survey items were explicitly written to explore real world integration of knowledge in keeping with the theoretical framework provided by Hammer [12]. Half of the items in this category were adapted from CLASS questions. The other half were new questions regarding the relationship between CS and other disciplines and between CS classroom instruction and our daily interactions with computers.

6.2.5 C5: Problem Solving—Confidence

The three items in this component embodied a notion of confidence or ability at being able to succeed in learning to program or solve computer science problems. Previous work has shown that one of the barriers to recruiting and retaining students in CS is that novices feel they do not have the skills necessary to be successful in an introductory course [17, 16]. Two of the three items had component loading values over 0.63. While the low number of items in this component may indicate some instability, the strong loadings indicate reliable measures. Example items include:

Q24 You must be creative to be good at solving computer science problems.

Q25 You must have strong problem solving skills to excel in computer science.

All of the CAS items here are new discipline-specific statements for computer science. Although the component "Problem Solving—Confidence" appears in the physics and chemistry versions of the CLASS, none of the items in their surveys clustered with those in this component.

6.2.6 C6: Problem Solving—Sense Making

The statements in this component captured how students use resources and strategies to help them solve problems. In particular, this component contains items about how novices

and experts grapple with and come to understand computer science problems. One item had a very good loading value (0.70), the remaining two were markedly lower ($\approx$ 0.4). Given the lower loading values and relatively small number of items, this component is potentially weak and unstable [7]. However, it was included in this preliminary analysis, and further data collection and analysis will help to refine and revise the component. Example items included:

Q35 I find that reading course materials (e.g., the textbook) in detail is a good way for me to learn computer science.

Q38 When I am working on a computer science program, I try to decide what reasonable output values would be.

Two of the three items in this component were adapted from original CLASS statements, and this component also appeared in both the physics and chemistry surveys.

6.2.7 C7: Abstraction

This component identified one of the key computer science topics that our experts highlighted in preliminary discussions. Abstraction is a fundamental concept in computing [27] and is emphasized in most introductory computer science courses. The items in this component reflected notions surrounding level of detail and information hiding. Two of the three items had very good component loading values (above 0.63). Example items included:

Q9 When working on a complex computer science problem, I have to understand all of the details of the program implementation before I am able to make progress on a solution.

Q50 In computer science, it is important for me to make sense out of algorithms before I can use them correctly.

While two of the three items were adapted from original CLASS statements, the subtle revisions modified them in an important way. Rather than referring to more general problem solving strategies (as in the CLASS-Physics), they now focus on a core computer science concept.

6.2.8 C8: Personal Interest & Enjoyment

This component was comprised of ten items related to personal interest, motivation, and engagement with computer science. Six of the items had component loading values ranging from 0.58 to 0.84, indicative of good to excellent measures. The remaining four items loaded much lower than the rest, indicating that the other six were better primary markers for the component. Example items included:

Table 2: Component Correlations

Comp.	1	2	3	4	5	6	7	8
1	1.0	-.07	.24	.06	.06	.05	-.09	-.07
2		1.0	.05	.02	-.03	-.01	.16	-.24
3			1.0	.21	.05	.02	-.12	-.27
4				1.0	.03	.06	-.01	-.18
5					1.0	.10	-.07	-.02
6						1.0	-.10	-.08
7							1.0	-.03
8								1.0

Q29 I find the challenge of solving computer science problems motivating.

Q30 When studying computer science, I relate the important information to what I already know rather than just memorizing it the way it is presented.

Q34 Reasoning skills used to understand computer science can be helpful to me in my everyday life.

The majority of the items in this component were adapted from original CLASS items, and "Personal Interest" is one of the components that has appeared in each version and adaptation of the CLASS.

6.3 Factor Correlations and Summary

The eight components discussed in the sections above should be considered preliminary. Further data collection and analysis with a full-scale pre/post term deployment will be required to refine and revise the candidate components. While some of the loading values and the low number of items in a few of the components may be cause for concern, the overall interpretability of the framework of components is quite reasonable—a key goal in factor analysis.

Component correlations can be found in Table 2. Although the oblique rotation used in the factor analysis allowed for inter-related components, only a few of the components were (minimally) correlated. There were weak negative correlations between the components related to problem solving strategies and personal interest (components 2 and 8, $r = -.24$) and fixed mindset and personal interest (components 3 and 8, $r = -.27$). Similarly weak positive correlations existed between transfer and fixed mindset (components 1 and 3, $r = .24$) and real world connections and fixed mindset (components 4 and 3, $r = .21$). Since statements could load on multiple components, such relationships were not unexpected. Further, as knowledge of the discipline is inter-connected [12], so should be the interpretation of the components. However, the relatively low values of the correlations indicate that each component measures a reasonably distinct aspect of the discipline and none are redundant.

While the modification of the CLASS-Physics for chemistry resulted in highly similar components, the CLASS-Bio and the CAS exhibit more uniqueness. We posit that this is tied to underlying changes in the survey statements across disciplines. In factor analysis any change in the statements can change the likelihood of groupings, and this is likely the main source of difference in the components identified here. CLASS-Chem and Bio only added $\approx$ 10 new statements, while CAS required the addition of 26 new statements. Thus the statement pool for CAS was quite different from the previous CLASS instruments.

All of the CLASS-style instruments have identified both "Real World Connection" and "Personal Interest" components from their analysis of student responses. The persistence of these components across the adaptations can be seen as a validation of the instruments against the theoretical framework on which they were all based [12]. Components related to problem solving—strategies, confidence and sense making, have appeared in some previous versions of the CLASS. These still appear in this analysis of the CAS but are comprised of a modified set of items that reflect a more discipline-specific nature of solving problems. Two new discipline-specific components, "Fixed Mindset" and "Abstraction" complete the set of candidate components that were identified on the CAS.

7. ONGOING WORK AND CONCLUSION

Development and validation of the CAS instrument is ongoing. The work presented in this paper is the initial, albeit critical, portion of the larger validation effort. Based on the results of the expert consensus process discussed in Section 5, we have further revised the CAS to eliminate many of the questions for which expert agreement could not be reached. This most recent version of the survey (version 3) contains 53 items.

We are currently analyzing additional data from students in introductory courses at the authors' institutions using version 3 of the CAS. Pre-term data was collected in January 2012 prior to the first week of instruction in the same set of courses described in Section 6 ($n = 437$). Post-term data was also collected in these courses ($n = 395$). Future work will subject the pre-term and post-term data to the same scoring procedure and factor analytic process described here. In addition, we will also compare pre/post data pairwise to examine shifts in individual student attitudes about computing as a result of the first course. Each of these analyses will seek to determine the robustness and reliability of the components identified here, as well as to identify survey items which do not consistently load on given factors for potential removal from subsequent CAS versions.

Beyond our immediate ongoing work, further revisions to the CAS could come from a variety of sources. Should we discover considerable variation in results from CS1 students completing the instrument in different terms, we may need to conduct additional think-aloud interviews with students. The nine student interviews described in this paper may not have been sufficient to fully depict how novices interpret each statement, and thus additional rewording may be necessary.

While the expert consensus levels obtained from our pool of computer science faculty are similar to those used in the CLASS-Bio, they are lower from those reached by faculty in both physics and chemistry. In order to further solidify expert consensus, we intend to gather additional data on newer versions of the CAS. We will recruit faculty more widely by using sources outside the computing education community. This will reduce the potential impact outlying opinions have and would ensure greater diversity and representation of expertise across all subfields of computer science.

Lastly, a critical piece to the final validation of the instrument is a large scale effort to gather data using the Web-based Computing Attitudes Survey from students at many different institutions worldwide. This will ensure that the final instrument is broadly applicable in a wide variety of institutional and pedagogical settings. Upon completion of this final validation effort, we plan to make the CAS publicly available under a Creative Commons license for use by instructors and researchers alike.

Having undergone several revisions already, the Computing Attitudes Survey is now entering the latter stages of the validation process to fully refine and finalize the instrument. In this paper we described the process for adapting an existing attitudes survey from physics, detailed the procedures for validating the instrument, and explored the discipline-specific variations in conceptualizing a domain. When complete, the CAS will permit a wide range of rigorous investigations related to student attitudes in computing, including the measurement of changes in attitudes resulting from curricular innovation, the identification of trajectories towards expert attitudes over time, and an in-depth study of the impact of student attitudes and beliefs on performance on standardized measures of conceptual understanding.

Acknowledgments

We thank all of the faculty and students who participated in interviews and surveys during CAS development and validation. We especially would like to thank the University of British Columbia and University of Hartford faculty and students who participated in the initial pilot. This work was funded in part by the Carl Wieman Science Education Initiative at the University of British Columbia.

References

[1] W. K. Adams, K. K. Perkins, N. S. Podolefsky, M. Dubson, N. D. Finkelstein, and C. E. Wieman. A new instrument for measuring student beliefs about physics and learning physics: The Colorado Learning Attitudes about Science Survey. *Physical Review Special Topics–Physics Education Research*, 2(010101): 1–14, 2006.

[2] J. Barbera, W. K. Adams, C. E. Weiman, and K. K. Perkins. Modifying and validating the Colorado Learning Attitudes about Science Survey for use in chemistry. *Journal of Chemical Education*, 85(10): 1435–1439, 2008.

[3] L. J. Barker, K. Garvin-Doxas, and M. Jackson. Defensive climate in the computer science classroom. In *Proc. of the 33rd SIGCSE Technical Symposium on Computer Science Education*, SIGCSE '02, pages 43–47, 2002.

[4] J. Biggs, D. Kember, and D. Y. Leung. The revised two-factor study process questionnaire: R-SPQ-2F. *British Journal of Educational Psychology*, 71(1).

[5] J. D. Bransford, A. L. Brown, and R. R. Cocking. *How People Learn: Brain, Mind, Experience, and School*. National Academy Press, Washington, D.C., expanded edition, 2000.

[6] A. L. Comrey and H. B. Lee. *A first course in factor analysis*. LEA, Hillsdale, NJ, 2nd edition, 1992.

[7] A. B. Costello and J. W. Osborne. Best practices in exploratory factor analysis: Four recommendations for getting the most from your analysis. *Practical Assessment, Research and Evaluation*, 10(7):1–9, 2005.

[8] C. S. Dweck. Motivational processes affecting learning. *American Psychologist*, 41(10):1040–1048, 1986.

[9] L. R. Fabrigar, D. T. Wegener, R. C. MacCallum, and E. J. Strahan. Evaluating the use of exploratory factor analysis in psychological research. *Psychological Methods*, 4(3):272–299, 1999.

[10] E. Fennema and J. A. Sherman. Fennema-Sherman mathematics attitudes scales: Instruments designed to measure attitudes toward the learning of mathematics by females and males. *Journal for Research in Mathematics Education*, 7(5):324–326.

[11] I. Halloun. Student views about science: A comparative survey. Beirut: Phoenix Series / Educational Research Center, Lebanese Univ., 2001.

[12] D. Hammer. Epistemological beliefs in introductory physics. *Cognition and Instruction*, 12(2):151–183, 1994.

[13] A. Hoegh and B. M. Moskal. Examining science and engineering students' attitudes toward computer science. In *Proc. of the 39th ASEE/IEEE Frontiers in Education Conference*, pages W1G 1–6, 2009.

[14] J. D. House. Student motivation and achievement in college chemistry. *International Journal of Instructional Media*, 21(1):1–11, 1994.

[15] J. D. House. Student motivation, previous instructional experience, and prior achievement as predictors of performance in college mathematics. *International Journal of Instructional Media*, 22(2): 157–167, 1995.

[16] C. M. Lewis, K. Yasuhara, and R. E. Anderson. Deciding to major in computer science: A grounded theory of students' self-assessment of ability. In *Proc. of the 7th International Workshop on Computing Education Research*, ICER '11, pages 3–10, 2011.

[17] J. Margolis and A. Fisher. *Unlocking the Clubhouse: Women in Computing*. MIT Press, Cambridge, 2002.

[18] K. K. Perkins, W. K. Adams, S. J. Pollock, N. D. Finkelstein, and C. E. Wieman. Correlating student beliefs with student learning using the Colorado Learning Attitudes about Science Survey. In *Proc. of the 2004 Physics Education Research Conference*, pages 61–64, 2004.

[19] V. Ramalingam and S. Wiedenbeck. Development and validation of scores on a computer programming self-efficacy scale and group analyses of novice programmer self-efficacy. *Journal of Educational Computing Research*, 19(4):367–381, 1998.

[20] E. F. Redish, J. M. Saul, and R. N. Steinberg. Student expectations in introductory physics. *American Journal of Physics*, 66(3):212–224, 1998.

[21] A. Robins. Learning edge momentum: A new account of outcomes in CS1. *Computer Science Education*, 20 (1):37–71, 2010.

[22] K. Semsar, J. K. Knight, G. Birol, and M. K. Smith. The Colorado Learning Attitudes about Science Survey (CLASS) for use in biology. *Life Sciences Education*, 10:268–278, 2011.

[23] E. Seymour and N. M. Hewitt. *Talking About Leaving: Why Undergraduates Leave the Sciences*. Westview Press, Boulder, CO, 1997.

[24] B. G. Tabachnick and L. S. Fidell. *Using Multivariate Statistics*. Allyn and Bacon, Boston, 5th edition, 2007.

[25] J. C. Valentine, D. L. DuBois, and H. Cooper. The relation between self-beliefs and academic achievement: A meta-analytic review. *Educational Psychologist*, 39(2):111–133, 2004.

[26] E. N. Wiebe, L. Williams, K. Yang, and C. Miller. Computer science attitude survey. Technical Report NCSU CSC TR-2003-1, Dept of Computer Science, NC State University, Raleigh, NC, 2003.

[27] J. M. Wing. Computational thinking. *Communications of the ACM*, 49(3):33–35, Mar. 2006.

A Statewide Survey on Computing Education Pathways and Influences: Factors in Broadening Participation in Computing

Mark Guzdial
School of Interactive
Computing
Georgia Institute of
Technology
85 Fifth Street, NW
Atlanta, Georgia 30332-0760
guzdial@cc.gatech.edu

Barbara J. Ericson
College of Computing
Georgia Institute of
Technology
801 Atlantic Drive Atlanta,
Georgia 30332-0280
ericson@cc.gatech.edu

Tom McKlin,
Shelly Engelman
The Findings Group
1201 Clairmont Road, Suite
305
Decatur, GA 30030
[tom,
shelly]@thefindingsgroup.com

ABSTRACT

In computing education, we have only just started developing methods for accurately measuring a student's understanding of introductory computing, let alone characterizing a whole classroom, school, or university system. As part of evaluating the impact of "Georgia Computes!" we sought an understanding the factors influencing undergraduate enrollment in introductory computing for an entire state in the United States of America. We gathered surveys from over 1400 undergraduate students in introductory computing classes from 19 higher-education institutions in a single state. The analysis provided insight into the impact of "Georgia Computes!", into the connections between stages of the computing education pathways, and how factors that influence students' pursuit of computing differ between genders and majority/minority group students.

Categories and Subject Descriptors

K.3.2 [**Computers and Education**]: Computer and Information Science Education — computer science education

Keywords

Assessment,statewide assessment,education pipeline,education pathways,broadening participation, women, under-represented minorities

1. MEASURING THE COMPUTING STATUS OF A STATE

"Georgia Computes!" (GaComputes) was a National Science Foundation funded alliance whose goal was to improve the state of computing education across the entire state of Georgia, and in so doing, improve the diversity of students pursuing computing-intensive degree programs [6]. It was funded 2006–2012 by the Broadening Participation in Computing (BPC) program in NSF. Our focus extended from motivating the learning of computing starting in Grade 4 (about 10 years old), through the creation of weekend workshops and summer camps for students in later primary and secondary school years, to professional development for secondary school and even higher education faculty.

All the public institutions of higher-education in the state belong to the University System of Georgia (USG), which is a partner in the GaComputes Alliance. When we originally started GaComputes, we planned to tap into data from the University System of Georgia to help us understand enrollment of computing education in the state and to measure the impact of our interventions. While they gather enrollment and demographic data from all the 35 institutions, including the 29 institutions that offer some form of computing (e.g., computer science, information technology, or information systems), the data are not aggregated. For our evaluation purposes, there was no systemwide data store.

Measuring across 358 high schools and 29 higher education institutions is an unusual challenge for computing education. We have been developing measures of the computing understanding of individuals [13, 14], and some on the progress of a whole class (typically, focusing on demographics and retention) [12]. We know of only one effort to measure progress on computing education goals (e.g., diversity, retention, and transfer from two-year to four-year programs) of a whole state, in Massachusetts through the Commonwealth Alliance for IT Education (CAITE) [1]. The CAITE effort focused on higher education, including community colleges. In our effort, we aimed to get some measure of the pipeline or formal education pathway from secondary school into higher education studies in computing education.

In 2009, we started a process of trying to measure the status of computing education across the entire state ourselves. All Georgia institutions offering introductory computer science courses were asked to administer a survey to their introductory computing students in Spring, 2010. Of the 35 colleges and universities in Georgia, 29 offer computer science coursework, and 19 participated in the survey. In total, 1,434 introductory computer science students (in either a first or second semester course, but all in the same semester without duplication of students) completed the survey[1]. In addition, we surveyed the instructors as well, but we are not presenting that in this paper. Georgia Tech is unique from other institutions in Georgia in that introductory computer science courses are required. Of the total number of introductory CS students completing the survey (1,434), 673 were identified as attending Georgia Tech (GT). At several points in the analysis, we separated Georgia Tech from the pool.

The survey was ten pages long. We gathered demographic data, and asked students about their middle school and high school experiences. We asked students for their major and about their college and university experience. We asked them about their interest in computer science, using the factors identified in studies like the ACM-WGBH teen survey[2]. We asked them about the factors influencing their engagement and how much support they felt that they had in studying computing. Finally, we asked them about their career aspirations.

In this paper, we look at these data to address three questions:

- Who takes computing in our state, and how computing experiences in middle school and high school influenced their choices?

- What impact has GaComputes' work in middle and high schools had on computing enrollment in Georgia?

- What influences the decisions of women and minorities to pursue computing?

2. DESCRIPTION OF POOL: DEMOGRAPHICS AND INFLUENCES

Overall, the pool was 31% female and 69% male (Table 2); 59% of the students reported their race/ethnic group as White, 15% Asian, 15% Black, 5% Hispanic, less than 1% Native American, and 5% Multiracial. 41% of the respondents were first year students, 29% were second year students. Perhaps surprising, given that the survey was given in the introductory course, 18% were third year students, 7% fourth year, and 2% fifth year, and 3% Other (e.g., graduate, or non-traditional/special students).

The majority of our respondents were at the beginning of their higher-education career. 40% had never taken a college or university computer science course, and 34% had taken only a singe one, and 12% had taken two.

Less than a third of students engaged in any computing activities in middle school. Only 28% of students said that they participated in middle school (grades 6–8, typically ages 12–14) computing activities (18% chose not to participate, and 57% were not aware of any being available). Only 14% engaged in computing activities out-of-school during middle school grades. GaComputes activities had little impact at the middle school level. Only 1% of respondents engaged in our Boys and Girls Club Activities, and 1% did Girl Scouts workshops, and those were the only categories with any respondents at all. 34% of the students said that

they were not interested in computing in middle school, 26% slightly interested, 25% somewhat interested, and 15% very interested. Some students did study computing in middle school classes, with 14% taking HTML basics, 13% web design, 10% database, 12% programming, and 13% robotics.

There was slightly more engagement with computing at high school. 32% of respondents said that they participating in computing activities or clubs in high school (37% chose not to participate in any, and 32% were not aware of any). 16% engaged in out-of-school computing activities or clubs. Only 21% of the students said that they were *not* interested in computing in high school, 22% were slightly interested, 28% were somewhat interested, and 29% were very interested – a big shift from middle school.

57% of our respondents said that they took computing courses in high school. 28% of those were "computing applications" courses, but the other 69% had courses whose learning objectives include significant programming. The Georgia high school computer science curriculum defines four courses [8]:

- Computing in the Modern World, which 9% of students had taken.

- Beginning Programming, 15%.

- Intermediate Programming, 4%.

- AP Computer Science, 5%.

In addition, 11% of the students had taken IT and systems management courses, 3% had taken game and animation classes, 3% had taken HCI design classes, and 17% had taken others, not-specified.

Because of the Georgia Tech (GT) effect, most of our respondents were not majors in computing, 52%. 31% were computer science (CS) majors, 3% were CS minors, 10% were in computing but not CS, 4% were undeclared. Table 1[3] describes students attitudes about factors that might influence a choice to pursue computing. Other than the factors related to programming, there is surprisingly strong sentiment about many of these factors.

We asked students, "If you are NOT a computing major/minor, indicate your reason(s) for not selecting computing." Below are the choices for that question, in the order that they appeared. These responses are valuable because of the large number of informed respondents, since they were currently enrolled in a computing course.

- Computing major/minor courses are too difficult, 12%.

- I don't want to do the kind of work that a computing major/minor leads to, 30%.

- I don't enjoy computing courses, 20%.

- I am not sure what jobs are available for students with a computing degree, 8%.

- I don't have confidence that I could succeed in computing, 16%.

- I have little interest in computing subject matter, 25%.

- It is too expensive to switch majors, 5%.

- My academic performance in computing to date is poor, 9%.

- The computing assignments require too much time, 8%.

- Computing is only about programming, 5%.

[1] A copy of the survey can be found on the Publications page at http://www.gacomputes.org.
[2] http://www.acm.org/press-room/news-releases/2009/nic-interim-report/

[3] The scale is Strongly Disagree, Disagree, Agree, to Strongly Agree.

Table 1: Student attitudes about factors influencing a choice to pursue computing

Statement	SD	D	A	SA
I have always wanted to be in computer science	25%	42%	23%	10%
I like to program in my spare time	31%	36%	25%	8%
I like solving complex logic puzzles	9%	18%	51%	22%
I would like to build cutting edge tools and applications that help people	10%	22%	35%	23%
I like talking with my friends about programming	27%	33%	28%	12%

To what extent do these apply to you?	Not at all	A little	Some	A lot
I am good at math or science.	5%	13 %	39%	43%
CS provides good financial opportunities after graduation.	4%	17%	35%	43%
CS allows me to be creative.	7%	15%	39%	40%
I am interested in helping people or society.	5%	18%	36%	40%
I have an interest in computer games.	10%	19%	25%	46%
Computing offers diverse and broad opportunities.	5%	13%	33%	49%
I am interested in solving problems with computing.	7%	17%	34%	43%
I like to program computers.	14%	22%	29%	35%
I enjoy working with computers.	4%	7%	24%	66%
I am interested in creating computer animation/movies.	17%	26%	26%	31%

- I don't think I belong in computing (don't fit the stereotype), 13%.

- Family, friends, etc. recommend that I not major in computing, 4%.

- Other (not specified), 13%.

2.1 Summarizing the Georgia Tech Effect

Georgia Tech *requires* computer science of all students, which leads to several interesting impacts on our results. Without Georgia Tech (GT), our pool is only 25% female (compared to 31% when GT is included Table 2). Without Georgia Tech, most students take the first course in CS in their second year, and are more likely to have taken a "bridge" course. More non-GT students report not having the option of out-of-school-time middle school computing experiences. 56% (vs. 57% with GT) of non-GT students took a high school computer science course. GT is a prestigious school, so students who go to GT may have had more enrichment opportunities and computer classes available.

Non-GT students were *more* interested in computer science in middle and high school. For example, 21% of students in the overall pool say that they had no interest in computer science in high school, but only 11% when GT is removed. Students from non-GT institutions were more likely to have engaged in middle and high school computing activities, when they were available (e.g., in high school, 32% of the overall pool, 38% of the non-GT pool). Likely, these results are due to students being forced to take computer science. The middle school to high school gap in interest is *more* pronounced without GT. In the overall pool, 15% of students say that they were "very interested" in CS in middle school, and 29% in high school. Without GT, 15% of students say that they were "very interested" in CS in middle school, and a whopping 41% in high school.

3. INFLUENCES OF GACOMPUTES ON PATHWAYS

One question that we pursued in this survey was an understanding of how students progressed from secondary school into higher education studies in computing, and if GaComputes professional development had any impact on that progression. GaComputes funds the Institute for Computing Education at Georgia Tech[4] which provides professional development for high school CS teachers. We asked all of the participants in our study about their high school experience. Of 2,244 schools in Georgia as of 8 February 2010, 422 offer 10th, 11th, and 12th grade classes (typically, students in the range of 15–18 years old). Most of these (358) are traditional high schools offering grades 9–12, and 16 offer grades 1–12.

Traditional introductory computer science students in our Spring 2010 study are most likely freshmen who attended high school during the 2005–2006, 2006–2007, 2007–2008, and 2008–2009 school years. Non-traditional students may have attended high school earlier, and the Institute for Computing Education (ICE) started training teachers in 2004. Therefore, any influence from the program would be from teachers who attended between 2004 and 2009 which was a population of 258 teachers from 53 public school districts in Georgia. Overall, these 258 teachers represent 152 public schools in Georgia. This group of teachers represents almost 36% (152 out of 422) of all schools in Georgia offering high school grade levels.

Overall, the introductory CS students surveyed came from 252 public schools in Georgia, and 107 of those schools had sent teachers for ICE training. While GaComputes had trained teachers at fewer than half of the schools sending students to introductory CS programs in Georgia, GaComputes schools are responsible for 60% of all Georgia students attending introductory computing courses. That is, of the 1,434 students taking the survey, 932 (64.99%) report that they attended a public high school in Georgia, and 531 (56.97%) of Georgia students attended a school that has sent a teacher to ICE training between 2004 and 2009. So, the 36% of schools with an ICE teacher produced 56.97% of introductory computing students in our survey who came from Georgia high schools. We did not have the data to track at a finer grain of detail, e.g., did those students have an ICE teacher in a class, talk to an ICE teacher, take a course from someone that an ICE teacher influenced, etc.

We conducted a separate analysis without Georgia Tech. 761 non-GT introductory CS students took the survey. Overall, the 761 introductory CS students surveyed come from 211 public schools in Georgia, and 98 of those schools have sent teachers for ICE training. Of the 761 students, 553 (72.67%) report that they attended a public high school in Georgia, and 291 (52.62%) of Georgia students attended a school that has sent a teacher to ICE training between 2004 and 2009, which is still disproportionate to the 36% of Georgia high schools that had an ICE teacher.

Gender Comparison: ICE schools produce more female introductory computing students than non-ICE schools, but

---

[4] http://coweb.cc.gatech.edu/ice-gt

Table 2: Number and percentage of male and female students in an introductory computing class from ICE and Non-ICE high schools

	Non-ICE Schools		ICE Schools	
	n	%	n	%
Female	120	29.92%	169	31.83%
Male	281	70.07%	362	68.1%
Total	401	100%	531	100%

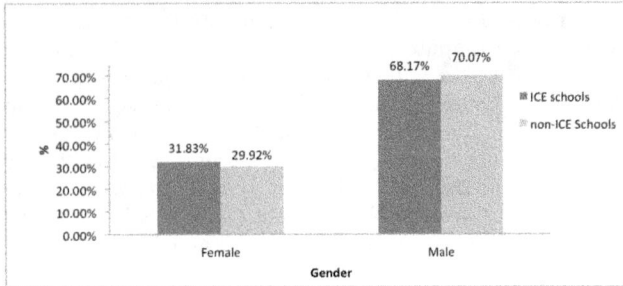

Figure 1: Bar chart of percentage of male and female students in an introductory computing class from ICE and Non-ICE high schools.

the differences between the production of female and male introductory CS students is *not* significantly different between ICE and non-ICE schools (Figure 1). We looked at the number and ratio of female and male students produced by each school (Table 2), and used a Chi-square analysis to compare ICE schools and non-ICE schools and gender, $\chi^2(df = 1) = 0.39$, $p = 0.534$.

Race/Ethnicity Comparison: ICE schools produced more minority students, both cumulatively and specifically for Black, Hispanic, and Multiracial categories, but not significantly, $\chi^2(df = 1) = 0.49$, $p = 0.534$ (Figure 2). More Asian introductory CS students come from ICE schools than non-ICE schools, and more White introductory CS students come from non-ICE schools than ICE schools. No differences were statistically significant.

4. INFLUENCING THE DECISION TO PURSUE COMPUTING

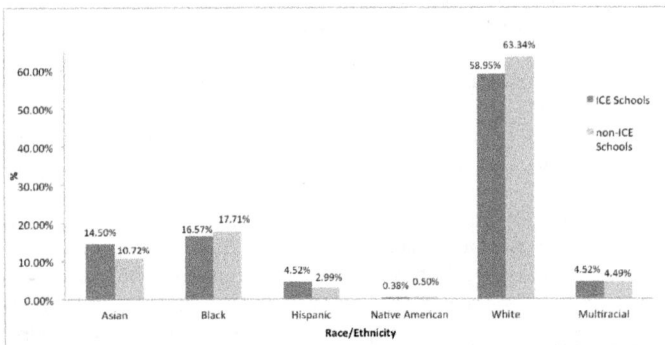

Figure 2: Barchart of percentage of students by race/ethnicity in an introductory computing class from ICE and non-ICE high schools.

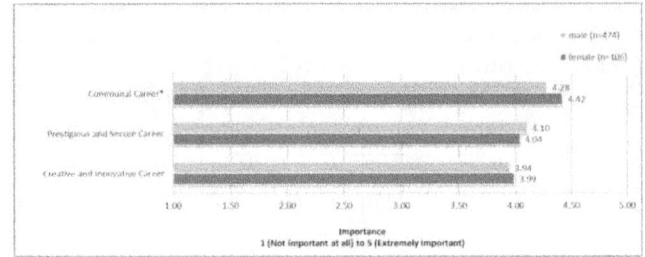

Figure 3: Important career characteristics, gender comparison (*$p < .05$, **$p < .01$).

We asked students about the characteristics of careers that were of interest to them. In the analysis in this section, we only look at participants who declared computing as their major or minor. Female respondents are significantly more likely than male respondents to place importance on communal career characteristics (Figure 3). That is, females are more likely to place importance on "being able to spend time with your family" and "having the power to do good and doing work that makes a difference" than males. Asian, Black, and Hispanic respondents are significantly more likely than White respondents to place importance on having a creative and innovative career and for achieving job security and prestige in their chosen professions (Figure 4).

As mentioned in the earlier section, we asked students about the factors for choosing a computing major or minor, and here we analyze those in terms of gender and race/ethnicity. Female respondents were more likely than male respondents to say that they chose a computing major/minor because of their "interest in helping people or society" (Figure 5). Male respondents were significantly more likely than female respondents to cite "interest in computer games," "interest in solving problems with computing," and "liking to program computers" as reasons for choosing a computing major/minor. Black respondents were significantly more likely than White respondents to cite "interest in helping people or society" as a reason for choosing a computing major/minor (Table 3). Asian and Black respondents were significantly more likely than White respondents (and multiracial respondents) to report "interest in creating computer animation/movies" as a reason for choosing a computing major/minor.

Perceptions of Ability and Relation to Encouragement in Predicting Success: We know that perception of ability plays an important role in students' decision to continue in computing (e.g., [9]). Recall that this survey was given to students who were mostly in their first or second computing course, and 69% of the students had taken a course involving computer programming in high school. So, when they tell us what they think about computer science courses and their abilities, they have experiences that inform their perceptions.

Female respondents rated their programming skills as significantly lower than male respondents did. On average, females rated their programming skills as average to slightly below average, whereas males rated their skills as average to slightly above average. Likewise, there was a significant difference between Black and White respondents in self-reported programming skills: Black respondents rated

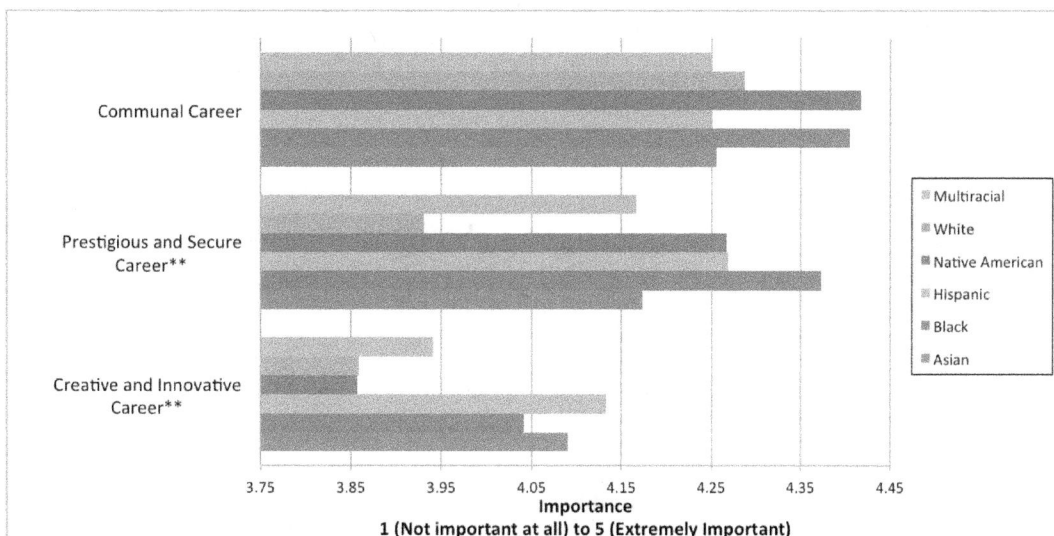

Figure 4: Important career characteristics, race/ethnicity comparison (*$p < .05$, **$p < .01$).

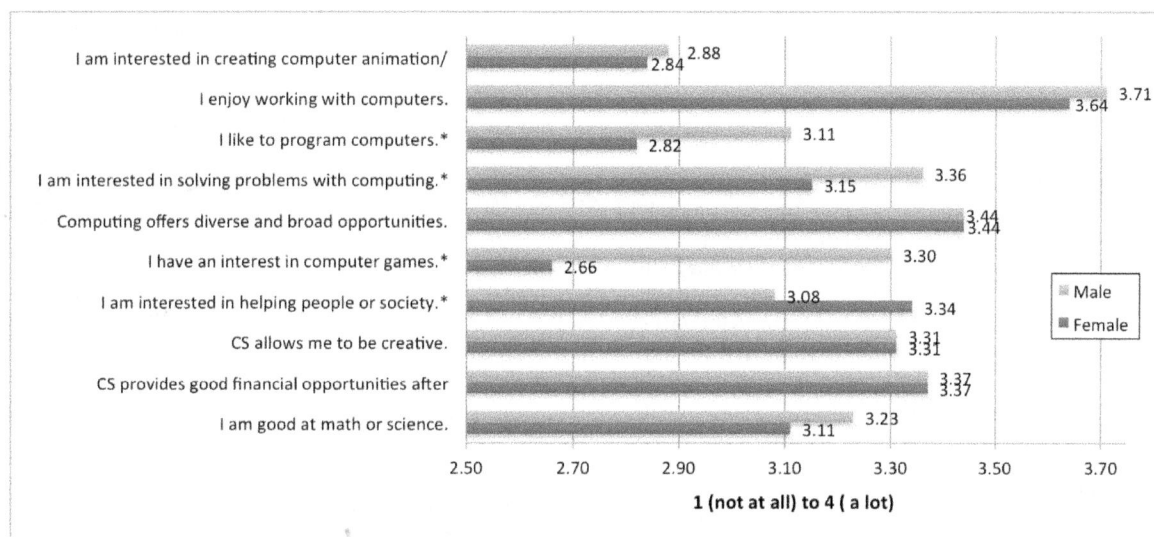

Figure 5: Reasons for choosing a computing career, gender comparison (*$p < .05$).

Table 3: 10 reasons for choosing a computing major/minor, race/ethnicity comparison. Numbers indicate mean responses, from 1 (not at all) to 4 (a lot). (*$p < .05$)

	I am good at math or science.	CS provides good financial opportunities after graduation.	CS allows me to be creative.	I am interested in helping people or society.*	I have an interest in computer games.	Computing offers diverse and broad opportunities.	I am interested in solving problems with computing.	I like to program computers.	I enjoy working with computers.	I am interested in creating computing animation/ movies.*
Asian	3.18	3.33	3.22	3.18	3.23	3.43	3.27	3.04	3.53	3.07*
Black	3.30	3.49	3.35	3.39*	3.15	3.52	3.30	2.93	3.74	3.04*
Hispanic	3.37	3.56	3.46	3.12	3.26	3.63	3.52	3.11	3.78	2.77
Native American	4.00	3.50	3.00	3.50	2.50	3.00	4.00	3.50	4.00	2.79
White	3.17	3.31	3.30	3.00*	3.18	3.38	3.33	3.12	3.71	2.79
Multi-racial	3.17	3.46	3.38	3.04	3.42	3.50	3.38	3.08	3.83	2.68

147

their programming skills as significantly lower than White respondents did.

We conducted a regression analysis [2] to assess the nature of the relationship among survey factors[5]. We hypothesized that self-reported *ability* (how students rated their programming skills) will directly predict (a) satisfaction in choosing to study computing, (b) likelihood in completing a computing major/minor, and (c) likelihood of pursuing a career in computing[6]. As perceived ability in computing increases, satisfaction and likelihood in completing and pursuing a career in computing will increase. However, we hypothesized that *encouragement* to belong and persist (e.g., construct includes responses to "Computing professors have offered me personal advice on how to succeed in computing" and "My parents/guardians encouraged me to take computing courses") will play a more important role than self-reported ability in predicting female and underrepresented minorities' outcomes. That is, we hypothesized that *encouragement* will statistically trump *ability* in predicting outcomes for female and minority respondents.

This hypothesis is based on previous research that investigated gender and racial differences in computer science (e.g., [5]). Previous research has repeatedly found that low affiliation and low interest in computer science assignments significantly accounts for the small number of women and underrepresented minorities in computer science majors and careers [3, 4]. In fact, Cohoon and Baylor [7] contend that increasing affiliation, confidence and interest in computing course work is equally, if not more, important as increasing ability in computing for females. Cohoon and colleagues [7] find that grades do not adequately explain why women and minorities leave CS at higher rates than men and majority group members. Strenta and colleagues [11] found that differences in introductory course grades did not adequately explain the effect of gender on willingness to persist in computer science.

To investigate the hypothesized meditational relationship, we conducted a series of regression analyses according to the guidelines stipulated by Baron & Kenny [2]. The numbers below reflect standardized Beta weights. The standardized Beta value indicates the number of standard deviations that the outcome will change as a result of one standard deviation change in the predictor variable. The standardized Beta value also provides information regarding the importance of a predictor in the model.

For females, encouragement fully mediates the relationship between ability and satisfaction, likelihood to complete computing major/minor, and likelihood to pursue a career in computing (Figure 6). When the outcome variables are regressed on both encouragement and ability, the direct effect of ability becomes insignificant. This suggests that while ability enhances female's satisfaction and likelihood to pursue computing, encouragement is driving this effect. For every one standard deviation increase in encouragement, there was a .598 standard deviation increase in satisfaction, a .458 standard deviation increase in likelihood to complete com-

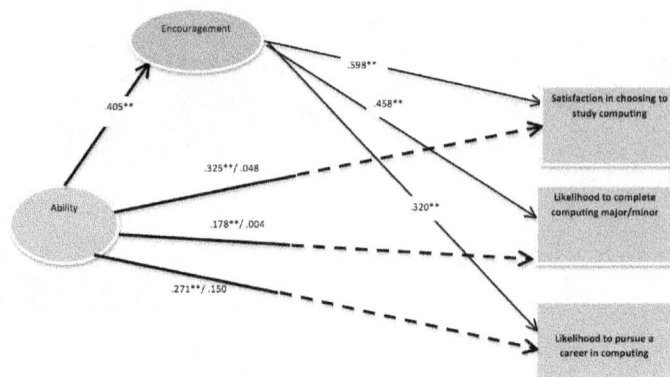

Figure 6: Mediation analysis for females (*p < .05, **p < .01).

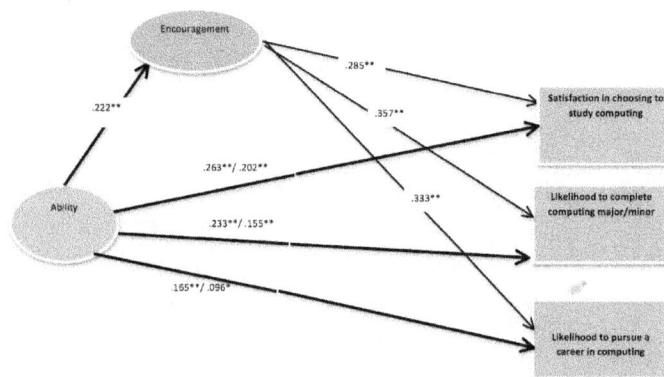

Figure 7: Mediation analysis for males (*p < .05, **p < .01).

puting, and a .320 standard deviation increase in likelihood to pursue a career in computing.

For males, both ability and encouragement equally predict satisfaction, likelihood to complete a computing major/minor, and likelihood to pursue a career in computing (Figure 7). When the outcome variables are regressed on both encouragement and ability, the direct effect of ability remains significant; thus, encouragement does not mediate the relationship between ability and the outcome variables for males.

Overall, for females, encouragement matters more than ability in terms of how satisfied they are with computing, how likely they are to complete their computing major/minor, and how likely they are to pursue a career in computing. For males, encouragement and ability were equally important in predicting their outcomes. These results indicate that improving outcomes for females entails improving their affiliation with the computing department and enhancing the relationship between computing assignments and female interests and career goals.

For underrepresented minorities (Blacks, Hispanics, native Americans), encouragement, once again, fully mediates the relationship between ability and satisfaction, likelihood to complete computing major/minor, and likelihood to pursue a career in computing. When the outcome variables are regressed on both encouragement and ability, the direct effect of ability becomes insignificant. This suggests that

[5]Due to space constraints, we have removed our the regression analysis tables and the analysis of correlations between the factors and the outcome variables. These are available in a technical report at http://www.gacomputes.org.
[6]Statistical tests revealed no significant differences by gender or race on these three outcome variables.

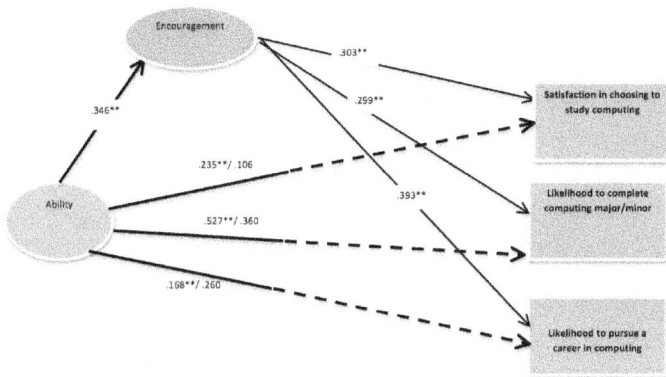

Figure 8: Mediation analysis for under-represented minorities (*$p < .05$, **$p < .01$).

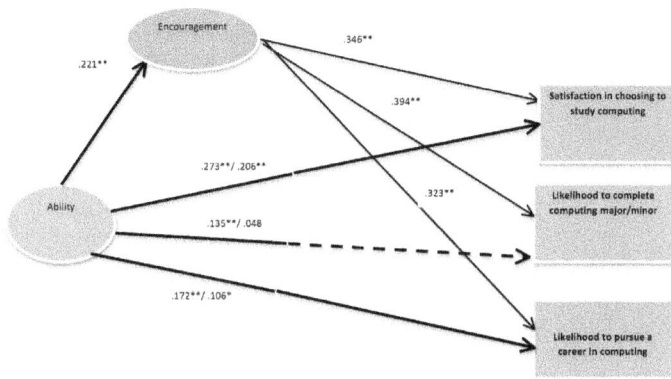

Figure 9: Mediation analysis for majority White and Asian (*$p < .05$, **$p < .01$).

while ability enhances underrepresented minorities' satisfaction and likelihood to pursue computing, encouragement is driving this effect. For every one standard deviation increase in encouragement, there was a .303 standard deviation increase in satisfaction, a .299 standard deviation increase in likelihood to complete computing, and a .393 standard deviation increase in likelihood to pursue a career in computing.

For White and Asian respondents, both ability and encouragement equally predict satisfaction in choosing to study computing and the likelihood to pursue a career in computing (Figure 9). When the outcome variables are regressed on both encouragement and ability, the direct effect of ability remains significant; thus, encouragement does not mediate the relationship between ability and the outcome variables. However, the relationship between ability and the likelihood to complete a computing major/minor was fully mediated by encouragement for White respondents. Interestingly, there was no difference between White and Asian respondents in their regression analyses, thus, for purposes of parsimony, they were combined.

Overall, for underrepresented minorities, encouragement matters more than ability in terms of how satisfied they are with computing, how likely they are to complete their computing major/minor, and how likely they are to pursue a career in computing. For majority group members in computing, encouragement and ability were equally important in predicting their outcomes. These results indicate that

improving outcomes for underrepresented minorities entails improving their affiliation with the computing department and enhancing the relationship between computing assignments and minority student's interests and career goals.

5. DISCUSSION

Recall that the majority of respondents did not engage in middle school computing experiences and did not report interest in computing in middle school, yet they are responding in an introductory computing course. Students in middle school already have been thinking about careers and have negative attitudes about computing [15]. What changed for our respondents, between middle school and higher education? It may be that there was a lack of *access* to middle school computing, and if there was more, we might see more interest and participation in computing experiences.

The fact that a majority (57%) of the student respondents had taken some computing in high school has several possible interpretations. Since all the respondents were in introductory computing, having *some* high school computing may have played a role in the decision to take that course. We do not have comparison data to see if university students *not* in introductory computing had much high school computing, to see if there was a causal impact. Other indications suggest that relatively few high schools in Georgia offer high school computer science [8]. Thus, these results are *consistent* with a belief that high school computer science had an impact in drawing students into computing, despite a disinterest in middle school, but the results are not definitive.

The greater proportion of women and under-represented minorities from ICE-affiliated ("institute") schools than non-ICE schools is trending in the right direction, but isn't yet significant. This result might suggest that ICE professional development has had an impact. There could be other factors other than ICE causing this effect, e.g., perhaps the schools that were most interested in promoting women and under-represented minorities in computing *then* sought ICE professional development. We also do not have a more detailed explanation of how the teachers who received the ICE professional development might have influenced those students, e.g., we do not know the names of student respondents' teachers. Nonetheless, the results described are consistent with GaComputes and ICE professional development having an impact on undergraduate enrollment of women and under-represented minorities in computing courses in Georgia.

The results on the factors that influence women and under-represented minorities in pursuing computing careers are not surprising. What is notable here is the scale of the study, and replication of previous findings (e.g., [10]). Women and men, and majority and minority students have had different experiences, and these lead to different values. Understanding these facts can help us understand how to serve those interests and how to recruit students into the major.

Particularly notable in this paper is the mediation analysis. Issues of student self-perception of ability are not new in computer science, but noting differences in gender and race/ethnicity is new, when supported with such a large study. The results are also promising for interventions. Changing students' self-perception of ability is challenging. Encouraging them is not. The mediation analysis suggests that encouragement has a larger effect on women and underrepresented minorities than it does on male and majority group students.

6. CONCLUSION

Taking a pulse on what influences the computing education formal pathways in an entire state is challenging. This paper describes one such effort, involving over 1400 students and 19 higher education institutions. In so doing, we increase our understanding on what interventions along the pathways might be having an effect, and where they might not be. We also gain a better understanding of where we should put further work, and what kind of work is most likely to succeed.

7. ACKNOWLEDGMENTS

This paper is based upon work supported by the National Science Foundation under the *Georgia Computes!* BPC Alliance, Grants #0634629 and #0940394. Any opinions, findings, and conclusions or recommendations expressed in this material are those of the authors and do not necessarily reflect the views of the National Science Foundation.

8. REFERENCES

[1] W. R. Adrion, R. Fall, M. Matos, and A. R. Peterfreund. Integrating evaluation into program development: benefits of baselining a NSF-BPC alliance. In *Proceedings of the 41st ACM SIGCSE Technical Symposium on Computer Science Education*, SIGCSE '10, pages 27–31, New York, NY, USA, 2010. ACM.

[2] R. Baron and D. Kenny. The moderator-mediator variable distinction in social pyschological research: Conceptual, strategic, and statistical considerations. *Journal of Personality and Social Psychology*, 51:1173–1182, 1986.

[3] S. Beyer. The accuracy of academic gender stereotypes. *Sex Roles*, 40:787–813, 1999.

[4] S. Beyer, M. Chavez, and K. Rynes. Gender differences in attitudes toward confidence in computer science. In *The Annual Meeting of the Midwestern Psychological Association*, 2002.

[5] S. Beyer, K. Rynes, J. Perrault, K. Hay, and S. Haller. Gender differences in computer science students. In *The 34th SIGCSE Technical Symposium on Computer Science Education*, pages 49–53, 2003.

[6] A. Bruckman, M. Biggers, B. Ericson, T. McKlin, J. Dimond, B. DiSalvo, M. Hewner, L. Ni, and S. Yardi. "Georgia Computes!": improving the computing education pipeline. In *Proceedings of the 40th ACM SIGCSE Technical Symposium on Computer Science Education*, SIGCSE '09, pages 86–90, New York, NY, USA, 2009. ACM.

[7] J. M. Cohoon and K. M. Baylor. Female graduate students and program quality. *IEEE Technology and Society*, 22(3):28–35, 2003.

[8] B. Ericson, M. Guzdial, and M. Biggers. Improving secondary CS education: progress and problems. In *Proceedings of the 38th SIGCSE technical symposium on Computer science education*, SIGCSE '07, pages 298–301, New York, NY, USA, 2007. ACM.

[9] P. Kinnunen and B. Simon. CS majors' self-efficacy perceptions in CS1: results in light of social cognitive theory. In *Proceedings of the Seventh International Workshop on Computing Education Research*, ICER '11, pages 19–26, New York, NY, USA, 2011. ACM.

[10] J. Margolis, R. Estrella, J. Goode, J. J. Holme, and K. Nao. *Stuck in the Shallow End: Education, Race, and Computing*. MIT Press, Cambridge, MA, 2008.

[11] A. C. Strenta, R. Elliott, R. Adair, M. Matier, and J. Scott. Choosing and leaving science in highly selective institutions. *Research in Higher Education*, 35(5):513–547, 1994.

[12] A. E. Tew, C. Fowler, and M. Guzdial. Tracking an innovation in introductory CS education from a research university to a two-year college. In *Proceedings of the 36th SIGCSE technical symposium on Computer science education*, SIGCSE '05, pages 416–420, New York, NY, USA, 2005. ACM.

[13] A. E. Tew and M. Guzdial. Developing a validated assessment of fundamental cs1 concepts. In *Proceedings of the 41st ACM technical symposium on Computer science education*, SIGCSE '10, pages 97–101, New York, NY, USA, 2010. ACM.

[14] A. E. Tew and M. Guzdial. The FCS1: a language independent assessment of cs1 knowledge. In *Proceedings of the 42nd ACM technical symposium on Computer science education*, SIGCSE '11, pages 111–116, New York, NY, USA, 2011. ACM.

[15] S. Yardi and A. Bruckman. What is computing?: bridging the gap between teenagers' perceptions and graduate students' experiences. In *Proceedings of the third international workshop on Computing education research*, ICER '07, pages 39–50, New York, NY, USA, 2007. ACM.

Enhancement of Learning Programming Experience by Novices using Mobile Learning

Wafaa Alsaggaf
School of Computer Science and IT
RMIT University, Melbourne, Australia, VIC
omafaf@hotmail.com

ABSTRACT
In order for computer programming students to acquire conceptual understanding as well as practical skills, it is important to follow a learning paradigm that includes a hands-on and practical approach. However, the traditional lecture format does not fully encourage active learning. While most students today own and use mobile devices (such as laptops), these devices are not obviously utilised as practical learning aids in lectures. This thesis evaluates the potential of a teaching approach delivers theoretical and practical components together in a lecture environment using students' mobile devices. It explores the potential enhancement of the learning experience of students in programming.

Categories and Subject Descriptors
K.3.2 [Computers & Education]: Computer and Information Science Education.

General Terms
Design, Experimentation

Keywords
Programming, learning enhancement, mobile learning, lectures.

1. RESEARCH QUESTIONS
Although there is criticism about the traditional lecture format, course delivery in lecture theatres is predicted to remain the main pedagogical method for the foreseeable future. In computer programming courses, using mobile devices with the lectures could make the learning environment more interactive and deliver knowledge in a more effective manner. Mobile learning is an evolving research area. Only a few studies have considered the use of mobile learning in computer programming education [3]. There is also a lack of research investigating the connection between classroom technology and student learning in traditional lectures [2]. There is a need to redesign introductory computing courses to deliver more effective learning. This study addresses the questions of 1) how the use of mobile devices in lectures can enhance the learning experience of computer programming for novices, 2) how do the instructors' perceptions about mobile devices affect the use of mobile devices as learning aids, and 3) how can classroom activities be designed to make an effective use of mobile devices in programming lectures.

2. RESEARCH METHODOLOGY
This study uses action research as its research methodology. Four research cycles were designed to answer the research questions.

2.1 Cycle 1: Background Study
The first cycle of the research involved a preliminary study with quantitative and qualitative analyses. It explored the perceptions of computer science students about the use of mobile devices during lectures. Majority of the students owned a laptop and were happy to bring it to university to use it during lectures. Advantages, disadvantages, opportunities and challenges have been discussed, and guidelines for proper integration have been devised.

2.2 Cycle 2: Interviews with the Lecturers
Research cycle 2 answered research question 2. It explored the perceptions of the instructors about using mobile devices during lectures. The majority supported the intervention. The results have been published in an international conference [1].

2.3 Cycle 3: Trial Experiment 1
This research cycle was designed and evaluated to answer research question 1. A trial experiment was conducted where students used their mobile devices with visualization software to simultaneously practice the lessons of the topic being taught during the lecture. Surveys were designed to measure student responses about mobile learning on seven principles of good practice in undergraduate education and distributed to the students pre- and post-trial. The findings showed that the participants reported improvement in four principles out of the seven. Overall, students were highly motivated during the lecture.

2.4 Cycle 4: Trial Experiment 2
To answer research question 3, cycle 4 will develop a framework to examine how classroom activities should be designed to make an effective use of mobile devices in the lectures. Finally, we will evaluate this framework in conjunction with the overall effectiveness of using mobile devices during lectures.

REFERENCES
[1] Alsaggaf, W., Hamilton, M. & Harland, J. (2012). Mobile Devices in Computer Programming Lectures: Are CS Lecturers Prepared for Mobile Learning? *Proc of the seventh International Conference on Computer Science & Education (ICCSE)*, Melbourne, Australia. IEEE.

[2] Kay, R., & Lauricella, S. (2011). Exploring the Benefits and Challenges of Using Laptop Computers in Higher Education Classrooms: A Formative Analysis. *Canadian Journal of learning and technology*, 37(1), 1-18

[3] Sheard, J., Simon, Hamilton, M., & Lonnberg, J. (2009). Analysis of research into the teaching and learning of programming. *Proc of the fifth international workshop on Computing education research workshop*. Berkeley, CA, USA, ACM, 93-104.

Automated Generation of Practice Questions from Semi-Structured Lecture Notes

Thushari Atapattu
School of Computer Science
University of Adelaide
SA 5005 Australia
(+61)883136196
thushari@cs.adelaide.edu.au

ABSTRACT

This paper describes the ad-hoc generation of study and practice questions from lecture notes, designed to assist computer science students in developing their understanding of lecture content.

Categories and Subject Descriptors

K.3 [**Computers & Education**]: Computer and Information Science Education.

General Terms

Human factors

Keywords

Computer science education, question generation, ontology

1. INTRODUCTION

Automatic question generation is an emerging area of research in computational linguistics and it is utilised in educational contexts (e.g. intelligent tutoring systems). This research studies the impact of content-oriented practice questions in developing students' understanding of the lecture content. We generate questions from semantic representation (i.e. ontology), where the ontology is produced automatically from PowerPoint lecture notes of computer science undergraduate courses in the University of Adelaide.

Our research hypothesises that reviewing lectures through practicing questions on lecture content will improve knowledge and skills. We focus on interrogative type questions (e.g. what, why), contributing to knowledge and comprehension levels of Bloom's taxonomy using multiple-choice, yes/no, and open-ended discussion questions. After analysing lecture notes, we intend to provide guidelines for lecturers to prepare semantically-rich lecture notes (e.g. maintain contextual relations between key concepts, arrange comparable data in one slide).

2. BACKGROUND

Automatic question generation in the educational context has little or no significant focus in the literature, particularly using lecture notes as a knowledge source. Tex-Sys [1] provides a tool for teachers to present domain knowledge, enabling the generation of an ontology and thereby generating template-based questions for students.

3. METHODOLOGY

This research generates an ontology from lecture notes by extracting a) key concepts using text mining and linguistic annotation techniques, b) the concept hierarchy using PowerPoint document structure [2], and c) linguistic relations between concepts using lexico-syntactic patterns. The reasoning of an underlying ontology selects the content of the questions and a template-based question generation approach will be used to generate practice questions (e.g. disjoint axiom of OWL DL generates 'compare and contrast' type question).

This research proposes to conduct several studies based on, a) lecturer's perspective on improving their lecture notes according to our guidelines, b) lecturer's agreement on computer generated overview of their original lecture notes, c) the rank of the generated questions according to fluency, ambiguity, relevance, question type and pedagogical value [3], and d) student's improvement of understanding of the key concepts in the lecture.

4. CONCLUSION

We believe that the ad-hoc practice question generation from lecture notes will improve students' understanding of material more broadly by clarifying misconceptions and complex sections on a regular basis.

5. REFERENCES

[1] Itko, B., S. Stankov, et al. 2009. Dynamic test generation over ontology-based knowledge representation in authoring shell. Expert Syst. Appl. 36(4), 8185-8196.

[2] Atapattu, T., Falkner, K., Falkner, N. Automated extraction of semantic concepts from semi-structured data: Supporting computer-based education through the analysis of lecture notes. In: S. W. Liddle et al. (eds): Dexa 2012, part 1, LNCS 7446, pp. 161-175. Springer, Heidelberg (2012)

[3] Rus, V., B. Wyse, et al. (2010). The first question generation shared task evaluation challenge. In Proceedings of the 6th International Natural Language Generation Conference. Trim, Co. Meath, Ireland, Association for Computational Linguistics. 251-257.

Understanding and Persuading Adherence to Test-Driven Development

Kevin Buffardi
Virginia Tech
114 McBryde Hall (0106)
Blacksburg, Virginia, United States of America
kbuffardi@acm.org

ABSTRACT

In computing education, students must learn techniques practiced in relevant professions. Test-Driven Development (TDD) is one such technique popular in the software industry. Preliminary reports suggest that TDD helps produce higher-quality code. However, motivating novice programmers to adopt TDD is also recognized as a distinct challenge. My studies and proposed work address this challenge with the following objectives: measuring adherence to TDD and its consequential outcomes; understanding students' reasons for non-adherence; and influencing students' attitudes and behavior via pedagogical interventions.

Categories and Subject Descriptors

K.3.2 [**Computers and Education**]: Computer and Information Science Education; D.2.5 [**Software Engineering**]: Testing and Debugging.

General Terms

Measurement, Human Factors, Verification

Keywords

Test-driven development (TDD), automated grading, adherence, affect, software engineering.

1. INTRODUCTION

In accordance with ABET accreditation requirements [1], computing programs teach students techniques applied in industry. Extreme Programming popularized Test-Driven Development (TDD), a software development technique that emphasizes an incremental "test a little, code a little" approach [2]. As TDD gained popularity in various software engineering methods, industrial case studies suggested that it improves quality of code. Consequently, by following TDD, students should develop better computer programs while gaining experience pertinent to potential professions.

However, current assessment practices do not account for students' adherence to processes such as TDD. Instead, programming projects are typically graded based on only the final product of students' work. To adequately identify adherence to TDD, it is necessary to observe students' work throughout its development.

2. RESEARCH PLAN

To explore how to address students' reluctance to adhere to Test-Driven Development (TDD), I must first understand students' software development habits and attitudes. After gaining this insight, I will investigate how pedagogical interventions can influence their behaviors and outcomes. The research plan depends on three studies, conducted in two primary stages.

2.1 Stage 1: Adherence and Attitudes

First, I will analyze data collected by Web-CAT [5], an automated grading tool that collects several submissions per assignment for each student. In particular, I will investigate relationships between metrics demonstrating TDD adherence and quality of outcomes. Meanwhile, I will use a survey [4] to summarize students' opinions of TDD and reasons for their (non-) adherence.

2.2 Stage 2: Leveraging Influence

Findings from the first stage will inform the design of adaptive, instructional technology with the purpose of encouraging adherence to TDD. The instructional technology will be applied in computer science courses. At the conclusion of the courses, I will investigate the influence that pedagogical intervention has on students' attitudes, behaviors, and outcomes with regard to following TDD.

3. REFERENCES

[1] ABET (2012). "Criteria for Accrediting Computing Programs, 2012-2013." Retrieved April, 2012, from http://www.abet.org/computing-criteria-2012-2013/.

[2] Beck, K. (2003). Test-Driven Development by Example, Addison Wesley.

[3] Bhat, T. and N. Nagappan (2006). Evaluating the efficacy of test-driven development: industrial case studies. Proceedings of the 2006 ACM/IEEE international symposium on Empirical software engineering. Rio de Janeiro, Brazil, ACM: 356-363.

[4] Buffardi, K. and S. H. Edwards (2012). Exploring influences on student adherence to test-driven development. Proceedings of the 17th ACM annual conference on Innovation and technology in computer science education. Haifa, Israel, ACM: 105-110.

[5] Edwards, S. H. "Web-CAT." 2012, from https://web-cat.cs.vt.edu.

Supporting the Virtual Design Studio through Social Programming Environments

Adam Carter
Washington State University
Pullman, WA 99164
cartera@wsu.edu

ABSTRACT

Incorporating alternative pedagogies into computing education has the potential to promote better engagement, outcomes, and retention than traditional methods. A limiting factor of many alternative pedagogies is that they target in-class activities, which constitute a small percentage of computing students' overall time. To achieve a more significant impact, we argue that computing educators need to find ways to innovate students' out-of-class activities as well. Inspired by the studio-based model used in architecture, we introduce the idea of *social programming environments*, which aim to simulate the design studio experience by enabling students to maintain an awareness of their peers' programming activities and to ask for and receive help.

Categories and Subject Descriptors

K.3.2 [**Computer and Information Science Education**]: *Computer science education*

General Terms

Design, Experimentation, Human Factors

Keywords

Social programming, Integrated Development Environment

1. INTRODUCTION

Over the next decade, the demand for software developers is expected to increase considerably. Unfortunately, the record numbers of incoming college students are not enrolling in computer science or decide to leave the major before graduating [1]. To address this issue, researchers have made attempts at bettering recruitment techniques, altering curriculum, and introducing new pedagogies. Building upon these past efforts, we believe that one solution lies in supporting socially-oriented pedagogies both within and outside class through the development of a social programming environment. To this end, we are exploring the creation of a "virtual" design studio by augmenting the integrated development environments (IDEs) in which computing students spend much of their out-of-class time working on individual assignments.

2. PRELIMINARY DESIGN

Our approach is to augment a traditional IDE with a social plug-in that transforms the IDE into a *social programming environment* (SPE). In developing such an SPE, our goal is to mirror the kinds of interactions made possible in socially-oriented pedagogies, such as Studio Based Learning (SBL) [2], and deemed important

by Situated Learning Theory (SLT) [3]. From this, we have derived the following requirements:

- *Activity Streams.* Activity streams are a method of organizing data in such a way that allows individuals to remain peripherally aware of other users' activities. On social networking sites, an activity stream allows people to connect by sharing and discussing their general life activities. Similarly, an activity stream embedded within an SPE would enable a learning community to connect by sharing and discussing their computer programming activities within the context of a specific programming assignment.

- *Code View.* In order to support the "over the shoulder" and impromptu reviews common in traditional SBL, our SPE allows students to view as well as comment on the work of their peers.

- *Chat.* While activity streams are useful for providing general classroom awareness, they lack the capability to facilitate effective synchronous discourse. Therefore, in addition to supporting messaging capabilities in both activity streams and social annotations, our SPE will include both group-wide and directed chat capabilities.

- *Achievements.* Long popular in various online social communities, achievements can be used to establish reputation, identity, and level of community involvement. According to SLT, achievements both help facilitate and provide evidence of learning.

- *Dashboard.* Similar in purpose to achievements, dashboards provide a history of community participation that is important to the Situated Learning process. In more practical terms, a dashboard provides a central location to display all of the aforementioned SPE features.

3. EVALUATION

Our SPE and its underlying learning theories will be evaluated through a two-semester study in our introductory computer science course. Upon completing data collection, we plan to draw comparisons between grades, self-efficacy, sense of community, IDE usage patterns, help-seeking behaviors, course evaluations, and student persistence.

4. REFERENCES

[1]   E. Seymour and N. Hewitt, *Talking about leaving: Why undergraduates leave the sciences.* Boulder, CO: Westview Press, 1996.

[2]   A. S. Carter and C. D. Hundhausen, "A review of studio-based learning in computer science," *J. Comput. Sci. Coll.*, vol. 27, no. 1, pp. 105–111, Oct. 2011.

[3]   J. Lave and E. Wenger, *Situated Learning: Legitimate Peripheral Participation.* New York: Cambridge University Press, 1991.

The Development of Knowledge in Novice Programmers

Nadia Kasto
SERL, School of Computing and
Mathematical Sciences
AUT University
Auckland, New Zealand
nkasto@aut.ac.nz

ABSTRACT

The doctoral research proposed here consists of a longitudinal study of novice programmers, which aims to explore the learning strategies they use, the ways in which they integrate knowledge, and the processes they employ when applying their knowledge and skills in different contexts.

Categories and Subject Descriptors

K.3.2 [**Computers & Education**]: Computer and Information Science Education.

General Terms

Experimentation, Human Factors

Keywords

Novice programmers, educational models, cognitive development

1. INTRODUCTION

A wealth of literature points to the fact that learning to program is difficult. However, we have little understanding about how students' cognitive processes develop. This is possibly due to the fact that many studies supported with the empirical evidence, have focused on a single snapshot of time and on naturally occurring data [3]. This research is based on the premise that in order to truly observe and identify the acquisition and development of knowledge, we must not only follow the same students during a significant proportion of their development as novice programmers, but we must also interview them and observe them undertaking tasks specifically designed to elicit this development.

A key aspect of this investigation into the development of skills takes its inspiration from Piagetian theory [4] , and focuses on eliciting how novice programmers integrate new programming structure, concepts or elements into their current understanding of code? As part of this investigation we wish to identify strategies that students apply when attempting to comprehend a piece of code or writing a piece of program code? And answer questions such as:

- Does a student's approach to integrating new knowledge change over time? And if it does what triggers this change?

- Can we develop a cognitive framework that describes the way in which novice programmers integrate new programming structure or elements?

- What existing frameworks, if any, can be integrated or adapted to describe the knowledge acquisition process?

- Do any of the existing models or theories of learning fit with our observations of the way in which novice programmers acquire knowledge and skills?

- How do strategies adopted alter depending on the students existing knowledge and/or the task type?

In this study, a mixed research method will be adopted. A novel framework has been designed that encompasses known educational taxonomies, models and software metrics (for example [2], [5] and [1]). This framework will subsequently be used to design a set of tasks to trigger situations that require some form of knowledge adaptation or acquisition. Students will be observed attempting to solve these programing tasks as well as being interviewed using a think-out-loud protocol We propose to map their strategies using the Block model and relevant theories regarding strategies used by computer programmers [5].

2. REFERENCES

[1] Cardell-Oliver, R. 2011. How Can Software Metrics Help Novice Programmers? *In Proceedings of Australasian Computing Education Conference, ACS, Perth, Australia, 55-62.*

[2] Lister et al. 2006. *Not Seeing the Forest for the Trees: Novice Programmers and the SOLO Taxonomy.* SIGCSE Bull. 38, 3 (June 2006), 118-122.

[3] Lister et al. 2010. *Naturally Occurring Data as Research Instrument: Analyzing Examination Responses to Study the Novice Programmer.* SIGCSE Bull. *41, 4 (January 2010), 156-173.*

[4] Piaget, J. and Inhelder, B. 1969. *The Psychology of the Child.* London, UK: Routledge & Kegan Paul.

[5] Schulte et al. 2010. An Introduction to Program Comprehension for Computer Science Educators. *In Proceedings of the 2010 ITiCSE working group reports* Ding, W. and Marchionini, G. 1997. *A Study on Video Browsing Strategies.* Technical Report. University of Maryland at College Park.

Communities of Practice and Situated Learning in Computer Science

Daniel Knox
School of Computing
University of Kent
Canterbury, CT2 7NF, England
dk242@kent.ac.uk

ABSTRACT

An overview of a body of work researching communities of practice and situated learning in computer science. The aim is to provide an insight as to how and why students participate in computing practice.

Categories and Subject Descriptors

K.3.2 [**Computers and Education**]: Computer and Information Science Education

General Terms

Human Factors

Keywords

Situated learning, communities of practice, motivation

1. RESEARCH QUESTIONS

This research is supported by two learning theories, communities of practice [6] and situated learning [4]; the two theories acknowledge learning as situated within authentic activity, experience, context and culture.

The questions examined by this research are:

- To what extent do situated learning and communities of practice occur in computer science? The desire to study this comes from the extensive literature within many practices, such as Xerox technicians [5] and neonatal nursing [3].

- What constitutes an authentic activity of computing practice in computer science? Brown and Duguid describe authentic activity as "the ordinary practices of culture" [1]. Furthermore, they suggest that, in the majority of cases and across different fields, contemporary formal learning limits students' engagement with a practice's culture.

- Can classical motivation theory be applied to understand why people practice computer science? This question is supported by the need to investigate the motivation of why engineers join and remain in the discipline [2].

2. WORK TO DATE

Two sites were selected as potential places of authentic practice:

2.1 Ethnographic Observations

For one week ethnographic observations were made of a technicians' room in a high school. The room provides a space for an employed support team to maintain the school's computer infrastructure. However, five students are frequently in the room during their free time.

2.2 Interviewing Apprentices

Interviews were conducted with apprentices from a computer support company for schools. These apprentices engage with on the job learning in a school technicians' room and also attend a formal college course once a week.

3. FUTURE WORK

First, to research the impact on learning when there is a transition between formal and situated learning. This aims to understand the effect of participating in different types of learning within the same environment; for example, a placement year in a degree programme. Second, to research whether a space dictates the type of learning that can occur there; to understand how computer science students utilise space and interact with peers to support their learning.

4. REFERENCES

[1] J. S. Brown, A. Collins, and P. Duguid. Situated cognition and the culture of learning. *Educational Researcher*, 18(1):32–42, 1989.
[2] T. Hall, N. Baddoo, S. Beecham, H. Robinson, and H. Sharp. A systematic review of theory use in studies investigating the motivations of software engineers. *ACM Trans. Softw. Eng. Methodol.*, 18(10):1–29, 2009.
[3] C. L. Hunter, K. Spence, K. McKenna, and R. Iedema. Learning how we learn: an ethnographic study in a neonatal intensive care unit. *Journal of Advanced Nursing*, 62(6):657–664, 2008.
[4] J. Lave and E. Wenger. *Situated Learning: legitimate Peripheral participation.* Cambridge University Press, New York, 1991.
[5] J. E. Orr. *Talking About Machines.* Cornell University Press, London, 1996.
[6] E. Wenger. *Communities of Practice: Learning, Meaning, and Identity.* Cambridge University Press, New York, 1998.

Assessing and Enhancing Computational Literacy in Basic Web Development

Thomas H. Park
College of Info. Science & Technology
Drexel University
Philadelphia, PA, USA
thomas.park@drexel.edu

ABSTRACT

Web development offers a motivating context for learning about computation. My proposed studies aim to identify computational skills and concepts at play in basic web development, and investigate how they can be measured and supported.

Categories and Subject Descriptors

K.3.2 [**Computers & Education**]: Computer and Information Science Education

General Terms

Human Factors

Keywords

Web development, computational literacy

1. INTRODUCTION

People from diverse backgrounds gravitate to programming by way of web development [2, 7]. Noting this motivational effect, many educators and researchers have used web development as a context for computing courses, largely in CS courses that make programming their focus [3, 4, 6].

However, web development encompasses a rich set of activities beyond programming. In introductory web development courses, students often grapple with a wide range of computing topics even before encountering their first programming language [5]. In particular, basic web development, defined as the use of markup and style-sheet languages like HTML and CSS, can provide many opportunities for teaching skills and concepts associated with computational literacy [1].

Building on this premise, my research explores how experiences in basic web development can be turned into more fruitful learning episodes. Specifically, I am studying how computational literacy can be assessed in basic web development, which aspects of computational literacy relate to success, and how learning of them can be fostered through design. These research questions will be addressed in two studies. A web-based code editor is being developed that will serve as a data-collection instrument for both studies, as well as a platform for exploratory design.

2. RESEARCH PLAN
2.1 Study 1: Identification

In the first study, I seek to explore key strategies that are applied by basic web developers. In a lab-based think-aloud study, novices and experts will be asked to perform a set of basic web development tasks. This will be followed by interviews that probe their strategy use and how they relate computational concepts to these tasks. This data will be analyzed to identify key strategies and conceptual knowledge that relate to task success.

2.2 Study 2: Assessment and enhancement

The goal of the second study is to assess computational literacy in students as they learn basic web development. I will conduct pre- and post-tests with students taking an introductory web development course. In both tests, students will be asked to use natural language to describe a set of computational concepts. During the course, we will also collect activity logs of students as they use our editor to complete assignments. This data will be analyzed for changes in their use of strategies and articulation of computational concepts as they advance in the course. The study will be conducted in multiple rounds, with subsequent rounds iterating on the design of the web-based editor to provide pedagogical support for computational literacy.

3. REFERENCES

[1] diSessa, A. (2001). *Changing Minds: Computers, Learning, and Literacy*. MIT Press.

[2] Dorn, B. & Guzdial, M. (2010). Discovering computing: Perspectives of web designers. *ICER*, 23-29.

[3] Lim, B. (1998). Teaching web development technologies in CI/IS curricula. *SIGCSE*, 107-111.

[4] Mercuri, R., Herrmann, N., & Popyack, J. (1998). Using HTML and JavaScript in introductory programming courses. *SIGCSE*, 176-180.

[5] Park, T. & Wiedenbeck, S. (2011). Learning web development: Challenges at an earlier stage of computing education. *ICER*, 125-132.

[6] Reed, D. (2001). Rethinking CS0 with JavaScript. *SIGCSE*, 100-104.

[7] Rosson, M., Ballin, J., & Nash, H. (2004). Everyday programming: Challenges and opportunities for informal web development. *VL/HCC*, 123-130.

ICER'12, September 9–11, 2012, Auckland, New Zealand.
ACM 987-1-4503-1604-0/12/09.

Programming and Neo-Piagetian Theory

Donna Teague
Queensland University of Technology
Gardens Point Campus
Brisbane Qld 4000
d.teague@qut.edu.au

ABSTRACT

Learning to program is very difficult for many students and we have seen failure rates in Queensland University of Technology (QUT) introductory programming units at over 40%. The reasons students struggle in this domain has been a widely debated topic for many years with little prospect of a 'silver bullet'. We do know that expert computer programmers operate at a high level of abstract reasoning. This research will map the documented stages of abstract reasoning according to cognitive development theory against the levels of abstract reasoning exhibited by novice programmers. Understanding how that reasoning is developed will enable us to influence and improve the transition of students from one stage to the next more complex level, of cognition in that domain.

Categories and Subject Descriptors

K 3.2 **[Computers and Education]:** Computer and Information Science Education

General Terms

Human Factors.

Keywords

Cognitive development, Neo-Piagetian theory, think aloud.

1. INTRODUCTION

Classic Piaget theory is based on age-related development through sequential and accumulative stages of cognitive growth [2]. Neo-Piagetian theory differs in the belief that cognitive development is domain specific rather than related to age [3]. Therefore a person operating at a high level of abstract reasoning in, for example, science or mathematics, may still show signs of operating at a much lower level of reasoning in computer programming. Neo-Piagetian theories have been useful in helping us understand misconceptions that students have with mathematical problems, but little is known about when, why and how abstract reasoning skills are developed in the programming domain.

The two main objectives of this research project are to:
1.   map the stages of cognitive development according to Neo-Piagetian theory to programming ability; and
2.   identify the manifestations of those stages from analysis of students' performance on computer programming tasks.

The outcome will be understanding of the sequence of cognitive development stages that programmers progress through while developing domain specific skills. For each of these stages, we will be able to assemble a set of behaviours likely to be exhibited, and artefacts likely to be produced by a programmer at this level of reasoning. The significance of this research will be in providing the basis upon which a pedagogical framework may then be developed to influence the progression of novices from one stage of cognitive development in programming to the next, more complex level.

2. RESEARCH APPROACH

Both qualitative and quantitative methods will be used including "think aloud" case studies, in-class paper-based tests and analysis of students' examination artefacts and final results.

Our case studies will involve observing students in the process of solving short programming exercises. The subjects will use a Smartpen, which will enable audio-visual replay of the programming exercises they complete while "thinking aloud". Case study data will take the form of verbal reports [1], pencasts (created by the Smartpen) and observations made by us about the subject's behaviour, mannerisms and remarks. We will also collect data from in-class tests of novice programmers using the same or similar programming exercises. In this way we can triangulate the qualitative and quantitative data to further validate the findings.

From the in-class test artefacts it will be possible to make generalisations about the entire cohort. Any difficulties encountered in these in-class tests will inform a specific investigation with case study subjects. Conversely, if we observe interesting behaviour or misconceptions in the think aloud sessions, we can deploy appropriate tests to the entire cohort in order to test a research theory or assumption.

Case study students will be categorised according to the skills they exhibit while completing tasks associated with concepts at a certain level of abstract reasoning. Analysis of the verbal reports will allow quantification of the time spent on specific tasks for each of the case study subjects, and allow comparison of students operating at the same and different levels of abstraction.

[1] Ericsson, K. A., & Simon, H. A. (1993). Protocol Analysis: Verbal Reports as Data. Cambridge, MA: Massachusetts Institute of Technology.

[2] Helmore, G. A. 1969. Piaget - A Practical Consideration. Oxford, UK: Pergamon Press.

[3] Knight, C. C., and Sutton, R. E. 2004. Neo-Piagetian Theory and Research: enhancing pedagogical practice for educators of adults. London Review of Education, 2(1), 47-60.

Author Index

www.ingramcontent.com/pod-product-compliance
Lightning Source LLC
Chambersburg PA
CBHW081532220326

41598CB00036B/6407